American Democracy
Under Pressure

DONALD C. BLAISDELL

PROFESSOR OF GOVERNMENT
THE CITY COLLEGE OF NEW YORK

THE RONALD PRESS COMPANY ~ NEW YORK

2

212648
ACLS

Library of Congress Catalog Card Number: 57–6827

PREFACE

I have written this book because I have felt the need for a treatment of American government in terms of the impact which pressure politics is making on traditional American democratic institutions.

American Democracy Under Pressure may be regarded as the first of a series on pressure politics in various countries. In the nineteen thirties it seemed to me that exposition of the governments of several countries of western Europe and North America in terms of pressure politics was not only more illuminating than the conventional approach through description of structure but also pointed to the dangers of pressure politics to democratic institutions. Hardly had the project been conceived than the Republic in Germany succumbed to internal pressures. In France, pressure politics weakened the Third Republic to a point where it fell an easy victim to Nazi Germany. Parliamentary government as practiced in the Low Countries, in Britain, and in Canada is by no means free of pressure politics. But the constitutional systems of these countries seemed better able to absorb the shocks of pressure politics without being destroyed by them. In the United States our history as a nation is replete with examples of political lobbies and pressure politics, some of which are referred to in the body of this work.

In 1941 I made an attempt to expound the American governmental system in terms of economic power and political pressures. Although not wholly untenable, the thesis implicit in that approach proved less and less satisfactory to me as I watched and felt the operation of pressure politics within the United States government. Accordingly, I shifted my approach from economic to social pressure. When separation from government service in 1953 made it possible for me again to speak and write freely, I revived my project of two decades earlier and undertook a complete revision of *Economic Power and Political Pressures*. The present volume is the result.

Briefly, it is an introduction to pressure politics as played in and exerted on the governmental institutions of American democracy. Pressures are of all sorts and intensities, and they come from varying directions. Several important constitutional issues are discussed. Political parties, public opinion and propaganda, public administration, the judicial system, Congress, the very structure of American national government—all these get careful treatment, though this is not a book on any one of these subjects alone.

The work is largely the result of individual effort. At one point I considered, but rejected, the suggestion that it be a collaborative work. Accordingly, the responsibility for the book is mine. But I would not leave the impression that I owe nothing to others. Dewey Anderson, executive director of the Public Affairs Institute, encouraged me to rework my monograph, *Economic Power and Political Pressures,* which I had prepared in 1941 for the Temporary National Economic Committee (Seventy-sixth Congress, 3d Session). Encouragement was also received from Ordway Tead, John Fischer, and Manning J. Dauer. My wife's fortitude was a constant encouragement when the preparation of the manuscript was begun after numerous delays. My daughter, Ann, has helped in many ways to perfect the manuscript, especially in proving the approach as a worthwhile way of instructing undergraduates in American government and politics.

I wish to acknowledge the courtesy of the holders of copyrights in granting permission to quote from their publications. The students of my seminar at Wellesley College helped collect and organize material on the making of public policy. The librarians at the University of Florida, Wellesley College, The City College of New York, and at the Library of Congress have cheerfully responded to many requests. Finally, I wish to thank Ralph K. Huitt of the University of Wisconsin for the help he rendered in reviewing the entire manuscript.

Laurel, Maryland   D. C. B.
    February, 1957

CONTENTS

American Democracy
Under Pressure

Chapter 1

THE PUBLIC INTEREST
IN THE ATOMIC AGE

> . . . How and how far a more general interest can utilize,
> discipline, and curb these special interests in the govern-
> mental process is a supreme test of a people's economic
> and political genius.
>
> —Ernest S. Griffith
> *Congress: Its Contemporary Role**

The American people are faced with the problem of adapting
their government to the requirements of the atomic age.

Shall we continue to jog along with our political institutions geared
to the needs of the eighteenth and nineteenth centuries? Then, we
could safely operate our political machinery according to the
calendar, renewing the Congress every two years, the Presidency
every four years. Even half a century ago the resulting problems were
not too serious. Nor has a two-party system based on our three
thousand counties produced too wide a gap between promise and
performance. But now, in combination with corporate concentration
and technology (the latter stimulated by large federal government
subsidies) and a luxuriant growth of political pressure groups, our
decentralized party system poses questions which every citizen
should face squarely. Has not applied science outstripped political
science? In the field of public policy do we have means for making
decisions which are abreast of the times? While we admonish
Europe to unite to save itself, do we neglect the modernization of
our own political machinery? The answers are to be found not so
much in scrapping or overhauling the machinery as in bringing our
institutions and ourselves to a state of political maturity which
measures up to the demands of today.

* New York: New York University Press, 1951, p. 113.

3

Government Under Pressure

Two Types of Pressure on American Government. *Internal pressure.* Government in the United States is government under pressure. Probably at least a thousand lobbyists and associations represented by them are operating in Washington to bring pressure to bear on the several branches of the federal government.[1] Some such effort is not without precedent in our history, but today this force is accepted as normal in the governmental process. These private associations, which are known as pressure groups, have become woven into the fabric of government, taking their place alongside the formal governmental organs and the political parties. The ideas embedded in our laws are in large measure their ideas. The opinions and views on public issues which daily travel the air waves are their ideas or reflect their ideas. The individuals who, as legislative representatives, public relations counsellors, or attorneys, speak for these groups in the halls of Congress, at the executive departments, and before the courts are their agents. And yet, so quietly and unobtrusively do they operate that, a few years ago, forty-five out of every one hundred persons interviewed could not identify the term "lobbying."[2]

External pressure. A different type of pressure is also exerted on the government, the pressure of communist imperialism. The threat to our institutions and our independence from this source is real. The consequences are enormous. They can be read in the fantastic size of federal budgets and expenditures. In a recent year, of the nearly seventy-five billion dollars of estimated federal expenditures, 70 per cent, or about fifty-three billion dollars, were required for six major parts of the national security program—military services, international security and foreign relations, atomic energy development, civil defense, shipbuilding, and defense production. "All but about twenty-one billions of federal expenditures" for the fiscal year 1953 (ending June 30) were "the direct result of programs designed to deal with the problem of communist aggression."[3]

American Democracy Under Pressure

American democracy is under pressure in the modern world because in trying to make the American dream come true it labors under a dual handicap. On the one hand is the threat of communism. On the other is the pre-emption of the field of defining the public interest by domestic pressure groups. And the unorganized citizenry can only watch from the sidelines.

Is THERE A GENERAL INTEREST? Both aspects of this handicap stem from differing philosophies of government. By philosophy of government we mean the sum of the things people strive for as citizens and the use they make of the procedures which are available for political purposes. Some would call it the set of values by which we put most store. Americans reject communism both as a philosophy and as a form of government, so it need not detain us. The kind of pressure on American democracy which needs sober thought arises out of the skillful way in which pressure groups have made their special interests appear to be those in the general interest.

The general interest, myth or reality? It is hard to escape the philosophical dilemma raised by the question, Is the general interest something real or is it imaginary? If we say that the general interest is real, we must be prepared to explain how it differs from the sum of the special interests. If we deny its existence and say it is only imagined, we must be equally ready to explain the universal practice of the leadership of every pressure group in the country in using the general interest as the justification for its political program.

Everyone has his philosophy of government, from the Founding Fathers to the President, from every member of Congress to every professional man, propagandist, farmer, industrial worker. Hamilton and Madison held that government was, essentially, the arena of opposing interests. According to this view, the general interest emerges as a by-product of the struggle of interests. In describing government in Washington in the 1880's, Henry Adams stated: "Democracy, rightly understood, is the government of the people, by the people, for the Senators."[4] This was, of course, before the Seventeenth Amendment changed the method of electing senators from indirect election by the state legislatures to direct popular election. In our own time, at the laying of the cornerstone of a new AFL–CIO headquarters building, President Eisenhower asserted that as a group increases in size and resources there is a corresponding increase in its responsibility to work for the good of all the people. The President took for granted a general welfare embracing the welfare of all the people.

A revealing glimpse of what a joint congressional committee thought on the matter was given by George Galloway in his testimony to the House Select Committee on Lobbying in 1950. Galloway, who was the staff leader of the joint (LaFollette–Monroney) committee on legislative reorganization in 1945, told the House investigators, five years later, that the earlier committee felt "the primary responsibility of Congress is to promote the general welfare and that no public policy could ever be the mere sum of the demands of the organized special interests. . . . the sum of the special interests, especially the organized special interests, is not equal to the total of all the interests of the nation, for there are vital common interests that cannot be organized by pressure groups. In other words, the general welfare is not the mere sum, for example, of Maine potatoes, Texas oil, Wyoming wool, Colorado silver, Mississippi cotton, and Georgia peanuts."[5]

A legislative finding that there is a general welfare or general interest that transcends the aggregate of producers' money income illustrates the difficulty of the problem. Although the existence of a general welfare was asserted, the legislators did not specify its nature beyond the statement that there were vital common interests which pressure groups could not organize. What these interests are was not stated. Presumably, since they are vital and common, that is, essential to the life of the people as a community, these interests are the twentieth-century counterpart of the more perfect union, the justice, the general welfare, which the representatives of the original thirteen states sought to promote when the Constitution was drawn in 1787. Probably it can be safely assumed that the specific meaning embodied in this general phraseology is to be determined by the appropriate organs of government in the light of existing conditions. In other words, it is up to each generation of Americans to determine for itself the meaning of the general interest.

Such argument begs the question, however. We may be confronting one of those bewildering situations in which a futile attempt is being made to bring an abstraction to life. Moreover, it may be that there is no totally inclusive interest. One student who has written realistically about public opinion and group interests believes so. David Truman, author of *The Governmental Process*, shares the view of Arthur F. Bentley, pioneer student of the nature of interests, that there is no totally inclusive interest.[6] Truman takes note of those who charge that a group interpretation of politics takes no account of or ignores or overrides the individual and the state (society) as well. Schattschneider, for example, although he blames pressure groups for much that is wrong with our operating political system, does not embrace the group interpretation of politics; such an interpretation, he claims, does not explain the politics of American democracy—for example, the politics of industrial mobilization since 1948. "The function of politics," he said, "is now very largely to explain to people why they must make greater and greater sacrifices,"[7] not to afford a method whereby competing interests can be accommodated in the making and carrying out of policy. For Truman, however, this criticism of the group interpretation of politics is not valid. To him, as with Bentley, "the individual and the group are at most merely convenient ways of classifying behavior, two ways of approaching the same phenomenon. . . . In developing a group interpretation of politics . . . we do not need to account for a totally inclusive interest, because one does not exist."[8] Thus, by looking at the same thing from different angles, or with different preconceptions, we can draw opposite conclusions: that there is or that there is not a general interest.

Those who value efficiency and economy in government, such as former President Herbert Hoover and the Citizens Committee for the Hoover Report, may find in this difference between an abstract public interest and the concrete interests of pressure groups with a stake in governmental programs an explanation of the reluctance of Congress to adopt proposals so eminently suited to promote economy and efficiency. Fear of offending an organized group or groups, instead of promotion of the abstract public interest, usually determines a Congressman's vote when administrative reorganization proposals are up for decision.[9]

In the larger setting of Western political philosophy an even more sweeping iconoclasm than Bentley's and Truman's holds comfort for neither those who proclaim nor those who deny a general interest based upon special interests. According to this view, the vocabulary of politics in the Western world has confused the forms of government with the purposes of government, with the result that the philosophical method employed leads to the false conclusion that one ideology is "better" than another, that democracy, say, is better than communism. Lest those who prefer the former to the latter become disturbed, the expounder of this view hastens to add that the discrediting of all political ideologies will produce no alarming consequences,[10] his plea being, apparently, for less chasing of myths and more concern for realities.

For the man in the street, in whose general interest believers in American democracy, both official and unofficial, professional and lay, are active, the bother over such philosophical questions arouses little interest. If he concerns himself at all, he probably tends more to the view that government should be responsive to certain of his needs which he feels simultaneously serve the general interest rather than believing that in this imperfect world it is possible for government to promote an all-inclusive general interest which can be defined and made real by some means other than practical politics. For him this is the best test of a philosophy of government: How much is my take-home pay?

DIFFICULTIES IN PROMOTING THE GENERAL INTEREST. Out of the confusion of values and the clash of interests emerges the central fact of our political life—the absence of permanent solutions and the prevalence of partial solutions to current problems, which result from the play of pressure politics on, in, and through our political and governmental institutions.

It would be naive to expect our political system to produce permanent solutions to the problems of the day. It is in the nature of these problems never to know final solutions. The basic rule of life is change. With each change a new set of conditions appears, requiring a readjustment to the new conditions.

But pressure group politics compounds the difficulties inherent in a world in which policy never produces solutions. This is the point at which the general interest suffers and special interests get undue consideration. Perhaps what is needed is a theory of interests which is both responsible and effective.[11] But it is doubtful whether Americans are value-conscious enough to work out such a theory. Politically, we are practical people. If something works, it is good. And a political system dominated by the ideas of pressure groups as to proper policies and programs works. There can be little doubt of that.

Mixed effect of pressure groups. More than a century and a half after the assumption of the state debts by the federal government, three-quarters of a century after an earlier era when the Presidency was eclipsed by lobbies,[12] and a short thirty-five years after radio began to provide these lobby groups with the means of nationwide propaganda, the effect of pressure groups on American democracy is neither all good nor all bad.

Pressure groups promote the public interest. This is the argument of every such group engaged in politics and of the lobbyists who represent them. Probably the great majority of those who know that lobbying and pressure politics are a feature of American politics would agree. While only an assumption, it accords with the theory of democracy as a belief in individualism which holds that each person knows what his own interest is and deliberately seeks to fulfill it, thereby promoting the interest of all; for it cannot be assumed that individuals would knowingly promote a public interest contrary to their individual interests.[13] Hence, only the cynic, that person guilty of what Henry L. Stimson called "the only deadly sin I know,"[14] would impute to groups active in politics and propaganda any motive less noble than that of promoting the interest of all.

It has been suggested by one observer that the catalytic pressure group (one stimulating and working through other groups) is in the best position to promote the public interest and to modify pressure politics in this direction. Groups of this type are sensitive to the subtle but important political difference between acceptance and support and between rejection and opposition. This is the difference between passive and active attitudes and is shrewdly exploited by catalytic groups. Rarely, if ever, strong enough in their own right to swing the balance of power when votes are taken in Congress and its committees, such groups form coalitions with stronger groups whose interest in the issue in question is only secondary, with other groups having a primary interest in the issue, and with minorities of still other groups whose majorities may be opposed to the issue. Admittedly, it is often difficult to use such tactics in an environment characterized by uncertainty and shifts of opinion. Yet it is a political maxim that, although sentiment for rejection of a proposal may be widespread, the lack of organized opposition will enable a small supporting group to obtain favorable legislation. The reverse is also true. Thus minorities seemingly at a disadvantage with others, because of the uneven distribution of knowledge and of wealth, may, on occasion, reach their goals. In view of the extensive acquiescence and tolerance toward policy-making known to exist among unorganized segments of the electorate, the hypothesis may be ventured that government in America "by consent of the governed" is really government by acquiescence.

It may be argued that such procedures are antidemocratic. To this it can be answered that legislation inconsistent with the general interest need not result. If we mean by democracy government by popular majorities, the American system of pressure politics cannot escape the charge of being undemocratic. On the other hand, pressure politics may be considered an essential part of the American type of democracy if democracy can be widened to include a form of responsible government which allows concessions to, and compromises among, strongly felt interests, in contrast to domination by any one special interest.[15] The public interest can be promoted, especially since "the system of pressure politics, while open to grave charges—and are not systems free of pressure groups also subject to serious abuses?—nevertheless grants to every interest a means of seeking relief, a safety valve whereby every minority may obtain a modicum of justice. Injustice cannot be eliminated, but at least it is not frozen into the political structure beyond any possibility of change."[16]

In contrast to this viewpoint, the opposing view holds that pressure groups do not promote the public interest. If conceived in terms of tangible values, the public interest is not served by pressure groups, because, at very least, they pose the general problem of private interests against the public interest and, more specifically, because these groups develop only partial solutions to economic problems confronting the country.[17] Whether the federal taxing process achieves the national interest is another question raised in this same connection. The process has given the country a highly productive system, but it has not invariably achieved the national interest as measured by any reasonable test.[18] It has not done so because the interests of the general public are inadequately represented in the pressures brought to bear on Congress by taxpayer groups.[19] The tendency of organized groups to place primary emphasis upon their own economic interests is noted by Ernest S. Griffith, with whose fundamental question this chapter was opened. He describes this tendency by such phrases as "the dispersive state," "government by whirlpools," a centrifugal type of "group utilitarianism."[20] A similar view is expressed by the editorial writer who entitled his criticism of "fair-trade" legislation, " 'Welfare,' Yes—But Whose?"[21] "The plain truth is," this writer asserted, "that the Fair-Trade Act, in Florida, as elsewhere, serves not the public welfare but the *private* welfare of certain manufacturers and retailers." The views of the committee of the Eighty-first Congress which investigated lobbying emphasized the shift in the basis on which combinations of industry or business massed their efforts to influence policy from the functional to the ideological or philosophical, that is, from tangible to intangible values.[22] This subtler and shrewder tactic is brought out by two other observers, both of whom see the community and the general welfare as threatened by what is called the imperialism of powerful groups.[23] The massive volume of data, information, and opinion in the ten volumes of hearings, the eleven special reports, and the two committee reports of the House Lobby Investigating Committee caused one of these observers to say that the threat to the general welfare posed by these groups thirty years earlier had not disappeared. Naming the National Association of Manufacturers as the outstanding example of such groups at that time, he states that "the imperialism of powerful groups . . . was then, as it is now (1951), a constant threat to the general welfare, or more exactly, the common interest of all the people." Differentiating the "narrow interests" of such groups and the "interest of the whole," he fixes the 1920's as the period when we began to learn, "the hard way," that "the never-ending problem of democracy is how to keep such groups under control and restrain them from placing their narrow interests above the interest of the whole. . . ."[24]

The destructive impact of pressure groups on traditional American values has not escaped notice. The lack of balance in public policy, the partial solutions to economic problems, the imbalance between what are called "tightly organized economic power blocs" and "more casually organized interests" and "a loosely patterned state"[25] are only one evidence of the material effect of pressure groups; less tangible effects are also to be noted, effects touching the valued qualities of honesty, forthrightness, and restraint. Tracing the effect of lobbying methods in modern times to the power of propaganda, Herring says that the contemporary lobby gives rise to the evils of deception and coercion, and that "misrepresentation and lack of balance are inevitable." He adds, "Propagandists and self-seeking promoters may exercise an influence far in excess of their relative social significance."[26] The existence of a general interest is assumed by Herring, and lobbies and pressure groups have an adverse effect upon it: "The cry of special interests tends to down the plea of the general interest. The public has no lobby."[27]

No simple, categorical statement can be made about the effect of pressure groups on American democracy. Only one thing is certain: the difficulty of determining the effect. It is doubtful whether the leadership and the rank and file of our great economic and other pressure groups will ever concede that a greater public interest is not served by promotion of their narrower, more immediate interests. Nor will any outside, objective observer ever be persuaded to give a blanket endorsement to the methods of promoting the public interest used by pressure politics. In neither case, however, is the sincerity of the opposing advocates to be questioned. In both cases, patriotism, as well as vision, wisdom, and purpose must be assumed, and in no less measure than that for the country as a whole.

THE PUBLIC INTEREST, AN ELUSIVE GOAL. To expect Congressmen and administrators to pursue fixedly the public interest when they are constantly under pressure is asking the impossible.

From California, strong in the nation's councils (as well as in its counsels) comes a statement of the impossible task placed upon the modern legislator. Since the nation embraces California, the statement applies, a fortiori, to the national political situation. In a democratic system the lobbyist is indispensable. How else, asks a committee of the California State Legislature, could legislators vote intelligently on the thousands of bills introduced annually, most of which are highly technical and relate to subjects in which the legislators have no experience. Explanation of these measures, which is all that lobbying is, according to this view, enables legislators to vote intelligently. But how shall they vote? Aye? Nay? Paired? Not voting? Here is the crux of the legislator's problem. Today his role has changed from that of an earlier day. An attempt merely to reflect the views of his constituents is not enough. On most issues his constituents have no views, or, at best, conflicting views; besides, nearly all issues transcend the boundaries of his district. "He must rather reflect the balance of interest of all groups in his community . . ." the committee states. But how is this balance to be determined? Quantitatively? Qualitatively? A combination of both? And how should the interests of all groups be weighted in the scales of the legislator's conscience? The statement is not very helpful in answering these crucial questions. The lawmakers are under an obligation, self-imposed presumably (how otherwise?), to "see that legislation as a whole is something like a composite photograph, in which there is a likeness of all and an image of none. . . ." If this guide leaves something to be desired, it does at least pose the further problem clearly when it states that "this is the most important and, at the same time, the most difficult task in a democracy. It requires men of breadth of view and integrity, men who are receptive to the claims of all and are the slaves of none."[28]

The dual position of the national legislator was brought out by Representative Charles A. Halleck (R., Ind.) in 1950. He believes that a Congressmen is charged "with exercising his own best judgment in the national interest. . . . he should be constantly tempering that judgment with what he can conceive the majority sentiment of the people he represents."[29] But this judgment and the degree to which it is tempered (modified?) by the Congressman's conception of his constituents' majority sentiment is not affected by the intrusion of external factors: ". . . in my observation," Congressman Halleck asserts, "any popular conception that some so-called lobbyist can persuade a member of Congress against his better judgment or against what he conceives to be the majority sentiment of the people whom he represents is just completely erroneous. . . . Our job is to find out what the real majority sentiment is and to distinguish between what is just some pressure operation or selfish-interest operation" (sic).[30]

Halleck's view deserves attention. However, few lobbyists are crude enough today to attempt to persuade a legislator against his better judgment or against what he believes to be the majority sentiment of the people he represents. In choosing his techniques the lobbyist is more adroit. If he approaches the Congressman directly at all, he finds more frequently than not that the legislator's judgment needs little attention. It has already been influenced in the way the lobbyist desires by those of the Congressman's constituents who count politically.

If we turn from the legislator to others in authority, the situation is not very different. A President must be courageous enough to say

No to pressure groups when their demands are not in harmony with the Chief Executive's conception of the general interest. But presidential vetoes can be overridden by Congress; when this happens it is clear indication of the strength of special interests. Moreover, Presidents, like Congressmen and Supreme Court Justices, come, stay a while, and go, departing from the political scene, leaving it to their successors, and handing over to them not only the seals of office but also the custodianship of the national interest. The threads of continuity and of interest in our American democracy are weaker and more subject to rupture in our governmental than in our economic and social groups.

Even if pressure politics produces partial, and not whole, solutions, a query still remains. Are not partial solutions, imperfect though they may be, preferable to the alternative? That, of course, depends on the alternative. There is but one. Only by a drastic overhaul of the party system could we obtain a unified expression of the national interest in policy terms. To gain greater unity in program planning, greater party unity would be required. To obtain greater party unity, more highly disciplined parties would be essential. To achieve disciplined parties, greater leadership and control would be necessary. The absence of effective leadership and control is due to the diffused and decentralized governmental authority over elections, electors, and parties, pursuant to constitutional requirements, and to the division of governmental power between the nation and the states. Only by amendment and innovation could such a drastic alteration of our constitutional and governmental forms be accomplished. Only then would coherent programs conceived in the public interest be possible; only then could parties, unified, disciplined, and strongly led and controlled, redeem in Congress platform pledges made in election campaigns. Strong parties are possible, but only at a price so high that many would prefer the system which they know, even with its existing imperfections, to the theoretically more perfect system which they do not know.

Moreover, there are few citizens and practically no groups without a stake in the existing system. To persuade them to surrender their stakes in return for a more rationally conceived notion of the public interest at some unspecified time in the future—and one of questionable value at that—might not be technically beyond the ability of our media of mass persuasion. But one must tax his imagination even to conceive of decision-makers acting in this way. The risks would be too great, too great in terms of lost or restricted freedoms, such as freedom from party control in voting, the exercise of state's rights, particularly local control over health, education, and welfare. A system of more responsible parties could be constructed in America, but only at the cost of a sweeping reorientation of our customs as well as of the structure of our political institutions.

SUMMARY. American government and democracy in the atomic age are under two types of pressure: internal pressure from our own citizen groups and external pressure from international communism. In such a situation pursuit of the general interest or welfare or public interest faces unusual difficulties. There is no consensus as to whether there is a general interest. Nor is there agreement on how to determine it. While it is generally assumed that the pursuit of their own interests by individuals and groups promotes the general interest, the results do not always justify this assumption. Each individual and each pressure group seeks his interest in his own way and as he sees it. But rarely is there agreement that the methods and goals promote the interest of all the people rather than that of the special groups. However, out of the hopes and fears, the concerns and expectations of the people, something recognizable as the public interest emerges, and is given shape and substance through various institutions of which government and politics are one. How the process works will be discussed in the remainder of this book. The next chapter summarizes the principles underlying our governmental system, giving it form and determining the efficiency with which it meets the problems created by domestic pressures at home and communist pressure abroad.

Chapter 2

AMERICAN DEMOCRACY
AND POLITICS

> . . . Our Republic embraces a great deal of virtue and a
> great deal of gangsterism, corruption, and crime. It em-
> braces tremendous altruism and tremendous hypocrisy
> about race relations and corporate greed. It embraces
> more true culture than ever before and a greater emphasis
> on the shoddy and vulgar. Defying the pattern-makers,
> it is the hardest democracy in the world to get inside a
> book.
>
> —Allan Nevins
> *The New York Times Book Review**

A summary statement of American democracy and politics would
emphasize two things: democracy as a creed and democracy as a
form of government. While every brief statement of this subject
necessarily emphasizes certain points and subordinates others, to
highlight creed and form helps bring out the essential features of our
democracy.

American Democracy as a Creed

As a creed, American democracy affirms a belief in the possibility
of growth of the individual personality. Everyone is to have an equal
opportunity to develop his talents to the utmost of his ability, free
from all restraints except those necessary for the maintenance of the
health, welfare, and morals of the community of which he is a part.
Nationally, the federal Bill of Rights sums up the rights of the individual. Supplemented by those rights proclaimed in the state constitutions, they express society's belief in individualism. The agencies of
society—governmental, economic, religious, educational—are not to

* March 14, 1954.

15

interfere with the individual's development. On the contrary, they shall nurture these rights for the good both of the individual and of society itself.

American democracy also affirms a belief in the necessity of government. But this affirmation is reserved and grudgingly made. Government can tyrannize as well as benefit. Government, hence, is not absolute, as in the days of absolute monarchy, but relative. There is a limit to the powers which a government should have and exercise. But this limit is not fixed for all times, places, and circumstances; it can be modified as these conditions change.

This relativity of government is a feature of uncertain status in the American creed. It arises from the basic fear implicit in the creed itself, a constant fear that government, even though based on the consent of the governed, can get out of hand. Belief in the value of the individual is stronger than belief in the necessity of government. Hence, subscribers to the creed are suspicious of government, and this results in a constant struggle, sometimes consciously, sometimes subconsciously, against government. But despite its resentment of government, this creed, at the same time, recognizes the need for government. Therefore the people's rights must be surrounded by safeguards to defend them and prevent arbitrary invasion by governmental authority. Since the individual is assumed to act in his own interest and since he is perfectible, the line between arbitrary and justified exercise of authority will always be clear in the wisdom of the people.

There is a potential conflict between these two basic elements in the credo of American democracy. As twin features of the American creed, individual rights and majority rule are always in an uneasy balance. Even theoretically, there is a logical inconsistency between them. A creed can assert the one or the other but not both. But this conflict between beliefs, though distressing to builders of logical systems, creates little difficulty for more practical persons. Expressing beliefs held and cherished in common, a creed need not be logically consistent to explain the motivations and proclaim the aspirations of a people. But principles of action grounded in incongruous beliefs can rarely produce the harmony, the balance, and the justice which adherents of a democratic creed profess. Man is rational, but not all the time. His emotions and instincts imbue his intelligence, producing behavior at variance with the dictates of pure reason. Nor need we, in affirming simultaneously belief in the individual and in majority rule, feel ill at ease because the democratic creed in America does not show the inner harmony to which "a more perfect union" aspires. For democracy in America is not only a creed but a form of government. It provides a set of principles for organizing government as well as a set of beliefs for motivating it.

American Democracy as a Form of Government

As a form of government, democracy in America is in a class by itself. While there are other countries with governments similar in form to that of the United States, there is none quite like it. Numerous examples of federal government can be cited: Canada, Australia, Mexico, Brazil, the U.S.S.R. (in a formal sense). There are also examples of what Woodrow Wilson called congressional government and what is now more commonly referred to as presidential government. Brazil and Mexico, to mention but two, both have bicameral congresses with an executive branch headed by a popularly elected executive. Many other countries operate under written constitutions. After World War I they became the fashion; similar practice was also followed after the second World War. In this respect India, Pakistan, Indonesia, the Philippines—all of whom have gained their independence since 1945—have followed the American example. Constitutional guarantees in the form of a bill of rights is another feature of many modern organic charters which reflects American practice. Other respects in which foreign countries have adopted governmental features on the American model are their vesting both the real executive power and ceremonial functions in one office and one leader; a fixed term for the real executive; fixed terms for members of both the upper and lower (the more representative) houses of the legislature; a judiciary appointed by the executive but independent of it; and universal suffrage.

The form of government of American democracy not only differs in one or more respects from that of other democracies, but it differs so markedly as to be in a class by itself. In no other government do all these features exist as in the American federal republic, for it combines all of the features found elsewhere only in varying combinations.

But there are additional differences which justify placing the American form of government in a separate category. So well implanted in custom is the practice of judicial review of legislative and executive acts that it can be regarded as part of the form of American democracy. Together with a written constitution, judicial review practically guarantees that sooner or later every political issue will become a legal question. Also, the President's Cabinet is a feature not found elsewhere in the same form. It is not mentioned in the Constitution; yet it disperses political responsibility and permits the

President, as the sole elected federal administrative official (except the Vice-President) to escape responsibility for the administrative acts of his Cabinet members. The doctrine and practice of the separation of powers in the form found in this country is peculiar, particularly its diffusion of executive and legislative power to the President, as the chief executive, and to the Congress, as the legislature. This is in contrast to the fusion of these two powers in cabinet government, as in Britain.

FEDERALISM. Also, American democracy is federal in form. Federalism is the belief in and practice of governance by power divided between a federal, or national, government and smaller units, such as states. In conjunction with formal features already mentioned, this division of power between Washington and the states has both advantages and disadvantages. Among the former are the relative ease with which new states can be brought into the Union; the opportunity for experimentation, as in Nebraska, with its unicameral legislature; in numerous western states, in an earlier period, with women's suffrage; and in Wisconsin, with social security, before the federal Congress established a system in which all the states may participate. But there are disadvantages, too, growing particularly out of the constitutional provision in the Tenth Amendment that powers not delegated to the federal government are reserved to the states or to the people. As a result, the many social problems which the industrial and technological revolutions extruded with explosive force have escaped adequate social control due to the doubt as to which government, federal or state, was constitutionally competent to deal with them. In the controversy over ownership of submerged lands, the need for petroleum to power the internal combustion engine for peacetime purposes as well as for defense created in a novel form a problem of federal–state relations which had not been adjudicated in more than one hundred and fifty years of judicial review. As a consequence of divided power between the federal and state governments the problem of the most efficient use of natural resources, such as land, water, minerals, and, now, atomic energy, has become so intricately involved with questions of ownership, control, and regulation as practically to defy solution in the general interest. Because of the force of custom and of states' rights in the Deep South, enforcement of Supreme Court decisions for full enjoyment of civil rights by all, regardless of race, threatens to test again the strength of the ties which make "one out of many." The repercussions of the public school cases, in which the Supreme Court ruled that segregation in the public schools on the basis of race is unconstitutional, are bound to be felt in the urban politics of such crucial northern electoral states as New York, Pennsylvania, Ohio, Illinois, and California.[1]

FEDERALISM AND THE PARTY SYSTEM. The peculiar nature of political parties in America can also be attributed to our form of government. The federal form made it certain that parties, when they developed, would be decentralized, not centralized. Moreover, from the Constitution the states receive the authority to determine who can vote and under what conditions; as regards representation, only the term of members of the House and of the Senate is fixed by the organic law. Also, it became customary for Congressmen to reside within the congressional districts they represent. While the states were not denied by the Constitution the right to elect representatives residing in other districts (as in Britain), in America this practice has never been adopted. This custom has reinforced the decentralization which the federal form, in effect, decreed. An additional consequence is that members of Congress think of themselves as delegates, rather than representatives, a tendency which has not been discouraged by the voters themselves, especially when groups, locally strong for economic or other reasons, are involved.

Still another factor has been the susceptibility of American parties to "bossism" or minority control. As the suffrage was extended by the states—first to adult males regardless of property, and then later to women—and as the size of the eligible electorate grew, much of it newly arrived from abroad, success at the polls came to depend more and more on organization, a feature accompanying and contributing to the leadership of an active minority. Abuse of the party caucus, of the congressional caucus, then of conventions, and today of the party primaries shows the oligarchical character of the parties at work. Successive reforms have been attempted on the theory that the cure for shortcomings or evils of democracy is more democracy. No doubt the reforms increased the opportunity for the party member to play his part. But in terms of deference, safety, and income, the prize of office is valued higher by organized interests than by unorganized voters; the result has been that the former have become more important in party affairs than the latter. The effect of the federal form on the party system can be seen, too, in the national nominating conventions, composed of delegates designated by state party organizations and run by the national party committee, which itself is made up of members selected by the state organizations.

The experience of America in building an economy of production, distribution, and exchange according to the creed of individualism is of only slightly less significance in illustrating the problems of a federal system with reserved powers resting in the states. Under corporate charters issued by the states, American enterprise has largely escaped effective social control, while it has benefited from a free-trade area of continental proportions. Likewise, the relations of cor-* porate management with its labor force have eluded control in the general interest. Judgment need not be passed on whether these facts are advantages or disadvantages of the form of government which American democracy takes. Some would argue vigorously that they are advantages; others, just as vigorously, that they are not. But they are, without question, the consequence of the federal-state system as we know it in America, a governmental setting in which the economic form of a creed of individualism is being worked out.

INTERGOVERNMENTAL AFFAIRS. Our form of government has consequences, too, for America in world affairs. Increasingly, foreign and domestic affairs merge into each other until it is becoming ever more difficult to find the dividing line. In some respects, however, the form of government makes clear assignments of power, while handicapping the effective use of that power.

In foreign relations the separation of powers is to be seen in the assignment to the President of the power to send and receive ambassadors and to negotiate treaties with other governments. But these can be checked by the Senate through its power to confirm presidential nominations and to consent to treaty ratification. Similarly, while Congress has the power to raise and support armies, to declare war, and to make regulations governing the armed forces, the President conducts foreign relations and is the Commander-in-Chief. Thus, while Congress declares war, the President and the executive branch, with congressional support or acquiescence, make war.

The rivalry between the legislative and executive branches, inevitable in a government built upon the doctrine of separation of powers, is nowhere more clearly seen than in the relations of the United States to other governments. The security of the nation is closely tied to the security of other countries. As a result of wartime cooperation, Anglo–American relations are inevitably "mixed up," as Sir Winston Churchill has said. The United States has signed mutual security treaties with forty-one other governments. The United States is a member of the United Nations and of the Organization of American States. In such a situation, the extent and complexity of American involvement abroad is obvious. But what it means in the conduct of American foreign relations is not so clear, so novel and unprecedented are these relationships. One thing stands out already. In implementing economic and military aid, American policy depends upon appropriations by Congress, thus placing the legislative branch in the middle of both formulation and execution of policy and increasing the rivalry between legislature and executive. In this way Congress tries to restore the balance and make itself co-ordinate with the President, a balance which in recent decades has gone steadily against the legislature due to wartime expansion of the President's powers, to authority delegated by Congress to the executive branch when legislating on technical subjects, and to the Chief Executive's public relations and leadership practices.

When the United States, during the latter part of World War II, decided to cooperate with other governments in relief and rehabilitation of Europe's population, speed was essential. Yet immediate action was impossible because of the separation of executive from legislative and appropriation power. This was in striking contrast to the dispatch with which Canada and Great Britain, with the parliamentary form of government, were able to act in joining the United Nations Relief and Rehabilitation Administration.

Because of the division of powers between the federal government and the states, foreign governments frequently wonder how firm a commitment can be made by the President and the State Department when treaties and agreements are negotiated. While the Constitution and court decisions leave no doubt that federal power in this respect is very wide—indeed, almost unlimited—and that it is clearly for the federal government, not the states, to make and carry out treaties, foreign governments, as well as federal officials, are sometimes exasperated by the handicap which federalism, with its rival partners, places on efficient conduct of intergovernmental relations.

The role of the states in enforcing equality of treatment of their citizens in education and in other civil rights has resulted in injecting the question of the division of governmental power into the conduct of foreign relations and making treaties. A proposed treaty outlawing genocide (the mass extermination of a people because of race) has aroused fears among those concerned with states' rights lest the federal government assume international obligations allegedly overriding rights of the states. Similar fears have been aroused by the human rights program of the United Nations, which consists of three parts: a Declaration of Human Rights, a Human Rights Covenant, and measures of enforcement. In 1948 the United Nations' General Assembly adopted the first part of this threefold program. Work on the second was proceeding when the Eisenhower Administration took office in the United States in 1953. As the result of a re-examination of American policy in cooperating with other governments with respect to human rights, the United States withdrew from the program.

Use of the executive agreement, which does not require Senate consent for its ratification, has further intensified the concern of those who would restrict the range of presidential discretion and power in conducting foreign relations. The President and State Department in 1948 subscribed to a set of principles for liberalizing international trading conditions, the General Agreement on Tariffs and Trade (GATT), and were thus able to continue for many years U.S. membership in the interim program established pending the enactment of the Charter of the International Trade Organization (ITO). But legislators, some business groups, and tariff protectionists complained that the United States was doing by executive agreement something which it would be unable, because of opposition in Congress, to do by treaty. (The ITO never came into being, the U.S. having never completed the treaty-making process on which it was based.) Only once in fifteen years, in 1953, did the United States complete treaty-making action on a convention proposed and developed under auspices of the International Labor Organization, action on all others having been prevented, at least in part, by the fear that federal treaty-making in such matters as raising labor standards, even with a federal-state clause safeguarding the position of the states, might invade an area reserved to the jurisdiction of the states.[2]

Inspired by what was felt to be an unconstitutional expansion of federal power by means of treaties and executive agreements, efforts were made in the Eighty-third and Eighty-fourth Congress to propose an amendment to the Constitution making the effective use of these powers in the conduct of foreign relations dependent on subsequent action by the Congress. Behind this proposed Bricker amendment[3] was the accumulated fear that unless the Constitution were to be amended formally, the federal nature of the American government itself would be permanently altered toward a more centralized form, and at the expense of the states.

SCIENCE AND POLITICS. There is great misunderstanding of the potentialities of science in human affairs and, particularly, of the applicability of the scientific method to politics. Unfortunately, for most people these are matters of no great moment. But the recent achievements of science have led even highly educated people to the false conclusion that reason applied by the scientific method will yield results in politics similar in significance to those achieved in investigating the nature and structure of matter. For example, one sociologist believes that the world in general and statesmen in particular can be accurately warned of dangerous international tension if only the measuring methods used in polling opinion were to be organized and used on a world-wide scale.[4] Surely this not only misinterprets the nature and proper scope of opinion surveys but also claims more for what reason can do in international affairs than is justified by our present knowledge of human relations.

Oppenheimer tells us that in our search for a secure peace "there are no equivalents of the experimental techniques of science."[5] While physicists like Oppenheimer may not be statesmen or even experts on politics, those who write on public affairs would do well to ponder Oppenheimer's words on the unavailability of methods for the study of politics identical or even similar to those available to students of the physical world.[6]

SUMMARY. As a set of beliefs, American democracy stresses the possibilities of individual growth, but insists upon limits to majority rule if such growth possibilities are to be fully realized. As a form of government, American democracy serves as a model for other peoples gaining their freedom in the contemporary world. Federalism is imprinted not only on the formal governmental structure but also on the political parties, giving them their localism and decentralization. In our relations with foreign governments federalism makes international cooperation less simple than it otherwise would be. Despite the need for federal power, the American fear of too much government asserts itself in attempts to make the power of the President to conduct foreign relations dependent upon formal action by Congress and the states. The technological marvels developed in America promise little for the solution of international problems. The methods of scientific research into nature require much fuller development than that yet attained before they can yield answers to such transcendent problems of human nature as the peace and security of the international community. Meanwhile, a closer examination of the dynamics of democracy in America is in order.

Chapter 3

THE DYNAMICS OF DEMOCRACY

> To attempt to discover the real rulers is one of the most
> important tasks of political science.
> —Westel W. Willoughby and Lindsay Rogers
> *An Introduction to the Problem of Government**

In discussing American democracy under pressure we are actually seeking the real rulers of American society, be they the Russian
Communists, as sometimes seems to be the case, the sovereign American electorate, as we like to think, or the lobbyist members of the
Washington Monday Lunch Club, as was asserted some three decades ago.[1] In any event, this search is a proper task for students of
government and politics.

A Modern Concept of American Government

For analyzing political conduct, a concept is valid and a method
is valuable to the extent that it produces results in conformity with
observation.

THE GROUP BASIS OF POLITICS. Governing in a democracy is a type
of activity requiring the making of decisions by individuals temporarily clothed with public authority. The decisions which have to be
made grow out of group activities in all parts of society. Exposition
of this activity, as it is manifested in the organs of politics and government, is the most revealing method of portraying the political behavior of the American people. This book is written in the conviction
that in politics it is the group that counts.

The group concept and group activity. The concept of the group
and the method of group activity as applied to government were first
presented systematically in this country by Arthur F. Bentley in
The Process of Government.[2] For roughly a quarter of a century after

---

* New York: The Odyssey Press, Inc., 1927, p. 11.

the book was first published in 1908 it was virtually ignored by students of government. Then slowly it came into its own. Little by little the significance of group activity organized for special political purposes began to be realized.

Political developments seemed to be explainable in terms of groups and of the activity of groups. Through congressional investigation in 1913, for example, information came to light on the way organized manufacturers had worked their agents into the law-making process.[3]

In the same year occurred President Woodrow Wilson's denunciation of lobbyists working in Washington for greater tariff protection for certain groups of industrial producers.[4] But other organized minority interests were able to secure the adoption of the prohibition (Eighteenth) and equal suffrage (Nineteenth) amendments in 1919 and 1920, respectively.[5] During this period the balance of power in Congress was held by a group, or bloc, of senators and representatives bound together by common economic interests. This bloc was the congressional counterpart of many agricultural producers who, because of low prices, had banded together in a nationwide federation of groups already organized on a county- and state-wide basis.[6] From 1933 to 1953 the Democratic reign was based on a loose coalition, often unstable, of blocs of northern urban workers' votes, those of farmers in the farm states, and those in the South.[7]

In addition, the prominent part played by economic interests and especially business in American life and politics was being clarified by viewing them in terms of group action and interaction. At the beginning of the twentieth century, a New York politician testified to this prominence. Richard Croker, head of Tammany Hall, New York County's Democratic organization, offered what has been called the best explanation of industrial America: "Ever heard that business is business? Well, so is politics business, and reporting, journalism, doctoring—all professions, arts, sports—everything is business."[8] Croker's analysis has been confirmed by more recent observers. In the 1920's the stamp of business on American life was so pronounced that James Truslow Adams characterized it as a "business civilization."[9]

An additional testimonial to the validity of the interpretation of politics as group activity was its prophetic character. Many groups were active in politics in 1908, when Bentley published *The Process of Government*. But they were few as compared with the tremendous expansion which was to occur in their numbers during the next forty years. By 1949 it was estimated that there were something over two hundred thousand distinct groups in the United States.[10]

The attempt to forge a satisfactory tool of social analysis was proved successful also by the test of events. By using it to analyze American society, it showed that the success of any one group or coalition of groups in dominating American politics and government was intermittent and partial, not permanent and complete. Obviously, it cannot be said with certainty that no one group or set of groups cannot permanently hold power, as witness the appearance to the contrary in the long span of Republican rule in Washington prior to 1933 and in the twenty years of Democratic rule thereafter. But in the struggle of different groups of varying weight in the political balance there seems to be a measure of safety against the domination of the government by any one of the contending groups.[11]

Finally, the value of analyzing political and governmental events and trends in terms of group activity was underlined by the increased recognition paid it by both practicing politicians and professional political scientists. Wittingly or unwittingly, four Presidents of the United States—Herbert Hoover, Franklin D. Roosevelt, Harry S. Truman, and Dwight D. Eisenhower—have acknowledged indirectly the value of the method in recognizing the significance (often adverse) of groups and of group activity in shaping governmental programs.

While valuing Bentley's method, certain scholars have criticized his conclusions as leaving no place for the general welfare in the group struggle for governmental endorsement of their particularistic aims.[12] Others, however, such as Bailey, Gross, Herring, and David B. Truman, welcomed the method if they did not subscribe entirely to the conclusions to be drawn from using it.[13] Herring, for example, in his *Group Representation Before Congress,* published in 1928, was among the first to identify groups as a factor in politics and government comparable with the formal organs and the political parties. Not long afterwards, Herring also made a contribution, one which the years have confirmed, namely, that propaganda was the new factor which made lobbying and pressure politics different from the lobbying of the past and greatly increased their importance relative to the political parties and the formal governmental organs.[14]

CLAIMS OF GROUPS PRESSED THROUGH GOVERNMENT. Having noted the cordial, although belated, recognition given the concept of the group and the tool of group activity as a means of social analysis, it would seem that by using them a more accurate and less misleading picture of American politics and government may be obtained. This is indeed the case. Viewed in its general outline, which will be amplified in the following chapters, the following analysis can be made. In peacetime America, politics and government offer a means, a process, of presenting the claims of groups upon American society. Only the overriding requirements of national security in wartime displace group politics, and then only partially and intermittently. If we look for the motivating force behind government today, we find it in the competitive struggle among political pressure groups striving to satisfy these claims. Like all other services, government costs money, and, while external events fix in large part the budgetary limits within which these claims are pressed, their origin is to be found in the varied aims of the politically active groups, each with its idealized picture of America. In political and governmental terms, the satisfaction of these claims takes the form of legislation, administration, and adjudication. For the decisions of government, political pressure groups are of equal if not greater importance than the agencies of government themselves and the political institutions of the parties, the electorate, and public opinion. In addition, the presence at the seat of government of large numbers of paid representatives of these groups, operating with large means for manipulating opinion, has so changed the guaranteed right of petition as to amount to an amendment of the Constitution. Finally, democracy in America works well or ill, depending upon the satisfaction or concern with which this extra-constitutional form of interest representation is viewed.

Nature of Control and of Power in Government

DIFFERENCE BETWEEN CONTROL AND POWER. The control of government differs from the power of government. In the governmental sense, power is a political term synonymous with authority and has no force, legally or otherwise, until its use is sanctioned by constitutional organs and procedures. As used here, control is used in the social sense, and refers to that group or those individuals who at any particular moment are dominant in the decisions of government. The power of government is inert or latent; the control of government is active, purposeful. Control is dynamic and constantly seeks new methods of limiting or using governmental power. Government may possess power and, at the same time, wield control, as in a totalitarian or authoritarian state. But, ordinarily, in a representative democracy power resides in the government, while control is exercised by the various citizens' groups, the most representative feature of the political landscape. Moreover, the extent of the government's power is limited not only by the Constitution but also by our traditional belief, which is still strong, that government should not

compete in the economic field but should act as umpire among the
competing groups in this phase of the struggle for control.

Pressure groups, on the other hand, organized for activity in politics and government, are never static; by definition, they are dynamic. This is particularly the case with the groups into which
businessmen and other producers are organized. Throughout our history, and especially in the last few decades, these groups have been
intent upon wielding not only economic power but also, where it
has been thought necessary, political power as well. Their purpose
is not solely profit, although in our money economy the making of
pecuniary profits is obviously of prime importance. Equally important is the satisfaction of ambition and of the urge to domination
and power, rationalized in terms of individual rights, private enterprise, and the general welfare.

Even today, when the purposeful use of governmental authority
for what is called the general welfare is widely accepted, there is not
found in the organs of government the fusion of power, purpose,
and will which is characteristic of our economic interest groups.

PARTICIPANTS IN THE CLAIMING PROCESS. But "power," "government," and "control" are general terms. To understand them, it is
necessary to determine who uses them, how, for what purposes, and
with what results.

Numerous groups, varying in size, official and unofficial. Groups
are the participants in the governmental process. This is not to overlook the part played by individuals and by the constitutional and
extra-constitutional organs of government. When we say that groups
are the participants in government, we mean that the concept of
the group is broad enough to embrace all the *effective* units in the
governmental process, no matter what their size, form, or structure.
We stress *effective*, for to do so takes account of citizens both individually and collectively. Individuals have weight in the forces pressing on, in, and through government to the extent that they are members of groups. Thus, as a voter, the individual is politically effective
as a member of that group known as a political party. Or, if one of
the groups to which he belongs has acquired political power, in
fact, if not in law, in the governmental structure, he is effective as
a member of the political ruling group, the government itself. Thus,
families which are members of county and state farm bureaus and
national banks belonging to the Federal Reserve System partake of
political power, although the groups of which they are members are
not strictly political but are economic and financial groups.

In diversity lies a measure of safety. In the number and variety of groups and in their constant change is to be found a safeguard against excessive domination of government by any one group. Even business, an aggregation of groups comprising the economically most powerful, does not have its way all the time. Few modern authors have dissected the basic relations between interests and government more cogently than Bentley. The great value of his study lies in his conclusion that no one group, not even business, can work itself into a position relative to other groups and the public authorities from which it can permanently dominate government. Bentley pointed out that "alliances were continually shifting and were, therefore, temporary. They were not the result of a fixed and determinate situation. For this reason, Bentley implied, pressure groups were not inevitably destructive of democracy; by their very nature they did not create an indestructible oligarchy."[15]

From the point of view of their effect on government and politics, the overlapping membership to be found among many pressure groups is likewise a safeguard against permanent dictation by any one group. The individual is often a member of many groups. This characteristic can be regarded as an automatic, built-in regulator of the political process, providing a check on parties, as on legislators and executives, and sifting out from the mass of protestations of support for the general welfare those which do least violence to it.[16] "Guardianship will emerge out of the affiliations of the guardians," is the way Truman puts it.[17]

CONGRESS UNDER PRESSURE. Table 1 (p. 30) lists some of the pressure groups which sought to influence the Eighty-second Congress (1951). In addition to general business groups, the large variety of other groups will be noted: lobbyists for war veterans; taxpayers; and those interested in internal improvements, foreign policy, agricultural and food products, labor, transport, retail and service, power and communications, extractive industry, financial affairs, building products and real estate, and the professions.

This enumeration by no means includes all the pressure groups. Some of them spring up for immediate purposes, and when those purposes are achieved pass from the scene. The Citizens Committee for the Repeal of Chinese Exclusion was such a group in 1943. Many of them are organized primarily for humanitarian purposes but find that they must act as political pressure groups in order to achieve their objectives; such were the groups formed after World War II seeking relaxation of immigration laws to permit entry of persons displaced by war and political change in Europe.

TABLE 1

REGISTRATIONS UNDER THE FEDERAL REGULATION OF LOBBYING ACT
82D CONGRESS, 1ST SESSION (1951)*

Type of Organization	Number	Type of Organization	Number
Business, general	6	Citizen groups	
Building products, real estate	16	Civic, civil rights	5
Financial	12	Welfare, religious	9
Food and agricultural products	28	Employee groups	
Oil, gas, and mining	18	AFL	10
Power and communications	12	CIO	4
Retail and service groups	23	Railway labor	4
Transportation, general	2	Other	6
Air	6	Farm groups	10
Highway	4	Foreign policy groups	8
Rail	4	Professional organizations	8
Water	4	Reclamation, rivers, harbors	4
Miscellaneous companies	24	Taxes	9
Miscellaneous trade groups	19	Veterans, military affairs	7
		Individuals, miscellaneous	7

* Prepared from data appearing in registrations.

CONTROL GAINS POWER THROUGH INFLUENCE. The purpose of the following discussion is to state how governmental authority as power is appropriated by those having nongovernmental control over resources and facilities and how it is manipulated by rival forces toward the attainment of specific goals.

Background or limelight. Groups seek to influence the making of official decisions in politics, whether acting as units or through individuals representing them. To do so they may adopt either or both of two alternatives: They may obtain a position from which it is possible to exercise their influence, thus remaining in the background, pulling strings, manipulating their own and related power groups on which their influence depends, and preferring to remain out of the limelight; or they may obtain official place, either by election or by appointment, in which case they control government directly, not through intermediaries, as in the first alternative.

The two alternatives are not mutually exclusive; it is not an "either-or" choice. The tendency is for a combination of the two to be used. The purpose is the control of government through influence; the means is secondary. This is a consequence of the preference of Americans, as a people, for pragmatic rather than doctrinaire methods in politics. The test is not, Does it find a logical place in some preconceived, intellectualized scheme or structure? The test is, Does it work in the existing circumstances? The political consequences and concomitants of both laissez faire and socialist economics have been

unacceptable to the American polity. The mixture of collective individualism and of limited government which characterizes American society today draws sustenance from the political theory of both
systems. But our democracy is a full embodiment of neither the one
nor the other.

The purchase of influence. In order to gain positions from which
they can control governmental decisions through their influence,
groups will employ any technique which money can buy. The uses
of money in politics are many and varied. Money can be used venally
to buy votes, to bribe legislators, to show gratitude for favors done.
Such unethical uses have not been unknown in American history.
Laws making such practices illegal and subject to punishment are on
the statute books, and when enforced fearlessly and impartially
bring offenders to justice and prevent the moral tone of the community from being lowered.

Far larger amounts of money, in all probability, are used in politics and government in ways that are not regarded as unethical. A
limit is fixed on the amount of money a candidate may legally spend
in his campaign for election to Congress. But no limit is placed on
the amount which can be spent by friends on his behalf. Likewise,
a limit is fixed by law on the amount a party can legitimately spend
in the electoral campaign of its presidential nominee. But, again, no
limit is placed on the expenditure by temporary committees on the
candidate's behalf. Limits are placed on the amount an individual
may contribute to a party's funds, but none on the number of committees or groups to which he may contribute. Contributions by
corporations, banks, and labor unions are prohibited by law, but
personal funds of officers of such organizations are not proscribed.
The setting up of numerous campaign organizations outside the
parties and the solicitation, receipt, and donation of such contributions are not regarded as evasions of the law; on the contrary, it
is argued that campaigns could not be financed otherwise. Political
campaigns have soared in cost with the adoption of advertising and
public relations techniques by candidates and party campaign
managers.

Money spent to influence elected and appointed officials and employees is disbursed for the same basic purpose as money spent in
political campaigns. By spending it somebody purposes to influence
the votes of legislators and the decisions of administrators. The law
does not say that citizens cannot spend money to influence Congress
indirectly through agitating or pacifying public opinion in general.
Nor does it say that citizens cannot spend money to employ lawyers
or public relations counsellors or others skilled in presenting and

promoting the citizen's point of view on pending legislation. To pro-hibit, control, or even regulate either of these techniques would vio-late the constitutional rights of citizens to speak freely and to peti-tion the government for redress of grievances. All the law requires is that those who wish to influence Congress should register; that is, identify themselves and the legislation they are interested in, the amount of money spent, whence it came, and the purpose for which it was spent in attempting to influence Congress. Likewise, those who are employed for such purposes are under an obligation to register. Congress has dealt with this problem of the purchase of influence on the theory that such information filed periodically and open to inspection will result in lobbying and lobbying activities being car-ried on in the open.

Conflict-of-interest laws are also on the statute books. These are congressional enactments aimed at disqualifying government offi-cials and employees from taking administrative action on matters in which their material interests are involved. But lobbying to influence administrative decisions is not covered by law. Here, as in the case of corrupt political practices and lobby information laws, public questions of great difficulty are raised. Enforcement of such legisla-tion is difficult, at best, and, at times, practically impossible.

Through the press and other information and propaganda media, it is possible for pressure groups to influence the political process. Political parties, likewise, and the government bureaucracy itself are also influential. While these means of disseminating information and ideas have been factors in the political process since our beginning as a nation, only recently have new inventions so expanded the ex-tent and deliberateness of their use. They are employed by all groups in the struggle for control. But, since they are geared to an economic system aimed at profit-making, they tend to reflect the viewpoints of businessmen more than those of others. Under pressure from the business community, the American democracy has not been congen-ial to the dissemination of news, opinion, and entertainment except on a basis acceptable to competitive enterprise.

As a factor in the political process, the press today differs funda-mentally from that of Jefferson's day. Its potentialities as a vehicle for use in petitioning the government are realized far more fully now than formerly. Although the unequal distribution of property helps to explain parties (the factions of Madison's day), contempo-rary groups controlling the means of production have political ad-vantages which Madison, when composing paper ten of the *Feder-alist Papers,* never dreamed of. The communications revolution of the twentieth century makes the press, radio, and other opinion-manipulating media far more important in the political process than ever before.

The development of the corporate form of business organization as a means of controlling production facilities necessitates ranking it, too, as an important factor in the political process. By this means ownership of much of America's industrial wealth has been separated from effective control of its property. Ownership is diffused; control is concentrated. Although more generally realized now than two decades ago, the facts and their effects on the operation of political and governmental machinery are not well understood even today. Enough is known, however, to warrant the statement that the concentration of corporate wealth is entrenched well enough to influence the power of government, thus subjecting the basic concepts of our democratic federal republic to great strains. Extending beyond political boundaries, in great national, even international, empires, corporate enterprises have grown greater than the states which chartered them. And corporations are the greatest contemporary proponents of the doctrine of states' rights.

SOME CHARACTERISTICS OF THE POLITICAL STRUGGLE. Among the noteworthy characteristics of the struggle for power are the invisibility of most of the activity, the continuity of the struggle, its varying intensity, and its constantly shifting site.

Invisibility. Although legislation under consideration in Congress is often spotlighted in the daily news; although the President's activities and the administrative decisions of the various government departments are frequently headlined in the press and radio; and although court decisions are a matter of widespread public interest—still it is true that a large and important part of the governmental process is hidden from the public's view.

To the initiated, it is a commonplace that the work of Congress is done not in the Senate and House chambers, where the spectators come to watch, but in the rooms of the congressional committees. Even this, however, is but an indication of the extent to which governmental activity is carried on behind the scenes. The factors which influence legislators only rarely include the opinions of their colleagues uttered in formal debate in Congress. Rather, they are the legislator's own political convictions, his mail from his district, the witnesses who appear before him in committee. The political effect of his vote, weighed in the scales of the next election, the expression of constituent opinion and its intensity, the state of public opinion generally—these are also factors. But none of these occurs with the same publicity as that focused on formal congressional action.

The callers at the White House are not widely publicized in the daily press. Callers upon the departmental officials subordinate to Cabinet members are subject to even less notice. The trade journal of an industry group may mention that its members went to Washington on a mission of benefit to the industry. But, if carried at all in the general press, it is tucked away in the financial pages. Letters, telegrams, telephone calls, personal visits, and the other contacts between congressional committees and their staffs, party officials, departmental officials, and representatives of interest groups are rarely of sufficient immediate dramatic content to secure public attention, even were it not the usual practice to conduct such activities without publicity.

Another reason for this invisibility is to be found in the territorial basis of legislative representation. This obscures the economic and social bases of legislative decisions, which are frequently far more compelling than geography. The political process is invisible also because citizens' groups are completely unprovided for by the written Constitution. Only in the living Constitution are they recognized as having significance along with the formal governmental agencies. They function on, in, and through the government structure, without, however, being subjected to the white light of publicity which surrounds it.

Not even the requirements of law since 1946 have exposed the governmental process to public view. Designed to bring lobbies into the open, the Regulation of Lobbying Act falls far short of regulating influence groups. It requires only that they register and that they file periodic reports of their receipts and expenditures. Although this information is of great value and is printed quarterly in the *Congressional Record*, it is practically ignored by the newspaper press, the periodicals, and the other information media. Hence its significance for the health of democracy and of government for the general welfare is not brought to the attention of the public generally. Moreover, since 1953 and 1954, judicial interpretations have limited both the number of groups required to register and the kinds of information to be filed. Thus the objective of Congress of obtaining publicity for the activities of pressure groups has by no means been achieved, and the process of government is still cloaked in obscurity.

Continuity. In addition to being invisible, the struggle for political power is continuous. From the first days of the Republic to the present the contest has never ceased. The increase and centralization of economic power has been accompanied by an increase (although not a corresponding one) in governmental authority. There have been periods which seemed relatively peaceful (1920–1928 is the most recent) but, for the most part, the peace was superficial and indicated control of the government by business-oriented legislators and officials—when the business community was not forced to resort to other, extra-governmental, methods, such as propaganda, to accomplish its will.

The continuity of the struggle is obscured by the constitutional requirement of periodic elections. The impression is thus created that, with new faces and new names in the *Congressional Directory*, new mandates have been received from the voters, or, at least, that specific programs in redemption of campaign pledges will be forthcoming. But this is true only in part. The strong, subsurface currents of the country's life are not stopped nor even greatly deflected by elections. These currents of activity go on regardless; and they are continuous as long as the country is safe and its independence secure. The eddies of these main currents which come to the surface to play upon the formal agencies of government are uninterrupted by the periodic renewal of the personnel of Congress, of the White House, and of the political posts of importance in decision-making.

A smooth or a turbulent process. Whether the struggle for control is smooth or turbulent depends on a number of factors. Obviously, military combat, whether global or localized, is a major factor. Another is the philosophy guiding the leaders of an administration. They are but temporary holders of authority, it must be remembered; even the twenty years of Democratic administration from 1932 to 1952 appears ephemeral in comparison with the durability of the philosophy of the business community. Wilson's New Freedom, Coolidge's and Herbert Hoover's faith in the wisdom of business leaders, the New Deal of Franklin D. Roosevelt and the Fair Deal of Harry S. Truman, President Eisenhower's liberal conservatism or conservative liberalism—each expresses a philosophy of government. By such varied sets of values do American Presidents steer the course of American democracy. By the extent to which each corresponds to or departs from the prevailing sentiment among the country's business leaders will the governmental process be smooth or rough. Rarely do these terms have value other than as political slogans. While they supply rallying points for campaigns, they have little of the quality of the social myth, expressing resolute and abiding determination to act. Moreover, each is indeterminate, each means different things to different men—even to officials of the administration supposedly guided by it—and each makes little pretense of embodying a consistent social philosophy. Also playing on the personalities of the nation's chief executives, affecting the intensity, the smoothness, or the turbulence of each administration, is the conception each one has of the general welfare, his political debts, his view of the future—intangible factors, to be sure, but no less important for their intangibility.

Constantly shifting site of the struggle. Where does the struggle take place? No simple answer is possible because it occurs simultaneously in all parts of the governmental structure but, at the same time, shifts constantly.

Suppose we stop the clock long enough to look at the situation in cross section, so to speak. In each of the three main branches of government hundreds of programs have been arrested in mid-air. Most of them are being administered by the departments, agencies, and commissions of the executive branch. Some of them, involving alleged violation of law or of rights, are being adjudicated in the courts even as they continue to be administered. The dockets of the Supreme Court, the appellate courts, and the district courts contain many other programs or parts of programs also in the process of having their validity under the Constitution and laws determined. The calendars of Congress, likewise, are full of bills in advanced and less advanced stages of consideration, as are the files of the congressional committees.

Every one of these products of government is the object of attention and concern by one or more of the dozens and hundreds of political interest groups which are determined to influence the course of government activity. (There were two hundred fifty-three in 1951, for example, see Table 1.) To these add the other groups not registered with Congress but pressing their claims in the executive branch, and those watching, as plaintiff, defendant, or friend of the court, the progress of the cases on the judicial dockets. (The lobby regulation law only requires registration by those trying to influence Congress; it does not apply to such activity in the courts or the executive branch.) Now, we have some idea of the volume of government work, its variety, the differing phases through which it is passing, and the manifold decisions in the making of which our hundreds of political interest groups try to take a hand. Now we see why no simple answer is possible to the question, Where does the struggle take place?

Now we can set this portrait of government, obtained by stopping the clock, in motion again. As time passes, out of the heat and pressure of such group activity, amorphous ideas embodying certain values and interests emerge and are shaped and reshaped as the process of government itself moves through its recurring cycle of elections, in which Congress, the President and his Cabinet, and other leading administrative officials account for their conduct of government to the people. Politics may absorb the daily interest and energies of only a fraction of the adult population. But the product of government is turned out on a scale so vast as almost to defy comprehension. In a typical year of the 1950's, government paid out sixty billion dollars in salaries and expenses. This is a measure of the magnitude of the operations which an observer must try to appraise if he would scrutinize the shifting site of the struggle for control of governmental power.

The Modern Right of Petition

PETITION WITH A NEW DIMENSION. In its modern form the ancient right of petition has acquired a new dimension. Formerly the length and breadth of a sheet of paper on which like-minded citizens placed their signatures, the modern right of petition has greater depth, the depth added by the revolution in communications.

Propaganda by petition. In nineteenth-century England, citizens petitioned Parliament by adding signatures by scores and hundreds until the petition rolls became too bulky for the mails to carry or even for the leaders themselves to present to Parliament. This was generating propaganda by petition, the legislature being pressed by weight of numbers to redress the grievances of the aggrieved.

Petition by propaganda. Today, in the United States, we have petition by propaganda, with the political parties hiring public relations and advertising experts to "sell" their candidates to the electorate by all the huckstering schemes devised to sell products. In much the same way, a group or a corporation (rarely an individual) that has the money will employ a public relations firm to "engineer the consent" of the people to support its program or to oppose that of his opponent. Thus a climate of opinion is created which blankets the country, including Washington. Coupled with the right of free speech, the right of petition has become a right, and one protected by the First Amendment, for those interests with the requisite resources to engage in political propaganda.

In this connection the business orientation of the newspaper press is a valuable asset. Newspapers have it in their power materially to influence opinion on specific issues. Most editors and publishers are men of the highest integrity. But they are also managers and owners of business enterprises, and their papers inevitably reflect, at least to some extent, their economic interests. When organized business deliberately propagandizes the country, using newspaper advertising as one medium, the press is a direct means of channeling business views into the public mind.

Pressure Within the Government

A CONGERIES OF RIVAL GROUPS. It must not be supposed that private persons, individual and corporate, organized and operating as pressure groups are the only ones who participate in the governmental process. While they are undoubtedly important and are sometimes decisive in the making of public policy, they are rivaled in power by the groups in the executive branch of the government. They are official, yet they behave in many respects like other pressure groups.

There is little doubt that Congress is subjected to pressure and propaganda originating within the executive branch of the government. The executive branch as a whole and all departments and lesser administrative units have a vested interest in maintaining intact the programs they have been authorized by Congress to administer. Private groups, also, and leaders and staffs of congressional committees have a similar, if not identical, interest, thus providing the bases of alliances which can be effective.

Moreover, not always do all units within a department maintain an undivided loyalty to the Cabinet member at the head and to his superior, the Chief Executive. The separation of legislative and executive powers, the strength of committee chairmen in Congress (due to the seniority rule and the absence of party unity), the diffusion of party leadership—all combine with the sheer size and heterogeneity of the executive branch to invite the development of a subsystem of tripartite executive-external group-congressional alliances within the executive branch yet not completely subordinated to it.

The Political Process

IMPORTANT, IF NOT PROMINENT, POSITION OF GROUPS. The position of groups in the political process is important. They are equally, sometimes more, important than the political parties and the bureaus of the executive branch in the policy-making process in Congress and an administration. It is not that they actually write the laws, make and execute the decisions, choose between the alternatives open to judges. Our governmental system still retains its original form. In many respects, it operates in much the same way it has traditionally operated. The new factor is the part played by groups, due to the way their influence has been multiplied by the dual revolution in communications and control of property. To a greater or lesser degree, government has always been a function of property, a reflection of the dominant ideas contained in the prevailing method of prop-

erty control. The situation in America is no exception. The failure of
Congress to deal resolutely with the issues involved in the control
of property through the corporate form of business organization
amounts to tacit acceptance of the situation as in the public interest.
(Here is an example, parenthetically, of policy-making by default.)

Relationships only partly understood. Although a relationship can
be found between governmental action and democratic elections,
this relationship is tenuous and difficult to establish, at best. Far more
important is the relationship between government action and the
desires and expectations of groups of citizens. Here the relationship
is often direct, although it is rare that it is causal. It is part of a more
complex relationship involving participants other than the officeholders and those in the groups themselves.

We depart here from the oversimplified notion that groups determine policy by threatening Congressmen with retaliation at the polls,
by pressuring government administrators, by intimidating the regulatory commissions and the courts. The relationship is more subtle
and complex. The making of decisions results not so much from the
direct pressure of groups as from the impalpable social pressures
compounded of deference and approval, fears and expectations, rationalized by propaganda in a business-oriented society. The political process is more than a political process, narrowly conceived: It
is a social process in the broad sense, a process by which society
through its articulate and active groups determines the division of
the social product. It is the answer to the question, Who gets what
of what there is to get?[18]

THE COSTS OF PRESSURE POLITICS. Accompanying the question of
the adequacy of the present system of making public policy is the
question of cost. In 1950, Congress itself raised this question. After
a detailed investigation, its committee concluded that the costs were
too high in terms of enactment of dozens of inequitable pieces of
legislation, and the defeat, delay, or emasculation of popular measures; too high in terms of the disparity in group pressures on the
policy-making process; too high in terms of the "ideological conflict
and public confusion" resulting "from the growing use of a charged
public opinion as an instrument of pressure"; and too high in terms
of financial cost. It concluded: ". . . the present demands of the
great interests total far more than the nation can afford." It defined
the problem of lobbying as "the great political imbalance between
tightly organized power blocs, such as big labor, big business, and
big agriculture, and more casually organized interests and a loosely
patterned state. . . ."[19] The Republican minority criticized the

Democratic majority not only for having issued its interim report just before the mid-term (1950) elections but also because of its views on lobbying, on the place of pressure groups in American democracy, and on the meaning of the right of petition.[20]

SUMMARY. In using the group interpretation of politics we can analyze the workings of the social process in American democracy. People join groups out of necessity and press their claims against society through the channels and by the procedures established by the Constitution and sanctioned by law and custom. This is the dynamics of democracy in America. With many and diverse groups and overlapping membership, American democracy avoids the risk of being dominated by one or another of the powerful groups which express the American genius for voluntary association. The struggle for political influence is marked by invisibility, continuity, smoothness or turbulence, and a constantly shifting site. The basic right of individuals and groups to request governmental action to redress their grievances has been transformed in modern times to a right to propagandize the country for special purposes. Over the years public policy-making has been strongly influenced by pressures originating within the nation's pressure groups—and not without cost to the country. The pattern of governmental power of which policy is so largely the reflection is discussed in the next chapter.

Chapter 4

GOVERNMENTAL POWER
IN AMERICAN SOCIETY

> . . . we lack and have always lacked any established
> theory as to the proper relationship and balance between
> private power and the power of government. . . .
> —House Select Committee on Lobbying Activities*

A study of the pressures to which the American government is subjected necessarily involves a discussion of power. Otherwise, only the skeleton of structure would engage our attention, an exercise of doubtful interest and of limited value. Pressures are manifestations of power; power is evidence of life. Therefore, to enlarge our understanding of American government, it is necessary to discuss governmental power in American democracy.

Fear of Power

Power in one form or other arouses fear in most Americans. A fear which appeared real to many occurred with the merger of the American Federation of Labor and Congress of Industrial Organizations.

FEAR OF LABOR'S FUTURE POWER. Early in 1955, the prospective merger of the AFL and CIO into one united group numbering perhaps fifteen million workers raised fears in certain quarters of the power which it could wield in both economics and politics. Speaking for the New York *Herald Tribune*, an editorial surmised that one emotion which the news would evoke in the public was "the spectre of a massed and alarmingly powerful labor group, bigger than anything 'big business' can show and more monopolistic than any of the monopolies against which government policy has been directed."[1]

---

* *General Interim Report of the House Select Committee on Lobbying Activities*, H. R. Rep. No. 3138, 81st Cong., 2d sess. (Washington, D.C.: Government Printing Office, 1950), p. 63.

It was observed in another editorial, in *The New York Times,* that the merger "alarmed disorganized masses of the people by evoking a vision of the largest and most effective pressure group in our history."[2]

Behind this alarm was the fear of an administration in Washington dominated by a merged labor group with many millions in its membership. Even without unity, according to *The Times,* organized labor in the 1930's had been effective in using its power politically. By supplying the margin of popular votes needed to swing the electoral votes of closely divided states in electing the President, labor had attained a position of influence in the governmental administration. "This electoral system," *The Times* editorial continued, "provides all sizeable pressure *blocs* with their opportunity to tilt the scales for the candidates of the party which they think or know will respond to their pressures for special consideration. Organized labor leaders, when their followings were divided, made the most of this opportunity. It is hardly to be expected that, united, they won't hope to do even better . . . in unity they raise the threat of absolute control of the economy."

There is little new in this apprehension over power except that this fear now arises out of the power which organized workers may be able to wield. Fear of power is old in American history. It was against the fear of a too-powerful government that in the Constitution only limited power was granted to the federal government by the states and the people. A system of checks and balances was built into the government against the fear of the power of popular majorities. Similarly, short and limited terms for elected representatives were also provided. Also it was to protect the individual citizen against the power of government used arbitrarily that the Bill of Rights (the first ten amendments, adopted in 1791) was embedded in the Constitution. A written constitution, a difficult amending process, and an independent judiciary are other constitutional features reflecting similar concern.

FEAR OF ANOTHER FORM OF ECONOMIC POWER. More recently, fears have arisen of the power of the managerial forces of business and finance. The trust-busting activities of the 1900's were directed against what was thought to be inordinate economic power. This was the era before 1913, during which, through the indirect election of United States Senators, whole industries were said to have been represented directly in the U.S. Congress.

One war and one depression later, both executive and legislative branches of the federal government were so concerned over the effects of concentrated economic power that an investigation was begun by the Seventy-sixth Congress, and volumes of testimony and analysis resulted. But the problem proved too much for the investigators. Although the advent of World War II undoubtedly created new problems which caused old ones to be set aside, nevertheless, the shortcomings of the *Final Report and Recommendations* of the Temporary National Economic Committee (TNEC) were clearly due to divided counsels as to how to deal with the effects of corporate concentration of industry on American democracy. To mention but one finding and the way the Committee handled it, the Committee revealed a disturbing impact of economic concentration upon representative government in the United States, an impact which one student has characterized as altering representative government to "a system of control by pressure groups."[3] Yet no legislation dealing with this finding was made. This is the more surprising, since the Committee recognized that "the rise of political centralism is largely the product of economic centralism";[4] that one result is that "individuals are no longer in contact with information which is essential to the formation of policy vital to their existence";[5] that the Committee's concern was with "the behavior of the huge collective groups which use the tools of the twentieth century and are not hampered by any of the limitations of the nineteenth century which retained the business of that era within local boundaries and to the jurisdiction of local government";[6] and that "it is lack of comprehension of this simple fact that is destroying democracy . . . in America . . . democracy which surely comprehends economic as well as political freedom for the natural person."[7] Despite the implications of these findings for traditional American democracy, the Committee went no further in its proposals for dealing with the situation and with its impact on representative institutions than to recommend, in some detail, "the maintenance of free, competitive enterprise by the effective suppression of the restrictive practices which have always been recognized as evil."[8]

As a whole, Congress seems unconcerned with the issue of big business. Individuals in Congress and a few committees, such as the House Judiciary Committee under Emanuel Celler (D., N.Y.), have displayed some concern. Spurred by the number of bank mergers in New York and corporate mergers elsewhere, a subcommittee of the House Judiciary Committee held hearings in 1956 and issued a report stating that free competition was being killed by the trend toward monopoly. Minority dissent pointed up the partisan nature of the monopoly issue. Also a Senate subcommittee investigated certain sales practices of General Motors, the largest manufacturing company in the world, and the subcommittee chairman, Joseph C.

O'Mahoney (D., Wyo.), renewed his personal recommendation, made originally at the time of the TNEC investigation, that corporations doing business in interstate and foreign commerce should be chartered by the federal government instead of by the states. But Congress did not respond to such a drastic departure from traditional principles, contenting itself with a law giving automobile dealer franchise holders the right to sue the auto-makers in the federal courts.

As compared with the shifts in the business community, the shift from Republican to Democratic control of the Eighty-fourth Congress emphasizes the frequency of change in the key leadership posts in Congress. Viewing such events from a wider angle than that of recent Congresses, observers of an earlier boom period noted this contrast:

> Compared to business enterprise in an age of great corporations, politics is a volatile thing. Executive, administrative, and legislative departments frequently change their personnel, while all political officeholders are subject to meteoric shifts in the attitudes and opinions of the voters. Of all the Cabinet members in 1921, only Andrew Mellon was in the same position in 1929. Three Presidents had been in office in that period, four Congresses had been elected, four Secretaries of State appointed, four Attorneys General, four Secretaries of the Interior, and so on down the list. Yet so profoundly pro-business was the national temper, and so successful were business efforts in keeping the favor of the public, that other groups might combine, publish, speak, and vote, and still industrial business could assert itself above all competitors for public favor. . . . The twenties were vexatious for large portions of our population. But nowhere, at any time in the world's history, had there been so much wealth so widely distributed. No wonder, then, that business pressures were most successful. No wonder that, while many groups in America won some laws in the twenties, very little legislation was passed that business opposed and very little legislation failed that business wanted.[9]

The Universality of Power

Power is everywhere, ready to be exploited. Like many common elements which occur widely in nature, power occurs widely in human society. Social power is the totality of the power of society. But it is not uniformly distributed throughout society, any more than the elements are uniformly distributed in nature. Individuals are the natural units of society, and, in one sense, the totality of the power of society is the aggregate of the power latent in each of the individuals composing that society. But this is misleading, for it leaves the impression that in his exercise of power each individual is or can be equal to every other individual. This is obviously not so. The key to an understanding of the unequal distribution of power in society is the position a person occupies relative to his fellows. Individuals are powerful in the degree and to the extent that they occupy positions in the organizations into which society is grouped according to interest.

POWER OCCURS IN MANY FORMS. Power resides in various areas. It is personal; it is social; and it occurs in all the gradations of individuals in groups, from one extreme to the other. Also, it is differentiated functionally as well as quantitatively. We have economic power, as in the power of industrial management to control production, the power of a labor union to strike, the power (almost completely unorganized) of ultimate consumers to boycott a product or a producer. We have financial power, employed to influence the behavior of others by granting or withholding credit. There is the power of government which is, in one sense, synonymous with the power of bureaucracy and, in another, only one of several different forms of governmental power—legislative, judicial, executive, political. Other forms of social power are the power of religion, as organized in the church; the power of a class, such as that of the nobility in the feudal system; the power of property, of the proletariat, of the capitalists, of the masses; the power of the press, of the other media of communication, of public opinion.

LITTLE KNOWN ABOUT POWER. Despite the confident assertions in the above paragraphs, it is doubtful that we know very much about power. In the United States it is a subject which has been neglected. It is almost always described in terms of interpersonal relations, for example, the capacity or ability of someone to effect action by someone else,[10] or as an attribute of society.[11] Such insights are suggestive. But they are inadequate in expounding a phenomenon which necessarily eludes complete description in a world where the determinants of group psychology are but partly understood.

More specifically, power can be described in terms of its sources —wealth, numbers, leadership and organization, and strategic position.[12] But most writers either emphasize the importance of the role of power or condemn it.[13] An adequate description or theory seems to be lacking.[14]

Our knowledge of power and society in the United States is imperfect. Both analysis and observation support this statement. At one moment, governmental decisions lend credibility to the thesis of the economic determinists that economic power controls political power. Yet, at the same time, further observation limits such generalization, disclosing many instances in which decisions go contrary to the apparent wishes of the wielders of economic power.

An example of the fallacy of comprehending society and power in purely causal terms is the decision of the Supreme Court that racial segregation in the public schools is unconstitutional. Here, two popular myths were shattered: first, that contentious cases get to the Court *because* some aggrieved individual believes his rights to be violated; and second, that the Court makes its decisions on legal grounds embodied in the Constitution. No individual citizen but an active organized group, the National Association for the Advancement of Colored People, initiated the cases. Grounds other than legal were used by the justices to justify their decision.[15]

Knowledge is largely lacking about the effect of economic power upon political power, or specifically, of the modern corporation upon political and governmental institutions. The corporation is far more than a device for raising capital, for creating an artificial personality separate from those of its owners, its managers, and its workers, and for organizing production, distribution, and exchange. As a form of property ownership, the corporation is outwardly the same today as it was a generation ago. But as a means for the right to use, control, and exploit wealth, it is quite different. Control is divorced from ownership. Also, the technology of communications gives control a new dimension.

To illustrate, the manufacture of public opinion is today one of the new powers of corporate boards,[16] as it is of anyone commanding the necessary resources. Obviously, as a result corporate power is increased. Also, it is expanded in a way which suffuses the environment within which government and politics operate. But knowledge of the effect, quantitatively and qualitatively, is lacking.

Again, corporation directors, as a consequence of the divorce of control from ownership, have greater discretion in the use of corporate funds. Not only are they able to manufacture public opinion but they are also permitted to subsidize private education,[17] and through officers' salaries, to finance political campaigns. Again, in both cases, the results may be guessed at but they are not yet known.

The practices permissible and followed under the corporate form are affecting government practices in still another way. Business values are imported into government by members of the business community appointed to political office. The results are far-reaching and the limits are invisible. The results range from attempted diversion of public business to business associates to the slowing down or reversal of entire governmental programs, such as public housing, public power development, resource conservation, mine safety, and foreign aid, among others, as events from 1953 to 1956 attested. Partisan opponents of the Eisenhower Administration termed such action "repeal by appointment." When the Secretary of the Interior in President Eisenhower's Cabinet says frankly that "we are in the saddle as an administration representative of business and industry," there is no reason for others to disbelieve it.

There is little mystery about the use of power for political purposes when government officials owing their position to political appointment abuse their authority. But the process by which economic power is turned into political power is more obscure. The impalpable quality of the process is suggested by the following remark of a Wilmington, Delaware, newspaperman. Commenting on economic power and its importance in politics, he said, "A billion dollars piled up, even if it remains immobile, casts a long shadow."[18]

Thus changes in the manifestations of power resulting from changes in the form of its source indicate its connection with the ways in which society is organized.

POWER IN AMERICAN DEMOCRACY. To test the hypothesis that power is a function of organization, the scope of the inquiry can be broadened to include the American economy.

The American economy. Careful analysis shows that more than half of all American industry, and the more important half at that, is operated by concentrates, that is, segments of the economy in which a few large corporations dominate the trade. On the basis of assets owned, some two hundred corporations own more than half of all American industry.[19] As of 1951, it was estimated that of all the industrial assets of the United States, 45 per cent were owned by 135 corporations.[20] This was nearly one-quarter of the manufacturing volume of the entire world.

Competent observers differ on the question of whether industry is becoming more, or less, concentrated.[21] They also fail to agree on what this concentration of ownership and power means to American society. To some the situation is ominous. They believe that concentration is approaching, if it has not already reached, monopolistic proportions and that democratic values are thus endangered.[22] At the other extreme, there are those who are not unduly disturbed by recent developments in corporate concentration. They assert that there is more, not less, competition. At the same time, even more competition is possible, they maintain, and would be desirable in the national interest.[23] Not far different are the opinions of those who plead for a re-examination of what is called the outdated structure of our feeling, our thinking, and our public policy toward bigness in business.[24] At an intermediate point in the critical scale are those who maintain that what we have is an economy characterized neither by monopoly nor by concentrates nor by competition but a mixed economy combining features of each, and with government itself an active participant in the market (the public sector).[25]

These viewpoints illustrate differing conclusions reached by students of the American economy. Aside from the extreme right and left of the critical spectrum, it is difficult to find any commentators who do not see some disturbing as well as some encouraging elements in the economy. A common element here is their recognition that the economy is now, and has been for some time, in a stage of rapid transition. It is evolving from a relatively competitive system to one characterized by relatively less competition in the traditional sense.

The meaning of the impact. The relation of economic to political power is the most acute problem faced by modern statecraft.[26] The question today is not so much the quantitative one of how much or how little competition there is in the American economy. Rather, it is one of the qualitative effects of economic concentration upon the political institutions of American democracy. It is difficult to deny that there has been some impact. Fifteen years ago the situation was noted by the TNEC in terms of the failure of political power, despite its putative monopoly of the power of government, to meet economic power on equal terms. In the meantime, the divergence of the axis of the economic from the axis of political power, noted at that time as the origin of the characteristic tension in capitalistic democracy, has not narrowed.[27] If anything, it has widened, thus increasing the tension. It shows itself in the fear of big labor by the business community and the press (as recounted at the opening of this chapter), of labor's fear of management and its conviction of the vindictiveness of business, in the partisan competition to redress the grievances of the rural farm population, and the reassertion by the states, ninety years after the crisis over slavery, of the power of the states and localities over the public schools. It is also shown in the revelation from time to time since 1950 of the power of wealth, subsidized by an income tax law loophole, to exploit state-controlled elections of U.S. Senators by campaign contributions in distant states.

The American Power Potential

Much waste and inefficiency occur in the process of converting the political power potential of the American democracy into governmental power. Only a fraction of the potential is realized. In an era when all groups seek to use their power politically, any major real or prospective change in the political potential of a particular group threatens to upset the existing adjustment, necessitating an all-around redistribution of power.

FRACTIONATED POLITICAL POWER. Underlying the fear of an enlarged labor movement is the apprehension lest a redistribution of political power result, one which could alter the existing distribution to the disadvantage of the groups presently favored, such as the business community.

Among present-day paradoxes, one of the most striking is the presence in the same country of fractionated political power with unprecedented governmental power. The needs of the people as a whole are reflected in a greater deposit of governmental authority in Washington and the states than ever before. At the same time, the division of power between the federal and the state governments, the structure and operation of the party system, the separation of powers and the scheme of representation, the desires of influential elements of the population—all combine to fractionate power. Any change in the power of one segment of society, such as organized labor, relative to that of other segments, is bound to be reflected sooner or later in a change in the political power, hence the governmental influence, of that segment. It is the prospect of an enhanced position of labor in terms of social, economic, and political power that underlies the fear of the AFL-CIO merger.

Divide and rule. The division of powers between the Washington government, the states, and the localities is central to the relation between economic power and politics. The significance lies in the fact of division itself. Divide and rule, one of the oldest political maxims, enables the managers of economic power to keep the political power potential unrealized, political power itself divided, and governmental power diffused.

Managers of all kinds of economic power follow the maxim. Producers, both industrial and agricultural, workers, service industries, transport, communications, finance—in all of these the managers are alert to the value of divided political power to their respective groups. Rarely does one of these segments of the economy act politically as a unit. Rarely is one of them so devoted to federalism as to overlook the advantages of states' rights. At one time and on one subject a group will claim the use of federal power, while at another it will make claims on state and local governmental power. This flexibility, by switching first to one, then to the other, enables each segment to squeeze the greatest possible advantage from our governmental structure and thus to defend and improve its relative economic position. Thus divide and rule enables agriculture and labor, as well as business, to exploit politics and government for their particular ends.

Federalism is particularly pleasing today to the managers of industrial enterprise. While their charters to do business are obtained not from the federal but from state government, under federalism they get the benefits of a trade area of continental proportions, at the same time escaping effective national regulation.

The TNEC's conclusion that most business escapes effective regulation by states and localities has already been noted. Here it should be added that the Committee's recommendation for national charters for concerns doing business nationally was a split recommendation, with some commissioners dissenting. In other words, it is a partisan political problem, although not an issue. Congress has never seriously debated the recommendation.

Numerous reasons serve to explain the lack of congressional attention: notably, defense and war programs, foreign aid, and foreign policy. But it is also relevant to note, in searching for reasons, that support from the business community is conspicuous by its absence. When to this is added the fact that the business community is successful, both in war and peace, in focusing attention of Congress on legislation it does want, it may be concluded that industrial managers do not want, and in fact are opposed to, even the modest degree of national regulation which would result from the requirement to obtain federal charters to replace or supplement state charters. A further conclusion is warranted. The absence of any such federal legislation is not displeasing to the business community.

Other examples of the preference for fractionated state control rather than unified federal regulation could be cited. One such is seen in the life insurance industry. It has effectively eluded social regulation, partly as a result of the nationwide lobby organization which the industry maintains. It is operated by the Association of Life Insurance Presidents and, at one time, represented "85 per cent of the legal reserve life insurance business in the United States. In one three-year period (1935-1938) it disbursed $559,751 for legislative activity. The staff of the Association analyzes about 10,000 bills a year, and where a particular bill is deemed adverse to the life insurance interests or otherwise objectionable, efforts are made through local representatives to quash the proposal in (legislative) committee or prevent its passage on the floor. Agents of member companies are frequently used to create sentiment and to communicate with legislators. The Association's organization is well integrated and effective. Its methods often are clandestine and devious."[28]

In addition, the farther away from Washington one gets in the federal-state-local hierarchy, the greater becomes the power of business leaders. While they are powerful in the national capital from time to time, at the state capitals the power of the business pressure groups is even greater. Also, overrepresentation of the rural areas in the state legislatures, together with conservative business interests in the cities, makes the pressure groups stronger than the governors and the legislatures themselves.[29] When we get to the local communities and the county seats, the power of the business leaders is greatest.[30]

Urban underrepresentation. Underrepresentation of the urban population in Congress and the state legislatures and overrepresentation of the rural population, hence of rural groups, is widespread. In many states the absence of equitable representation is accentuated by the similarity of views on economic and social matters held by representatives of the rural population and of those from urban districts where business interests are strong. Thus the disproportionately large political power of rural areas is reflected in the lack of control of legislatures by any substantial proportion of the people, thus facilitating the exercising of political power by pressure groups.[31]

No altruistic devotion to the laborer's right to work is behind the movement to embed a declaration of that right in the constitutions and laws of the states. In Florida, for example, the Associated Industries of Florida, an NAM affiliate, initiated the movement which led to a right-to-work amendment to the state constitution. By 1955, seventeen states had such laws on their statute books, evidence of a more widespread and coordinated effort than usually occurs without some centralized stimulus. Fear was expressed in 1955 by the American Civil Liberties Union lest these laws restrict the civil liberties of individuals, particularly the right of association.

Moreover, the partnership idea so prominent in the philosophy of the Eisenhower Administration as the basis of cooperation between the federal government and the states in natural resource development and management is explainable only in part by any theoretical preference for states' rights. Equally important is the political strength of localities and private groups at the state capitals and the desire to protect it. Such interests are eager for power development, reclamation, and navigation. With Cabinet members and legislators in Washington sharing their point of view, these interests are able to press for single, rather than multiple-purpose, dams and works, thus keeping the profitable projects under local control but with the federal government paying the capital cost. The possibility that this partnership principle might be extended to include irrigation, reclamation, and river and harbor development, in contrast with the policy of federal control based on federal financing, was broached by an Administration official to a national reclamation group in 1955.

The party system. The structure and operation of the party system, both inside and outside Congress, also contributes to fractionated political power.

It may be "the business of politics to produce power,"[32] but politics in the United States fails to generate enough power to support a system of responsible party government able to cope with nationwide conditions and problems. Pressure group government is the consequence. It is the result of unrealized political power potential; the dissipation and nonconsolidation, due to the localism of party control, of the power that is generated; the absence of party discipline;[33] the county basis of party organization;[34] the spasmodic efforts of the national parties; and the unrepresentative character of single-member constituencies.[35]

Emergence of pressure groups. Political potential unrealized by the parties, or generated by them only to be dissipated, is taken up by pressure groups. The rise of such groups has been an accompaniment of increasing economic specialization and changes in the level of economic activity, together with such factors as decentralized political parties, Presidents making less than full use of their political power, high taxes, the expansion of the country, and concentration of economic power.[36] Organization techniques, consciously perfected and practiced, and the technological revolution in communications, with its contribution to the propaganda art, have also played their parts in this development.

SOME UNSOLVED PROBLEMS. Political power fractionated by the Constitution, by law, and by custom is complicated further by the impact of economic power on society at large.

Freedom from responsibility. In the overlapping margins of economics, politics, and law, an analogy can be drawn between corporate managers and political officeholders. The tenure of the former, as does that of the latter, depends on the continued good will of the governed. But there is a vital difference. Political officeholders are subject to periodic scrutiny by the electors at the polls, while corporate managers are not. The former are responsible to the people, who are the source of political power, even though that system of responsibility may break down or continue to work inefficiently. Corporate managers, however, are beyond the effective control of the corporate electorate. In general, corporate ownership is divorced from control.[37] It may be difficult for a representative in Congress from a "safe" congressional district to be removed by dissatisfied constituents. But Congressmen are unseated more frequently by dissatisfied constituents than corporate managements are ousted by dissatisfied minority stockholders.

Others have drawn attention to the irresponsibility of corporate management in the political use of economic power.

> It is impossible to operate an individualistic economic system in which the power of some individuals is not subject to any quickly effective check. This is obvious in the realm of political individualism, and it must be equally true that an arrangement of checks and balances is required in any system of economic individualism. Or if unlimited power is granted to the executive, the system must provide for the immediate dismissal of the executive when he loses the confidence of the electorate. And that provision we do not have. Even if production plans are well laid, and the rewards paid to themselves by control groups are moderate, we cannot depend on a planning system that may be upset at any time by the actions of one group in the system. The presence of a benign and intelligent autocrat does not create a system of economic or political democracy.[38]

The irresponsibility of concentrated economic power sharpens the dilemma of the politics of control. Government draws most of its support from the very particularistic groups which it must attempt to control.[39] When the economically most powerful of these groups can operate outside the political system, thus evading the responsibility which must always accompany political authority, it becomes almost impossible to perform the task of government.

Political thinking not up-to-date. Outmoded thinking is a handicap to fruitful understanding of the penetration of political by economic power. One reason is our habit of thinking compartmentally, that is, of economics as separate from politics and of economic power as distinct from governmental power. Also, in our time the uses of power are not always obvious, but are subtle and are not easily fitted into our conventional thought patterns. Another reason is the short memory span we have for any but the most momentous events. Congressional investigations which reveal the inner workings of economic power in government do not hold our attention long enough to permit us to grasp their full implications.

Our imperfect understanding of the terms "power" and "politics" is shown in the constant use of the phrase "power politics"—as if politics were participated in for any purpose other than power, and as if politics were limited to public affairs and were not characteristic of human relations in all groups. The wide area of political ignorance and unawareness is the result of popular failure to grasp the fact of economic power, its range, its impact on family incomes and on the terms under which all goods and services are offered for sale, as well as the default of the new means of popular communication in their duty to disseminate these facts.

There is no sharp line dividing economic from political power. To understand how economic power has pervaded American life, how it uses political power, while resisting its use by others, we must be prepared to replace much of our conventional thinking about politics by new ideas and new concepts. Together with the marvels of technology, we must adopt a new attitude no less revolutionary in the world of social thought than the insights of scientists into the world of material things.

There is a widespread notion that all political power is localized in government. A little thought shows this is not so. Much political power lies latent in the people. Some of it is in the political parties outside Congress, some in the political pressure groups, the press, the politically urbane segments of the people. Organization, multiplied by prestige, gives these groups political status. Yet Americans dislike and reject too much organization. Although we have a genius for it, few would claim that America is completely organized. Indeed, when organization reaches a certain point in any sphere of activity, the suspicion arises that organization has gone too far. Society at large, as well as individuals and groups, no longer benefit from it; they may be harmed. The point beyond which Americans do not want organization to extend is the point at which individual enterprise is stifled and personality frustrated.

We also like bigness. But, at the same time, many of us become suspicious of bigness when it overshadows personality and acts impersonally. The suspicion of bigness in business and in labor has already been mentioned. One should add bigness in government, too. But federal government is in fact limited, and government as a whole is divided, although federal government and big government are synonymous to many Americans. The separation of powers within the federal government, the division of power between it and the states, the further subdivision of power among the cities, the states, and school and other special service districts and three thousand counties are proof of the great diffusion which exists. This atomization of that part of political power to be found in government is an accurate reflection of the basic American preference for decentralized power.

There has been no similar preference for atomized economic power. In their preoccupation with maintaining curbs on political power in government, the American people have unwittingly permitted the assumption of political power by economic institutions.

It is likely that "the stability of republican government depends upon considerable dispersion of economic control."[40] But it also depends on material resources and a consciousness of purpose which, as the Lobby Investigating Committee in 1950 said, government, for all its vaunted power, may not have.[41] A fuller exposition of government as the action and interaction of political pressure groups with the more formal governmental organs is called for. To this part of the subject we turn in the next chapter.

SUMMARY. The present chapter has discussed governmental power in American society. Government does not monopolize power in American democracy. Power is widespread and occurs in all parts of society but not everywhere in the same proportions. While Americans innately fear power in government, in labor, and in the business community, they have been more tolerant of power exercised by producers than by any other segment of society. As a whole, Congress does not seem concerned by concentration of economic power in industry and finance. The political power potential of the American democracy is not fully realized due to default of the political parties, the emergence of pressure groups, underrepresentation of urban populations, and the diffusion of governmental power by the American federal system. The freedom of corporate managers from any responsibility to the political electorate and the lag in the development of up-to-date thought patterns are two problems with which the American democracy has not yet come to grips.

Chapter 5

THE PLACE OF GROUPS
IN GOVERNMENT AND POLITICS

> You yourself are doubtless a member of a lobby group
> and are represented in Washington by a lobbyist, or two,
> or three. If you are not, then it shows that you are not a
> very active citizen. . . .
>
> —W. M. Kiplinger
> *Washington Is Like That**

The distinction made by Kiplinger between active and passive
citizens, points up several points of crucial importance in politics.
Viewed broadly, government and politics are the action and interaction of groups of people in their political capacities. The leaders of
groups get and are able to retain their positions because of the inertia
of the mass of members of a group. All formal governmental agencies,
not just legislatures, are the object of, and are themselves participants
in, group activity for political reasons.

The purpose of this chapter is to examine in some detail the first
two of these features of government and politics in the United States.
The third is examined in later chapters.

Political and Group Activity

In mid-twentieth century America the impulses and other evi-
dences of social activity which we call politics and government are
the impulses and activities of social groups. The selection of candidates for public office and the choice made from among these candidates at elections are actions of individuals acting as groups. Likewise, the decisions of legislatures are decisions of transitory groups,
majorities formed for the moment, when conditions are ripe for decisions. In the offices of the bureaucracy, administrative decisions are

* New York: Harper & Bros., 1942, p. 279.

the result of the pressures from varied groups brought to bear on the decision-making officials. Even in the courts the judgments and the decisions handed down are actions of groups of men approving or rejecting the arguments of social groups.

THE GROUP NATURE OF SOCIETY. Whether the term "group politics" is used in the sense of public politics or private politics, its quality of activity is its most characteristic feature.

Dual role of the individual. In politics groups supply fundamental human needs. While the individual is never wholly absorbed in the group, it is, nevertheless, the support which sustains him. There are two major characteristics of human society: human beings everywhere are members of groups; yet the individual is never wholly absorbed in his society. Despite his membership in groups, he never ceases being an individual.[1]

Cooperation essential. People everywhere strive for a feeling of security that their basic needs—food and shelter, health, protection, and companionship—will be satisfied. Moreover, people seem to crave a chance to increase their standard of living. They are, apparently, never satisfied with what they have, but always want more.

From the primary group, the family into which he is born, the individual learns of his need for security and of his craving for better things. As he grows older he finds that by joining with others in secondary groups he can advance his own aims. In time, his aims become absorbed into those of the group; he identifies himself with the group not only as a member but also as a supporter and promoter, potentially at least, of the aims of the group as embodied in its programs. Maximum satisfaction of his basic and learned needs now comes from the group of which he is a part. As witness Hadley Cantril told a committee of Congress in 1950: "Man is so constituted apparently that he must live and work with other people if he is to survive and get this maximum satisfaction."[2]

The importance of cooperation is worthy of emphasis. No society can exist without some measure of cooperation according to rules regulating behavior which reflect a spirit of give and take. It is not the individual but the primary group which is the basic unit of society. Society is composed of a network of these groups. It is not the individual but the social controls of the groups to which he belongs which make up the major instruments of control in society.[3]

Importance of group experiences. Through his group experiences and affiliations the individual understands, explains, and reacts to the larger social whole of which he is a part. Within limits, the group instills uniformities in behavior and attitudes in the individual, uniformities which tend to regulate all of the individual's attitudes toward other groups, and his work. They also regulate, in a sense, his political attitudes and behavior.[4]

Politics as a process. If politics is based on groups, then, in studying politics we study a process rather than static concepts, power rather than the state. We study groups as they function in private and official spheres, rather than individuals. We study groups as organizations of power, because groups combine for a purpose—to control their environment—and in so doing to fulfill the function of the group. Their purpose is the fulfillment of the individual's need for self-expression and a sense of security, and groups attempt to achieve it through the manipulation of their environment. According to the group basis of politics, the state is an association of power which has been approved by the "official" consensus of the people in order to establish and enforce norms of permissible behavior in group relations. This is done by establishing various points for reaching compromises among the social groups (legislatures), for execution of the rules (executive agencies), and for defining these rules and their applicability (the judiciary). There are also group interests and frictions within and among these branches of government.[5]

In America the individual's role in society is thus based on group relations. Similarly, political pressure groups can be regarded as basic elements in the contemporary political process. American social behavior can best be understood as the more or less conscious struggle of an almost infinite number of groups striving to realize their aims and ideals through group action. This is "groupism," the belief that the individual can best achieve his purpose in life by associating himself with, and working through, groups.

Thus the scope of groups in American life is wider than their effect on politics and government. Freedom of association, a right guaranteed by the First Amendment to the Constitution, goes far to explain the central place of groups in American life. Describing this right as a freedom full of danger, one observer sees in voluntary association a key to the understanding of America.[6]

GROUPS AS MASS ACTIVITY. If government is a certain kind of group activity, it is pertinent to ask how many groups there are, and in what variety. Generally speaking, the number is legion and the variety is infinite, or nearly so.

No one knows how many groups there are in America. The federal census is not very helpful here. While certain of its classifications, such as urban, rural farm, and rural nonfarm, are suggestive, the categories in which people are classified for census purposes are not very informative for our purpose. Nor does classification by age, sex, and color, by states and regions, by military or civilian status, or by major occupation groups help very much in providing an answer.

The number of groups. Statistics as such are not very helpful; what is needed are statistics which will provide some insight into the range and penetration of government in society. By the term "group," we mean "a certain portion of the men of a society" engaged in "mass activity."[7] Our search must lead us to the data on groups whose activities influence the public, for it is then that we have discovered the stuff of government.

Estimates of the number of groups in America, on this basis, range from a few dozen to many millions. At the lower limit, one writer estimated sixty as the number of groups with enough money or votes back of them to have political strength.[8] At the upper limit, in all probability, would be the number of spending units in the population —an estimated fifty-two million in 1951, and probably more now.[9] Between these two limits, different estimates are made. One writer, whose attention is centered on groups which "influence opinion outside their own memberships," notes the absence of accurate information on the number of such groups, as well as information on their memberships. However, he enumerates as of importance for opinion-influencing purposes the 1810 organizations estimated in 1947-48 as having Washington offices, and mentions a 1950 estimate of 150 national labor groups, 40,000 to 50,000 local labor groups, as well as more than 3000 national business groups and some 2000 local ones.[10] These and other groupings are of significance to another commentator, who also added 30,000,000 families, 250,000 local religious congregations, 12,000 agricultural marketing associations, 175,000 local and *ad hoc* governmental authorities in an enumeration illustrating the multiplicity of interests.[11] For the U.S. Department of Commerce, the test for inclusion in its 1949 compilation of national associations in the United States was "economic activity." On this basis, "there were in the United States approximately 4000 trade, professional, civic, and other associations, the majority of which are national in scope, while, if locals and branch chapters are added, the figures mount to 12,000 trade associations, 4000 chambers of commerce, 70,000 labor unions, 100,000 women's organizations, 15,000 civic service groups, luncheon clubs, and similar organizations of businessmen and women."[12] Additional data, such as the 1090 societies and associations, the 97 labor unions with a membership of 25,000 or over, and the estimate of 262,000 manufacturing establishments, listed in a recent issue of the *World Almanac,* corroborate the figures already given as to the vast number, running into the thousands or millions, of groups in the United States.

The variety of groups. Groups exist in almost infinite variety. Fifteen main categories, each based on a general interest, are used to classify the 4000 associations on which the U.S. Department of Commerce published information in 1949. These comprised the following: associations of manufacturers, of distributors, and of businessmen in the fields of transportation, finance, insurance, and related fields; professional and semiprofessional persons; labor unions; women; veterans and military; commodity exchanges; farmers; Negroes; public officials; fraternal associations; sports and recreation; and, finally, a blanket category "all other fields."

National associations, thus divided into main categories, are built on varied interests. Also, each of these main categories itself embraces a variety of interests and each of these, in turn, a variety of interests. When it is recalled that activity is evidence of interest and, further, that activity includes not only men's actions but also their mental and emotional reactions, the rich variety of grounds for the coalition of people into groups is obvious.

The changing nature of groups. In the study of politics as mass activity by men in groups, two more points to note about groups, in addition to their number and variety, are change in their composition and differences in the rate of change. Regardless of the kind or size of a group, it is constantly undergoing change. Only in the statistician's data do groups lose their vital characteristic of change and become static. Here lurks a danger: Reading such figures in a reference book, one may too easily mentally transfer the static quality of the data to the groups to which they refer, and thus be led to the mistaken conclusion that the group, too, is static. Nothing could be further from the truth. The spending unit expands or contracts in activity as its membership increases or decreases in size. Similarly, the massive group known as government undergoes daily change, both in size and in composition. Also, at varying rates, other groups of differing sizes and varieties are changing continuously, but are unlike in their respective rates of change. These rates differ from group to group: Some groups flourish longer than others; some renew themselves, wholly or partially, at different periods, but, again, at different rates.

Pressure Groups

In view of the interpretation given here—that politics and government are certain kinds of mass activity by men in groups—some discussion of the emergence of pressure groups is needed.

THE NATURE OF PRESSURE GROUPS. The term "pressure group" is one of recent origin, in fact, of the past thirty years or so. Neither the term "group" nor "pressure group" is to be found in a political dictionary published in 1924.[13]

What is a pressure group? Writers on pressure groups do not agree on a definition of their subject. Two examples may be given. According to the *Encyclopedia of the Social Sciences*, a pressure group is any "aggregate, organized or unorganized, which applies pressure tactics."[14] According to this source, a distinction should be drawn between an interest and a pressure group, a musical organization and a philatelic society being cited as examples of interest groups which are not pressure groups. Another writer, however, holds that there is no difference and asserts that interest groups are also pressure groups and, moreover, that the distinction is not maintained consistently in the literature of political and social science.[15]

The differences over what constitutes a pressure group are a little unreal. To cite musical and philatelic societies as examples of interest groups which are not pressure groups is not convincing. At one time they may not have engaged in pressure tactics. But nowadays the public (as well as the group) politics of organized musicians and philatelists are politically significant. Moreover, the distinction overlooks the potential nature of interest groups as pressure groups, a potentiality which has become an actuality for almost all groups that were purely interest groups two decades ago. Today, interest groups are pressure groups, and vice versa; the earlier distinction was a matter of degree and kind of pressure exerted rather than a difference in the bases of the groups themselves.

Oligarchical tendency of groups. Like all groups composed of individuals, political pressure groups develop undemocratic tendencies, particularly as regards control. Although in the United States they owe their existence to the individual's right to associate freely with his fellows, the corresponding opportunity to participate in the group's decisions is used by only a small minority of its members. This is the active minority, or, in other words, the oligarchy which controls the group's affairs.[16]

The tendency to oligarchy in groups was first erected into a law of society in an analysis of the working of political parties.[17] Once an organization reaches a certain size and degree of complexity, its leaders cannot be controlled positively, but only in a negative way: ". . . the executive or leadership activities in an organization are free from control by the other activities; or, putting it another way, the people who hold positions of authority within an organization are not checked by those who hold subsidiary positions within the organization."[18]

As in political parties, so in other social groups, each group is led by an active minority, while the majority is acquiescent. This acquiescence is not the "consent of the governed" of the Declaration of Independence, whence the just powers of government are derived. On the contrary, consent implies activity; acquiescence, passivity. The former presupposes some prior participation, the latter, default on such activity. Although outwardly similar, the two qualities are inwardly quite different.

In fact, as well as by their charters, minorities, not majorities, rule in our most important pressure groups, such as the National Association of Manufacturers,[19] the American Bar Association, and the American Medical Association.[20] In labor unions much the same situation prevails. The day-to-day administration of labor unions would be difficult if the unstated assumption of majority acquiescence in leadership policies were not operative.[21] The management of organizations apparently presupposes the acceptance by the great mass of members of the form, rather than the substance, of democratic rule.

If the law of oligarchy is true of pressure groups, as for groups generally, the implications for politics in America are disturbing. The party system and congressional districts determined on a territorial basis represent the individual voter but imperfectly, at best. Likewise, the individual learns sooner or later that even if he is an active citizen, he is similarly poorly represented, if not actually disenfranchised, in the groups to which he belongs. The operating principles of his groups leave little scope for his individual interests and energies unless he happens to emerge, in time, himself a member of the active minority. Moreover, in the groups to which he belongs, a management class is evolving a class of paid experts who, because of their experience and technical knowledge of politics, assume the role though not the title of directors. Although hired and fired by the nominal directors, much of the time the paid managers supply the initiative, the ideas, and the program direction of the group's actions, which are accepted by these same directors. This, too, leaves little room for the ordinary member to become active. The more organization, it would seem, the less chance there is for the organized to realize their full potentialities. Thus in politics, the political man is, in effect, less than a full man.[22]

MODERN DEVELOPMENT OF PRESSURE GROUPS. Pressure groups are modern in name, but the conditions which gave rise to them go back in history.

A modern biographer of Thurlow Weed describes him as the "Wizard of the Lobby." Weed died in 1882, at the age of eighty-five, having lived through the breakup of the Democratic Party over slavery, the rise of the Republican Party, the Civil War, and Reconstruction. The period in which he flourished was one of money-making, of gaining office by whatever means it took to win, of bigotry, of political mudslinging, and of personal vituperation. It was in this same period that Weed won his title of "Dictator" and "My Lord Thurlow." Although he served in the New York State Assembly, office-holding was less to his liking than putting others in office: "His job was getting other men the nominations for Governor, President, Senator, or Assemblyman, and then influencing or controlling them and their fellow-executives or legislators."[23] As a lobbyist, Weed practiced the art of politics, lobbied scientifically, influenced the influential.

But Weed typified the "old lobby" which has passed; in its stead stands the "new lobby," with propaganda its characteristic feature. But it cannot be said that all of the conditions which produced the "Wizard of the Lobby" have vanished; neither can it be said that the new lobby owes its development entirely to the rise of the propaganda art. The new lobby, too, has its roots in the past.

The origin of pressure groups in their contemporary form can be traced to three principal and several minor sources. The main ones are economic factors, particularly specialization; psychological factors; and the weakness of political parties.

Economic specialization. Society in the United States is built upon economic specialization and organization. Both have contributed greatly to the rise of pressure groups. Specialization fosters the growth of groups and of subgroups in the field of management as of labor. Moreover, in order to advance their particular objectives, all such groups and subgroups resort sooner or later to political action and influence. In the United States they have not founded labor parties or parties representative of management, as in some European countries. On the contrary, group leaders have, by and large, worked within the parties, while the groups work autonomously but in cooperation with them, throwing their weight first to one party, then to the other, depending on which party seems to offer more.[24]

The effect of specialization on the social structure results in a subtle reshaping of that structure. Even more important is the effect of specialization on the whole scheme of government. The processes set in motion by specialization in modern society effect "as great a transformation in the character of government as can be attributed to the most world-shaking of revolutions. . . ." They are even more enduring and more universal, "for these processes are persistent, irreversible, and cumulative in their impacts, not subject, like revolutions, to revulsion and countermovement."[25]

Psychological factors. Psychological factors associated with economics are the second of the main factors explaining the modern development of pressure groups. In modern industrial society there is a high degree of group consciousness.[26] Psychological factors are strong influences in making unorganized masses of people coalesce into groups of large number and variety. Men join groups to overcome the fear of having to battle hostile forces single-handedly. Group action in the economic field is more natural among men than the classical economists thought or admitted. The individual achieves a sense of security when he joins with others. This drive toward groupism has been further intensified by industrialization and the greater independence among the several parts of the economic system.

Furthermore, men join groups to achieve a sense of belonging, thus compensating for the loss of this sense induced by industrialization.[27] Pressure groups also act as safety valves for individual frustrations.[28] The desire to protect or advance an existing position in the economy is another psychological factor favoring the growth of pressure groups. Here the psychological and economic factors merge in a powerful motivating force to do something to meet a threat, or to prevent its emergence. Individuals are thus drawn together into a group to protect its real or fancied interests, seeking the power of government to hold the position already gained, to advance it, or to protect it from new threats. Group organization becomes desirable, even necessary. The threat may come from any one or a combination of a number of sources—domestic or foreign competition, transportation rates thought to be too high, power developed from a new source, such as atomic energy, or from new tax proposals. High taxes are a strong inducement to form groups and for the development of and intensification of conflict among groups, and for efforts of such groups to find haven in partial relief from taxation.[29]

The birth of many of our pressure groups can be traced to origins such as those just mentioned—commercial farmers, manufacturers, transportation groups, producers of tobacco, wool, cattle, peanuts, wheat, soybeans, citrus fruit. Similarly, industrial laborers at trades or industries, transport workers, truck drivers, motor vehicle manufacturers, contractors, and many more have joined together in recent times to advance the interests of its individual members and of the group collectively. These economic interest and political pressure groups evolved with America's economic development in such a way as to create the impression that such a movement was inevitable. George Galloway, for example, calls the presence of these numerous interest groups in an industrial society like that of the United States "an inescapable feature."[30] He also describes the complex industrial society of the United States as being "made up of a 'mosaic' of interest groups. . . ." Perhaps kaleidoscope would be more accurate. A mosaic is static; a kaleidoscope is always set in motion when sufficient pressure is applied.

All segments and parts of society are caught up in the activity of groups so characteristic of industrial society. There are not only industrial producer and labor and farm groups, but also groups based on profession, on sex, on religious belief, on ethics and morals. If the laboring men of the late nineteenth century made the discovery that organization can "counterbalance or outweigh the power attached to property or prior privilege of any kind," as MacIver says, the extension of this discovery to the professions is evidence that they, too, have learned the advantages of organization for political activity.[31] Already organized for professional purposes, the country's physicians, for example, pressed their way into the legislative struggle when they thought their status was threatened by the proposal of what they termed "socialized medicine," which was advanced to bring the costs of adequate medical care within the reach of the country's middle-income groups.[32] "Improper" public opinion about the federal Constitution, and about political matters generally, underlay the addition of a new article to the constitution of the country's organized lawyers in 1936, thus making the bar a more active factor in the generation of "proper" public opinion on these matters.[33] Lobbying and pressure politics is not new among the churches, but a recent survey concludes that there is a new tendency for agencies to be formed to represent denominational and interdenominational bodies before the federal government.[34] Commercial and investment bankers are likewise organized into national and state organizations which are active in Washington and at the capitals in their respective states.[35] The influential role of the life insurance industry on, through, and in government, uncovered by Charles Evans Hughes in New York State in 1906, was found in 1940 to extend to many other states, as well as to Washington, and has already been mentioned.[36] There are many women's groups whose origins antedate the adoption in 1919 of the equal suffrage amendment to the Constitution, as well as some founded after that date which inject themselves into the legislative process.[37]

Operation of the party system. Still another reason for the rise of pressure groups is the operation of the party system. It is not a strong system, that is, it is not strong enough to provide responsible party government. Pressure groups would not have attained their present status as a recognized part of the governmental system if the political parties had come closer to the high ideals of the party government enthusiasts. In the one-party states and districts the party system does not provide vigorous competition for popular support for different programs. Also, in the country as a whole the party system operates to foster the growth of pressure groups. This was pointed out in 1950:

> Pressure groups thrive on the inability or unwillingness of political parties to exercise the powers of government which they have lawfully gained at the polls. The advantages of this situation to the lobby group are obvious: lack of cohesion in the parties enables well-organized private interests to secure some of the advantages of political power without having to submit to the democratic electoral process by which this power is usually attained.[38]

Other contributing factors. Popular lack of knowledge about lobbyists may be a contributing factor in the rise of pressure groups. Fewer voters know about lobbyists than vote in general elections (but more than in primary elections).

Freedom of association, the right of petition, the complex nature of government and international war have also been advanced as reasons for the rise of pressure groups. All of these contributing factors, plus loyalty to the memory of a departed leader, probably operated to bring Americans for Democratic Action into existence. The importance of the right of petition lies in the invitation it offers to those who would employ it with modern techniques.[39] Similarly, the complexity of government baffles rich and poor alike, but the former have means of surmounting the obstacles not available to the latter. The rich can buy the "knowledge and skill," which the Supreme Court itself has said is required in dealing with the government and its departments.[40] World War II contributed greatly to the mobilization of group interest. In 1950 it was noted the impact of the war on lobbying had a "marked increase in the number of organized groups having an active and continuous interest in shaping policy to their own ends."[41]

Given the form of our government, the energy of the people, the resources and physical location of the United States, there is something inevitable in the growth of pressure groups in American society. The natural development of lobbies is seen in the fact that there are no significant interest groups in this country which do not seek something from the government.[42] Pressure groups and lobbies are the "inevitable co-product" of our form of government, necessary as an outlet through which people can vent their grievances and press their claims between biennial elections.[43]

THE ROLE OF LOBBYING IN REPRESENTATIVE SELF-GOVERNMENT. In theory, the United States is a federal republic, a union of states, in which ultimate political power rests in the people and is exercised on their behalf by representatives chosen periodically in free and open elections.

In the United States we have self-government. But neither in theory nor in fact is political power exercised directly by the people. On the contrary, ours is representative self-government. While the people govern themselves, they do so not directly but indirectly, through elected officials chosen by the electorate in democratic elections. The people permit themselves to be governed by officials chosen from among candidates for political office who are themselves designated by political parties according to devices such as direct primaries, conventions, and party caucuses. Although parties were frowned on by the Constitution's framers, our early leaders soon found indispensable to the operation of the government some means of designating candidates and of organizing the unorganized power of the people. The parties have been performing this function ever since.

Within this system of government the lobbying techniques by which pressure groups influence government and politics have reached their present stature.

By lobbying is meant all substantial attempts to influence governmental decision for pay or for any consideration. This definition is a modification of the one used in 1950 by the House Select Committee on Lobbying Activities. But the modification is a major one. The Committee adopted a more restricted definition: ". . . all substantial attempts to influence *legislation* (italics mine), etc."[44] The wider scope suggested is believed to be more in line with the facts, and, indeed, was suggested by the Committee Chairman, Frank Buchanan (D., Pa.), when he said, at the outset of the inquiry, that the subject of inquiry was "pressures in a democracy."[45] Furthermore, to limit lobbying to attempts to influence legislation ignores the efforts to influence administration and the judicial process, both of which are subject to intense pressures.

In the United States lobbying has four roles: representative, advisory, protective, and promotional.

Representative role of lobbying. In its representational aspect, lobbying is an adjunct to territorial representation. In our "polity of pressure groups," to use Walter Lippmann's phrase,[46] representation based on territory is inadequate to represent the individual both as an individual, and as a member of an occupational group. Lobbying meets this need for more complete representation.

The individualistic conception of political representation is not adequate for contemporary needs. From the early days of our government it has been more an ideal than a reality. With westward expansion, population growth, the Industrial Revolution, and the revolution in communications and the accompanying specialization of labor, the gap between fact and ideal has widened. One author has put it thus: "The rise to power of unrecognized pressure groups in America was an example of how ill-adapted individualistic conceptions of representation were to deal with the necessities imposed upon politics by modern life."[47] Nowadays, representatives in Congress often act more like representatives of groups in their districts than they do of the constituents considered as individuals.

The demands made on present-day members of Congress to represent their constituents in their occupational and related capacities is stressed by a committee of the California State Legislature which studied lobbying:

> Territorial representation as provided by the federal and state Constitutions is inadequate because it makes no provision for the common interest of individuals and groups living in different constituencies; it fails to give all the varied interests affected by legislation a voice in that legislation; it means that important minority interests, if widely scattered, have no voice at all; it makes the representative appear in the false role of speaking for or on behalf of his constituents on most issues, when in fact there cannot be any common interest or opinion among his constituents on those issues.[48]

Advisory role of lobbies. In advising Congressmen, lobbyists appear in another role. Present-day legislators have to act on highly technical matters. Lobbyists are often better informed on these matters than the legislators themselves. Under these circumstances it is not surprising that Congress and the state legislatures find useful the information supplied by lobbyists. Such information, however, although useful in promoting understanding, is also selective and is developed for purposes of persuasion along a certain line. Indeed, it is the job of the legislative representative or lobbyist, when he testifies before a legislative committee, to keep the legislators' attention focused on that information which will most effectively promote the lobbyist's point of view. Thus there is a dual aspect to the advisory value of lobbying. Lobbyists advise legislators not only as representatives of people as such, but also as representatives of people in their occupational or functional capacity.

Information for the legislature supplies the need to explore the far-reaching but not always readily discernible effects of many legislative proposals upon economic life. Using the information thus supplied, the legislator still has a difficult role to perform. This is attested to by the same committee of the California Legislature quoted above. After noting that "groups of farmers, businessmen, taxpayers, public employees, labor representatives, and many individual citizens engage in legislative lobbying in one way or another," the committee offers this definition of the legislator's task: "to achieve something constructive out of the conflicting claims and demands and explanations of all groups that make up our society. The legislature should not become merely an efficient machine to grind out laws for this group or that, or for this governor or that, but a sort of marketplace in which, by the slow process of debate, the wares that each group has to sell are truly valued in the terms of public demand and need."[49]

In this connection, the educational value of lobbying, both to Congress and to the public at large is noteworthy. The role of pressure groups and lobbyists in the formulation of public opinion is discussed elsewhere.[50] Here it is sufficient to mention the educational value of lobby activity. The evils of lobbying are incidental to its positive values, it was maintained in 1949 by the *Washington Post*. After noting a *New York Times* editorial in which the Eighty-first Congress was reported to have been "more hag-ridden by pressure groups and pleaders for special interests" than any in recent times, the *Post* editorial expressed no surprise at "this excessive activity"; it went on to point out the "highly useful purpose" which lobbying serves "under our representative system of government, by providing a means of communication between lawmakers and their constituents and marshalling arguments for and against measures." Lobbying, it stated, is "an effective molder of public opinion not to be despised because lobbyists are usually spokesmen for special interests." The chief danger from lobbying "arises when a few powerful organizations are able by sheer force of numbers or superior powers of persuasion to silence the voices of opposition groups." But this danger is usually offset by counterarguments from rival groups "with the result that both Congress and the public are better able to judge the effects of pending legislation. Lobbying is, in short, educational when all interested parties have an opportunity to present their case."[51]

Protective role of lobbies. When we pass from the representative and advisory roles of lobbying to its protective role, it becomes related to even larger matters of public policy. As has already been noted, pressure groups originated and developed largely, if not wholly, as mechanisms for both defense and offense, the latter, to improve the situation in which a group found itself, the former, to defend an advantageous position vis-à-vis other groups. And lobbying continues to perform this dual role efficiently.

Here, we deal with a subject which touches the roots of political theory and practice. Political pressure groups have both an affirmative and a negative function. Paradoxically, some groups operate negatively when they operate affirmatively, that is, in taking the offensive to correct what they think is a maladjustment, they try to deny to other groups some benefit or privilege, right or value, already attained. Conservative groups often act in this way. Such groups view America's current development and future in traditional terms, setting a premium on the values of the past. They want to deny to other groups, possibly less privileged economically or socially, positions, rights, or income which they feel are rightly theirs. In other words, political pressure groups are sometimes negative pressure, or veto, groups, which want to, and do, veto proposals of other groups for public policy or action. As such, they have much power in American society, and in exercising this negative power they are, in effect, able to influence the course of government and politics.[52]

Groups possessing such veto power use it. In fact, in this veto power of pressure groups there is the same minority veto of majority rule which John C. Calhoun erected into a philosophy of government, over a century ago, in his theory of concurrent majorities. Only when majorities of groups, sections, or states can be gained concurrently, argued Calhoun, should we have the prerequisites to policy and to program. In effect, this gives a veto not only to any one group or section but to little more than half of any group or section. Although Calhoun's theory was never formally adopted, it has been, to some extent, realized in practice, since it is almost impossible to force through measures that are deeply resented and opposed by any large minority of the people.[53]

Sometimes groups believe their status can be recognized and their positions assured in the institutional framework only by some addition to the formal governmental structure. This is another form assumed by the defensive aspect of lobbying: the establishment of new executive agencies or bureaus and of new congressional committees. By itself the group's desire is usually not sufficient for success, but, when combined with the need for specialized organizations to deal with the ever-expanding burdens of the federal government and with the interest of Congress and of executive officials in building instruments of personal power and prestige, the new agencies and committees usually materialize.[54]

Pressure groups have come to be termed the third house of Congress. As such they have become respectable.[55] Pressure politics are now an inseparable part of the representative process in American government.[56]

The Impact on American Society

There is impressive evidence that pressure groups are effective. The large number and variety of groups in themselves testify to this effectiveness; otherwise, there would not have been the phenomenal growth which has already been noted. Moreover, the denunciation of pressure groups by almost every recent President is additional testimony to their strength.

Famous lobbies which have influenced public policy have been listed by an expert on the legislative process in Congress—the protective tariff lobby, the Pennsylvania Railroad, the National Grange, the Anti-Saloon League, the American Legion, the shipbuilding, private electric utilities, banking, and the securities-exchange lobbies, the housing lobby, the lobbies for and against the St. Lawrence Seaway, and the atomic energy lobby.[57] "Pressure groups and their lobbies," the editors of *Fortune* have asserted, "have long been the despair of patriots. They have been responsible for most of the worst, most damaging governmental acts in U.S. history: the Hawley-Smoot Tariff, the Silver Purchase Act, the bonus grabs, the Chinese Exclusion Acts, et al., et al."[58]

The costs of pressure politics also measure group effectiveness. Although these costs have already been cited,[59] the question of absorbing the impact of "clusters of private power" on American government puts the problem in another form. The House Select Committee inquired in 1950 whether our kind of popular government can indefinitely absorb the impact of an inherently expansive system of organized pressure; whether we can continue to afford the social cleavages, the clusters of private power of which this mounting pressure is both cause and symptom, and went on to say: "This is no abstruse problem in political theory. . . . The way in which these questions are resolved is the key to our institutional future."[60]

Legislation. For decades Congress has been under pressure from organized interests to adopt legislation favorable to their objectives or to refrain from adopting legislation which these interests think would affect them adversely.

The following is a list of typical examples of legislation and tax measures expressive of public policy—either positively in the form of laws, or negatively in the form of legislative default—in which pressure groups have been active in recent years.

1. Public policy in the form of laws enacted
   Wagner Labor Relations Act (1936)
   Fair Labor Standards Act (1938)
   Repeal of Chinese Exclusion Acts (1943)

Emergency Price Control Bill (1942)

Employment Act (1946)

Labor-Management Relations Act (1947)

Atomic Energy Act (1946)

Price and Rent Control Act (1946)

Basing Point Legislation (1950)

Tidelands Oil Legislation (1953)

Income tax, estate, gift tax legislation (various dates), but particularly retention of oil depletion allowance by 83d Congress (1952-1954)

Shipping quotas in European Recovery and Military Assistance Program legislation (1948-1949)

Defense Production Act Extension (1952)

Restriction of foreign oil imports (1955)

Extension of reciprocal trade agreement amendments to Smoot-Hawley Tariff Act (1934, and at successive three-year periods and shorter intervals)

2. Public policy continued through failure to adopt proposed legislation

Proposed Missouri Valley Authority (1944)

Proposed National Health Insurance (1948)

A series of laws favoring agricultural producers, not included in the above list, may also be mentioned. One of the characteristic features of legislative output over the years has been this "response of government to agriculture."[61] Nor does the list include the rivers and harbors (pork barrel) legislation which Congress enacts every session. Any complete list would have to include as well the amendments to the 1946 Atomic Energy Act, adopted in 1954, and the continued failure of Congress to admit Hawaii and Alaska as states in the Union.

The above list, necessarily incomplete, shows clearly one thing about pressure politics: As shown in legislation passed or defeated, pressure politics is largely concerned with economics. This is not wholly the case, as the Chinese Exclusion Act repeal, the rejection of health insurance legislation, and the failure to admit Hawaii and Alaska testify. These instances undoubtedly reflect strictly political motivation in varying degrees of intensity. But even in these, economics is by no means lacking. The labor groups had to be neutralized in the case of Chinese Exclusion Act repeal.[62] Physicians' fears that professional income would suffer from the adoption of health insurance legislation no doubt figured in the pressure which prevented its passage. As for admission of Hawaii and Alaska, the partisan struggle over this issue can be explained not only by the fear of disrupting the political balance in the Senate but also by the fear of its effect on the sugar, timber, and fish cannery industries, among others.

Table 2 (pp. 74ff.) attempts to illustrate the results of political pressure group activity in the origin, development, and approval of the Revenue Act of 1951. It presents in parallel columns (1) the proposals prompting resistance or pressure, (2) the groups resisting and pressuring, (3) the groups' positions on the proposals, (4) where the positions were made known (in the formal process, that is), and (5) the fate of the proposals as reflected in the measure signed by the President.

Admittedly, the tabulation presents only a partial picture. It is doubtful whether a complete picture is possible. Moreover, reducing living pressures to cold type, in this way, risks leaving a partial, if not a wrong, impression. Also, the impression conveyed is too much that of a mechanical process, whereas tax legislation in American society is the modern counterpart par excellence of the cruder and less peaceful forms of earlier days in dividing up the gross national product. In a society such as ours, which depends on money (primarily in the form of credit), any new impulse imparted to the taxing process is certain to galvanize all elements of society. This is no sluggish, slow-moving process, but a dynamic, constantly changing swirling of streams and currents of activity originating among the population and rushing into the legislative seas where political decisions are made.

SUMMARY. In this chapter three main topics have been discussed: political and group activity, pressure groups, and the impact of pressure groups on American society. The group nature of society was emphasized and the need for cooperation, the importance of group experiences to the individual, and politics as process were considered. Also, groups were described in terms of mass activity, including the large number and variety of groups in America and the constantly changing nature of groups. In considering pressure groups, the alleged difference between interest and pressure groups was found to be invalid. The strong tendency, amounting almost to a law of society, was also noted for the affairs of groups to be decided and run by a small minority of the members. Factors contributing to the growth of pressure groups were enumerated: economic specialization, various psychological factors, the weakness of the political parties. Finally, the role of lobbying in representative self-government has several different but related aspects—representative, advisory, protective, and promotional. The impact of pressure groups on American society was presented in terms of legislation enacted and legislation denied passage due to the activity of pressure groups. Be-

TABLE 2

TAXES—REVENUE ACT OF 1951

APPARENT EFFECT OF GROUP PRESSURES ON ELEMENTS AND INCIDENCE OF TAX POLICY

(1) Proposals Prompting Pressure	(2) Pressures Exerted by	(3) Position	(4) Pressure Points	(5) Bill as Signed
1. Pay-as-we-go program	National Grange	Favored	House Committee Hearings*	President asked $16 billion increase, later $10; expected yield as passed $5.691 billion
	American Farm Bureau Federation	Favored	House	
1a. Stiffening of capital gains tax	N. Y. Cotton Exchange	Critical	House	Increase maximum rate on long-term capital gains for individuals and corporations from 25 to 26 per cent
	American Cotton Shippers' Association	Critical	House	
	National Association of Real Estate Boards	Opposed; relax treatment of certain home sales	House	
2. Tax retained earnings of cooperatives	National Grange	Favored	House	Exempt rural electrification co-ops and certain mutual insurance companies from a provision requiring informational return on patronage dividends and other such distributions
	Illinois Bankers' Association	Tax amounts distributed as dividend by building and loan associations	House	
	National Savings and Loan League	Opposed to proposal of Investment Bankers' Association	House	
	Cooperative League of U.S.A.	Opposed	House	
	Grain and Feed Dealers' Association	Favored	House	
	National Tax Equality Association	Favored	House	
	National Milk Producers' Federation	Opposed	House	
	National Council of Farm Coops	Opposed	House	
	Missouri Farmers' Association	Opposed	House	

3. Increase in regular income tax rates†

4 per cent on individual incomes in all rate brackets

8 per cent in corporate normal tax, from 25 per cent on first $25,000, and maximum on income over $25,000 from 47 to 55 per cent

Individuals: Increase by 11 per cent tax on first $2,000 of income after deductions and personal exemptions. On income over $2,000 an increase of 11.75 per cent on present tax liabilities or 9 per cent after present taxes, whichever is less. Maximum effective rate limitation 88 per cent

Corporation: Increase normal tax to 30 per cent. Set ceiling of 18 per cent on amount that can be taken in excess profits taxes. Make taxes effective 4-1-51 and terminate 3-31-54. Reduce average earnings credit for excess profits tax from 85 to 83 per cent of earnings in 3 best years of 4-year period, 1946-49. Effective 7-1-51

Group	Position	Chamber
Federal Tax Forum	Opposed—substitute higher excess profits	House
United Electrical Workers	Opposed—reduce by $4 billion on low-income brackets	House
National Federation of Independent Business	Opposed—no further taxes on small and independent business; or, if taxes increased, permit offsets	House
CIO	Favored even higher rate on higher income sources	House
Pennsylvania Power and Light Company	Opposed to corporate income tax increases; if enacted, propose authority be granted to pass increases to consumers	House
	Senate Committee Hearings	
Americans for Democratic Action	Favored high corporate and individual tax rates	Senate
National Farmers' Union	Increase tax rates in upper income brackets, increase corporate taxes, close loopholes; opposed retail sales tax	Senate
National Association of Shoe Chain Stores	Opposed to limiting related corporations to a single surtax exemption and excess profits tax credit	Senate
National Retail Furniture Association	Requested relief for businesses paying corporate income tax on installment basis	Senate
Committee of Investors of America, Inc.	Protested tax burden imposed in House bill in regard to capital gains	Senate

TABLE 2 (continued)

(1) Proposals Prompting Pressure	(2) Pressures Exerted by	(3) Position	(4) Pressure Points	(5) Bill as Signed
	Committee on Federal Tax Policy	Critical of House bill as inflationary and aimed at middle- and upper-income groups	Senate	
	Committee for Constitutional Government	Opposed—eliminate all taxes on corporations; adopt 45 per cent limit on personal income	House Committee Hearings	
	Council of State Chambers of Commerce	Opposed—finance defense by a uniform tax on individual incomes after deduction for taxes in effect; no further corporation taxes	House	
	National Retail Dry Goods Association	Opposed—fix corporate tax rates at 50 per cent upper limit	House	
	National Association of Manufacturers	Recommended "broad consumption tax" rather than increased corporate income taxes	Senate Committee Hearings†	
	American Farm Bureau Federation	Favored tax increases rather than wage and price controls to combat inflation	Senate	
	Smaller Businesses of America	Relieve small businesses under the Excess Profits Act; increase income tax rates on larger business firms	Senate	Provide for taxing life insurance companies for 1951 at rate of 3.75 per cent of adjusted normal tax rate income, not in excess of $200,000, and 6.5 per cent of amount over $200,000

4. Increased excise rates on passenger automobiles from 7 to 20 per cent; gasoline from 1.5 to 3 cents per gallon; cigarettes from 7 to 10 cents a pack; distilled spirits from $9 to $12 a gallon; beer from $8 to $12 a barrel; television, radio, and phonograph sets from 10 to 25 per cent; and increases in manufacturers' excise on various electrical appliances	American Federation of Labor	Opposed—instead, eliminate split income provisions	House Committee Hearings	Increase tax on passenger cars and motorcycles from 7 to 10 per cent but exempt house trailers; trucks, buses, and truck trailers from 5 to 8 per cent; parts increased similarly
	United Electrical Workers	Opposed—eliminate old and proposed new taxes on beer, cigarettes, transportation and household appliances	House	Cigarettes from 7 to 8 cents per pack
	Congress of Industrial Organizations	Opposed—no new excises		
	Committee for Constitutional Government	Favored financing of defense by comprehensive system of excise taxes	House and Senate Committee Hearings	Distilled spirits—from $9 to $10.50 a gallon proof
				Beer—from $8 to $9 a barrel
	American Farm Bureau Federation	Opposed increased excise on gasoline; instead tax electrical energy by public-owned utilities, co-ops for domestic or commercial use	House and Senate	Wine—about 12.5 per cent
	Americans for Democratic Action	Opposed—any excise tax increase	Senate Committee Hearings	
	National Retail Dry Goods Association	Opposed—advocated federal retail sales tax instead of manufacturers' excise tax	Senate	
	New York Board of Trade Committee for Economic Development	Opposed (same reasons)	Senate	
		Favored federal retail sales tax	Senate	
	Independent Investors, Inc. Investors' League, Inc.	Favored	Senate	
		Favored	Senate	
	Council of State Chambers of Commerce	Favored—go further and balance budget, primarily through excise taxes	House Committee Hearings	

TABLE 2 (continued)

(1) Proposals Prompting Pressure	(2) Pressures Exerted by	(3) Position	(4) Pressure Points	(5) Bill as Signed
	National Committee on Fair Emergency Excise Taxation	Opposed—substitute a retail sales tax on everything except food, medicine, nuts, alcohol, tobacco, and gasoline	House	
4a. Raise excise tax on cigarettes from 7 to 10 cents per pack	Burley Leaf Tobacco Warehouse Association	Opposed	House	Increase—see above
	Burley Tobacco Growers' Cooperative Association	Opposed	House	
	Farmers' Federation of Asheville, N.C.	Opposed	House	
	Middle Tennessee Burley Tobacco Growers	Opposed	House	
	Kentucky Farm Bureau Federation	Opposed	House	
	Virginia Farm Bureau Federation	Opposed	House	
	North Carolina Farm Bureau Federation—Senators Hoey, Smith (N.C.)	Opposed	House	
4b. Increases in taxes on whiskey, beer and wine	Liquor Industry Representatives	Warned of increased moonshining and bootlegging if new taxes were voted	House	See above
	Kentucky Alcohol Beverage Control Board	Cut tax on whiskey instead of raising it	House	
	U.S. Brewers' Federation	Opposed—beer an essential food "necessary for public and military morale"	House	
	Wine Conference of America	Opposed—"wine is not a luxury"	House	
	Pennsylvania Alcohol Beverage Study, Inc.	Opposed	House	
	Kentucky Revenue Commission	Opposed	House	
	Schenley Industries, Inc.	Opposed	House	

4c. Increase in auto excise taxes	Automobile Manufacturers Association	Opposed	House	See above
4d. Increase in federal gasoline excise tax from 1.5 to 3 cents per gallon	Air Transport Association	Opposed	House Committee Hearings	No increase in federal gasoline tax
	American Trucking Association	Opposed	House Committee Hearings	
4e. Increase on vacuum cleaners, sewing machines, food freezers	Vacuum Cleaner Manufacturers	Opposed	House	Apparently vacuum cleaners exempt; sewing machines and food freezers apparently also exempt
	Amana Refrigeration, Inc.	Opposed	House	
	White Sewing Machine Company	Opposed	House	
	Institute of Cooking and Heating Appliance Manufacturers	Opposed	House	
	American Retail Federation	Opposed—instead, would accept a retail sales tax with few exemptions	Senate Committee Hearings	
	International Union of Electrical Workers—CIO	Opposed increases in radios, cars, and gasoline	Senate	Repeal electrical energy tax
	National Appliance and Radio Dealers Association	Opposed increases on radio and television sets	Senate	Apparently no increase on radio and television sets
	National Association of Broadcasters	Opposed increased excises on radio and television sets	House Committee Hearings	
5. Repeal of tax exemption for state and municipal bonds	New York City Mayor	Opposed	House Committee Hearings	Tax exempt status retained
	Spokesman for N.Y., Pa., Fla., N.C., Iowa, Maine	Opposed	House	
	Conference of Mayors	Opposed	House	
	Association of Ohio Municipalities	Opposed	House	
	American Municipal Association	Opposed	House	

TABLE 2 (*concluded*)

(1) Proposals Prompting Pressure	(2) Pressures Exerted by	(3) Position	(4) Pressure Points	(5) Bill as Signed
5. Repeal of tax exemption for state and municipal bonds	Dallas (Tex.), Enid (Okla.), Birmingham (Ala.), Mayors	Opposed	House	
6. Cut percentage depletion allowances on oil and gas producers from 27.5 to 15 per cent, with corresponding cuts on mineral products	National Coal Association	Opposed	House and Senate Committee Hearings	No change in depletion allowance on oil or gas producers
	Lake Superior Iron and Ore Association	Opposed	House Committee Hearings	Provide 5 per cent depletion allowance for sodium chloride, calcium and magnesium chlorides, potassium chloride, bromine, sand, gravel, slate, stone, brick and tile clay, shale, oyster and clam shells, granite and marble; 10 per cent for coal, asbestos, lucite
	Freeport Sulphur Company	Opposed	House	
	Potash Company of America	Opposed	House	
	American Mining Company	Opposed	House	
	Gulf Oil Corporation	Opposed	House	
	Independent Petroleum Association of America	Opposed	House	
	Arkansas Oil and Gas Commission	Opposed	House	Dolomite, calcium carbonates, magnesium carbonates (including magnesite) wollastonite and perlite; and 15 per cent for apatite, garnet, refractory clay, fire clay, metallurgical grade limestone, chemical grade limestone, borax, Fuller's earth, tripoli, quartzite, and diatomaceous earth
	Texas State Board of Education	Opposed	House	
	Texas Railroad Commission	Opposed	House	
	Congressmen from Southwestern States, Nevada and Illinois	Opposed	House	
7. Pegging price of government securities	American Farm Bureau Federation	Condemned	House	

* Some 260 persons asked to be heard at House Ways and Means Committee Hearings, February 15–March 19, 1951.

† More than 100 persons testified before the Senate Finance Committee Hearings, June 27–August 16. Appearing in favor of Administration program were (1) Secretary of the Treasury Snyder; (2) Eric Johnston, Economic Stabilization Director; (3) Charles E. Wilson, Director of Defense Mobilization; (4) Anna M. Rosenberg, Assistant Secretary of Defense; (5) John D. Small, Munitions Board Chairman; and (6) W. J. McNeil, Assistant Secretary of Defense.

cause of the veto role they play, pressure groups are so effective that some members of Congress and private citizens alike are convinced that they play too dominant a part in American government and politics. On the other hand, the educational value of lobbying and its value to the public at large was pointed out.

Only one of the many attempts made by Congress to deal with lobbying resulted in legislation. In the next chapter, the dilemma which faces Congress and the country in any attempt to regulate lobbying by law is presented.

Chapter 6

THE DILEMMA OF
LOBBY REGULATION

> . . . the chief reliance for restraining the pressure groups
> must be on education.
>
> —*Fortune**

Regulation of lobbying has been attempted by Congress on the theory that filing of information by lobbyists and lobby groups would produce the publicity necessary to keep Congress informed and lobbyists in hand. There is a wide gap, however, between theory and fact.

Efforts of Congress to Regulate Lobbying

THE BASIC DILEMMA. The title of the law requiring registration of lobbyists is the Federal Regulation of Lobbying Act.[1] But the title is not descriptive. While the law requires registration and the filing of information, it does not regulate. The difference between the title and the text reflects the dilemma in which legislators find themselves in dealing with this subject. They would like to establish regulations, it would seem; therefore, they label the law a regulatory law. But they realize, at the same time, they cannot actually regulate an activity based on a right guaranteed in the First Amendment against abridgment by Congress. Thus the text of the law is enacted in terms falling short of regulation.

Lobbying is one of those activities which periodically agitates Congress and gives rise to demands to "do something about it." But in "doing something" about lobbying one is faced with the basic question of how lobbying can be regulated for the good of all while steering clear of the First Amendment's guarantees of freedom of speech, press, and petition.

* "Our Form of Government," Supplement to *Fortune,* November, 1943, p. 10. By permission of *Fortune.*

This question was posed in 1950, and an inconclusive answer was given by the House Select Committee on Lobbying Activities. The recognition by the Committee that effective regulation cannot be limited to lobbying involving direct contact with legislators but must include indirect efforts to influence legislators highlighted the problem. From the record of the Committee's inquiry one gets the impression that the majority realized they were dealing with a question which goes to the very bases on which the Constitution and the government of the United States are grounded. After probing deeply and amassing quantities of data on lobbying methods in the mid-twentieth century, much of it new and hitherto undisclosed, the majority agreed that lobby and lobbying information should be fully disclosed, but concluded that lobbying should not be regulated.[2] Like its Committee, Congress, too, has shown no enthusiasm for tackling this problem. Although five years have passed, the Committee recommendations still have not been adopted or even debated by Congress. Efforts to draft a law going beyond registration and filing of information, although reported, have apparently been unable to reconcile semiregulatory objectives with the constitutional prohibition against congressional abridgment of the right of petition.[3]

LOBBY REGULATION ACT. *Provisions.* The Regulation of Lobbying Act (Title III of the Legislative Reorganization Act of 1946) applies to those who collect or spend money or anything else of value for the principal purpose of aiding or of influencing the passage or defeat of any legislation by the Congress of the United States. Such persons (the term is defined to include an individual, partnership, committee, association, corporation, and any other organization or group of persons) are required to keep detailed accounts of contributions. They are supposed to file quarterly reports with the Clerk of the House of Representatives giving the names and addresses of persons making contributions of five hundred dollars or more and of persons to whom payments totaling ten dollars or more in any calendar year are made, and the amount, date, and purpose of such expenditures. Quarterly and cumulative annual totals are also to be filed. Such statements are to be preserved for two years by the Clerk and are to be open to public inspection.

Similarly, persons engaging themselves for hire for the purpose of attempting to influence the passage or defeat of legislation must register with the Clerk of the House and the Secretary of the Senate before engaging in such activity, and must supply information about their employers. They also must file quarterly reports of money received and spent, to whom paid, the purposes, and the names of papers, periodicals, magazines, or other publications in which they have had articles or editorials published, and the legislation they are employed to support or oppose. Such information is to be compiled jointly by the Clerk of the House and the Secretary of the Senate and published quarterly in the *Congressional Record.* Registration requirements do not apply to persons who merely appear before congressional committees in support of or in opposition to legislation, to public officials in the conduct of their official duties, or to newspapers. Persons violating the law are guilty of a misdemeanor, and are liable to fine or imprisonment, and, for three years after conviction, are prohibited from attempting to influence the passage or defeat of legislation and may not appear before congressional committees. Those violating such prohibition are guilty of a felony, and are subject to a fine of ten thousand dollars, imprisonment for not more than five years, or both.

Weaknesses. The Regulation of Lobbying Act is based on the theory that publicity resulting from the information supplied by lobbyists and lobbying groups will alert public opinion and thus keep such activities within bounds and correct any transgressions. However sound it may be theoretically, the law contains many weaknesses. It is poorly drafted. It is not clear to whom it applies. The reporting provisions call for information in such volume and detail as to make it difficult to comply. The reporting provisions also make it possible for names and addresses of those who make contributions of less than five hundred dollars to lobby groups to escape publicity. Although registration data are published in the *Congressional Record,* and other information is open for inspection in the office of the Clerk of the House, the law neither designates any existing agency (not even the Department of Justice) nor sets up any new agency to assure compliance. Nor does it authorize specific appropriations to be used in its enforcement. Moreover, the law contains a serious contradiction. In the section defining lobbying there seems to be authority to require information to be filed on indirect lobbying, that is, "grassroots" lobbying and propaganda. At the same time, the applicability of the law is limited to those who use money principally to accomplish the passage or defeat of legislation. Until the Supreme Court clarified this ambiguity in 1954, many organizations used it to defend their failure to file information.[4]

PROPOSED SUGGESTIONS FOR MEETING THE PROBLEM. *Publicity, official aid, advisory role for lobbies.* The filing of information by lobbyists and lobbying groups is already required by the Lobby Regulation Act. Although admittedly of small value, a law based on the publicity theory was the main recommendation made to Congress in 1951 by the House Investigating Committee.

Another proposal discussed by the Committee was government support for those interest groups without adequate resources to compete with more affluent lobbies. The idea that in a free society excessive power in one interest group would be offset by competition from other groups gave some weight to this proposal. However, the Committee decided that making government support available would only produce more pressure, and would defeat the purpose of the legislation. Therefore, the Committee rejected this idea.

A third suggestion considered was the inclusion of organized private groups in the formal policy-making process. By this arrangement they would have been accorded a position similar to advisory councils, administrative bodies, and similar groups testifying before congressional committees. Again, the Committee decided against this proposal. The value of more streamlined legislative and administrative processes in reducing the bottlenecks which add to the complexity of dealing with government was also discussed. The first steps in this direction had been recommended by the Hoover Commission on Reorganization in 1947. The aim of such streamlining would be to create a clearer pattern of government for the public to appraise, and hence one with fewer dark alleys in which lobbies could operate.

Stronger parties. A more fundamental remedy discussed was the value of strong political parties and party discipline. The Committee acknowledged that here they were dealing with the basic cause of lobbies: Lobbies move into the picture whenever the political parties do not accept the complete responsibility of governing. The Committee recognized the difficulty of attaining stronger party cohesion, but stated that the final answer was to be found along this line. "Ultimately, however, responsible parties are the essential requisite of responsible government."[5] This attitude was strongly supported by a number of witnesses who argued that increasing party responsibility would have the greatest impact in the direction of minimizing the effectiveness of private pressures on congressional behavior.[6] Among others advocating this approach is Schattschneider who states: ". . . it is a waste of time to talk about controlling the depredations of pressure groups by other means than adequate national party leadership."[7]

All these proposals were rejected and the majority of the Committee agreed to recommend the retention of the existing legislation without major amendments.

DIFFERENCES OVER LOBBYING. A basic difference of opinion appeared between the Democratic majority and the Republican minority over the meaning of lobbying. The majority defined lobbying as "all substantial attempts to influence legislation for pay or any consideration."[8] The significant aspect of this definition was the assumption that lobbying was not limited to direct contacts but included indirect efforts to influence legislation. The minority objected to this definition and argued that, if accepted, it would apply to any activity by anyone designed to influence another or designed to inform another on any question which might be submitted to any Congress at any indefinite time in the future; that all sums spent on institutional advertising or in the form of contributions of any sort to business organizations would be legislative expenditures.[9] Such scope was apparently, however, just what the majority had in mind.

Information refused. When Edward A. Rumely, Executive Secretary of the Committee for Constitutional Government, refused to supply the Committee with a list of the purchasers of its widely distributed publications, he challenged the authority of the Committee to require the submission of this information. On recommendation of the Committee, Congress found Rumely in contempt; he was tried and convicted for contempt, but his conviction was overturned by the Supreme Court. Meanwhile, the Committee completed its investigation, submitted its reports to Congress, and went out of existence.

The opposing points of view on lobbying were crystallized by Rumely's refusal to supply the requested data. The question was, according to a Committee member, "whether the money was used for lobbying."[10] One point of view held that large-scale purchase and distribution of books published by an organization admittedly trying to influence legislation (an organization registered and filing information under the Lobby Regulation Act) constitutes indirect lobbying, since the purpose of these activities—the publishing, transfer, and distribution of certain books—is to influence readers to accept the point of view contained in them; moreover, the readers, in turn, will be influenced by the ideas in the books in their own political activities, in voting in congressional elections, and in exerting their personal influence on Congress. The opposing viewpoint held that such a practice is not lobbying, since the organization is, in reality, a publisher, and as such is protected by the First Amendment from being compelled to disclose the names of persons who made possible the large-scale distribution of the books in question by their purchases (contributions). Therefore, simply reporting the total sum received for such book distribution is sufficient to fulfill the requirements of the law as to receipts and expenditures of funds, despite its requirement that the names and addresses of those contributing more than five hundred dollars must be filed.[11]

On June 27, 1950 Mr. Rumely told the Committee that "our lobbying consists of going out with a viewpoint to the country, and informing people and letting the people talk to their members of the Congress . . . *The Chairman:* 'The grass-roots approach?' *Mr. Rumely:* 'It is helping people get the facts on which to do their thinking.' "[12]

In its *Report*, the Committee concluded that it would be futile to attempt to frame a law distinguishing "good lobbying" from "bad lobbying."[13] Laws regarding lobbies, it maintained, should identify pressures, not regulate them. Both the majority and minority agreed that pressures should be identified, but there was almost complete disagreement as to what constituted "pressures," the disagreement stemming from the difference over what constitutes lobbying. To the majority, identifying pressures meant identifying the sources of financial support of the pressure groups which seek to influence Congress.[14] Both agreed, too, on the matter of regulation—there should be none. But here, again, the basic disagreement over what constitutes lobbying appeared in what the majority and minority, respectively, meant by regulation. To the majority, an attempt to require the Committee for Constitutional Government to disclose the purchasers of its publications was a legitimate function of the Select Committee, because such information could be required under the Lobby Act provisions calling for filing of information. The filing of such information was a part of identifying pressures; it was not regulation. The minority, on the other hand, appeared to agree with Rumely. Based on its restricted definition of lobbying as direct contacts with Congress, its committees, and its members, the minority argued that the Select Committee had no authority to require Rumely to disclose the names of purchasers of his organization's publications, and that refusal to do so did not constitute contempt of Congress or violation of the Lobby Act. On this point the courts finally decided in Rumely's favor.

Lobbying, according to the Supreme Court. The Supreme Court set aside Rumely's conviction for contempt of the House Select Committee on Lobbying because, under the resolution (H. Res. 298, 81st Cong. 2d sess.) Congress was authorized, the Court declared, to investigate activities that involved only direct lobbying in Congress, and not activities that involved efforts to influence the thinking of the community generally. The majority of the Court construed the resolution in this way in order to avoid the constitutional issue, for, the majority held, an inquiry into the efforts of private citizens to influence public opinion through publications would raise doubts of constitutionality under the First Amendment. The dissenting justices,

Douglas and Black, maintained that the resolution was intended to vest broad powers and was unconstitutional.[15]

The Supreme Court's definition of lobbying emerges from its opinion in the Rumely case. As used in the resolution establishing the House Select Committee, lobbying activities meant direct lobbying —not indirect lobbying, as the Committee majority contended. The Court argued:

> As a matter of English, the phrase 'lobbying activities' readily lends itself to the construction placed upon it, namely, 'lobbying in its commonly accepted sense,' that is, 'representations made directly to the Congress, its members, or its committees', and does not reach what was in the Committee Chairman's mind, namely, attempts 'to saturate the thinking of the community.' . . . Certainly, it does no violence to the phrase 'lobbying activities' to give it a more restricted scope. To give such meaning is not barred by intellectual honesty. So to interpret is in the candid service of avoiding a serious constitutional doubt. . . .[16]

And although the Regulation of Lobbying Act does not use the word lobbying or lobbying activities, the Supreme Court, in upholding the registration provisions of that law, defined lobbying in similarly restrictive terms.[17]

Lobbying by the executive branch. The Committee, in its *Report and Recommendations*, stated its belief that the existing law (18 U.S.C. 1913) prohibiting lobbying by executive agencies—a matter which the Committee was authorized and directed to investigate— meets the situation and that no amendment for this purpose to the Regulation of Lobbying Act was necessary. In reaching this conclusion the Committee pointed out that the latter Act was directed to obtaining information, while the former was prohibitory in character. The minority of the Committee expressed vigorous dissent from the conduct of the Committee's investigation of lobbying by executive agencies. In the course of the hearings, one member referred to the executive influence on the legislative process as a conflict between bureaucracy and the representatives of the people. According to Congressman Brown (R., Ohio), "The whole question involved was whether bureaucracy should rule through pressure."[18] Congressmen frequently draw a parallel between lobbying activities by private citizens and those by officials of the executive agencies, and ask, according to a witness from the Bureau of the Budget, If the former have to register, why not the latter? This point of view received support from some witnesses, one of whom went further and suggested registration of all executive and congressional personnel receiving more than a certain amount of outside income.[19] The proposal was not supported by the Bureau of the Budget representative. He pointed out that any listing of executive officials, such as that in the *Official*

Register of the United States or in the *Congressional Directory,* is, in effect, public notice that anyone listed therein may be given a specific job to do by his superior, up to the President, which could probably be construed, if so desired, as an effort to influence legislation.[20]

Applicability of existing law. The applicability of the Regulation of Lobbying Act was discussed by the Committee in its *Report.* The Committee reasoned along the following lines. Expenditures for pamphleteering, including costs of printing and mass distribution, should be reported, since these are "anything of value" and are included within the concept of a contribution. Multipurpose organizations should file, even though lobbying is not their principal or one of their principal purposes, and financial outlays which cannot be clearly designated as either legislative or nonlegislative should be reported and a percentage estimated for legislative expenses. Expenditures for legislative activities by business firms should be similarly handled. An individual doing both legislative and nonlegislative work should file a report and calculate therein the percentage of income received for legislative work. The Act's applicability to attorneys and to public relations counsellors should be decided in the same manner. However, mere contributors to an organization need not ordinarily file unless the organization acts as a front to cover the activities of such a contributor, or unless the contributor cooperates with the organization to escape the Act's requirement of registration by contributors of five hundred dollars or more. Research institutes which emphasize one side of controversial issues in their fact-finding should file, since they do not qualify as educational or publishing institutions. Finally, publishers do not come under the Act; they are specifically exempted. But the Committee concluded that the mass distribution of books for purposes of influencing legislation does come under the Act.[21]

Reluctance to register and file. Some persons and organizations were apparently subject to the Act but declined to register and file information. For some time after the Act went into effect it was common knowledge that many organizations which received and spent money to influence legislation had not filed the necessary information. In fact, it was not until 1948, when a special section was set up in the Department of Justice by the Attorney General to survey compliance with the law, that organizations like the American Federation of Labor, the Congress of Industrial Organizations, the Chamber of Commerce of the United States, and the National Association of Manufacturers began to file information. There was real doubt among some organizations whether they should supply information. And it was true that the Act was not a model of legislative drafting. But there were others, both individuals and organizations, who postponed registration and filing, some who filed under protest, and some, like the Committee for Constitutional Government, who had their lobbyists register and filed certain information but who failed and refused to file other information.

Improved enforcement. The House Select Committee recommended that a Joint Committee on the Legislative Process should be established to scrutinize attempts to influence legislation. It was to work closely with the committees of the two houses set up after elections to investigate conduct of elections in the light of the Corrupt Practices Act. Another select committee was to be set up by Congress to investigate attempts to influence the executive branch of the government in such matters as attempts to obtain contracts and priorities, an area from which the Lobby Activities Investigating Committee was barred by the terms of the resolution authorizing it. Important recommendations were made both to the Congress and to the Department of Justice for better use of the information filed under the law.

A final recommendation of the House Select Committee was addressed to the educational institutions of the country and to the press. In calling attention to the responsibility of these two institutions in connection with lobbying, the Committee made a tacit admission and uttered an important corollary of the principle on which the existing law is based. The Committee admitted, in effect, that the theory of regulating pressure group activity by publicity was in itself powerless to correct defects and remedy wrongs. It appealed for help from the schools and from the press to publicize the information filed under the Lobby Regulation Act, and thus make possible the working of public opinion as a corrective to pressure group abuses.[22]

REGULATION NOT ACHIEVED BY PUBLICITY. Some opinion, both official and private, has held that the federal and state lobby regulation laws have failed and have been ineffective because of the sheer mass of data filed.

Regulation of lobbying by publicity has not been achieved, concluded the state legislative committee which investigated lobby activities in California. It examined the operation not only of the then existing California statute but also that of the federal act and corresponding laws of other states. It found that all legislation proceeded on the principle that "undesirable activities can best be controlled by publicity. But, it concluded: "The result is frequently to open the door to what might be called concealment by overdisclosure."

The same committee also concluded that the publicity given to activities of this sort by the various acts now in effect throughout the country is more illusory than real. The danger always exists, it said, that any special publicity for the mass of detailed material required to be filed would result only at times when certain groups come under attack by opposing interests. Deliberate or even careless use of such information, without its being properly analyzed and evaluated, creates a constant threat for the use of false and distorted conclusions as a weapon injurious to legitimate enterprise.[23]

Another observer also testified to the ineffectiveness of existing legislation. Most antilobbying laws are like prohibition laws, observed Carl J. Gilbert, official of the National Municipal League and Vice-President of the Gillette Company, Boston. Everyone was well aware of them, he added, but that did not prevent their being freely violated.[24]

The Right of Petition

Despite the enactment of legislation by Congress, and despite Supreme Court approval of this legislation, pressure groups and lobbyists carry on their varied activities without regulation. It appears to be impossible to regulate lobbying without impinging upon constitutional rights of freedom of speech and of petition.

THE CONSTITUTIONAL PROVISION. "Congress shall make no law," reads the First Amendment to the Constitution, "abridging . . . the right of the people . . . to petition the government for the redress of grievances."

The right of petition became part of the federal Constitution with the adoption of the first ten amendments—the Bill of Rights—in 1791. In the minds of the framers of the Constitution, representation of the population in Congress was not sufficient to satisfy the needs and desires of society viewed as a sphere of competition and conflict. To satisfy these needs, a guaranteed right of petition to the government itself was necessary.[25]

British background. The right of petition has a long history. Originally, it was a means whereby loyal subjects of the British monarch brought to his attention the grievances which they wished remedied. In colonial America, the right served to bring to the attention of the colonial governor, the representative of the British monarch, the grievances for which the colonists sought redress.

In Britain, in the nineteenth century, monster petitions, drawn up and pressed upon Parliament by irate citizens, had the power to persuade and even to threaten. Over a period of years, four developments occurred in England to rob petitions of this power to threaten or persuade. They were the extension of the suffrage, the development of the press, increased use of questions in the House of Commons, and the greater competence of the police in handling petition processions.[26] Thus, with the rise of alternative methods of relieving popular discontent, methods which signified acceptance and wider extension of basic principles of representative, democratic government, the right of petition declined in relative importance as a means of bringing pressure to bear on the legislature.

Similar developments can be noted in the United States. Here, too, the nineteenth century witnessed a great extension of the suffrage and a rapid development of the press. Both served to diminish the relative importance of the right of petition in the practical, political sense, although in the United States, as in Britain, there was no legal impairment of the right itself. The United States did not develop anything comparable in importance to question time in the British House of Commons until the presidential press conference became established in 1913. Certainly, the parallel is not exact. Question time in the Commons is effective because of the direct responsibility of the government to Parliament (because of the fusion of legislative and executive powers), whereas in the United States we have separation of legislative and executive powers. But the forum of presidential press conferences has afforded an opportunity for questioning which has significance in lessening the importance of the political aspect of the right of petition.

In connection with the right of petition, we do not find in American political history any development comparable in significance to the increased efficiency of the British police in handling the monster processions petitioning Parliament. Reasons for this lack are numerous, but only one need be mentioned here. Enforcement of law and order has been traditionally a responsibility of the localities in the United States, not of the federal government. In this respect, American experience, such as it is, does not compare favorably with the British. In instances when aggrieved citizens tried to exercise the right of petition, public authorities did not show particular efficiency in dealing with them. In 1894, at a time of severe depression, a few hundred of Coxey's Army marched to Washington to ask Congress for relief. They were arrested for walking on the Capitol lawn and were thus denied the right to present their plea. A generation later, in 1932, fifteen thousand unemployed World War I veterans who had marched on Washington demanding payment of adjusted compensation certificates were ousted from federal property, on orders of the President, by federal troops under command of Douglas Mac-Arthur.

In American politics the right of petition, in the modern sense, is associated with the history of the tariff. Prior to the first tariff measure in the 1830's, this right was interpreted very broadly as meaning that government should be accessible to any citizen for a hearing of his complaints. With the beginnings of the Industrial Revolution in the United States, the particular value of the right of petition to those wishing to establish and, later, to protect infant industries was clear. Protection for new industry from foreign competition could not be obtained from state and local governments; it was only through congressional use of the powers of taxing and regulating commerce with foreign countries that the desired protection could be gained. Moreover, ever since Hamilton's famous *Report on Manufactures* in the 1790's the value of new industry to the growing nation had been emphasized. Hence, by using the individual's right of petition the national interest would be served if individuals and groups promoting new industries could persuade Congress to levy duties on imported products of foreign countries. Thus it was through the promotion of national interest by individual petitioners that a new practice, lobbying, and a new profession, lobbyist, arose in Washington.[27]

Safeguard of modern lobbying. The right to petition the government for a redress of grievances safeguards varied methods which have developed in more recent times and are available to citizens and citizens' groups to enlist public help for the correction of private inequities. Propagandists are the modern counterpart of citizens of earlier generations who petitioned Congress in person. Welding the right of free speech and a free press to the right of petition obviously multiplies many times the range and force of the single voice or the few voices which formerly reached Congress through written petition.

Although the effects of the mass media in transforming the meaning of the right of petition are discussed elsewhere, it deserves emphasis here, because this result of the revolution in communications is often not fully understood. It is a subtle change and has come about quite rapidly. The right of petition, in its historic sense, has pretty largely gone the way of the old-time village opera house, the vaudeville show, and the summer Chautauqua. These institutions have been outmoded by motion pictures, the radio, and television.

Two decades ago a revolution in political thinking occurred, according to Carmine G. De Sapio, New York Democratic leader, as exemplified by the introduction of the regularly scheduled presidential press conference and the fireside chat of President Franklin D. Roosevelt. This revolution was the result of the development and availability of new techniques of communication. Similarly, the availability of these same techniques has resulted in so overshadowing the old-fashioned form of petition that resort to the latter by the Ten Million Americans Organizing for Justice in an attempt, in 1955, to forestall censure of Joseph R. McCarthy (R., Wis.) by the United States Senate was regarded as something of an anachronism.

The lack of legal interpretation. Few cases have arisen involving interpretation of the constitutional right of petition. For many decades no occasion arose for an interpretation of that part of the First Amendment. Cases reaching the Supreme Court in 1876 and in 1937 considered the right of petition but only in regard to the right to assemble peaceably. In the first of these cases, the Court gave freedom of assembly and petition a restricted meaning, holding that the First Amendment guarantees citizens the freedom to assemble *in order* that they may petition Congress for a redress of grievances.[28] Later, in 1937, freedom of assembly was freed from dependence upon the right of petition and was held to be as fundamental as freedom of speech and of the press.[29] But the meaning of the right of petition was not the issue in either case.[30] This basic right of a free people seems to occupy a secondary position. In a decade when other individual rights have been the subject of great public debate and legal controversy, little attention has been given to the right of petition in its modern form.

It is chiefly the use of propaganda by pressure groups, by political parties, and by governmental agencies which raises the question whether the right of petition today is the same as it was when the Bill of Rights was incorporated into the Constitution. Until thirty years ago, propagandists had only limited means of communications —principally, the newspaper and the political pamphlet. Since then the electronics revolution has placed mass media at the disposal of the propagandist. This has introduced new factors, such as the possibility that lobbying as an exercise of this right may use the new mass media for deception and coercion. And yet, in recent times, the courts have not been called on to rule directly on the right of petition. Although the idea of freedom to petition the government unrestricted by statutory abridgment has not changed, its meaning has changed, with the changed context. It is this changed meaning which calls for further discussion.

MODERN MEANING OF THE RIGHT OF PETITION. When the Supreme Court construed the constitutional provision in its modern form, it came about not as a direct interpretation but as a result of the attempt of Congress to regulate lobbying by statute and to investigate it by resolution in its direct and indirect forms. National associations engaged in lobbying and propaganda denied the authority of Congress to regulate these activities of pressure groups by claiming the right of petition as well as those of freedom of speech and of the press.

Regulation of Lobbying Act. The Regulation of Lobbying Act was enacted by Congress in 1946. Along with several other national associations which, for many years, had tried to influence Congress, the National Association of Manufacturers was of the opinion that it did not have to register as a lobby organization or file reports under the Act. When the government claimed that it was subject to these provisions of the lobby regulation law, the NAM in 1948 sought, and in 1952 obtained, an injunction restraining the government from holding it liable for non-registration. Although the Supreme Court in 1952 disagreed with the lower court and restored the Act to full force, the NAM for three years had not filed quarterly financial reports, as required of organizations trying to influence Congress by other means than direct employment of legislative representatives. Since it held that it did not have as a principal purpose the influencing of Congress, it declined to report to Congress as allocable to such an activity more than a small fraction of its expensive public relations program financed by member contributions.

Domestically, organized labor and the Truman Administration had suffered a setback, and organized management had gained a victory in congressional enactment of the Labor Management Relations (Taft–Hartley) Act in 1947 over the veto of the President. Moreover, it was clear to many that this new legislation was the statutory embodiment of antilabor sentiment consciously generated and manipulated by management propagandists. And calm consideration of public issues was not aided by reckless charges of official "softness" toward communism.

In international relations, this was the period preceding the conflict in Korea. Although the United States was still not wholly convinced of the existence of an international communist conspiracy, the obstructive role of the U.S.S.R. in the United Nations, the communist civil war in Greece, the 1947 coup d'etat of the Czech communists, and the Berlin blockade were rapidly forcing the American government to conclude that such a conspiracy existed and threatened the security of the United States.

The specific grounds on which the NAM claimed exemption from the requirements of the Lobby Regulation Act were (1) that the Law was unconstitutional because it deprived the Association of its constitutional right to petition Congress, and (2) even if the Law were found to be constitutional, the NAM was exempt, in any case, because its principal purpose was not to influence Congress directly or indirectly in the passage or defeat of legislation.

A lower court agreed with the contention that the penalty depriving guilty defendants of their right to appear before congressional committees for three years after conviction was unconstitutional because it deprived them of their right to petition. But even before the Supreme Court could pass on the merits of this case, it declared in another case under the same Act that the law was constitutional.

In the Harriss case, the government charged that Harriss and others had violated the law by failing to register as lobbyists. The Supreme Court rejected the defendants' contention that the Act's provisions were too vague and that its penalty provisions violated constitutional rights guaranteed by the First Amendment. In upholding the right of Congress to require registration and information from persons subject to the Act, the Court, however, construed lobbying narrowly as including only direct representation to members of Congress.

> Present day legislative complexities are such that individual members of Congress cannot be expected to explore the myriad pressures to which they are regularly subject. Yet full realization of the American ideal of government by elected representatives depends to no small extent on their ability to properly evaluate such pressures. Otherwise, the voice of the people may all too easily be drowned out by the voice of special interest groups seeking favored treatment while masquerading as proponents of the public weal. This is the evil which the Lobbying Act was designed to help prevent.[31]

Lobbying construed narrowly. In the Harriss case, the Supreme Court said that for a person or organization to be subject to the Act, they must have solicited, collected, or received contributions; a main purpose of such activities and of such contributions must have been to influence the passage or defeat of legislation by Congress; the intended method of accomplishing this purpose must have been through direct communications with members of Congress. In upholding the registration and filing requirements, the Supreme Court said that "to rule otherwise would be to deny Congress in large measure the power of self-protection."[32]

In construing lobbying narrowly as including only direct representation to members of Congress, the Supreme Court rejected the definition of lobbying as indirect influence on Congress, such as that which might be focused on the legislature by generating propaganda through the use of the mass media.

A similarly narrow construction was placed on the term "lobbying" by the Supreme Court in 1953 in the Rumely case, as we have seen.[33]

Division within Congress. The congressional investigation from which the Rumely case issued gave considerable attention to the right of petition in connection with its inquiry into lobbying.

There was never any question that the right of petition should be maintained in all of its original vigor. At numerous points in its deliberations, the right of petition was stated to be the basic constitutional aspect of the investigation.[34] The real question, however, was the meaning of petition and how far Congress could go in identifying persons using the right. The answer to this question turned on the answer to a prior question, What is lobbying? Here, as we have already seen, there was no unanimity within the Committee. The resolution establishing it authorized and directed it to investigate lobbying, direct and indirect. Having drafted and sponsored the resolution, the Committee Chairman, Frank Buchanan, brought to the investigation his preconceptions of what lobbying was and how far Congress, in clarifying the vagaries of the law, could go in requiring information without running afoul of the constitutional injunction against congressional abridgment of the right of petition. The majority agreed on the theory that lobbying meant not only representations made directly to Congress but also representations made indirectly by propaganda or, as the Supreme Court later said, by "saturating the mind of the public." In line with this concept, the Chairman proposed and the Committee adopted a definition of lobbying as "any attempt by individuals or groups to influence governmental decision," and proceeded forthwith to conduct its investigation on this basis.

The Committee minority, however, was not persuaded. In its report the minority also summarized its ideas as to the proper nature and scope of policy. Regulation by Congress, it said, through identification and registration of sources of support should be required *only* of individuals whose "principal purpose is to attempt to persuade individual members of Congress to follow a certain course of action." The minority doubted whether any lobbying statute could go further than this.[35] Thus the Republican minority forecast more accurately than the majority the stand which the Supreme Court would take on the meaning of lobbying in the Rumely case. But the minority was proven less accurate than the majority in its ideas about the scope of the power of Congress to require information. Information not only from lobbyists but also from principals employing them, as well as the sources of support of such principals, is within the "protective" power of Congress to require, said the Supreme Court in the Harriss case. While the ambiguity of the provisions requiring information from persons whose "principal" purpose is to influence legislation was not clarified, the Harriss case decision has been used since 1954 by lobbying organizations to justify submission of more limited information on expenditures for lobbying than before.

SUMMARY. Several approaches to the problem of lobbying were listed in this chapter: government aid to restore a theoretically attainable balance among economic groups; streamlined government and government operations; advisory roles for occupational groups; and more responsible political parties. Whatever the approach, the problem is complicated by a disagreement over the nature and scope of lobbying. The existing law assumes that regulation can be achieved by publicity. Congressional action going beyond this is prevented by the constitutional guarantee against abridgment of the right of petition. Supreme Court decisions are based on the premise that lobbying is petition in the traditional sense; they do not take account of the propaganda content of lobbying, which is the most up-to-date form of lobbying. The next two chapters deal with the various techniques, including the generation of propaganda, of lobbies and pressure groups.

Chapter 7

THE TECHNIQUES OF LOBBIES AND PRESSURE GROUPS—I

[Lobbying means] representations made directly to Congress, its members, or its committees.

—U.S. Supreme Court

The gentle art of applying political pressure is the stock in trade of lobbies and pressure groups. They exist in order to help the government make up its mind and to see that it stays made up. To this end our political pressure groups have employed a large number and a great variety of techniques. Some of them are as old as politics itself; some are as new as last night's television program. Some of them are unobjectionable; others, although not illegal, overstep the bounds of propriety. In early 1956, President Eisenhower gave the lobbyists and the country a yardstick with which to measure the ethics of lobbying. He withheld his approval from legislation freeing natural gas producers from direct federal regulation, citing as his reason "the arrogant" lobbying of the oil and gas lobby. Since he approved the purpose of the bill, presumably he would have signed it had lobbying for it not been "arrogant." Hence lobbying which is not arrogant is to be accepted, that which is arrogant is to be deplored.

It is the purpose of this chapter to list and discuss briefly some of the techniques which are used by groups to bring political pressure to bear on public officials. A comprehensive exposition would require a book in itself.[1] But we cannot be certain, in a matter of this kind, that we know all the devices of pressure which have been used. The material that follows is believed to be a fairly complete enumeration of the methods now in use.

Uses Made of the Right of Petition

Most of the methods devised and used by pressure groups can be regarded as different ways of using the right of petition.

GATHERING OF INFORMATION. Any group which would influence the course of politics or of government must have information before it can act. Without it, a group is like an army lacking intelligence about the enemy. An information-gathering service is indispensable to success in pressure politics.

DISSEMINATION OF PROPAGANDA. Closely related to the gathering of information is the preparation and dissemination of propaganda. One observer, in a position to know, says that there is one technique and one rule of pressure politics; make a noise like the clamor of millions, but never permit an investigation of the claims. "Exaggeration is the life of pressure politics."[2] This view is corroborated by two others: claim boundless support, and identify one's special interest with the national interest.[3] Identification of a proposed course of action with the public interest is the goal of most successful and effective lobbying, according to another observer.[4] The technique of raising a clamor is not the only successful technique used by lobby groups. As we shall see, the legislative victory sometimes goes to the quietest group. But the high value of identifying one's special interest with the general interest is unquestionable.

Generation of propaganda is synonymous with exaggeration. The mass media, as applied to politics, developed from methods of communicating information and news into means for promoting the acceptance of ideas and persons. As in advertising, so in politics superlatives and other grandiose adjectives are used to blunt the discriminatory faculties in order to make people ready or acquiescent victims of a sales campaign.

A wide variety of methods is used to disseminate propaganda. They range from skywriting to prompted postcards and telegrams to Congressmen; from canned editorials and folksy columns in rural and suburban newspapers to purchase of newspaper advertising space in the metropolitan press and the setting up by economic and other interest groups of so-called research and educational foundations. To illustrate, skywriting was used by the organized electric power companies in the 1930's in their attempt to prevent Congress from enacting the public utility holding company bill. Faked telegrams to members of Congress, with signatures of names taken at random from telephone directories, were used in the same campaign.[5]

The House Select Committee on Lobbying Activities was told by one witness that the National Association of Manufacturers sends material ready to print to 7500 rural weekly newspapers and maintains a service called "Farm and Industry," a release which is sent to 35,000 farm leaders. "Since the editors and publishers of small-town and rural papers are generally important members of the local community and since Congressmen pay a good deal of attention to the home-town press, editorial decisions to select for publication handouts from the national opinion machines of big business have considerable significance."[6] The same witness pointed out to the Committee the relation between business and agricultural opinion, noting that the Pew family in Pennsylvania (Sun Oil Company) was behind the *Farm Journal* and *The Pathfinder,* two of the most widely read farm magazines, and that Frank Gannett published the *American Agriculturist* and was the prime force behind Edward A. Rumely's Committee for Constitutional Government.[7]

Under the headline "Pressuring the Ways and Means Committee," readers of the January 31, 1955 issue of *The New York Times* could read a news story about the advertising campaign of the American Tariff League against H.R. 1 of the Eighty-fourth Congress (first session), a bill providing for a three-year extension of the Reciprocal Trade Agreements Act—if they had not noticed the advertising bought by the League in the same issue.

In reading the column "Washington and Small Business," in Maryland's county seat (Howard County) weekly, *The Ellicott City Times,* observers have wondered whether the copyright owner, the National Federation of Independent Business, was as independent as it purported to be in the news and opinion it disseminates.[8]

Business firms have spent considerable sums of money for the establishment and support of cause groups, institutes, and foundations. Their primary purpose was found by a congressional committee to have been the dissemination of literature. A large part of their income is in the form of contributions received as payment for the sale and distribution of books and other literature.[9]

The carrying on of propaganda was found by the Court of Tax Appeals in 1950 to have been the primary reason for the organization and operation of the National Tax Equality Association, a group said by its president, in testimony in 1947 before the House Ways and Means Committee, to be "devoted solely to research and educational activities."[10]

To these examples of propaganda techniques should be added pamphleteering, advertising, and other public relations activities.[11] Straight news stories have propaganda value, too, such as, for example, *The New York Times* story of November 21, 1955 on the new lay-off plan of the NAM which was "designed to take the steam out of union pressure for a guaranteed annual wage."

The social lobby. In this section on information-gathering, special mention may be made of social contacts. Washington is said to have more cocktail parties than any other city in the United States. As the seat of a national government raising and spending some sixty-odd billion dollars annually this is perhaps not too surprising. In any event, the "social lobby" is popularly supposed to be one of the most effective ways of influencing governmental decisions. Periodically, stories and articles appear in newspapers and magazines of national circulation which purport to give details on how insidious the social lobby is. One such story appeared in *The New York Times* for April 17, 1938, just after Congress had adopted a bill for reorganizing the executive branch of the government. Under the title "The Lobby on the Job," S. T. Williamson wrote, "when important legislation is up, it [the lobby] swings into action and national lawmakers squirm." His description of the social lobby continued: "No Congressional committee has investigated it; it wouldn't know where to begin, for the social lobby has no organization, no office space. It keeps pace with its own era . . ." Williamson also quoted Ben "Perley" Poore, who, in his autobiography published in 1886, provides details of the working of the social lobby in an era described as one in which even the Presidency was eclipsed by the great growth of lobbies.[12]

There is no unanimity of opinion about the effectiveness of the social lobby. A Republican member of the 1950 House Select Committee on Lobbying Activities, later to become one of the top three in the House Republican hierarchy, was troubled by the social lobby, because, as he said, it "has a great and very direct influence many times on legislation."[13] On the other hand, because it is unorganized, as Williamson pointed out, and hence cannot be considered a lobby in the sense in which the term is used here, it can hardly be more than the disunited efforts of real lobbyists and real lobbies in their hypergregarious manifestations. And, if the female sex plays more than its due role in the social side of politics, the reason is not far to seek. Women have an intuitive sense for news, and news is what people—lobbyists or laymen—who would wield influence in politics must have for survival.

There is nothing new about the so-called social lobby. Picking up or exchanging information or arranging political deals at dinner or at some other social gathering is a time-honored way of "politicking." Hamilton and Jefferson did just this when, over the dinner table, the one agreed to support a location of the new federal capitol on the banks of the Potomac in return for the other's agreement to support federal assumption of state debts.[14]

PROMOTIONAL CAMPAIGNS. *Grass-roots lobbying.* "Grass-roots" lobbying is the kind of lobbying which the Supreme Court says is not lobbying in the legal sense. However, it could no more be omitted from a catalogue of techniques of influence than an expense account from an advertising executive's budget. Contemporary politics draws much of its sustenance from the lines of influence and of authority between Washington and congressional districts throughout the country, by which it is made to appear that what the Washington lobbyist wants, the constituents want.

Grass-roots lobbying takes many forms, just as the right of petition has assumed different forms. Grass-roots lobbying is probably the most characteristic contemporary means of exercising the right of petition.

It would be a mistake to assume that, because of the localized, down-to-earth adjective used to epitomize this form of lobbying, its practice is confined to the grass roots, that is, to the legislator's district. Nothing could be further from the truth. Grass-roots lobbying is coextensive with the country, because such activities are country-wide in scope and influence action, or aim at influencing action, the country over.

Grass-roots lobbying is what the House Lobby Committee in its *Interim Report* in 1950 and its final *Report and Recommendations* the following year called indirect lobbying. It may be defined in the words used by one of its most active practitioners, the Committee for Constitutional Government: "The place to persuade Congressmen is back home."[15] But lest some reader hold to the incorrect idea that even this revealing admission discloses the whole story, let us hasten to add that the pressures designed to persuade the Congressman originate in places far removed from his home or his district. In its ultimate effect, the most important component of grass-roots lobbying is the distribution of printed matter bearing on public issues. The printed matter is specially prepared. Textbooks written from the "right" point of view are inspired by the group engaging in grass-roots lobbying. Educational institutions are persuaded to offer special courses. Prominent educators are included among the group's officials. The printed matter thus prepared is distributed in a number of ingenious ways. Material is channeled into editorial and news columns, periodicals and radio, editorial advertising; or sold to a membership group, then distributed to local groups and individuals, thus gaining greater impact because of its apparent local sponsorship. Distribution is made according to two principles; the saturation principle, and the principle of a carefully placed sprinkling.[16] The difference between the two principles is obvious. It was distribution according to the saturation principle about which the House Lobbying Activities Committee wanted to learn more than its originator, Edward A. Rumely, Executive Secretary of the Committee for Constitutional Government was willing to disclose.

An adjunct of grass-roots lobbying is the organization on a nation-wide basis of a pressure group's legislative committee. In identifying the distribution of printed matter on public issues as the most important component of grass-roots lobbying, the House Select Committee on Lobbying Activities did not exclude other components. But the local work directed by a pressure group's legislative committee should certainly not be omitted from discussion of grass-roots lobbying. By combining the subtle, intangible influence of local opinion—itself shaped in part by indirect efforts—with the overt action of prominent citizens in a Congressman's district, maximum persuasive power is brought to bear on the member of Congress at the proper psychological moment. This pattern is not followed uniformly by pressure groups, nor do all groups utilize both variations of grass-roots lobbying. The CCG's efforts are concentrated almost exclusively in influencing the opinion of solid citizens, while the American Medical Association relies mostly on citizens strategically placed, both geographically in congressional districts and socially, being alerted by the group's general lobbyist in Washington to communicate directly with Washington legislators.

Even more ingenious, probably, than the methods of distributing specially prepared material are the methods of financing employed. Three devices were used by the CCG, apparently with the intent of circumventing the Lobby Regulation Act's provisions calling for names and addresses of contributors of more than five hundred dollars. One method used was to have the printing costs paid for directly by the firm making the contribution. The second method had a larger purpose; to cover up the support by large business firms of organizations purporting to act for small business. According to this device, the large concern would pay membership dues in such organizations for its customers, officers, or employees. These payments were not subsequently reported as contributions under the law. The third device aimed at educating the public. The CCG prepared, circulated, and sold to purchasers contributing less than five hundred dollars, books and pamphlets for distribution to recipients designated by the contributor. Such contributions, called sales, were not reported under filing provisions of the Lobby Regulation Act.[17]

The various forms of grass-roots pressure just described justify the term "indirect lobbying." The testimony gathered in 1950 from Rumely, although not as full as desired, was nevertheless sufficient to corroborate the suspicion that devices were being used and practices engaged in which the users and practitioners would prefer not to disclose. For several years after the enactment of the Lobby Regulation Act in 1946, many national associations with public relations programs keyed more or less directly to legislation pending in Congress had claimed that they were not lobbying organizations, hence did not need to register under the law. This casuistry, joined with the recollection of the devious methods used by the power lobby fifteen years earlier, caused some observers to wonder whether the right to petition Congress was not being pushed beyond its legitimate limits.[18] Even when, in 1948, a special section in the Department of Justice was established to oversee compliance with the Lobby Regulation Act and many of the national associations who, up to that time, had claimed exemption began to supply information, doubts persisted as to the propriety of some of the techniques being used. In 1950 these doubts were found to be well grounded. While the majority of a House Select Committee thought that lobbying was a legitimate use of the right of petition, the ways in which it was being used raised important questions of democratic procedure. Its report pointed out that the right is usually not exercised for its own sake but as a means to an end, and an end which is not always consistent with the principles of democracy.[19]

PRESSURES ON CONGRESS. Pressures on Congress through direct representations may be exerted in several ways; by forming blocs, by proposing legislation, by appearance and testimony before congressional committees, and by working through a catalytic group.

Forming blocs. A congressional "bloc" is a loose aggregate of members of one or the other or both houses of Congress, united more or less firmly in their attitude on some particular question of public policy and usually tied by bonds of interest to pressure groups outside Congress. There have been many blocs in Congress at different times—the farm bloc in the early 1920's, the silver bloc in the 1930's, the anti-civil rights bloc of southern representatives, and the reclamation bloc of Congressmen from eleven western states.

It is customary to refer to such loose groups of lawmakers by using the French word *bloc* rather than the English term *block*. Such usage is significant. Rather than a two-party system the French have a multi-party system. They tend to represent interests even more than American parties—to the satisfaction of the interests, no matter how small or how localized, but to the despair of those who deplore this kind of particularism. Because there are so many parties, it is necessary to form working alliances in order to obtain a majority on which a ministry can be built. These alliances have gone by the name of *blocs;* sometimes they are formed in the preparliamentary, that is, the electoral stage, when the electoral laws have held out advantages to such coalitions of candidates. At other times in French history they have been formed within the Chamber of Deputies or the Assembly. But, since they are easily formed, they are also easily dispersed; hence the characteristic of the bloc is its rapidly changing character, differing from the stability associated with the English term *block* to describe a number of voters or votes in the Congress.

Blocs are difficult to form without the assistance of pressure politicians within the legislature itself.[20] In the legislative process in Congress, the members of the two houses are not inert, passive objects, pushed here and there by forces outside the Congress. On the contrary, members of Congress are themselves active spokesmen. The concept of representation prevailing in the United States is one in which the member of Congress serves in the dual capacity of representing both interests and locality. Thus pressure groups in many, if not all, instances have their own representatives in Congress, alert to protect the interests of the group, ready to go into action to advance its interests. An example is found in the Senate Banking and Currency Committee in 1946, when proposals to extend wartime price and rationing controls were before Congress. Members behaved more as participants in the struggle between different producers' groups than they did as impartial judges during the debate among the participants who appeared to testify before the Committee.[21] The same point is made by a veteran reporter of Washington affairs, W. M. Kiplinger, who wrote of the inaccuracy of newspapermen in reporting Congressman A or B as doing so and so; it would be more accurate, he said, if they would report pressure group A or B.[22] A reason for the close relationship is suggested by another veteran journalist, Frank R. Kent, who has stated that on entering office the successful candidate finds himself under an obligation to some group or interest in his constituency that has helped financially in a close contest. In most cases the voters do not know of this obligation.[23] Bailey concludes that the Congressman feels the pressure within himself as well as experiencing pressure from outside sources. His finding is based on an analysis of the cultural background of legislators involved in the enactment of the Employment Act of 1946.[24] And even when, in unlikely cases, lobbyists and pressure groups are noticeable by their absence, the pressure politician will himself recruit support, warning lobbyists of the threats in pending legislation to interests or positions of the groups they represent and generally prodding groups into action—instead of groups prodding the legislator into action.[25] In this way the pressure politician becomes, in effect, a one-man pressure group, but, obviously, of much greater influence than any one-man group outside the legislature.[26]

Because business groups more often seek to prevent than to encourage action, strategic bottlenecks in legislative procedure account for much of their success, according to the House Select Committee in its 1950 *Interim Report*.[27]

Blocs are generally difficult to keep together, and, consequently, they are always trying to develop wider public interest and support than that possible for the particular groups concerned. The need for this wider support was illustrated in the fall of 1954 when the National Reclamation Association's board of directors took heed of the question being raised by members of Congress from eastern states. Why, they are reported to have asked, should we vote to tax our constituents to obtain interest-free money to build reclamation projects in the West, when we already have a food surplus? The facts were different, the Association's president maintained. Speaking at their annual meeting, he declared that people in the East "are paying less taxes, not more, for the development of the West." Although they themselves were divided over such projects as the Upper and Lower Colorado development schemes, the Association's directors wanted to get the facts down on paper and publicized widely, since the congressional delegations in the seventeen states concerned, by themselves, were not a majority in Congress. By gaining allies, or at least neutralizing some of the eastern opposition, they improved their chances of gaining the necessary additional votes in Congress.[28]

LEGISLATIVE PROPOSALS. Political pressure groups and their lobbyists take an active part in the drafting and proposal of legislation. Some discussion of this method of exerting pressure on and in Congress has already been given.[29] Despite the increased importance of the President as initiator of legislation in recent years, the separation of powers in the American government and the working of the party system invite disunity, rather than unity, in legislative programs. In Britain, the Cabinet has complete control over legislation; Parliament debates the subjects which the Cabinet permits it to debate. In America, by contrast, Congress cherishes the role of legislative initiative given it by the Constitution and is reluctant to share it with the Chief Executive. In fact, as the Presidency has increased in power and prestige, Congress has shown even more tenacity than usual in holding on to its power to initiate legislation. The result, so far as the place of political interest groups in the process is concerned, is to give such groups a larger role relative to both Congress and the Presidency than they otherwise would have. Under House and Senate rules, any member of Congress can propose legislation. In effect, this means that any pressure group can introduce legislation, inasmuch as no Congressman, given the short two-year term, remains long unaware of the direct relation between success in election and pressure group attitudes. Pressure group support in a Congressman's district at election time may not be necessary to success; opposition, however, makes success more difficult to attain. Given the inertia and nonparticipation of much of the electorate, particularly in party primaries, the relative significance of pressure group attitudes is thus enhanced. Thus Congressmen rarely refuse to introduce legislation desired by groups, although it may take a little "shopping around" before an agreeable Congressman is found. Lobbyists are paid to inform themselves on the outlook and philosophy of legislators; knowledge of Congressmen is high on the list of job specifications for the group representative in Washington.

Where bills actually originate is a matter of some dispute. For the hypothesis that the actual (as distinct from the apparent) origin is mostly in groups outside Congress there is not much documentary support. Chamberlain concluded, after analyzing ninety major statutes enacted by Congress over a half-century period, that some two out of five were chiefly the product of Congress, one out of five originated with the executive branch, three out of ten could be traced to joint legislative-executive influence, while but one out of ten originated with outside interest groups.[30] Galloway gives the impression that a larger proportion originates with the outside groups.[31] It is believed that this estimate is closer to the actual situation. There can be little doubt that few Congressmen would hold themselves so aloof from the constant stream of ideas on public policy as to refrain from introducing legislation desired by a pressure group. What will happen to a bill once introduced is another matter.

Of the five sources of legislation listed in an official House document, one is the member's constituents. The other four are the member of Congress himself, executive communications, executive departments and independent agencies, and commissions or committees appointed by the President or one of his Cabinet officers. Little information can be obtained from this document on the relative importance of these sources beyond the statement that "in modern times the 'executive communication' is a prolific source of legislative proposals." Proposals from a member's constituents are transmitted pursuant to the right of petition; such proposals may come from constituents "either as individuals or by corporate activity such as bar associations, labor unions, manufacturers' associations, and chambers of commerce." In a foreword to this document, the Chairman of the House Judiciary Committee expressed the hope that citizens and organizations would be better informed as a result of its publication "on the so-called 'behind-the-scenes' background of the legislative process. . . ."[32]

Legislative committee hearings. The appearance of witnesses at legislative committee hearings and their testimony on pending legislation is a common method of transmitting pressure to Congress. For both legislation and appropriations the committees of Congress do the real work. It is likely that in no other legislature in the world is the committee stage of legislation as important as in the United States Congress. It is natural, therefore, that those who speak for citizens' groups and national associations, whether as paid lobbyists or officials of the groups, should ask and, many times, be invited to appear and speak for their groups. This is but one form among many of using the right of petition; but next to the anachronistic petition in document form, it is the most direct way of asking Congress to hear a citizen's complaints. Citizens in their individual capacities use this means of getting their views before Congress. Any law abridging this form of petition would no doubt be struck down by the Supreme Court as a violation of the First Amendment. As we have seen, however, few opportunities have ever arisen for the courts to pass on this right of the individual even generally, much less in the form of appearing before legislative committees. The danger of abridgment comes from other more practical considerations, such as the volume of business which the committees must handle, the personal prejudices of committee chairmen, the number of group representatives seeking to be heard, the pressure of time, the question of whether the individual has anything worthwhile to tell the committee. But here, too, as in the matter of originating legislation and getting it introduced, access to the legislative process at the committee stage is not too difficult to arrange, particularly for group spokesmen. They have a knowledge of legislators and of legislative ways which almost invariably enables them to gain a hearing.

Not voluntary, but involuntary, appearance before congressional committees has become the problem for citizens today. In their investigating zeal some congressional committees have gone beyond the legitimate search for information for use in legislating. They have exposed past associations of witnesses and associates and have tried to get them to inform on others. A witness can be compelled to attend by subpoena. Although he is protected by the Fifth Amendment from being compelled to testify if his testimony would tend to incriminate him, a witness can be subsequently cited for contempt, tried, and punished. The question seems to be the limits of the power of congressional committees to obtain information needed to perform their legislative functions.

In recent years, Lincoln's test of loyalty seems to have been completely forgotten. In his dispute with Congress over the form of loyalty oath to be required of citizens in the seceded southern states before again permitting them to participate in politics, Lincoln rejected the idea that loyalty should be tested by past performance; rather, he thought future conduct should be the test.[33]

Private persons who work at the business of legislation have a decided advantage over common citizens who have little contact with the officials involved or knowledge of the procedures. It is necessary to know the well-worn paths by which committees carry on their business. It is even more necessary to know the staff personally. The job of receiving inquiries from lobbyists and from other group representatives and, generally, of handling contacts with them is assigned to committee staff. Expert by long experience if not by training, the staff of a congressional committee is rivaled only by veteran newspapermen in their knowledge of legislative details. How to arrange for an appearance, whom to contact, what is the best time, when will a particular bill receive hearings, what is the history of similar legislation, where did the bill originate and under whose sponsorship, is the chairman sympathetic or not, would it be better to testify before the Senate or before the House committee, or both, or neither? All these questions and many more require answers which the staff of a committee can answer if they will, for without answers to these questions any person interested in influencing the passage or obstruction of legislation is under a handicap.

A knowledge of procedures and acquaintance with the staff allows full use to be made of tactics. Appearance before a committee with an unsympathetic chairman can be avoided in favor of one before a more sympathetic committee leader. Sometimes it is better not to appear; sometimes no hearing is indicated. Sometimes the time of a committee can be monopolized in order to freeze out a rival or opposing group. Or strict observance of committee procedure is sometimes more advantageous. The kind of witnesses is important, as well as the nature of the testimony and the order in which witnesses are called.[34]

One thing about committee hearings which is hard to explain is the indifference of most committee members to the question, Whom does the witness really represent? In one sense, the entire theory of hearings stands or falls upon this question. The system works best when everyone who may be affected by the pending legislation is informed of the hearings and is given an opportunity to testify either individually or through the representative of some group of which he is a member. The system works badly to the extent that this ideal is not reached. That it does not work as well as it should is claimed by

Blough, who believes that producers are overrepresented and consumers underrepresented in hearings on tax proposals.[35] A similar complaint characterized testimony of many of the expert witnesses who testified before the 1950 House Select Committee on Lobbying Activities on the subject of the role of lobbying in representative self-government.[36] Suggestions that existing lobby regulation legislation be amended to require the filing of complete information on the representative character of organizations filing under the law were not accepted by the Committee.[37] Yet such information would seem to be essential if the claims of witnesses to represent large segments of society are to be analyzed. But congressional committees show little interest in asking for substantiation of such claims. For example, authority to speak for American industry is claimed by the National Association of Manufacturers, whose spokesmen appear frequently in the testimony in the transcript of congressional committee hearings. But the evidence of this authority is rarely, if ever, requested, much less analyzed. If it were to be subjected to scrutiny, the accuracy of the claim would be open to serious doubt.[38]

Organization of Congress. Making an impact on Congress by influencing the organization of legislative committees is a particularly effective way of focusing pressure on the legislature. The role of committees in legislation is critical. Hence the goal of every pressure group is to obtain a position from which the composition of committees can be affected to its advantage. There are limits, of course, beyond which even the most influential group cannot go. Due to the seniority rule, groups cannot influence the selection of the members of Congress who get committee chairmanships. Length of service helps to determine committee memberships, too. But the membership of any two Congresses is never indentical; death, resignation, retirement, defeat—all result in new members coming in, with resulting changes in composition of the standing committees. With every new Congress, too, both houses organize anew. It is at such times that pressure groups are most active in trying to get assigned to committees those members who it is thought will be of most aid in the coming legislative struggle. National officials and legislative representatives of Americans for Democratic Action tried in this way in 1948 to affect the make-up of the House Ways and Means and Labor Committees, and not without some success.[39]

Chapter 8

THE TECHNIQUES OF LOBBIES
AND PRESSURE GROUPS—II

[Lobbying is] . . . any attempt by individuals or groups
to influence governmental decision. . . .
—*Yale Law Journal**

In this chapter the survey of lobby and pressure group techniques begun in the previous chapter is continued. There, various methods of petitioning Congress were described. Here, other forms which the right of petition may take to influence government decision are surveyed; in addition, a particular type of pressure group which warrants special mention and the participation of pressure groups in election campaigns are described.

Additional Forms of the Right of Petition

THE CATALYTIC PRESSURE GROUP. Influence exercised quietly differentiates the tactics of the catalytic from those of many other pressure groups. Although pressure groups in general work behind the scenes as well as in the arena of politics, catalytic groups usually avoid open appearances. They come into being to solve two problems; first, how to coordinate the pressure activities of several groups sharing the same primary concern or interest; second, how to increase to a point of action the intensity of a group's interest in a question falling within its secondary sphere of concern. These groups may be formed in different ways: an established pressure group may assume the function of a catalytic group, or it may set up a committee to assume this function; several pressure groups may set up a coordinating center, or they may set up a committee of individuals to serve on a

* "Improving the Legislative Process: Federal Regulation of Lobbying," LVI (1947), 306.

personal basis; or there may be informal consultation among interested individuals, sometimes followed by more formal organization.

What a catalytic group does. The two major aspects of the work of a catalytic group are to deal directly with pressure groups in an attempt to obtain all possible support and neutralize opposition, and to establish the main outlines of strategy and expedite the step-by-step tactics. Strategy is the broad planning of a legislative campaign, and includes agreement on specific goals, the definition of chief arguments to be used, analysis of existing social forces and agencies with a view to maximizing support and minimizing opposition, and the choice of timing for various moves. Tactics involves the detailed implementation of strategy: timing of the campaign and its various steps, securing sponsorship, modifying the social forces at work to augment the favorable and diminish the unfavorable forces, and focusing the efforts of available pressure groups to get optimum results. Groups within the government structure, in administrative agencies in particular, are important. Whether or not an administrative agency plays a primary role depends on whether the subject is basic (in a policy sense) or technical. The likelihood of administrative agency involvement is greater as the subject becomes more technical. Also the standing committees of Congress, regional sentiment, and the political parties are important factors.

Catalytic groups may be temporary or permanent. Examples of temporary groups are the Citizens Committee to Repeal Chinese Exclusion, Citizens Committee on Displaced Persons, Committee for Equality in Naturalization, National Committee for the Enactment of the National School Health Services Act, National Council for a Permanent Fair Employment Practices Commission, and the National Council Against Conscription. The following are examples of permanent catalytic groups: the National Council for the Prevention of War, Committee for the Extension of Labor Education, National Tax Equality Association, and the Committee for Constitutional Government. A group urging the national committees of both parties to agree to take the issues of the Middle East out of domestic politics came into being in early 1956 in response to what was regarded as a danger that partisan debate of such issues would hinder the formation of sound foreign policy.

The Citizens Committee for Chinese Exclusion is of particular interest as the prototype of the catalytic pressure group. It was eminently successful in achieving its goal, the repeal of the provisions of American law excluding Chinese from general immigration. This success was obtained in a phenomenally short time—a little over two months. President Franklin D. Roosevelt on October 11, 1943, asked

Congress in a special message to pass a bill then before the House "to correct an injustice to our friends." On December 17 he signed the bill. In this way, laws which had formed a part of U.S. foreign policy for sixty years were repealed. Yet mention of the Citizens Committee never appeared in the records of the House Committee on Immigration and Naturalization. Planning the legislative campaign and conduct of tactics were done by an executive committee consisting of representatives of pressure groups directly or indirectly interested in repeal of the legislation in question. Both planning and execution took place between May 25 and October 13, 1943. The Committee did not try to manufacture public opinion, as a labor organization or a manufacturers' group might have done, but left that job to constituent groups. Committee expenses were less than five thousand dollars for the job of erasing "laws which realists said could not be tampered with during the war and not for a long time afterward, if ever."[1] The Citizens Committee "could not have succeeded if that (manufacture of political pressure) had been necessary. Rather, as a catalytic group, it released forces which already existed but were largely inoperative or not specifically directed."[2]

A question might be raised as to the use of the adjective *catalytic* to describe this special kind of pressure group. According to Webster, *catalytic* is the adjective form of *catalysis,* a process in physical chemistry, in which a reaction is accelerated by a catalytic agent, the catalyst. A catalytic pressure group, then, would be a pressure group causing acceleration of a reaction which otherwise would have proceeded at a slower rate. Whether a political reaction is accelerated by a group or whether it is made to occur when otherwise it would not occur at all, can be determined only by analyzing the particular case. Even then the issue may remain in doubt. In any event, and although usage has begun to sanction the phrase in political discussion, whether the use of terms appropriate to the physical sciences advances serious political discussion is open to question.[3]

Significance of the catalytic pressure group has already been discussed. Additional comments may be made at this point, however. Large resources, particularly money, are not always necessary for success in pressure politics. Nor does success go to the group which makes the loudest noise. In fact, if conditions are right, success can be achieved without fanfare, and in a short space of time. Able leadership, which need not appear publicly, is essential to success.

ELECTION CAMPAIGNING. Taking part in election campaigns is another way in which organized interests and pressure groups strive to affect the course of political events.

The American system for choosing responsible federal officials comprises biennial party primaries and elections for the House and one-third of the Senate and quadrennial elections for the Presidency and Vice-Presidency from among candidates nominated by party conventions of state-designated delegates.

Pressure groups do practically everything in political campaigns that the parties do except the nominating of candidates for public office. They endorse candidates nominated by the parties or withhold endorsement, depending on the candidate's record. They raise money and spend it on behalf of particular candidates or set up committees to do so. They ring doorbells, make telephone calls to get voters to register, publish electioneering material, and use all the known devices of propaganda, including radio, television, newspapers, periodicals, as well as other advertising, not excluding using airplanes to shower leaflets favoring endorsed candidates and opposing their opponents. The latter method was used in 1950 by members of the American Medical Association to defeat candidates for re-election to Congress who had previously favored President Truman's proposed plan for compulsory health insurance.[4] For many years, Labor's League for Political Education worked for the election of candidates endorsed by the American Federation of Labor, while the Political Action Committee of the Congress of Industrial Organizations electioneered for its favorite candidates.[5] The same formula of rewarding its friends and punishing its enemies is apparently to be followed by the merged AFL-CIO.[6] Attempts to defeat a member of Congress who voted "wrong" on a pending bill are not unknown, as for example, that attempted by the National Retail Lumber Dealers in the case of an Ohio member who voted against its interests, even though the NRLD's legislative counsel later thought the attempt was ill-advised.[7] State units of Americans for Democratic Action are active in varying degree on behalf of candidates nominated by the major parties. In some states, New Jersey, for example, the state ADA endorsed the senatorial candidates of both parties in 1954. In other states, the candidate of neither party has been endorsed. In presidential campaigns many groups are active in their support of one or the other candidate, among other reasons because they have attempted to make their imprint in the party platform. In 1948, for example, farm groups were successful in getting an agricultural plank acceptable to them. But neither party adopted the health plank advocated by the Committee for the Nation's Health.

Unusual candor was shown in the 1954 New Jersey senatorial campaign when Clifford P. Case, the Republican candidate, asserted his independence from all pressure groups. He distinguished between individual voters, who he thought would support him even though they might not agree with him on all issues, and pressure groups, with whom, he said, one must apparently go down the line or lose their support. Convinced that elections are not decided by pressure groups, Case declared his independence from them and, in effect, defied them to defeat him. He won the election in a tight race.

Pressure groups avoid political responsibility by letting the parties nominate candidates, thus resisting the temptation to form third parties. Whenever economic discontent, political reform, dissatisfaction with the two major parties, or factionalism suggests to a group that it enter the political arena by nominating its own candidates, the result has been failure in the long run. On a national scale, even sectionally and regionally, third parties have not flourished in this country.

In an electoral system based on single-member districts, third party candidates are at an inherent disadvantage, one accentuated by the way state election laws invariably discourage third parties. Both experience and observation reinforce the truth of the rule that success in pressure politics turns on neutrality as between the two parties.

PETITIONING THE EXECUTIVE BRANCH. The scrutiny which pressure groups give to administration, the alliances they often form with executive bureaus, and the working arrangements entered into among themselves can all be considered as variations of the right of petition, which has been focused on Congress for a longer period of time than these more modern applications.

Watching the administration. Representatives of the auto workers, of railway trainmen, and of some agricultural producers were scrutinizing the administration of President Eisenhower's economic policies when, in 1955, they criticized these policies before a joint Senate-House committee studying the country's economic condition.[8] Such testimony was the normal result of the constant watch kept by the staff economists of these groups over the statistical indexes maintained by the Bureau of Labor Statistics and other government agencies. Dissatisfied with what they found, particularly in the way of backward instead of forward-looking economic policies, falling farm income, and unemployment among railway workers, these group representatives hoped to generate enough pressure behind public opinion to force a change in policy.

Formation of alliances. To obtain the aid of a governmental agency in its legislative campaign is the new rule of lobbying now generally followed by pressure groups whenever possible.[9] Most government departments (including the State Department) have vested interests in maintaining intact existing programs authorized and supported by laws on the statute books. Many government bureaus are ready to join with like-minded pressure groups to align themselves behind a legislative program aimed at promoting mutual interests. A legislative campaign supported by executive agencies alone, or by private organizations alone, has difficulty in making headway. But one backed by both executive agency and outside groups has force behind it, particularly if local interests stand to benefit in a large number of congressional districts, as is the case with rivers and harbors improvements, reclamation projects, wildlife projects, defense projects. The Rivers and Harbors Congress, the National Reclamation Association, the Izaak Walton League, among others, are examples of national organizations with friends in both administrative and legislative branches of the government with whom effective alliances in their special interest are possible. New national organizations have grown up since World War II—for example, the National Defense Industrial Association—to extend into industrial production and the military part of the national defense budget the same pattern for political success that the Army Engineers, the Rivers and Harbors Congress, and long-time Congressmen and Senators have developed in the Army Department's civil appropriations budget. Unrelieved international political tension in the atomic age thus reproduces a set of vested interests not unlike those resulting from prolonged domestic economic tension two decades ago, a duplication which not even a Bureau of the Budget under strong executive direction has been able to prevent.[10]

Alliances with other groups. When Americans for Democratic Action, in 1950, mobilized support in its campaign to prevent the House Rules Committee from regaining the tight control it previously had over legislation going to the floor of the House, nine other national organizations joined in this action. In letters sent to all Congressmen and released to the press, representatives of these ten groups stated: "We will regard a Congressman's vote against the new Rules Committee recommendation as proof that he has kept faith with the American people. We will regard a Congressman's vote to restore dictatorial power to the Rules Committee as a vote against the best interests of the American people."[11]

PETITION TO THE COURTS. Appeals to the courts, both direct and indirect, must now be included among the methods adopted by pressure groups to influence the formulation of the rules by which society lives.

Initiation of cases. The success of the National Association for the Advancement of Colored People in its resort to the courts over the past few years has brought this particular technique into public view. Even before the first (in 1915) of the many successes of the NAACP in winning cases which it sponsored, litigation before the Supreme Court, although cast in terms of individuals as plaintiff and defendant, was nonetheless essentially part of the process of formulation of rules governing the relationships between groups of the population. When the NAACP turned to the courts in its campaign for fuller recognition and observance of Negro rights, it was adopting a technique which had already been adopted and used by other social groups and their organizations for some time.

When a group petitions the government for a redress of grievances by enlisting the support of the courts, there is an advantage in setting up a separate group to fight the cases. By so doing it can attract financial support from contributors who can deduct their contributions from their taxable income. (Confusion over the real nature of court actions has been perpetuated by Congress in maintaining an unreal distinction between organizations receiving contributions for conducting propaganda for the purpose of influencing legislation and those obtaining funds for seeking redress of grievances through the courts.) Thus the NAACP in 1939 established the NAACP Legal Defense and Education Fund for the exclusive purpose of conducting legal action, while the NAACP proper has devoted itself to legislative activities.[12]

The amicus curiae brief. Of assistance to one group fighting cases in the courts is the filing of briefs by other sympathetic groups as friends of the court. In the four racial restrictive covenant cases reviewed by the Supreme Court in 1947, nineteen briefs were filed by friends of the court, including racial, ethnic, and religious minority groups, two large national labor unions (the AFL and CIO), religious organizations (the Congregational Church, the Human Relations Council of the Protestant Council of New York City, and the American Unitarian Association), and many liberal associations, such as the American Civil Liberties Union, the St. Louis Civil Liberties Committee, the American Association for the United Nations, the American Veterans Committee, the National Lawyers Guild, and the Non-Sectarian Anti-Nazi League to Champion Human Rights. The Department of Justice also filed an *amicus curiae* brief.[13]

Fighting cases and filing briefs as friends of the court may both be described as direct appeals to the courts. A third variation of the basic technique of petitioning the government is somewhat different but has the same purpose. The preparation of articles for publication which are or can be useful as legal briefs has another purpose as well; it facilitates favorable decisions by judges. In justifying their decisions, judges do not confine themselves to the strict text of the Constitution and of the laws but seek guidance and justification elsewhere. Law reviews are a favorite place to hunt new ideas on or about the law. Groups which turn to the courts to gain enforcement of their rights can assist their cause by simultaneously inspiring publication of articles which, in effect, argue their case. Moreover, such publication may have an effect (admittedly, one difficult to measure) on lay opinion as well, and such opinion, in turn, may have some minor effect on court decisions.

RESOURCES. All the techniques listed above cost money; hence the spending of money should be included if one is to have a fairly complete list of the various methods used by groups to influence public policy. But the money spent must first be raised. The last, and in some respects, most important method—raising money—is in a very real sense the primary method, since without it few of the others are possible.

Raising and spending money. If this discussion of raising money were to be confined to that part of the total amount raised for lobbying as legally interpreted, the sums involved would be relatively small. For example, in 1948 the NAM submitted to Congress the figure of $146,186.12 as the cost of its lobbying in 1947.[14] By what methods this sum was raised was not stated. However, a full statement was made of the method whereby it was decided that this was the part of its total expenses properly allocable to activities intended to directly influence the passage or obstruction of legislation.[15]

According to the NAM's calculation, expenditures for influencing legislation amounted to 6.2 per cent of the NAM's total expenditures, excluding the cost of its public relations program, which was $1,947,-362.34. (Total expenditures without public relations program, $2,-367,500; with it, $3,314,862.) Obviously, the raising of a sum of money amounting to less than $150,000 from the membership of the NAM did not tax their resources unduly.

However, the real question is not whether or not the NAM has any trouble in raising the funds it spends for the narrow interpretation of lobbying. The problem is the volume of expenditures for purposes which are bound to have an impact on the government of the United States. In reporting to Congress its 1947 expenditures for lobbying purposes, the NAM meant by "direct efforts to influence Congress" the following: (1) communication with Congressmen through letters from NAM officers, (2) appearance of witnesses representing the Association before committees of Congress, (3) personal visits to members of Congress by members of the NAM's office and staff, and (4) direct communications to members of the Association suggesting that they communicate with their representatives in Congress.[16] All such activities will be recognized as normal for an up-to-date lobbying group to engage in. They do not differ from those methods of influencing Congress which were in common use before the invention of radio, television, and motion pictures revolutionized communications; before advertising, public relations, and propaganda in their present breadth and depth blanketed and penetrated all parts of the country and all levels of activity. The same resourcefulness which led the NAM in 1913 to put a House committee employee on its payroll to obtain congressional intelligence while tariff legislation was pending has been shown in the urbanity with which NAM lawyers, with an assist from the Supreme Court, have managed to make the country believe that the Association's expenditures for political lobbying purposes are much less than they are in fact.

Other resources. There are still other resources which enable national organizations to influence the course of legislation yet avoid the necessity of reporting them as contributions. One is indirect revenue, that is, revenue in the form of services performed for a nominal sum which in the regular market would fetch a much higher price. The NAM, for example, as part of its program of educating the public in the days preceding the election of the Eightieth Congress, the Congress which enacted the Labor-Management Relations (Taft-Hartley) Act, received billboard advertising and other similar services for $50,000 which would normally have cost $3¼ million.[17]

Indirect subsidy. Another device, already referred to in connection with the NAACP, is, in effect, an indirect government subsidy. Here, the internal revenue laws permit contributions to educational organizations to be deducted from tax payments to the federal government. Here, too, may be a clue to the reason why the NAM calls its propaganda program a "public education program." More likely such subtlety is not necessary, inasmuch as the ordinary and necessary expenses of firms doing business are deductible; and these expenses include regular dues (as distinct from special contributions), fees to law firms and public relations firms, expenditures for institutional advertising, and entertainment of government officials. Contributions to research organizations are similarly exempt. Moreover, contributions to organizations are deductible if "no substantial part of the activities" involve the conduct of propaganda or other attempts to influence legislation. It is estimated that some fifty thousand organi-

zations qualify as such organizations, as, for example, the NAACP
Legal and Defense Educational Fund. Since the line between education and propaganda is often hard to define, and since propaganda is
not lobbying, according to the Supreme Court, the temptation is
great for national organizations to keep lobbying expenses low in
relation to other expenses; or when this is difficult, to set up educational, research, or legal aid affiliates and to solicit contributions on
assurance of tax exemption. And individuals, both real and corporate,
can lessen their taxable income by responding to such solicitation.

Since the groups sponsoring public education programs include
government agencies and departments, it may be added that executive agencies get their funds for legislative campaigns from appropriations themselves. With their large budgets, the major agencies
are at an advantage as compared to smaller agencies, since their large
budgets allow ample room for the personnel and public relations expenditures needed. Congress enacted legislation in 1919 attempting
to prohibit legislative campaigns by executive officials, but it has
been ineffective. It has resulted only in the use of more caution and
indirection.[18]

The profession of lobbying. In connection with the resources available to private associations lobbying as a profession should not be
overlooked. Practicing lobbyists are available for hire, just like legal
talent, advertising skill, or publicity know-how. Obviously, in this
respect private groups possessing or having access to great resources
have a corresponding advantage over groups with few resources.

The role of the lobbyist is often misunderstood. Congressmen, as
well as the public at large, often do not understand the lobbyist's
role. If Robert Luce, the late veteran Congressman from Massachusetts, and author of books on parliamentary procedure, misunderstood the real role of lobbying, others can be excused for similar
misapprehensions. Yet the distinguished Congressman from Massachusetts failed to grasp the essential point. While it is true, as Luce
said, that retention of their position depends on getting results, lobbyists must not get too great results: If they do, they are out of a
job. In other words, the main principle of lobbying is never to do
the job of lobbying too well.[19]

One lobbyist, who is reported to have violated this cardinal tenet
of the craft, did in seventeen days what his employers had been
unable to do in seventeen years. According to the report, subcontractors on construction jobs had been trying during the previous
seventeen years to obtain legislation from Congress forcing contractors to make known the names of subcontractors and the amounts
of their bids. Since they were not required to name their subcon-

tractors, contractors could get bids from subcontractors, and then when awarded contracts, could subsequently go to them and force down their bids on pain of excluding them. The lobbyist thought he could help. He persuaded the organized electrical, heating, piping, air conditioning, and plumbing contractors to divide the expense. He then went to work and in seventeen days' time had bills long stymied in both Senate and House committees acted on and favorably reported to the two chambers. Here was the lobbyist's error: he had done his job so well that his employers no longer needed him and he was out of a job.[20]

COMMENT. Public policy in the matter of lobby regulation leaves much to be desired. The strict interpretation of the existing law by the Supreme Court is unrealistic. The shortcomings of the revenue laws and the difficulties encountered in administering them call for remedy. The encouragement of evasion and subterfuge is not healthy.

In many quarters the idea that the situation calls for review because it favors groups with large resources is not given much weight. For example, one scholar, examining this idea, sees no reason for concern in the fact that some groups have far larger resources than others for propaganda campaigns aimed at influencing Congress through manipulating the views of the electorate.[21] More difficult to understand, perhaps, is the widespread lack of concern about the existing situation. Little attention is paid, apparently, to the mass of information filed with the Clerk of the House even under the restricted meaning of the Lobby Regulation Act. Even before 1954, when the Supreme Court approved the Act as a valid exercise of the authority of Congress to protect itself from anonymous pressures, there was little public interest. One group investigated by Congress in 1950, the ADA, complained that it never knew whether the data it filed met the Act's requirements, and nobody, not excluding the Department of Justice as the government's law enforcement arm, seemed to care.[22] On the other hand, other groups, the NAM, for example, investigated by the House Select Committee objected to the volume of information required and even to the right of Congress to require the production of certain information.

The 1950 House investigation, the new lobbying practices and devices disclosed, the large volume of information collected and analyzed, and the recommendations, even though modest, have been treated with indifference. No doubt the Supreme Court's confirmation in 1954 of the NAM's interpretation of the lobby regulation act's requirements regarding expenditures for lobby activities and of its method of deciding what part of its total expenditures were allocable to lobbying help explain the substantially smaller amounts filed since

1954 as lobbying expenditures. And since there was little public concern over the larger amounts, with accompanying detail, submitted before the meaning of lobbying was defined, there is even less reason to believe that the smaller figures filed following the clarification of the meaning of lobbying will attract attention. It cannot be claimed in defense of the Supreme Court that it made its definition of lobbying in 1954 without full knowledge of the adoption by contemporary petitioners of all the modern devices of public relations, advertising, and propaganda, since Earl Warren, the Chief Justice, was Governor of California when the California Legislature, with his approval, undertook an exhaustive investigation of lobbying in that state. The Court can hardly be excused for ignorance of the situation within which the law operates any more than the citizen can be excused because of ignorance of the law.

Public indifference may be due to confusion rather than apathy. One method of confusing the public, as the California Legislature was reminded by its lobby investigating committee, is to submit so much data when filing reports under state lobby regulating laws that the public turns from the problem in confusion.[23] But a confused public is not a disinterested public; the fault lies in the lack of interest and concern in responsible quarters. The educational institutions and the press, to which the House Select Committee attached "responsibility of increasing public knowledge as to the nature and extent of pressure group operations,"[24] cannot be said to have acknowledged this responsibility or to have responded to this appeal. For the press to accept such a responsibility would require the prospect of some financial gain in playing up the problem as a "publicity stunt," like the crime wave which the old-time newspaperman Lincoln Steffens claimed he could engineer at any time by merely reporting to his city editor all the entries on the police blotter. There is small prospect of public interest being aroused by nonpartisan, objective investigation financed by public funds. Nor is there much likelihood of the contemporary public unconcern being dispelled by grants from corporations, since the exercise of the right of petition by corporations, particularly large corporations, is certainly not at stake. It is interesting, but probably idle, to speculate what could be accomplished in the way of increasing public interest in the problem of lobby regulation if some foundation were to become aroused, or if some aggrieved group, such as the NAACP, were to start working on the problem. Other pursuits, however, absorb too much thought and too many resources for most of them to be devoted to this aspect of the problem of American democracy under pressure.

SUMMARY. In this and the previous chapter the techniques of interest groups and of their lobbies have been discussed, particularly the manifold use made of the constitutionally guaranteed right of petition. Such groups gather information and use it in many ways to generate propaganda. The social lobby is one method of lobbying. Others are grass-roots lobbying, bringing pressure to bear on Congress by forming blocs in Congress, with pressure politicians as their nuclei, proposing legislation, appearing and testifying before legislative and appropriations committees, influencing the composition of committees when Congress and committees are being organized. As a special form of pressure group, the catalytic group works quietly and without much clamor, adds the power of one group to that of others, and thus obtains results in legislation which would otherwise be beyond the reach of any of these groups acting separately. Also, the activities of groups in the election phase of politics were discussed. Nowadays, the courts also are subject to pressure from external groups which have found that the judicial process offers an opportunity to correct grievances not available in the legislature. Resources of national associations available for lobbying were discussed, particularly the effect of existing law as construed by the courts and enforcement agencies. Finally, some tentative reasons were suggested for the public indifference to this aspect of American democracy under pressure.

Chapter 9

POLITICAL PARTIES OUTSIDE CONGRESS

> We must recall that American parties are founded on no ideological or social bases, that they include elements and doctrines that are completely heterogeneous, that fundamentally they are simply organizations for the conquest of administrative and political offices and for the nomination of candidates in primaries, which are often more important than the real elections. . . .
>
> —Maurice Duverger
> *Political Parties. Their Organization and Activity in the Modern State**

American government is partisan government. Despite the silence of the Constitution on the subject, our formal governmental system is operated by political parties. At the same time, it is a system of government in which the interests of people are not wholly represented either by the parties or by the organs of government, the gap having been filled by political pressure groups. In this and the following chapter the political parties are discussed, first, as they exist and operate outside Congress, and then, as they are organized and operate in Congress.

Federalism and Decentralized Parties

To call American political parties a system probably dignifies them too much. Rather, they are an unsystematic and not too well organized set of groups held together uncertainly in the states and known nationally as the Republican and Democratic Parties. They strive on a nationwide scale to elect their candidates to national office; hence

---

* Trans. by Barbara and Robert North, with a foreword by D. W. Brogan (London: Methuen & Co., Ltd., New York: John Wiley & Sons, Inc., 1955), p. 210.

the rewards and perquisites of office, rather than differing principles and programs, hold the parties together. There are no uniform answers which are acceptable throughout the nation to the question, Who is a Republican and who is a Democrat? Moreover, the party organizations, national and state, draw forth little sustained interest and support from among the mass of citizens. This is the more surprising because the major parties are decentralized and owe their existence to party organizations in the counties.

PREDOMINANCE OF THE STATES. The importance of the federal nature of our government to the kind of parties we have is nowhere better illustrated than in local organizations and membership.

Under authority of the federal Constitution, the state legislatures determine the qualifications of the voters, hence of party membership.

Party membership. Party membership in the United States is generally not distinguished from voting affiliation. A voter is a Republican, a Democrat, or an independent, depending upon which way he registers in the party primary, and depending on the kind of primary provided by state law.

There is generally some kind of test to determine the voter's party affiliation. This is the essential feature of the closed primary, which is used in about three-quarters of the states, the remainder having open primaries.[1] There must also be some authority—the party itself, the national committee, the states—by law, on the basis of past allegiance, present affiliation, or future intention to prescribe what the test shall be.

Party size. There is a widespread belief that there are more Democrats than Republicans in the country. This belief is based on registration figures. But registration figures are an unreliable measurement of actual party strength. In many states more voters are registered as Democrats than as Republicans, yet Republican candidates are more often successful at the polls. California is an example. The fact is that the membership strength of the two major parties is not accurately known and cannot even be estimated without difficulty.[2] "In view of the loose rules with respect to members in the major parties," Berdahl observes, "and the failure to distinguish clearly between loyal membership and mere voting affiliation, the strength in actual membership of the major parties cannot be accurately determined and becomes very difficult even to estimate." There are three bases on which such an estimate might be based: active work for the party; contributions; party enrollment or registration, where such enrollment or registration is provided for.[3]

One attempted estimate is worth noting. There may be 500,000 local workers for the two major parties together—county chairmen, county committeemen, district leaders, township and precinct captains and workers. There are perhaps as many again who are party workers who do not hold party office. This would indicate that there are about a million professional party workers who are active participants in political organizations.[4]

Voters' independence. Strict rules for party membership, including payment of dues, have never been popular in the United States. In fact the view is widespread that there is something "un-American" about hard and fast regulation of membership in a political party. ". . . it is doubtful," Berdahl says, "whether American opinion would tolerate such a departure from the traditional looseness of our two-party system; and in fact, a congressional committee has already indicated that, in order to be truly American, a party must be loosely organized, with complete freedom on the part of the party members to do as they like at any time, to refuse to work for the party, to refuse to contribute to its support, to vote against its candidates, to quarrel with its principles, and yet presumably to remain within the party organization as members in good standing."[5]

"Under our political system," a committee of the Seventy-fourth Congress stated, "any citizen having proper residential qualifications cannot be denied the privilege of joining a party, nor can he be expelled from it. He is not even bound to vote for the candidates of his own party; in truth, under the American system of parties the initiative rests wholly with the individual and assures his complete freedom of political action . . ."[6]

Consequences of voters' independence. The emphasis upon the voter's right to join a party (privilege, according to the House Committee just quoted), while assuring him complete freedom of action, at the same time has undesirable consequences as regards party organization. It contributes to control by the few and encourages factionalism. In the United States some 800,000 offices are filled by elective officials. Most of these are state and local improvement and school district offices. With so many offices filled by election, and with politics taking so little of the average citizen's time and attention, the road is open to domination of organization by a few people.[7] Also factional fights occur within a state political party which can disrupt its machinery, divide and weaken it at the polls, and lessen its value and usefulness to the national organization. An example of its lessened usefulness is the failure to meet a state quota for campaign funds fixed by the national committee. In states where one of the two parties is superficially the stronger, there is a temptation for one faction to bolt the party at election time, while striving to gain or keep its control of the state organization, especially in a state with an open primary. Texas in 1954 had a two-party system operating within the framework of the Democratic primaries.[8]

Another consequence of emphasizing the political independence of the voter is opposition to outside interference or control. Voters who are nominal members of a party in a state are a law unto themselves. They refuse to be controlled or led by leaders—state or national. Particularly, they resent the attempts of national party chairmen to lay down the law. Thus the Democrats of California in 1954 reacted violently to an attempt by Democratic National Chairman Mitchell to guide them in their choice of candidates.

Instead of limiting themselves to the textbook definition of a party as a group of like-minded individuals, some observers see in the variety of opinion which the parties try to embrace a valuable feature, since it tends to discourage third parties.[9] Even when third parties arise and become established, sooner or later they are under pressure to abandon their separate identity and merge it with that of one or the other of the traditional parties. The New York Liberal Party was under such pressure from the Democratic organization in the Bronx in 1955, but rejected the suggestion.

There are other consequences of emphasizing the voter's freedom of action as the highest value in politics. In the Democratic Party it lies at the base of the "loyalty oath" issue. State party leaders, particularly in the South, guard zealously their right to determine who are Democrats and who are entitled to appear on the ballot as candidates of the Democratic Party in their respective states. There are two developments to be noted—the Dixiecrat (States' Rights) Party in 1948, and the only partially successful attempt at the 1952 nominating convention to bind delegates by a loyalty oath to work for the election of candidates nominated by the convention for the office of President and Vice-President.

In 1948 the party organizations in Alabama and Louisiana were controlled by anti-Truman Democrats (Dixiecrats) who refused to permit the names of the Truman-Barkley ticket, the convention nominees, on the ballot. Instead, the Democratic Party emblem, the rooster, was printed on the ballot with the Dixiecrat candidates for presidential electors. To avoid a repetition, the Democratic National Committee's advisory committee on convention rules recommended that in those states whose laws permit the state party organization to repudiate the party's nominees, the legislatures act to prevent this practice. The authority to make state party organizations comply with the convention's choice rests with the state legislatures. There is no way that the national convention, the highest organ of the national party, can assure by a "loyalty oath" the support of state organizations and party members who resent the attempt of the convention to require them to support and vote for the convention's nominees.

Dissatisfied Democrats and Republicans from thirteen southern, border, and mid-western states gathered in Memphis in the fall of 1956 to organize another states' rights party on a broad base and to nominate candidates for the Presidency and Vice-Presidency.

Some results of voter independence are also to be seen in the 1952 Republican Convention. Nominal Texas Democrats played an important role in Eisenhower's nomination. His nomination was practically assured when the report of the credentials committee, recommending the seating of Taft delegates from Texas, was rejected by the Convention in an unprecedented move and Eisenhower delegates were accepted instead. Election laws in the one-party state of Texas permitted nominal Democrats to vote in Republican primaries and many did, with the result that both Taft and Eisenhower delegates were supported by many Democrats in the selection of delegates to the state Republican convention. The victory of the Taft forces in the state convention, reflected in the credentials committee's report, could not be made to stick in the Convention itself, where Taft sentiment was in the minority. The so-called "Texas steal" of delegates by the Eisenhower forces did not sit well with some delegates.

About one-fifth of the eligible voters are independents, the so-called floating vote. This is also a consequence of the independence permitted to the American voter to use his vote or refrain from using it—wherever and whenever he chooses.

The Two Major Parties

Of the eighteen organizations which qualify as parties under state law and place candidates on the ballot in at least some of the forty-eight states, only two—the Republican and the Democratic—are major parties. They are major parties because of their size (although size is hard to measure, as already noted); because of their long history and of their success in electing candidates to the Presidency; because of their widespread organization; and because of their ability to enlist at least the transitory support at the polls of large numbers of citizens and to raise large sums of money with which to fight political campaigns.

Probably only one minor party, the Liberal Party in New York, could qualify as a third party at present, and it is doubtful whether it should be so designated. It must not be overlooked, however, since it holds a key position in the Empire State. For example, in the 1954 gubernatorial election, the Democratic candidate, W. Averell Harriman, would have been unsuccessful in his campaign without Liberal Party votes (it placed no candidates of its own in the field). The Liberal Party vote for Harriman was 250,000; his plurality over Senator Ives, the Republican nominee, was 11,000.

THE DUAL NATURE OF PARTIES. One feature characteristic of both the Republican and Democratic Parties is their duality. There are two Republican Parties and two Democratic Parties, in effect; each has a party in Congress and a party outside Congress.

PARTY ORGANIZATION. The parties outside Congress, the so-called central party organizations, are loose groupings of the several state parties.

National party committees. The national committees are composed of representatives from the state parties. On the Democratic side, the national committee is established by the national party convention and consists of one man and one woman from each of the forty-eight states, the District of Columbia, and the territories, in accordance with the laws of the respective states and territories. Officers of the national committee are the chairman, three vice-chairmen, a secretary, and a treasurer. They are elected by the committee. The committee meets periodically at the call of the chairman to transact committee business. The most important items of business are the following: to fix the date and place for the convening of the national nominating convention once every four years; the quadrennial call for the convention, together with fixing the number of delegates and votes to which each state or territory is entitled; the preparation and recommendation to the convention of its rules; the maintenance of a staff at headquarters, which is greatly enlarged in presidential election years, and the raising of funds, both for the maintenance of the staff and for fighting of campaigns.[10]

In the Republican Party, the national committee is elected by the national convention. It, too, is composed of one man and one woman from each of the states, the District of Columbia, the territories and territorial possessions. In addition, the state chairman is a member if his state cast its electoral vote for the Republican candidate for President at the last election, if a majority of the congressional delegation from his state is Republican, or if the governor is a Republican.[11]

National committee chairman. In the party outside Congress the most important party official next to the chief of the party (President or defeated candidate) is the national committee chairman. He is responsible for the work of the national committee. If the party has been successful in electing its candidate, the chairman becomes the chief dispenser of patronage under the President's supervision. If appointed to public office by the President, the chairman resigns and is succeeded by another chairman, likewise chosen by the President and holding office as long as he retains his confidence. If not appointed he continues as chairman until replaced by the committee at the President's request. The chairman chooses the committee's staff, oversees the committee's activities, and raises funds for the party's treasury. During mid-term elections the national committee is less important than during a presidential campaign and election. At both times, candidates for Congress are quite free of the national committee, preferring to run their own campaigns with such assistance as they can get from congressional campaign committees set up in both houses of Congress.[12] During presidential campaigns, however, the national committee under the chairman is responsible for the conduct of the entire campaign. If the party wins, the chairman is in a position to claim a reward, as noted above. If the party loses, the chairman must face the likelihood of being asked to resign, although the Chairman of the Democratic National Committee, Stephen A. Mitchell, stayed on for some time as chairman after the Democratic defeat in 1952.[13] The post of national committee chairman pays well, when there is money in the treasury with which to pay, but it cannot compare with the rewards offered in private business.

When the party has lost a presidential election, much of the blame, whether justly or not, must be accepted by the national committee chairman. Like the defeated candidate himself, the chairman is discredited. He usually resigns, to be replaced by someone who can undertake the task of reconstruction without the onus attaching to defeat.

American parties after defeat must fight an uphill struggle to rehabilitate themselves. The first test of rehabilitation comes at the mid-term elections. But the test is inconclusive. At mid-term elections the "outs" do not have the leadership or the inspiration supplied by a presidential candidate. Moreover, mid-term elections bring the party outside Congress and that in Congress together in little more than a formal sense. Liaison between the national committee and the party in Congress is rarely satisfactory, the congressional campaign committees rendering their assistance to party candidates largely independently of the national committee and the latter unable to be of much help to the candidates.

An opposition party between presidential elections is usually divided and disrupted. No one is authorized to or can speak for the party. No suitable organ exists for identifying public questions and making issues out of them. Nor is there any party organ for exploiting to the full the mistakes and errors of the administration. Issues do arise and potential issues multiply, but the dispersed party machinery and organization is not able to capitalize on them.

A defeated presidential candidate is often referred to as the titular leader of his party, as Adlai E. Stevenson was after 1952. He has difficulty, however, in maintaining leadership in the party organization, particularly from committee chairmen and other leaders in Congress. One role a titular leader can essay is to mediate differences among different wings or factions or bolters from the party in an attempt to unify the party for the next presidential campaign. Stevenson made some attempts to do this in 1955.

NATIONAL PARTY CONVENTIONS. The national party conventions are a unique feature of American politics. They are unique because of the fixed term of the President in the American political scheme. The President's term is fixed by the Constitution at four years. The question of candidacy, therefore, arises only quadrennially. More important, the President, with the Vice-President, is the only official of the federal government who is elected, in effect, by the people directly. (The electoral college, provided for by the Constitution, still operates formally, but its members, the presidential electors, long ago lost the independence of judgment contemplated for them by the Constitution, and now vote automatically for the party's nominee to whom they are pledged.) Thus only once in four years does an opportunity arise for the American democracy to choose the candidates from among whom their President is chosen.

Call from the national committees. The national conventions are held on call of the respective national committees. The call is signed by the national committee chairman, and informs the chairmen of the state party organizations of the place, the date and time, and the purpose of the meeting. Their purpose is to nominate a candidate for President and a candidate for Vice-President of the United States, to promulgate a platform, and for such other matters as the convention may decide. The call also notifies each state and territory of the number and distribution of votes to which it is entitled, and the basis on which the distribution of votes is made.[14]

In deciding the date for convening the nominating conventions, the national committees must take account of the laws of the various states. These laws fix the period within which party nominees for President and Vice-President *must* be certified for the ballots. For the most part, the state legislatures enacted these laws before the days of radio and television, and before travel by air became common, when it was thought that several months were necessary to conduct an election campaign and particularly to "build up" a candidate over the country. Nowadays, with quick means of communication and transportation available, the need for holding conventions several months in advance of the balloting in November has largely disappeared. Yet the state laws fixed a limit beyond which it was not possible to move the convention dates. In order to hold their 1956 nominating conventions later than usual, that is, in August, the national committees of the two major parties had to request four states —Massachusetts, South Dakota, Connecticut and Ohio—to alter their laws to permit later certification of the party nominees.

Choice of delegates. Delegates to the national nominating conventions are chosen in party primaries, by state conventions, or by state party committees. In 1952 the voters in seventeen states selected delegates by the primary method; all the others used either conventions or state committees. In 1953 and 1954, Nevada, Indiana, and Montana joined the earlier seventeen states in providing for selection of delegates by primaries.

Selection of delegates by party primary also gives an indication of the relative appeal which various candidates for the nomination have for the voters. Only nineteen states conduct presidential preference primaries, that is, party elections in which candidates for convention delegates favor a particular candidate for the party's presidential nomination. However, in some of these states, such as Wisconsin, Minnesota, and California, voters of one persuasion can vote in the primary of the other party, with results that are sometimes interpreted as showing a preference among the voters of one party for the candidate of the other which will be most easily defeated. In addition, only small percentages of the eligible voters participate in such primaries. Also, they take place long before the party nominating conventions and even farther away from the national election. All these things combine to make the preference primaries of limited value as indicators of the actual preference of the total electorate.

Nominations. The nomination and election of a candidate for the Presidency is the main purpose of parties in America. All the party activities during the preceding four-year period point to the day when the nomination takes place. The moves of the aspirants for the nomination; the politics in three thousand counties, in forty-eight state capitals, and in Congress; the maneuvering for designation as delegates to the convention and the designation itself, whether by party organization, popular petition, or convention; the caucusing and voting; the making of pledges and construction of the intangible but strong loyalties in hundreds of political factions; the influence of special interest groups and of their leaders, who ordinarily play a marginal role as to the selection of candidates, although they display more interest in platforms—all these factors combine to produce the glamour, the excitement, the tension of the moments when the convention finally has before it the names of the persons put in nomination, and the voting begins.

No attempt is made here to describe fully the course of a national party convention. On the appointed day, the convention is called to order by a temporary chairman. A permanent chairman and other officers are then proposed and elected. A credentials committee, a resolutions committee, a platform committee, are established. A "keynote" speech, glorifying the party and its leaders, is made. Other speeches are made while the credentials committee passes on the credentials of the delegates. Their report is then submitted and acted on by the convention as a whole. The platform committee completes its work, submits its report, and the convention acts on it. Only then do nominating speeches begin, and are names placed in nomination. When completed, the voting starts, by states, in alphabetical order, and continues until one of the candidates obtains the necessary majority of votes. He is the party's nominee, the one who will carry the party's banner into the campaign for the Presidency. The proposal of persons for the vice-presidential nomination is always anticlimactic, for the convention's chief purpose is already completed. After the vice-presidential candidate is nominated, the delegates usually begin to disperse and the convention adjourns.

Platforms. Platforms of American parties are constructed to appeal to the greatest possible number among the diverse groups of the electorate. Racial, religious, and occupational groups in urban areas in populous states are objects of special appeals. Such groups are thought to, and may, hold the balance of power in some key states. The platform is also drawn in such a way as to alienate as few voters as possible. With these considerations in mind, the convention's platform committee hears party members and leaders, state and local officials, distinguished private citizens, and representatives from most of the nationwide organizations, such as those representing farmers, labor, and industry, who wish to be heard. The committee is usually authorized by the national committee to convene and conduct hearings before the convention. The platform committee is composed of one representative from each state delegation and is presided over by a chairman elected by the committee. The drafting of the platform is usually well advanced by the time hearings are held and is finalized soon after. It is then presented to the convention for adoption.

The platform of the party adopted by the national convention has value only because it comes from the one party organ authorized to determine the party's stand on public issues. On all other grounds it is of doubtful value. Voters disregard it in favor of the stands taken by the party's nominees; the parties in Congress find it of only limited value as a guide in the legislative struggle. Frequently, it has no value as such, for the issue or problem involved has arisen since the platform was drafted. As the impact of convention recedes and new situations develop, the platform's value diminishes to the vanishing point. It is then valuable only to the opposing party as something to attack—a stick with which to beat the dog.

Party conventions and pressure groups. Party conventions are party meetings held primarily for the nomination of candidates for public office. The pressure groups, being more interested in issues than in the nomination of candidates, do not figure directly in the conventions. But indirectly they do have a certain importance. Since the groups work through the parties or through particular party leaders both in and out of public office, lines of influence run from pressure group officials to political and governmental officials. The reverse is also true. Thus leaders of labor groups, of industrial, business, and farm groups, of the banking and financial community, as well as of nonoccupational groups, such as those interested in civil rights, are active at national party conventions and no doubt wield some influence. The exact amount is not readily ascertainable.

Local and sectional issues often become national, as in the case of civil rights and ownership of submerged offshore lands. Consequently, groups interested in the governmental treatment of such issues work to make themselves felt in the choice of delegates to the conventions. Before the 1952 convention, for example, Governor Adlai E. Stevenson's opposition to state ownership of submerged offshore lands no doubt influenced the stand of many Texas and other southern Democrats toward him. The issue of enforcement of the Supreme Court's decision outlawing segregation on the basis of race in the public schools played a similar role in the preconvention days of 1956. In both cases, the influence of groups with strong feelings was merged with that of party in determining delegates to the party conventions, there to be exerted in the convention's platform drafting, votes, and proceedings. The influence of local groups, both in their own right and as parts of wider associations, may be of greater weight than hitherto supposed in view of the finding in 1954 that the county, although a governmental anachronism, was the real basis of the state party organizations and, consequently, of the national party organizations as well.[15]

Value of the national convention. As a central institution of the party system, the national convention has its defenders and its critics. Among the defenders the first argument is that it works. The convention, despite the ballyhoo and carnival atmosphere and mob rule aspects, nevertheless, turns up competent candidates. Such defenders point to the candidates named by recent conventions; Eisenhower and Stevenson, Truman and Dewey, Roosevelt and Willkie, Cleveland, Wilson, *et al.* At the same time there are those who, while defending the convention as a means of nominating candidates, would, however, prefer to have delegates selected by direct primaries, under instructions to vote for given candidates. Other critics would like to see presidential candidates nominated by the voters in national presidential primaries, a suggestion made formally by President Woodrow Wilson in addressing Congress in 1913.

The national conventions are needed, say its supporters, to adopt platforms and select nominees for the Presidency and the Vice-Presidency. The conventions help the parties feel their way toward nomination of presidential candidates who can best unify them and have the best chance of commanding the support of independent voters, who hold the balance of power in the electoral college. The convention promotes unifying compromises, runs the argument, rather than sharp intraparty struggles.[16]

THE CAMPAIGN. Since the candidate for the Presidency who gets elected is the one with the majority of the votes in the electoral college, the national committee puts forth its greatest effort on behalf of the party candidate in those states with the largest electoral vote. A big electoral vote is dependent on large population, since the electoral vote of each state equals its total representation in Congress. Moreover, the popular vote in such states is fairly evenly divided between the two major parties. The vote of the independent voter and of voters organized in groups and taking sides is of crucial importance; such groups may hold the balance of power between the voters attached by tradition or choice to one or the other of the major parties. Organization is essential not so much to be able to vote large blocks of votes as to get out the vote among those who are unorganized and need prodding to do their civic duty.

The national committee chairman and his lieutenants manage the campaign and advise the candidates on the type of campaign to wage. Each campaign is different from its predecessor, for at no two times are the conditions identical. Much present-day campaigning is done by radio and television. In fact, Republicans and Democrats in New York in 1954 estimated that 70 and 80 per cent, respectively, of their funds were absorbed by television costs.[17] Political rallies of the old-fashioned type are not held very frequently. In a presidential campaign, candidates have to appeal to a nationwide electorate. At least one and usually two swings around the country are made by plane or train. The whistle-stop technique with its opportunity for many face-to-face contacts is still a powerful campaign method. Locally, doorbell-ringing is regarded as the most effective way of stimulating voter participation.

Campaign tactics never appear the same to both sides. Both assert that they carry on their campaigns on a high level, that there is no exaggeration in the charges hurled at their opponents, and that all such charges are justified by the conduct of the other party. The situation in 1954 is not unlike that of other campaigns: ". . . what seems 'unfounded' and 'without justification' to us Democrats (Republicans) is apparently somehow justifiable to Republican (Democratic) consciences. . . ."[18]

Radio and television time is the most important single item of expense in electoral campaigns. In the generation that has passed since 1920, when KDKA first broadcast the results of a presidential campaign, the mass media have come to be used as a matter of course in primary and election campaigns. Moreover, as communications improved, the associated fields of advertising and public relations were developed, so that today all the art and artifice of these two groups are used to "sell" candidates to the voting public. The underlying assumption here is that the same methods which are suitable for the sales promotion of products are also suitable for the promotion of candidates for public office. The assumption is put into practice in political campaigns, both for candidates and for ideas.

Some observers feel that a deeper issue is involved: "The political issue is the health and direction of the whole community, not just the satisfaction of an individual consumer's desire."[19] With radio and television absorbing a greater proportion of available funds than any other aspect of campaigning, it is obvious that political campaign managers think of these media as the best channels to the people as voters. Thus a double revolution has come about: No longer does the voter make up his mind on the basis of a remote, impersonal relation with the candidates, rather, he does so following a period in which he has been bombarded with arguments, appeals, and solicitations embodying all the devices of radio advertising; second, persuasion and social pressure by means of these new media have replaced the informational function of the earlier media, such as the newspaper, the pamphlet, and the political tract.

During campaigns voters become surfeited with political argument and debate. But if the existing legal restraint on free radio time for the candidates of the leading parties were removed, the volume would be even greater. At present, if time is donated to any candidate, the same station or network is required by law to offer equal time to the candidates of all other parties for the same office. Eight parties put candidates in the field for the Presidency in 1952. If any radio network had given time to any candidate, it would have had to offer similar time to all eight candidates. This the chains would not do, since the candidates for the minor parties would not gain the audience commanded by those of the two major parties. In order to encourage face-to-face debate by the candidates, the suggestion has been made that the law be amended to permit this "Lincoln–Douglas type of debate."

The outcome of a campaign is not due entirely to the efforts made by the candidates, the party managers, and party workers. Slow developments over a period of time contribute to the result, too. One such development was the skillful attack during 1930-1932 on the Hoover Administration by the publicity director of the Democratic National Committee, Charles Michelson, and the close collaboration between him and members of Congress in finding and probing deeply into the Administration's weak points.[20] An attempt in 1955 to emulate this earlier success was seen in the critical analysis made by the Democratic National Committee of President Eisenhower's State of the Union Message. Although prepared as a private paper by the Committee's research staff for Democratic members of Congress, it became public and was subsequently published. But it showed few of the earmarks of the successful collaboration with the Democratic Party in Congress which characterized Michelson's efforts.

When the party is not in control of the White House the party committee chairman and his staff are faced with the problem of what and when to attack. One of the most delicate aspects is the relationship between the party outside and the party inside the Congress. Members of Congress are not beholden to the national committee for their success in election; they are independent thinkers when it comes to deciding what part of the administration's program and of the conduct of that program should be selected for criticism. The party chairman and his staff are even more eager to criticize vigorously than the party in Congress. Like so many aspects of the relationship, this one of establishing liaison and working effectively by both the central organization and the party in Congress holds out dangers as well as opportunities. In an effort, apparently, to close the gap and mobilize the full potentialities of the Democratic Party's machinery, reports were current in late 1954 that a policy planning staff would be established by Paul M. Butler to bring the congressional leaders and the national committee together on policy matters in the preparatory phases of the 1956 campaign. Since staff changes at party headquarters in Washington usually occur upon the assumption of his duties by a new chairman, there was reason to place some credence in these reports. Focusing the Democratic Committee's attack on the President as party chief and government leader, instead of on his subordinates, would work in the same direction.

The national committees and candidates for Congress. Two factors guide the national committees in their relationships to congressional candidacies. One is the unwritten rule against intervention by the national committee in party primaries; the other, the meager financial resources usually available to the national committees to assist candidates for Congress in their election campaigns.

Intervention by the committee in a party primary would signify a much more tightly knit party organization than is apparently desired in the United States. Also, a greater sense of obligation to the national party would be implied in greater financial support of candidates by the national committee. Yet neglect of congressional nominations and elections by the national committees weakens party unity in Congress more than any other factor.[21]

The national party organization is tied in loosely with state party organizations. This loose relationship reflects different needs. The national party needs the votes which the state and local organizations are in a position to deliver more than they need the national party. The primary effort of the national organization is directed to the presidential campaign. Congressional campaigns in presidential and in mid-term election years are secondary in importance to conducting a successful campaign for the party's nominee for President. Moreover, since the national committee, particularly the chairman and his staff, stay out of primaries as a rule, there is no feeling of mutual aid between the national organization and the candidates winning the party designation at the primaries.

An additional factor underlining the weakness of the tie between the national and the local organizations is the variety of primaries authorized by the various states. At one extreme is the closed primary, permitting participation only by voters registered as party members; at the other, the blanket primary inviting independence by the voter and by candidates alike. Under Texas law, for example, all citizens have the right to choose the party primary in which they vote, thus opening the Democratic primary to Republicans and vice versa. In other words, the primacy of the states in the determination of the means by which the parties select their nominees, particularly for national offices (Congressmen and Senators), makes impossible the development of a uniformly strong tie between the national, the state, and the district organizations.

Still another factor is the indifference of the national committee to the "safe" districts in which it is almost certain that the incumbent, whether Democrat or Republican, will be returned. There are many of these districts in the North, as well as in the South. Perhaps in all there are more than three hundred such districts.[22] The Republican National Committee ignores the dozens of safe Democratic districts in the South, while the Democratic National Committee ignores the numerous Northern districts where there is no chance, or practically no chance, of electing a Democrat. One reason, apart from any other, dictates this course. There are insufficient funds with which to fight all district campaigns. Obviously, in such a situation the strength of the national party organization varies greatly from state to state and from district to district within each state. This variation shows clearly the nature of American political parties as loose groupings of state parties. The organization is national only in the sense that all states of the Union, the District of Columbia, and territories are entitled to representation on the party organs, the national committee and the national nominating convention, constituted on more than a state-wide basis. The persons who come from these parts of the Union bearing the same party label in fact represent a great variety of "parties," differing not only in strength, numbers, and organization, as well as in cohesion and freedom from factionalism, but also on the basic question of the party itself. The two so-called wings of the Democratic Party, the southern and the northern, stand for differing conceptions of party: the one embedded in "states' rights" with all the historical associations attached to that phrase; the other, in the primacy of the majority, nationally computed, in party affairs.

Cost of elections. Campaigns are expensive. It was reported that over twenty-three million dollars was spent in the 1952 presidential and congressional elections.[23] How much was actually spent is not known, since many state and local groups are exempt from reporting their expenditures.

There is a limit on the amount which any individual may contribute to any one national group. It is illegal, under the Hatch Political Activities Act, to give more than $5000. But this limitation is evaded by setting up additional committees for a candidate which are independent of the national party committees. In this way, the same individual can make contributions to as many committees or groups as have been set up. Big gifts were the principal source of party funds in the 1952 presidential election. The six top Republican and Democratic political committees received 55 per cent of their total receipts in 2047 contributions of $1000 or more during 1952.[24] As constituted at present, parties are not satisfactory as member organizations for the raising of funds necessary to conduct electoral campaigns. In order to decrease the relative importance of large gifts, it has been suggested that contributions up to $100 to a political party be allowed as deductions from income for tax purposes, on the theory that this would stimulate small gifts and consequently enhance member interest in party affairs.

Although labor unions, corporations, and banks are prohibited by law from contributing from their regular funds to candidates in primaries and regular elections, members and officials of labor unions, corporations, and banks and their families are important sources of funds for electoral campaigns. Under the law, political campaign expenditures must be reported to the Clerk of the House of Representatives. But federal law does not extend to state party primaries nor to conventions nominating candidates for federal office. Proposals to bring these activities within the scope of federal law were made during the Eighty-fourth Congress.

Nor are state political committees covered by federal law regulating limitations on spending. Federal statutes of 1925 and 1939 fix the amount that can be spent by any candidate for the House of Representatives at $5000, and for the Senate at $25,000. These limits would also be raised under proposals submitted to the Eighty-fourth Congress.

THE BEHAVIOR OF VOTERS. Today we know little about voters and why they behave as they do. There is much speculation and pseudo-scientific analysis carried on, but it is doubtful that our knowledge is very complete.

Present-day psychologists are wary of making flat statements about political behavior. Over the past half century they have broken away from the atomistic approach in favor of the integrated study of the whole man. Also, they tend now to consider man and his environment together rather than as separate absolutes. They seek more and more to simulate actual life situations in their laboratory experiments. While there are many theories of behavior and wide agreement on reasonable explanations of life, there is little scientific proof; hence the difficulty in putting one's finger on what the social psychologists say about political behavior.[25]

Mental characteristics. Mental characteristics go far to explain voters' behavior, according to Overstreet. "The news today," he says, "is that politics is a thing of the mind—of everybody's mind."[26] By this he means that our political attitudes and modes of action are largely governed by psychological characteristics which have developed within the American people as a whole.[27]

Other observers accept only in part the view that "politics is a thing of the mind." According to them, voting is not rational but is irrational. The impossibility of an intelligent appeal to the voters is the chief difficulty in our political system, according to this view. A verdict on the merit of candidates and issues is therefore impossible. No remedy for this state of affairs is visible. To such observers it appears to be part of the price we pay for universal suffrage.[28]

In the 1952 presidential campaign, Adlai E. Stevenson recognized the crucial place of the parties in dealing with pressure groups and discussed it rationally with the voters. It did not help him in his bid for the Presidency. In campaign speeches he identified and spoke directly to groups of veterans, of labor, of management, of bankers, and of tidelands oil-states' righters. He did not evade issues raised by the demands of these groups. Speaking of "The Nature of Patriotism" as putting "country above self," he referred to "some things in American life today of which we cannot be proud" and asked his American Legion audience, on August 27, to "consider the groups who seek to identify their special interests with the general welfare." "I find it sobering," he said, "to think that their pressures might one day be focused on me. I have resisted them before and I hope the Almighty will give me the strength to do so again and again. And I should tell you—my fellow Legionnaires—as I would tell all other organized groups, that I intend to resist pressures from veterans, too, if I think their demands are excessive or in conflict with the public interest, which must always be the paramount interest."[29]

Social characteristics. Still another view holds that political preference is determined by social characteristics: age, income, education, religious affiliation, occupation, information level, and population class.[30] To these, according to one commentator, should be added what is called a psychological characteristic: attitude.[31]

Conclusions based upon analysis of a sample of the voting population in the 1952 presidential election showed that the candidate, rather than party allegiance or issues, was the determining factor.[32] More voters who ordinarily leaned to the Democrats shifted their vote from Democratic in 1952 than did Republican-oriented voters. The shift was made less because of party allegiance and issues than because of the personality of Dwight D. Eisenhower, the Republican candidate; Eisenhower's personality attracted more votes than that of his opponent, Adlai E. Stevenson. Although the Democratic candidate claimed to "talk sense" to the voters, it is clear that factors other than straight intellect operated to produce the victory of the Republican nominee.

Political activity. If opinion samples are to be trusted, the extent and intensity of political activity in America is not very great. By political activity is meant voting, membership in groups with possible political interest, personal communication with legislators, political party activity, and habitual dissemination of political opinions through verbal communications with others. In one test of political activity so defined, little more than a quarter of those tested were very active or active, while the rest—nearly three-quarters—were either inactive or very inactive.[33]

Of the ninety-eight million civilians old enough and otherwise eligible to vote in 1952, a record of sixty-one and a half million cast their ballots in the presidential election, and fifty-seven and a half million cast ballots for representatives in Congress.

In February, 1951, President Truman found the explanation for the lack of interest in the right to vote in "plain laziness" and the idea of "letting George do it."[34] This lack of interest or sporadic interest plays into the hands of those who are interested in politics and make a living in it or make it their business to know the technical details of the election laws. It is a matter of common knowledge, which each citizen can test for himself, that even the most elementary political facts—the identity of representatives in Congress, state legislatures, municipal councils, voting qualifications, party structure, the methods of selecting party officers—are all matters not within the range of information of most citizens.

Political Organization and Pressure Groups

From the above exposition of political parties outside Congress it must not be concluded that structure is all-important. Party structure and organization are important not as ends in themselves but as means to an end. That end is the "conquest of the power to govern."[35]

To conquer the governing power the party must elect its candidate for President, and to this end parties build the structure and maintain the organization discussed above. The party organization in the county is the basic unit. There is an association between counties and rural areas which tends to obscure the county's political importance in the urban, metropolitan areas as well. Here, too, the county is the basic area for party organization.

Moreover, in the metropolitan areas individual citizens are effective in the degree that they identify themselves with groups. "Political participation today is determined primarily by the individual's identification and association with the group and social structure of our society."[36] This finding suggests that one political consequence of the rise of pressure groups has been to facilitate the control exercised over the party organization and elections in urban areas by the political machine, whether it be a boss, the organization, an oligarchy, or active minority. Machine rule in American cities is one of the deep-seated characteristics of the politics of American democracy. Far from decreasing in importance, the political boss, the machine, or organization leader who is in a position to deliver votes on election or primary day has been aided by the growth of pressure groups. "The collection of voters into their thousands of associations and societies, the gathering of voters who could not be induced to join political clubs, makes the work of the boss easier; his work of organization has been done for him—he can more readily deal with the leaders of the groups than with the members as isolated individuals. . . ."[37] In the future this relationship will probably become even more prominent, with the continued growth of groups, particularly economic groups in the market.[38] "As associations multiply, and grow in size it seems reasonable to expect that they will not affect political machines adversely, although leaders of machines may perhaps more often appear from the leadership of private groups. . . ."[39]

Thus the structure of parties is a framework through and by which leaders and groups pursue their interests. This is not the place to expound the intricate network of relationships which tie together interests and parties through organization and otherwise. It is pertinent to note, however, that here we are dealing with the real, as distinct from the apparent or theoretical, source of political power. In the political sense, power is policy as it manifests itself through governmental activity. The pressure groups are interested in policy, while jobs, prestige, and deference are within the gift of party leaders. "Bosses will readily leave policy to the pressure groups in return for group support in terms of money, publicity, or votes which produce the patronage and the power in which the bosses are interested."[40] Unlike titular leaders who "enjoy power in theory," pressure groups "exercise it in reality or share it with titular leaders. Here we touch upon the general question of the real repositories of power. . . ."[41] The organization which the parties set up and maintain for the purpose of gaining control over the governing personnel is thus the vehicle by which interests are able to share power with the titular leaders. As a means of gaining the power of governing, party structure and organization serve not only the leaders nominally in official and party positions but also the pressure groups.

SUMMARY. Parties outside Congress have been considered in this chapter. They are organizations for determining those candidates for the Presidency and the Vice-Presidency from among whom the voters will choose their leaders. Federalism and the high value placed on the voters' independence of party control have produced a party system in the United States which is more a combination of two loosely articulated confederations of state parties than it is a set of tightly knit national parties. Except during presidential and congressional elections political activity is neither extensive nor intensive. The running of American politics is left largely to the party organizations and the leaders and active minorities of the pressure groups who share political power and use it with the acquiescence of the electorate as a whole.

Chapter 10

POLITICAL PARTIES IN CONGRESS

> . . . the parochialism of the men who make up Congress
> and render it the most parochial of national legislatures
> is a direct and unmistakable result of the parochialism
> of the American political system.
>
> —Clinton L. Rossiter[*]

The political parties in Congress differ so sharply from the parties outside that it is advantageous to treat them in a separate chapter.

Party organization within Congress is largely the result of the American system of electing Congressmen from single-member districts. Each Congressman holds his office from a district, one of the four hundred thirty-five into which the country is divided. The party outside Congress is the machinery for nomination and election of a President who holds his office from a nationwide constituency. The member of Congress secures his election with little if any help from the national party organization. He tends to think of the organization responsible for the President's election as an expert regards an amateur. Even more strongly, party organization in and out of Congress reflects the rivalry between the Congress and the Chief Executive growing from the constitutional separation of powers. In such a system, rivalry between these two branches of government is inevitable. Hence, entirely aside from factional considerations, complete harmony between the Democratic organizations within and without Congress and that between the Republican Party within and without is unattainable. In effect what we have is a multi-party—a four-party—system operating behind the facade of the two major parties.

[*] Review of James M. Burns's *Congress on Trial* (New York: Harper & Bros., 1949), in *American Political Science Review*, XLIII (December, 1949), 1280.

Party Organization in Congress

COMPOSITION OF THE PARTIES. Outwardly, all candidates elected to the House as Republicans and, similarly, all elected as Democrats are members of the Republican and Democratic Parties, respectively, in the House. The same is true of the Senate.

Composition determined by party label. In fact, however, this is true only for Democrats in the House, and even there it is more nominal than real. Although House Democrats organized themselves into a caucus and adopted rules in 1909, the force of the rules today is not great. The Republicans in both Houses and the Democrats in the Senate apparently have no formal rules for party membership.[1]

The custom of apportioning committee assignments among the parties roughly according to party strength and the actual assignment of members within the agreed proportion makes it necessary to determine who are the Republicans and who the Democrats and, in case of doubt, what are the criteria of Republicanism and the Democracy respectively.

In the absence of formal rules, determinations *ad hoc* are necessary. Until 1936 a rule of thumb for the House Republicans had it that a bona fide Republican was one who supported his party's candidate for the Presidency. Since then the Republicans have had more difficulty, principally in the Senate. Until fairly recently the Democrats in the House and Senate were not plagued with the difficulties experienced by the other party. Following the 1948 and 1952 conventions, the Democrats, particularly in the Senate, differed over the definition of Democratic orthodoxy. Since the Democratic Senators from southern states joined with northern and western Republicans in the Senate on many issues, serious doubts were raised about their membership in any national Democratic Party. Yet in their respective states and among many of their colleagues there was no doubt as to their party label. They were Democrats.

Lack of other criteria. Is there any standard or criterion other than the party label under which a candidate runs in an election by which his membership in a political party can be determined? An examination of party insurgency (independence) in Congress and of the attempts made to deal with it leads to the conclusion that there are no other generally accepted criteria.[2]

The matter of party membership is important to the operation of party, of Congress, and of government. An extended survey of legislation and of practice led Clarence A. Berdahl to conclude that there is still need for "some better definition or understanding of what is meant by a loyal Republican and a loyal Democrat, that the lack of such definition is at least partially responsible for the loose and irresponsible nature of the party organizations, for the mass of glittering generalities in party platforms, and for the failure to offer the voter anything like clear alternative programs." And there are more consequences that can be traced to the absence of definition or understanding as to political designation: "If it is also understood that the respective party organizations in Congress are almost completely independent of the national party organizations, and, still more, that the respective party organizations in House and Senate are almost completely independent of one another, the problem of party membership, in its relation to party organization and methods in Congress, clearly deserves attention."[3]

PARTY CONFERENCES. Nowadays, candidates elected to Congress under the Democratic and Republican labels meet together in party conferences in the two houses of Congress. Meetings are infrequent, however.

Nominating and electoral bodies. At the beginning of each new Congress, the conferences of the parties in the House meet to nominate their candidates for the Speakership. When the House meets formally, the outcome is known in advance, for this is one occasion when the parties vote solidly for their respective candidates. The conferences also elect their leaders, the majority and minority leaders in the House and in the Senate. In addition, the conferences name their candidates for the office of Secretary of the Senate and Clerk of the House; election is by the Senate and the House. The conferences also elect the Committees on Committees which recommend, on a partisan basis, the size of congressional committees and distribution of party strength within them for subsequent ratification by the two houses themselves.

Policy committees. In the Senate the two party conferences designate their policy committees, a majority and a minority policy committee, each with a chairman. In 1946 the House eliminated a section of the Legislative Reorganization Act providing for the setting up, for each session, of majority and minority policy committees. In spite of this, the Senate, acting on its own initiative, decided to set up such committees. In the Senate, the highest officer next to the presiding officer, who is the Vice-President, is the President *pro tem;* he is a Senator, usually the oldest in service, and is nominated by the majority conference and elected by the Senate.

In the Eighty-fourth Congress the size of the Senate Republican Policy Committee was doubled from twelve to twenty-four. The expansion was made by the Senate Republican Conference, composed of all Republicans in the Senate.

In addition to the Secretary of the Senate and Clerk of the House, there are numerous other officers of the two houses who are designated by the majority conferences and whose designation is formalized by election by the respective houses. There are also some seven hundred employees of the Congress, who are designated by the majority party—Capitol police, elevator operators, pages, clerks, messengers, doorkeepers, postal clerks and carriers.

Party whips. Another important action of the majority conference in the House is the designation of the party whip and his assistants. In the Democratic House organization, the job of the whips is to keep Democrats in line. Under a chief whip and his deputy, appointed by the Democratic membership, seventeen assistant whips are supposed to get and keep Democratic representatives on the floor when they are needed, estimate their probable reaction to pending legislation, and keep the membership informed when important votes are to be taken.

Instructing members how to vote is not part of the whips' duties. In this respect the whips are misnamed. They have no authority to tell the rank and file how to vote, as their counterparts do in the British House of Commons. In this contrast is to be found one reason for the existence of party government in Britain and the absence of it in the United States.

Committee chairmen. Chairmen of the great legislative committees in Congress are not named by the party conferences. Although elected by each house, they are designated more or less automatically according to length of service, that is, seniority. This practice is a matter of custom. There is no provision for it in either the Senate or House rules nor in the rules of the House Democratic caucus. But it is as strong or stronger than many of the written rules of Congress and is ignored or departed from much less frequently than many procedures which were written into law by Congress in the 1946 reorganization act.[4] Through a joint committee of the Seventy-ninth Congress, the Congress itself wrestled with the seniority method of designating committee chairmen, following testimony both supporting and condemning it. But the committee made no recommendations, "because of a lack of agreement within the committee as to workable changes in existing practices."[5]

Combined with safe districts and states, the seniority system operates to put members of Congress from southern and border states in most committee chairmanships when Democrats are in control of

Congress, thus placing disproportionate power in their hands to the disadvantage of many other Democratic districts and states with much larger population. In the Eighty-fourth Congress, for example, in which Democrats had majorities in both the House and the Senate, the chairmen of twenty-two of the thirty-four legislative committees came from southern or border states.

Assignment of members to committees is usually determined by length of service and preference. Departure from the seniority rule sometimes occurs, knowledge and experience as well as length of service being advanced as reasons. In this way Lyndon Johnson (D., Texas), Senate Majority Leader when the second session of the Eighty-fourth Congress convened in 1955, explained the assignment of former Vice-President Alben Barkley (D., Ky.) to the Foreign Relations Committee and of Joseph C. O'Mahoney (D., Wyo.) to the Judiciary and Interior Committees after an interruption of their service in the Senate. In the rare case of a Senator switching parties, as Wayne Morse of Oregon did in 1954, from Republican to Democratic, preference of assignments was respected, despite the return to the foot of the list which a strict application of the seniority rule would have required. In this case, the adherence of Morse to the Democratic side gave it a majority of two, a development which no doubt figured in the decision to accede to Morse's request.

LEGISLATIVE CAUCUS. *Theory.* In theory the legislative caucus is the machinery through which a political party is able to conduct itself in a politically responsible manner and thus to account to the rank and file of the party's membership, to the electorate, and to the country as a whole for its stewardship of legislative power. Under its legislative leaders and rules of conduct, democratically adopted, the party in Congress can discharge the responsibility it assumes when it receives popular power from the electorate.

Practice. In practice the legislative caucus in the United States Congress has had a mixed history. Forty years ago it was effective. In the Presidency of Woodrow Wilson, and under his vigorous leadership, the House Democratic caucus lived up to its name. It did not treat cavalierly the platform adopted by the party's national convention, but, working with the President and under able leadership in Congress, it made the platform the basis of a legislative program and enacted it. Although Democrats in the Senate had no organization or rules to compare with those in the House, they, too, took part in carrying out the party program which was forecast in the convention platform and in the presidential campaign, and translated it into specific legislation which was approved by the President.

Since the heyday of the legislative caucus in the years preceding World War I, it has been less effective. In the 1920's it was noted that while "the caucus rules have been somewhat relaxed . . . party government machinery in this country would by no means be perfected even if they were applied in a most rigorous manner."[6] Now, as then, the situation is not conducive to party responsibility. Party platforms are made by national conventions and not by those who have the authority to carry them out. The declarations in such platforms are not generally held mandatory on the parties. The four-year interval between conventions prevents platforms from being kept up to date.

To these reasons for the decline in the legislative caucus, valid a generation ago, others have been added: the operation of the single-member district system of electing Congressmen, the rise of mass means of communication,[7] and the development of the art of public relations.[8] In fact, Congress itself has noted the rise of "a new political order which constitutes a basic change in the federal design,"[9] one with "a breach between the government and the people."[10] Pressure groups, already active a generation ago,[11] are a characteristic feature of the new order, and "government by administration is the object of group pressures which weaken its protection of the public interest."[12]

In recent years the caucus, as a device for binding members of Congress to a party position, has been little used. In 1953 the senior specialist in American government of the Library of Congress Legislative Reference Service reported that the last time the Democrats had held a binding caucus was in January, 1949.[13] Testimony of members of Congress consulted by two other scholars in the same year corroborates what is generally known; namely, that the right of parties to make binding decisions is widely denied by members of Congress, is especially disavowed by the formal rules of one of the four caucuses (those of the Republican Senate Conference), is not asserted for two of the others (Senate Democratic and House Republican Conferences), and is only asserted in what has been an unworkable form by the fourth (House Democratic Caucus).[14] Newspaper reports have appeared of the use of the Senate Democratic Policy Committee in making pending measures matters of "party policy" and "clearing" them for Senate action.[15] Such action, while susceptible of interpretation as fixing a party position, falls short, nonetheless, of constituting one which is binding upon party members on pain of punishment. "There is no evidence in recent years of control by party organs in Congress over their members in the sense of restraint which prevents members from taking what they would otherwise regard as expedient actions."[16]

PARTY CAMPAIGN ORGANIZATION. Party campaign committees in Congress are maintained by both Republicans and Democrats in both Senate and House. They are organized to assist members in their campaigns for re-election. While the committees are in touch with the respective national committees they are independent of them. Nor are the national committees represented in the congressional campaign committees.

Democratic campaign committees. The history and organization of the Democratic campaign committees will illustrate the place of the congressional campaign organization in the party organization in Congress.

In the House, the Democratic National Congressional Committee traces its origin back to 1866. At that time Democratic members of both houses appointed a National Congressional Committee to manage that year's campaign. The Committee was formally organized in 1882, and is composed of one member from each state with a Democratic delegation in the House. In 1954 there were thirty-seven members. The Chairman of the Committee is designated by the House Democratic Leader, but state delegations pick their own members. The purpose of the Committees in House and Senate is to elect Democrats to the two Houses of Congress. In this they work in harmony with the Democratic National Committee, according to a statement in the *Democratic Digest*.[17] With small staffs (five for the Senate, six for the House Committee), they compile the record of Republican promise and performance as set out in campaign pledges, legislative votes, and other statements. This material is furnished to Democratic candidates challenging Republican incumbents as well as those seeking re-election. Neither the Senate nor the House Committee engages in primary contests.

The Democratic Senatorial Campaign Committee was established in 1916, following the adoption of the Seventeenth Amendment to the Constitution, providing for the direct election of Senators. The membership of the Committee includes all those Senators elected under Democratic labels who are not themselves up for re-election. The Committee chairman is named by the Democratic Leader in the Senate; in turn the chairman picks seven other Senators to serve with him.

The two Democratic Congressional Campaign Committees have little money to spend. In addition to their opponents' records, the Committees supply candidates with advice and assistance on press and radio coverage, campaign literature, use of speakers, and other technical phases of conducting a campaign. Neither Committee should be regarded as a campaign strategy board. Chairmen of the

two Committees have been known to say that there is no over-all
Democratic campaign strategy. Individual candidates are presumed
to be competent to conduct their own campaigns as they see fit, in
the light of their understanding of their districts, their opponents,
and the issues. The Committees assist them with information, advice,
and, to the extent possible, funds, but on each candidate falls the
responsibility for financing his own campaign.

Party campaign committees in the two houses of Congress are not
inactive between political campaigns. For example, in 1955 the Republican Senatorial Campaign Committee conducted what was
called by its chairman a "grass-roots analysis of political trends since
the 1952 election." The results of this analysis were made available
to the Senatorial Campaign Committee, to individual Republican
Senators seeking re-election, and to the Republican National Committee.[18]

At campaign time a spirit of mutual forbearance apparently prevails among certain members of the Senate. In the 1954 campaign,
it was reported that Democratic campaign organizers had difficulty
getting Democratic Senators to campaign in states in which their
Republican colleagues were candidates for re-election. No difficulty
of this sort was admitted, however, by the Republican party organization.[19]

Safe and marginal seats in Congress. In national elections the
parties, both within and outside Congress, concentrate their efforts
on winning the marginal districts. These are the districts in which
the winner of the last election received less than 55 per cent of the
votes. In many districts and in some states there is really no contest
at election time. These are the so-called "safe" districts, those in
which the incumbent won by more than 55 per cent of the vote cast,
or in which there was no opposition candidate, thus indicating that
the seat is safe for the incumbent, short of some upheaval in the local
organization, some politically inexcusable mistake, redistricting,
mass movement of voters, or the death or resignation of the incumbent. In such districts there may be and often is a working organization of the opposition party. But the division of the votes is clearly
into a majority of over 55 and a minority of less than 45 per cent.
In the 1954 congressional election it appears that three-quarters of
the 435 seats were in this category. (See Table 3, page 154.)

Leaving aside the question of the accuracy of the term "two-party
system," to describe such a situation, it is clear that campaign managers have a much simpler job in contesting only a quarter to a fifth
of the seats than if they were to contest a larger number. It is not,
however, a matter of shirking a duty, although some cynics might

TABLE 3

OPERATION OF THE TWO-PARTY SYSTEM
Safe and Marginal Seats in the House—84th Congress—1954

	Democrats	Republicans	Total
Elected by			
Less than 55 per cent	31	63	
More than 55 per cent	122	138	
With no opposition	79	2	
	232	203	
Competitive seats	31	63	94
Safe seats	201	140	341

suggest that the parties, or some sections of them, have a vested interest in the status quo and do not wish it changed. Campaign managers never have enough money to fight campaigns in all districts. Therefore, they operate according to the law of most results for the least expenditure, and concentrate their efforts on the districts where there is a good chance, on the basis of the last returns, of victory.

PARTIES NOT STRONG ON POLICY. The parties in Congress are not so organized as to control the votes of individual members. To do so would require, in the first place, the determination of party policy. But it is difficult to know what party policy is. There is no organ within, or procedure used by, the parties to determine policy. In a sense, the quadrennial conventions determine party policies and positions in the platforms adopted. But, as has already been noted, the value of the platform as indicative of party policy is rarely clear, because of the way the platform is made. In hearings of the convention platform committee, planks are prepared so as to attract the most, and offend the least, number of voters and groups. Moreover, whatever value the platform may have at the time of its adoption is transient. The issues change, so that the platform is out of date almost as soon as it is adopted.

The national party committees do not make or determine policy on pending issues. They are not set up to do so, nor are they authorized to do so. From what is known about the party policy committees in the Senate, they do not operate as policy-making bodies for the parties. Nor do the parties have any such organ in the House.

Regional party meetings or conferences held by Democrats and Republicans are not suitable places for declaring or interpreting policy. Such gatherings are useful as pep rallies, as morale builders, as safety valves, and as places for party leaders, great and small, to make statements and exchange views and to criticize the policies and positions of the opposing party. But they are not meant to be policy-making organs.

Policy is not determinable by analysis. Quantitative analysis of roll call votes in Congress is one method used to discover party positions. But both the method and the conclusions are of dubious value. The analysis of over one hundred roll call votes in recent Congresses showed that in nearly nine out of ten cases there was a division in which a majority or more of those Republicans or Democrats voting voted on opposing sides. The method equates the position gaining a majority of Republicans or Democrats with the position of the party on that issue. The number of times a member is found to have voted with the majority is his index of loyalty. From this it may be concluded: "Party pressure seems to be more effective than any other pressure on congressional voting. . . ."[20]

The Workshop of Congress

So far as the federal government is concerned, the term "congressional government" is sometimes used to describe government in the United States. While this is an apt description, it does not emphasize the really important part of Congress, the standing legislative committees.

THE LEGISLATIVE COMMITTEES. The legislative committees constitute "the workshop of Congress," the term used by the Joint Committee on the Organization of Congress.[21] Their importance in the legislative process was brought out clearly by this Committee in its report. It estimated that "about 90 per cent of all the work of the Congress on legislative matters is carried on in these committees." Their key importance is obvious when we read that "most bills recommended by congressional committees become laws of the land, and the content of legislation finally passed is largely determined in the committees."[22] In fact, the test of the will of Congress to reorganize itself was its willingness to strengthen its organization to carry the tremendous work load that present-day governmental problems placed upon it by reorganizing "its present obsolete and overlapping committee structure." In passing the Legislative Reorganization Act, in 1946, Congress acted on the recommendation of its Joint Committee by realigning the respective fields of competence of the committees and reducing them from forty-eight to nineteen in the House and from thirty-three to fifteen in the Senate.

Little Congresses. The importance of the standing committees in considering legislation has grown to the point that they have been called "little Congresses."[23] The shortcomings of party organization in Congress appear here as well as in Congress itself. Contrary to the popular impression, the effect of party leadership on committee decisions tends to be more nominal than real. It is generally thought that in three ways committee decisions can be and are affected materially by the party leadership and the organs through which it operates: selection of committee members and committee chairmen; control of floor schedules; and use of the caucus. The popular understanding is hardly in accord with the facts. As has already been pointed out, only in a nominal sense is the structure of congressional committee power to be found in the party leadership, since seniority usually determines membership and always chairmanships. So far as floor schedules are concerned, the Rules Committee of the House is a strong rival to party leadership. As for the caucus, its weakness as a device for party control and its infrequent use have already been pointed out.[24]

The House Rules Committee. The House Rules Committee is technically not a legislative committee. It should function, as some would have it, as a "director of traffic on the legislative highway,"[25] or, according to another view, as "an instrument of party control over the legislative program."[26] While good arguments can be made for both points of view, the chief difficulty, as the *Washington Post and Times Herald* points out, "is that in practice the Rules Committee has frequently adhered to neither course. It has often used its control over procedure to thwart the leadership of the party in power as well as the legislative committees and the House itself."[27]

Rather than as a technical committee working with the party leadership in scheduling and promoting a party program, the Rules Committee has tended to become another legislative committee. It rehears the arguments pro and con already heard and passed on by the appropriate legislative committee, duplicating its work, and under leadership which may or may not see eye to eye with the House majority leadership, makes its own decisions, irresponsibly, as to whether legislation acted upon by committees should be granted a rule for consideration by the House itself. The "twenty-one-day rule" is a device available to any Congress by which the majority of the House membership may gain the right to get bills to the floor from the Rules Committee when it will not or cannot act. The rule was adopted in 1949 by the Eighty-first Congress and remained in force for two years. According to this rule, any legislative committee chairman can take a favorably reported bill before the House if the Rules Committee rejects it or fails to rule upon it within twenty-one days after being reported out of committee. Eight bills were taken to the floor under this rule and passed by the Eighty-first Congress; the existence of the rule, in other cases, was enough to cause the Rules Committee to act.[28]

WEAKNESS OF CONGRESS UNDER PRESSURE. Congress is still not strong enough, despite the 1946 committee reorganization, to protect itself against or deal with the problems raised by the activities of the pressure groups. This subject has already been considered in some detail.[29] Here it is mentioned because of the effect of structural, electoral, and party organization inadequacies upon party responsibility.

Pressure from propaganda. The Joint Congressional Committee on the Organization of the Congress recognized in its Report in 1946 that modern propaganda methods used by pressure groups created problems, such as distortion of public opinion, and, as a consequence, that Congress and the parties were confronted with difficulties in legislating for the nation as a whole. At the same time, the Committee was hesitant to recommend control over pressure groups lest the right of petition be attenuated or curtailed. The Committee recommended, nevertheless, and Congress approved, legislation requiring registration by those attempting to influence the Congress by the expenditure of funds collected for that purpose.

In an earlier chapter, the situation following the passage of the Regulation of Lobbying Act of 1946 was examined fully.[30] We should say here that it appears doubtful whether the structural and procedural changes wrought by Congress in 1946 have had any appreciable effect upon the ability of Congress to deal adequately with the problems of government under pressure. The 1946 reforms did not extend, nor could they, to the mixture of constitutional, social, economic, and political factors which together determine the conditions in the nation. These are reflected in the loose national party organizations, in the duality of parties in and out of Congress, the single-member district system, the safe districts, and in the differing conceptions of party and of majority rule versus individual rights.

Pressure from local interests. An extreme view, perhaps, but one for which there is some justification, is that it is not inefficiency nor ineptitude but "parochialism" which sums up the state of Congress.[31] In other words, the American political system produces in our legislators an outlook dominated by local considerations. This localism resists enlargement to accommodate wider national considerations.

Pressure exerted via procedures. In earlier chapters the techniques of pressure groups were discussed to clarify the many methods available to lobbyists for keeping the attention of legislators trained on special, particularistic, and local interests. It is pertinent here to discuss additional points about the organization and procedures of Congress which render it unduly vulnerable to pressure from private groups.

Favorable opportunity for exertion of pressure is created by the absence of effective presidential and party control over assignment of members of Congress to committees. Similarly, the tradition of selecting committee chairmen according to length of service is not always sufficiently precise to clarify seniority rights, thus opening another channel for private groups to exercise influence. Still another opportunity arises when legislative committees clash over jurisdictional rights over bills. Formal techniques, such as motions to instruct committees or discharge them from further consideration of bills, are also of use to private groups. The working out of compromises in committees and the preparation of conference reports are additional points where influence can be used, the latter being regarded as a vital operation by participants in the legislative struggle. The scheduling of witnesses and the rationing of time by committee chairmen; diversion of witnesses from the bill in question to other, unrelated bills; assistance, in conjunction with executive agencies, in helping to defeat filibusters in the Senate—all are examples of key points in legislative procedure where outside groups can wield influence. They can also exploit the Senate rules which permit unlimited debate, delay, and obstruction.

Congress does not reorganize itself very often. When it does, as in 1946, one factor in gaining majority support is the effect on committee leadership. Thus, a reason for winning support among the conservative majority in both houses and among the conservative pressure groups was the prospect that the number of chairmanships held by liberal members of Congress would be reduced by the proposed amalgamation and consolidation of committees.[32]

Why the Congressman votes as he does. If there is no party policy and the parties in Congress do not instruct the members how to vote, it is pertinent to ask what the determining factors are in congressional votes. Only the Congressman himself knows why he votes as he does. But there is no unanimity on this point. Some hold that, in deciding how to vote, the member of Congress makes his own decision: "It is not the decision of someone who pulls the strings or gives the signals."[33] However, the determining factor or factors may lie far from the floor of Congress. Votes in Congress are largely determined by fear, according to another observer, fear which arises from the "persistent and unrelenting pressure from the groups and elements in their (the members') communities" which they do not wish to offend.[34] The view of another who was once a member of the New Jersey legislature is not quite so explicit. On the effectiveness of groups in determining the votes of legislators, no one knows what the factors are. Even if they were known, it would be impossible to weight them.[35] Personal and sectional interests of the member of Congress are no doubt factors. A long-time member of Congress asserts that it is the timidity of Congressmen, rather than the cupidity played upon by the old-time lobbyists, on which present-day lobbyists capitalize.[36] It is clear that the process by which a Congressman decides how to vote is a complex one.

Pressure politicians. Pressure politicians are not unknown in the Congress of the United States. Their number varies from Congress to Congress; yet in any particular Congress it is probably quite high. They act as if they represented groups, classes, or sections more directly than the electorate of their districts as a whole. Or, more likely, pressure politicians and other members of Congress act in a variety of ways. This is the conclusion reached by one who analyzed the performance of members of a Senate legislative committee on extension of price controls in 1946: ". . . members of the committee behaved in a variety of ways, depending upon the roles they chose to play."[37] The role of pressure politician is one which legislators find difficult, if not impossible, to avoid.

Responsible Party Government

Any discussion of the American political system leads sooner or later to the question of responsibility. The term is used in at least four different yet related senses.

One sense in which the term "responsibility" is used is the British one of responsible parliamentary government.

As applied to Democratic party politics in the American democracy, the term is used in a quite different sense. When former Democratic National Committee Chairman Stephen A. Mitchell referred to state government and state party leaders who failed to support the party's presidential nominee as "irresponsible," he had in mind their departure from responsible conduct conforming to the will of the party majority as expressed in the national convention.

A third sense in which the term "political responsibility" is used is to refer to the goal of those who want more responsibility in party government in the United States. According to this view, developments of the last three-quarters of a century have produced a pressure group state in which the parties fail to realize the political power which they ostensibly strive for; thus they default to the private associations who exploit the political power which the parties themselves fail to mobilize.[38]

In a somewhat broader sense the term "responsibility" is used to refer to the relationship of accountability between government and people existing in those democracies in which the party in charge of the government is held to account periodically at free elections for its conduct of public business. In this sense the term has broader application than in the first sense, above, where it applies to Great Britain and the Commonwealth governments who have adopted parliamentary institutions from Britain for their own use. In the present sense it would apply to such countries as France and the Federal Republic of Germany, which, although operating under a parliamentary system, nevertheless differ in fundamental respects from Britain.[39]

THE PROBLEM OF POLITICAL RESPONSIBILITY. It is difficult to get to the heart of the problem of responsibility. Two aspects of the situation must be emphasized; the apparent and the actual. It is generally believed that within Congress the parties are well organized, especially in the House, and that such party agencies as caucuses, floor leaders, whips, and steering or policy committees are powerful authorities controlling procedures, committee structure, and legislative schedules, and that frequently they dictate to members how they should vote.

It is with this apparent situation that the real situation should be compared. Party leadership is disunited and divided between that part within and that without Congress. Congressional procedures, committee structure and composition, and legislative schedules are only partly controlled by party leaders in Congress. Strictly speaking, there are no party positions on issues. Discipline is weak because members themselves, and not the party organization, are primarily responsible for success at election. Organizationally, the parties themselves are divided into the parts within and those without Congress. None of these facts is conducive to responsible party government.

Due largely to the peculiar nature of the American political ideal, in which conflicting principles of majority rule and minority rights are both highly prized, the concept of responsible political parties is a little understood principle in American democracy. It is generally believed that the American two-party system is a responsible system. Popular faith is strong in the capacity of the system to produce responsible government. At the same time, the political ideal affirms an even stronger belief in individual rights. The political result is insistence on individual freedom of political action, a freedom which is tacitly recognized and guaranteed by the Constitution and is implemented on a decentralized basis by the individual states. To this insistence must be attributed many of the shortcomings of the party system.[40]

Emphasis on the right of freedom of individual political action has resulted in undervaluing the corresponding obligations and duties of voters. Politics does not operate in the realm of abstract values, unrelated to the individuals and groups who participate in it. On the contrary, politics embraces and embodies social as well as individual values. Insistence on individual rights without an equal observance of individual duties results in social values being overlooked.

Why parties are not more responsible. The best groundwork for party responsibility in Congress results when congressional districts are so organized by the parties as to provide alternative choices for the voters, both as to candidates and issues. Neither of these conditions prevails generally in the United States. As has already been pointed out, in well over half of the districts the organization of either the Democratic or Republican Party is nonexistent or is so weak as to present no clear choice to the voters on either candidates or issues. This is not a new condition but has prevailed for many years. Moreover, ". . . the party primary is not an effective substitute for two-party competition. . . ."[41] In congressional districts the two-party system works very unevenly and provides the country only imperfectly with a Congress composed of legislators chosen from among candidates opposing each other on clear-cut issues.[42]

Whether or not issues or party platforms have any significance in the constituencies depends on the location of the district, the independence of the press, the number and strength of its groups, its occupational and racial composition, its regional or sectional importance. Also, in those districts in which no opposition or no effective opposition exists, it is unlikely that issues will figure at all in a campaign. In others, the candidates themselves are often the issues. This situation is accentuated by the tendency of candidates to dodge or straddle the issues or take equivocal positions on them. Intraparty factional struggles in one-party districts are obviously personal fights and are not differences over issues. With national conventions on a quadrennial basis and with congressional elections held biennially, it is obvious that, at best, the convention can define issues for the constituencies only half the time.

The limited success of the parties outside Congress and in the constituencies to provide guideposts as to party policy is duplicated within Congress. Strictly speaking, there is no enforceable party position on bills and other actions of Congress. The right of parties to make binding decisions on members of Congress is not asserted by the party organs within Congress and is denied by members of Congress themselves. If party positions were being made and enforced unknown to the party rules, there would be evidence of it. But there is not. Leaders of the same party in Congress are rarely, if ever, in complete agreement on program and, in fact, are often in disagreement. Moreover, guides to party positions on pending matters would be circulated to the party membership by congressional leaders if such positions existed. (Such guides, called "whips," are evidence of the control exercised by the government over the party rank and file in the British House of Commons.) But such guides are not found in the Congress of the United States. This is further evidence of the absence of enforceable party positions.[43]

Parties in Congress are not coherent voting units, because the party is neutral in the matter of discipline. The party neither supports nor disciplines its members in Congress; it neither rewards them with support at election time nor withholds such support as a sanction against insurgency. And this party neutrality regarding discipline contributes to the strength of minorities and pressure groups. "Congressmen succumb to pressure by organized minorities, not because pressure groups are strong, but because Congressmen see no reason for fighting at all; the party neither disciplines nor supports them."[44]

The establishment of official party agencies in Congress according to the principle of seniority further explains why parties are unable to be more responsible. Although noncontroversial, as a basis for choosing congressional leaders, seniority does not assure a party the loyal and undivided leadership it needs to guide legislation through Congress. Seniority is a consequence, probably accidental, of the aim of the party organizations, both inside and outside Congress, to acquire or preserve a formal majority of seats in Congress. As long as the party organizations have this aim it is unlikely that the seniority principle will be replaced by some other means of choosing legislative leaders.[45]

COMMENT. One test of party responsibility is the ability of the parties to enact into legislation planks in the platforms adopted at their quadrennial conventions.

Applying this test to the 1952 platform pledges on civil rights, one group in 1955 charged both parties with failure to carry out their pledges. In testimony before a House Judiciary subcommittee studying civil rights legislation, the legislative representative of the Americans for Democratic Action raised a question as to "the good faith of the political parties, the President, and the members of Congress . . . by the failure to produce civil rights promises (sic)." Both Democrats and Republicans were "spellbound by the pro-discrimination anti-civil rights forces of the South" who have "arrogated to themselves a veto power over legislation which involves provision for equality of treatment."[46]

Another incident in the Eighty-fourth Congress illustrates how the majority party falls short of operating responsibly. Congressional action was involved on a proposed twenty-dollar-per-family income tax reduction. The measure was passed by the House but was defeated in the Senate. Although Democrats controlled both houses, the Democratic Party was without a party declaration on the matter, the party platform adopted three years earlier providing no real guidance. Even had there been a clear-cut position, the control of Democratic leaders in the two houses is not strong enough, nor is discipline tight enough, to produce majorities in favor of such tax reduction.

At the basis of this situation in Congress is the over-all constituency of the Democratic Party. In theory this constituency is a majority of the electorate which has agreed on a body of principles and through its party organization loyally backs its representatives in the legislature in enacting legislation in accord with these principles. But the theory and the reality do not correspond. In the Eighty-fourth Congress the majority in Congress represented the Democrats in thirty-seven states; the Democratic voters in eleven other states had no representation in the House of Representatives (Iowa, Kansas, Maine, Nebraska, New Hampshire, North Dakota, South Dakota, Utah, Vermont, and Wyoming). Thus a sizeable block of the Democrats of the country had no way of registering their views on legislation. Moreover, the Democratic voters in the remaining thirty-seven states were not a homogeneous group in any way. There was no cohesion among them as voters, even though they all voted the Democratic ticket. Specifically, there was no consensus on civil rights or on income tax reduction. Furthermore, within the party organization there was no technique for discovering and welding together a majority of those with the same views on any subject. Nor did the party provide them any means of participating in the formulation of party program or the debating of issues. Finally, there was apparently no agreement between the House and Senate Democratic leadership. A Republican President in the White House would serve to explain differences between leaders of the executive and of the legislative branches. But it can hardly explain the absence of agreement between leaders of the two houses of Congress who are, in name at least, members of the same party.

Would a more tightly knit, more responsible, better disciplined party system be desirable? Would it be acceptable to the American people? One hesitates to answer in the affirmative, for one must note the many respects in which the existing system satisfies present-generation Americans. Whether any more responsible system is possible in a democratic, federal republic is also doubtful.

Moreover, one cannot escape the impression that a nostalgia for British parliamentary institutions of pre-World War I days has resulted in an idealization of responsible party government; and when compared to it, American congressional-presidential government seems to suffer. But British parties are not monolithic entities. The Labor Party in Parliament, for example, is not under the control of the Labor Party outside Parliament, as the arguments of some party government advocates for America might lead us to believe. Herbert Morrison, former deputy Labor Party leader in the British House of Commons, tells us why. The constituency Labor parties would never be allowed by the parliamentary Labor Party leaders to dictate or control its action on matters pending in the House. To do so, Morrison states, would be to submit to a party dictatorship, such as that of the Communist Party in the Soviet Union.[47]

Also, one distrusts proposals for structural and organizational reform. Such proposals reflect too great a faith in rational power to effect change, too little understanding of the nature of social processes. Perhaps these explain the coolness with which most party leaders greeted the *Report* of the American Political Science Association's Committee on Political Parties. Perhaps they also explain the similar reception accorded a proposal of Chester I. Barnard to increase party responsibility. He would accomplish this, among other things, by having 20 to 30 per cent of the membership of the two houses of Congress elected at large for four-year terms at the same time as the presidential elections.[48] This proposal has not made any more headway than those of the APSA's Committee on Political Parties. In another connection, Barnard himself admits the limited role of intelligence in public affairs. In taking to task a fellow member of the business community who abandoned official Washington in disillusionment after six months in 1953, Barnard suggested that intelligence has but a limited role in politics and that one should not expect too much from attempts at reform based on rational analysis.[49]

SUMMARY. In this chapter three subjects have been considered: party organization in Congress, the legislative committees as the place where Congress does most of its work, and the problem of responsible party government. The parties in Congress are largely independent of those outside. While they appear to be strongly organized, party cohesion and discipline are lacking, program-making bodies are weak or nonexistent, leadership within Congress is divided, and the leadership which the national party might exert over Congress is resisted by the parties in Congress. Legislative committees often succumb to outside pressure, and outside groups are able to penetrate congressional procedure at many points. While American government is partisan, it is not party government in the sense of responsible government.

Chapter 11

THE PRESIDENCY AND THE BUREAUCRACY

> Of course, any time any group believes, and particularly
> with reason, that they are falling behind the average of
> the nation in their products, there is trouble. We ought
> to do something about it.
>
> —President Dwight D. Eisenhower*

In March, 1940, President Franklin D. Roosevelt met at the White House with his Interdepartmental Committee to Coordinate Health and Welfare Activities. At the conclusion of the meeting, and as the members were about to return to their respective departments and agencies, the President directed them to prepare a new and more politically appealing statement of the administration's goals for the health and welfare of the American people. "Make it something," he said, "that could go into the party platform."

The American President is many things. He is the head of the government, leader of his party, an initiator of legislation. President Roosevelt was all of these in the incident just described. The President is also chief of state and Commander-in-Chief of the armed forces, hence the principal maker of foreign policy. As head of the government, he has a dual role to play as national program administrator and as chief of the bureaucracy. Because of the power of the Presidency, he is exposed to the diverse pressures from foreign governments and domestic groups, from the party, the bureaucracy, and the press, in short, all the influences which stand to gain or lose from the way the President plays his part. These numerous and sometimes discordant aspects of the Presidency and of the bureaucracy are examined in this chapter.

* Press conference, January 25, 1956, in answer to a question as to whether the political aspect of the farm situation is a real or an imaginary problem for the Republican Party.

The President's Many Roles

Perhaps the quality most needed by the people from the President is guidance. The President can choose whether or not he will guide the people. His other roles, however, are thrust upon him. As the President he is head of state; he cannot avoid this role. As the only elected federal official (other than the Vice-President) he is simultaneously tribune of the people and chief of the party. He cannot sidestep either of these roles. As the Chief Executive he is head of the government; again, he cannot escape its duties. But the role of leader in the sense of providing guidance he can accept or reject. He need not accept it if he conceives of his office as that of administrator. But if he conceives of his office as something more, he can hardly fail to see the possibilities of using it as a means of guidance. To succeed in this role, special qualities are required: "Almost superhuman skill and nobility are required if the President is to be an effective national leader."[1]

THE PRESIDENT AS HEAD OF STATE. As head of the state, the President is the symbol of the American nation, the ceremonial or titular executive, the director of American foreign relations, and the representative of the United States before the world.

In this capacity it is hard to overestimate the importance of the President. He is the American counterpart of the British sovereign, both as ceremonial head of state and as the embodiment of the abstraction known as the "American people." But he is far more than the British sovereign, in whose name the ministry of the day carries on the affairs of state. The President is the titular executive and the working executive combined, the prime minister and the sovereign considered together, the head of the government as well as the head of the state.

During the last quarter century, the office, already large, has expanded enormously. Today, with the whole world alert to America's every word and deed, it is unlikely that the Presidency will ever again contract to its size during, say, the Coolidge era. It may be occupied by a President whose conception of the office is a limited one. But, by the Constitution, by the laws—particularly the law which places in the President's discretion the sole right of deciding on the use of atomic weapons—by the interpretations of the laws, and by usage, the President, regardless of personal ideas, is almost forced to be as large as the office.

Neither Franklin D. Roosevelt nor Harry S. Truman abstained from using the vast powers of the Presidency. While Dwight D. Eisenhower had a more restricted conception of the office (as shown in his request for advance congressional authorization to use the armed forces in the defense of Formosa), later he, too, did not hesitate to use all the powers of the office when in his judgment the situation demanded it. When he flew to Korea after his election and, later, to Geneva to the conference of heads of governments, President Eisenhower appeared in all of his multiple roles—ceremonial executive, working executive, Commander-in-Chief of the armed forces, director of foreign affairs, and Republican party chief.

The eminently political character of the Presidency is shown clearly in the way he abandoned his earlier opposition to the 1955 Geneva conference in order to strengthen the hand of Sir Anthony Eden, his British counterpart as working executive, in his electoral campaign in May, 1955.[2]

Foreign relations. As head of state and, in that capacity, principal maker of foreign policy, the President is subject to pressures, as he is in his other capacities.

The decisions on prime questions of foreign policy and foreign relations, on war and peace, are the result not of logical, straight-line, rational intellectual activity, but of a mixture of reason and emotion, thought and instinct, formulated under pressure of time, place, and circumstance.

It is difficult, if not impossible, to inventory all the factors present and operative in any particular foreign policy decision. Even persons highly trained in the weighing of historical evidence arrive at different conclusions as to why Presidents act as they do in making decisions. "On how Presidents really function," we are told, "there is probably greater interest and less knowledge than on any other phase of government."[3] Moreover, the size of the government's administrative organization is so great that dispersal of strength and lack of discipline inevitably lessen the President's influence. Cohesion is not achieved by the parties, whose composition and operation, as already noted, are such as to make them unwieldy in enforcing responsibility. Functional specialization of career officials is perhaps the most serious impediment to unified leadership.[4]

There is no disagreement over why Franklin D. Roosevelt led the American people to fight back, in both the Eastern and Western worlds, after the Japanese attack on Pearl Harbor. But there is no unanimity on the weight to be assigned to President Roosevelt as the cause, either proximate or ultimate, of the Japanese attack.[5]

Domestic groups outside the government are also operative, but with what effect it is hard to say. In 1940, in the exchange of British bases for American destroyers, for example, the weight to be attached to the America First Committee, which opposed the deal, and to the

Committee to Defend America by Aiding the Allies, which advocated it, is not known. Both were active in creating "public" opinion, both had access to the White House, both were able to generate considerable newspaper support for their respective points of view. Yet, simply because the deal was made, it would be less than accurate to assert that the latter was more influential as a pressure group than the former, given the many other factors which are known to have operated and which not even an incomplete inventory would fail to enumerate.[6]

Other illustrations will underline the risk involved in trying to measure influence in the making of foreign policy. In 1955 a former State Department official told the "inside" story of the way the decisions underlying the Truman Doctrine, the Greek-Turkish Aid Program, and the Marshall Plan were made. But an outsider, a journalist, added much information about these decisions.[7] The point is illustrated further by the decision in June, 1950 to assist the government of the Republic of Korea in resisting the military attack of the North Korean forces. While the decision was Harry S. Truman's, as President and as Commander-in-Chief of the armed forces, nevertheless, the complete story of the influences on the President at the time of decision still remains to be told, particularly since Korea was not within the strategic frontier of the United States as traced by the Secretary of State barely three months earlier.[8] Nor apparently was it so considered by either the plans division of the War Department general staff or the Commandant of the Naval War College, who, not long before, appeared unconcerned over Korea but quite concerned about the security of Formosa.

In considering the origins of policy, fuller treatment will be given this subject, particularly the role of groups in it.[9] Here it may be said that, while groups are not inactive in this connection, their relative weight is less than it is in connection with domestic politics. Some years ago a preliminary finding indicated that this was the case.[10] More recently, a similar conclusion was reached about the importance of pressure groups in the period immediately preceding the Pearl Harbor attack. They were relatively unimportant.[11]

It is doubtful, however, whether analysis can be quite as penetrating in this field as in the related field of domestic policy decision. Zionist leader Chaim Weizmann importuned the President many times to conduct American policy so as to achieve the establishment of Israel. Harry S. Truman was the first head of state to recognize the State of Israel after the proclamation of its existence. However, not even this sequence of events establishes a clear case of *post hoc ergo propter hoc*. Nevertheless, this was a case in which leadership of a group strong in foreign as in domestic politics was able to gain access to the decision-maker and a decision was made which was highly gratifying to the group in question.[12]

THE PRESIDENT AS PARTY LEADER. The President is the undisputed leader of his party. He attains this position by virtue of his success at the polls.

Owing his position as party chief to those who voted for him, the President is always solicitous of the welfare of the groups which combined to make the winning combination at the polls. He wants to keep this combination intact to repeat the performance at the next presidential election. This is one constant factor in a field of variables. It makes him pay particular attention to the pivotal states and, within those states, to the voters who tend to vote as groups in the large cities and suburban areas. It is to them that he appeals for support at election times; in between, he is careful not to alienate them.

The relationship between the President and these voters is a reciprocal one. He needs them because he wants to be re-elected or to have his party's candidate (in the naming of which the President can be decisive) be successful at the next election. On the other hand, the voters in question need the President to represent them in the executive branch of the government.

One way the President has of keeping their support is to give them such representation. From among them he appoints his Cabinet, and his "little cabinet" (the under and assistant secretaries), and they, in turn, fill by appointment the many policy-making and confidential positions which are exempt from civil service rules. Collectively, they form the "party in the government," or the administration. The nominations for heads of the departments and agencies and their principal assistants require confirmation by the Senate; the others do not. Thus the appointing power, the basis of patronage, enables the President to reward the leaders of those who voted for him at the polls.

The link between the party without and the party within the government is the chairman of the national committee of the party. He is the link because he owes his position to the President who, if he does not appoint him, nevertheless chooses him for formal election by the committee as a whole. Under the chairman is the staff which dispenses the patronage. The chairman is in touch, through the staff, with the state and, through them, with local party officials. They, in turn, provide most of the names of worthy party workers, supporters, and sympathizers from whom suggestions for appointment to federal positions are made to the President. Persons thus appointed can be of great help to the President as party chief, to the national committee chairman as campaign manager, and to many party workers during campaign and elections. All presidential appointees whose nominations require Senate confirmation are, by definition, political, hence do not fall under the legislative ban against political activity contained in the Hatch Act. This legislation has probably made more difficult the building up of a bureaucratic machine under the domination of either of the two major parties, although this danger has been perhaps exaggerated. Also, central party control over members of Congress is weak. Even the President as party chief is not able to enforce decisions upon the party in Congress.

Because he is President of the United States, the view is sometimes argued that in him, rather than in Congress, is to be found that aloofness from politics and freedom from pressures essential to an objective formulation of the general welfare. The argument does not hold water. The President and the executive branch which he heads are by no means immune from the pressures of the same groups which ask Congress to protect them against the inroads of other groups. In fact, because of the different clienteles represented by the Congress and by the President, some groups are more effective with the Chief Executive than with Congress.[13] As President Eisenhower, in the quotation with which this chapter was opened, said, when any group in the country falls behind other groups in its share of the national income, "we ought to do something about it."

But no single principle or rule can explain the responses of the President to the myriad pressures which are exerted upon him. As undisputed party leader, a President in office can lay down a campaign line almost single-handedly, as President Eisenhower did in the 1954 mid-term campaign. But the election outcome determined the extent to which the hopes and fears of the electorate which voted Eisenhower into office in 1952 influenced him. A Congress controlled by the opposing party, as was the Eighty-fourth, assisted a Republican President in some respects and balked him in others. The groups and their leaders experienced no more difficulty in gaining and using access to the President than when the Republicans had controlled Congress. But the necessity of agreement among both branches of the government will mean that it will be reached with more difficulty. Thus the President, as one of the contestants in the legislative struggle, finds his role as party leader modified and altered.

Even when the Presidency and the Congress are both held by the same party it is not too often that the President as party chief can really lead his party. From time to time it happens, as with Wilson during his first term. Then, under the influence of long study of the British parliamentary system, Wilson faced Congress in person, and by patronage and with cooperative party leaders in Congress, used the legislative caucus as a means of converting party platforms into laws, thus going far toward bringing the New Freedom to maturity. Also, during Franklin D. Roosevelt's first term leadership of Congress by the President as party chief was realized.

As party chief, a President with a strong sense of the party in the program-making and administering activities of government can make party government approximate the ideal in the United States. A weak President, on the other hand, or one with a different concept of the role of party, by the same token causes government to falter in its program-making activities, and by failing to stress the role of party opens the way to pressure groups. And while the President is, in effect, elected directly by the people, a fact which complicates the multiple role he occupies, at the same time it gives him an independence from Congress. He is not responsible to Congress, as the British Cabinet is to the House of Commons, nor is he under its control. His responsibility is to a different electorate.

THE PRESIDENT AS LEGISLATOR. In the technical sense, the President is not a legislator. He is not a member of Congress, neither of the House nor of the Senate. Yet, constitutionally, he is part of the legislative process, and customarily he is the originator of many proposals which become law.

According to the Constitution, legislation adopted by both Houses of Congress becomes law either with the written approval of the President, or if he fails to act on it within ten days, or if he vetoes it and returns the proposal to Congress without his signature, and it is then re-enacted by a two-thirds vote of both houses. If Congress adjourns within the ten-day period following submission of legislation to the President and he has not yet signed it, it fails to become law. This is known as the "pocket veto."

Even more important in the President's role as legislator is his right, acquired through usage and custom as much as through any constitutional provision, to initiate proposed measures. It is his constitutional duty to acquaint Congress with the "State of the Union"; he may also call Congress into special session. In discharging the former right, he often makes proposals for new or changed laws. The purpose in calling Congress into special session is usually to place emergency legislative proposals before the members.

Much of what is called "positive government" owes its origin to Presidents whose philosophy of the public good called for active rather than passive, or laissez faire, government. From a long list which might be drawn up, a few examples will suffice. As President, in 1913, Woodrow Wilson initiated the proposal which became the basic legislation regulating the volume of credit. Laws for industrial and agricultural recovery, for currency reform, for tariff bargaining, for the whole group of measures known collectively as the New Deal, originated with Franklin D. Roosevelt. How the basic ideas of health and welfare programs originated has already been mentioned in the opening paragraph of this chapter, where the outcome is narrated of a meeting of FDR with his "little cabinet" aides in these two fields. Upon his death in 1945, his successor, Harry S. Truman, was the originator of many proposals which were enacted into law—economic and military aid for Greece and Turkey, European recovery, self-help and mutual aid for defense for the countries allied in the North Atlantic Treaty, and defense production, following the attack in Korea in 1950. Dwight D. Eisenhower as President has also actively sought Congress's help in legislating for education, transportation, highway construction, and health. In fact, it is difficult to see how a President of the United States in modern times can refrain from leading in the legislative process. It is doubtful whether any Republican President in the future would pattern his conduct in this matter after that of Harding, Coolidge, and Hoover, Eisenhower's Republican predecessors in the White House.

Willy-nilly, the President is caught up in the "legislative struggle," as Gross calls the process of enacting laws. If rivalry between Congress and the President was not the intention of the Constitutional convention, it has been the result of a century and a half of constitutional development. Today, the legislature and the executive are normally in a state of rivalry. Moreover, the form of this rivalry is affected by the modern movement of group organization and by modern methods of communication. Organized groups, particularly those whose relative economic status appears threatened, seek the powers of government to assist them to protect their position or to advance it. As this book has endeavored to show throughout, these groups are as important in the whole governmental process as are any of the formal agencies of government. The Chief Executive and the vast bureaucracy over which he presides, no less than the Congress, attract the attention and are subject to the pressures of these groups in their manifold efforts. But the process is not a one-way street. The President is also an active agent. He will often, or infrequently, plunge into the conflict of influences, depending upon his concept of the presidential office and the over-all political situation at the time.[14] In drawing up and confronting Congress with measures, the role of the President is vital, as it is in mediating among the organized minorities.[15] From time to time the President must press on Congress issues on which Congress as a whole or its members may be neutral or even oppose, including those measures not enjoying universal popularity. He must also give thought to what support is likely to emerge for his proposals in Congress.[16] The ability of the President to appeal to the people over the heads of Congress is one of the methods available to the executive in the legislative struggle. The White House is strategically located for generating propaganda. It is also a way of organizing the unorganized for political purposes, particularly in the pivotal states and metropolitan areas to which the President must look for so much political support.[17] Loyal aides can also be of help to the President; for example, a Cabinet member may be the "spark plug" in generating administration and group influence strong enough to overcome opposing group advocacy of a particular measure in Congress.

Group influence impinges most strongly on the President once a bill has been sent from Congress to the White House for action. The President's signature, his veto, whether by withholding his approval or by pocket veto, each is a major process by which the aims or objectives of some groups are advanced and those of other groups retarded. In making these decisions, personal interviews and letters to the President are used by members of Congress and leaders of groups in attempting to influence the President. Memoirs and biographies sometimes cast revealing light on this phase of the legislative struggle. Walter White, late Executive Secretary of the NAACP, relates in his autobiography his conferences on legislation with Franklin D. Roosevelt and Harry S. Truman.[18] Weizmann's autobiography, already cited, narrates his experiences with an even larger number of American Presidents. Biographies of labor leaders, such as the late Sidney Hillman and of John L. Lewis, for example, are similarly revealing.[19]

There are numerous reasons why Presidents are under pressure to lead, or try to lead, Congress. The constitutional separation of powers makes it desirable; similarly important is the change in the mood of the people evidenced when Congress is controlled by the opposite political party. There is also the inability of Congress to provide its own leadership, the nature of the times (with their need for technical analysis and information on policy-making), and the President's unique role of representing the people at large. No Congressman can claim this latter role,[20] for each Congressman is, in a sense, an ambassador from his district to Washington. It is in the districts where the groups are strongest—the groups whose respectable but limited concepts of the general interest rarely, if ever, coincide with the President's. While no Congressman fails to feel a primary loyalty to the country at large, or at least to that part of the electorate which placed him in office, the range of these differently focused loyalties complicates the hammering out of policy and makes the President's role as legislator a necessary but uncertain one.[21]

The uncertainty surrounding the President's role as legislator is increased by the frequent changes in the executive branch of responsibility for preparing policy recommendations. In an administration headed by a military leader, extensive use is made of the staff principle. In addition to staff aides with a statutory basis, such as the Bureau of the Budget, the National Security Council, the Office of Defense Mobilization, the Joint Chiefs of Staff, and the White House Office, numerous examples are to be found in the establishment of aides without specific statutory authority, such as the presidential assistant for foreign affairs, the presidential assistant for disarmament and a presidential advisor to review foreign economic policy. The last was named at a time when foreign assistance programs were under the direction of a Mutual Security Administration and the Department of State was the President's primary advisor on matters of over-all foreign policy. Some confusion and rivalry is bound to result from this diffusion of responsibility.

The President as Chief Executive

By the Constitution, the President is the head of the executive branch of the government, and it is his duty to "see that the laws be faithfully executed." In effect, he is elected directly by the voters, thus he is the only federal official directly responsible to the people. Also, by the Constitution, he is independent of Congress, being neither dependent upon it for the tenure of his office nor responsible to it.

NATIONAL PROGRAM ADMINISTRATOR. The President is the head of of the executive branch. It is he upon whose shoulders rests the responsibility of administration of the large number and variety of governmental programs which have accumulated over 160 years of national life and which permeate so many interstices of individual and group life in America.

The budget embodies programs. As Chief Executive, no statutory duty affords the President such opportunity to review administration as the preparation of the annual budget.

Public policy and programs are impossible in our system of government without, first, congressional authorization of the activity or program, then, appropriations for financing and carrying them out. These two prerequisites to administration mean that where the activity or program is already authorized by existing law, the citizen groups sympathetic to it or supporting it tend to ally with the bureau responsible for its administration in expanding the program, or at least in protecting it against budget cuts. With them are usually to be found individual members of Congress. Chairmen of committees, both legislative and appropriations, are in key positions. In other cases, where a new activity is proposed or an existing one altered, sympathetic groups with allies in Congress try to obtain permanent legislation authorizing the activity. Here, too, appropriations are necessary, even after the authorizing legislation is approved.

Under the provisions of the Budget and Accounting Act of 1921, the President must send to the Congress in the early days of each session a full statement of the estimated expenditures for the fiscal year beginning July 1.

In placing this duty on the President, Congress brought the Chief Executive into the appropriations process and, in so doing, expanded the area for the operation of political interest groups. Estimated expenditures and programs are but two aspects of the same thing. Estimates are the financial reflection of on-going programs; programs cannot continue without the appropriations issuing from the estimates. Programs, as already indicated and as will be detailed later on, are, in large part, the evidence in public policy of the successful efforts of groups put forward in Congress and sanctioned by opinion and law. Groups which have gained their ends in the adoption of programs and in the establishment of administrative agencies to administer them recognize in the budget process the first line of defense in maintaining the victories they have won. Similarly, organizations interested in winning the war of administration, after having lost the legislative battle, see an opportunity to gain their ends in the budget-making process. The agencies themselves have jobs and careers at stake, to say nothing of professional pride and satisfaction in the successful execution of a job to which its personnel is devoted, and they usually want to increase their funds, or at least to maintain them at existing levels.

There are other points mentioned by Frederick J. Lawton, a former Director of the Bureau of the Budget. After noting that ". . . the major determinant in any budget is whether a given activity should be conducted at all, and if so at what level," he continues: "All decisions on individual activities must be made in the light of broader factors—primarily the expenditure and revenue outlook, the international scene, economic conditions, and the provisions of existing law. . . . Long before detailed estimates are prepared by the agencies, the basic decisions have been reached which, together with mandatory expenditures under existing law, control the broad outlines of the forthcoming budget."[22] The budget of estimated expenditures, as it is finally submitted to Congress, indicates the approval, or tacit acceptance, by the President of the thousands of individual items representing the decades of achievement by successful groups, along with the inevitable accumulation of public services made necessary by the growth of the nation.

Recurring nature of the budgetary process. The preparation of the annual budget is but the first in a series of steps taken annually to provide funds for carrying on the government. After receiving the budget from the President, subcommittees of the two congressional appropriations committees, first the House, then the Senate, examine carefully the estimates of expenditures, and on the basis of the recommendations resulting from this examination, Congress passes the necessary appropriation bills. These are the final stages of the supply process. Hardly are Congress and President finished with the process for one fiscal year than the spending agencies, at the direction of the President and the Bureau of the Budget, set the process in motion for a new fiscal year.

At all stages the influence of citizen groups may be seen. In the executive stage, when bureau chiefs, department heads, and fiscal officers carry forward the work of preparing the estimates, groups may be either active or passive. If active, it is through their Washington representatives. Members of Congress belonging to the group allied with a bureau may be the source of pressure. If groups are passive, it may be because the officials responsible for the performance of services in question are sympathetic to the group's point of view. In greater or lesser degree, every executive agency lobbies for expanded functions and increased funds. When the departmental estimates are assembled by the Budget Bureau and are presented to the President for his review and decision, the influence of the citizen groups may again be actively exerted. After the estimates are submitted to Congress, the groups continue to exert influence actively, openly, and covertly.

Defects in the process. In the budget and appropriation process, as in the legislative process generally, the United States government operates under the system of separated and divided powers and checks and balances, as provided by the Constitution and as modified by law and custom. By themselves the constitutional requirements are formidable enough. Responsibility for execution of the laws is separated from the authority to supply the funds on which successful execution depends. By law, Congress has imposed on the President the responsibility of preparing a budget. But, falling back on the Constitution, Congress withholds from him the power to exact from the Congress the funds necessary for putting the programs embodied in the budget into effect. Congress requires the President to systematize budgeting in the executive branch. But Congress itself fails to systematize budgeting in the legislative branch. Despite the call in the Legislative Reorganization Act of 1946 for a legislative budget with income and expenditure in balance, Congress has complied only once with its own requirement (1947–1949). Nor have steps been taken to coordinate the actions of the money-raising and appropriating committees with those of the substantive, legislative committees in the two houses of Congress.

Not the separation of powers alone but the whole electoral process and the party system are held by Lawton to explain the complications of budgetary relationships between Congress and the executive branch. The electoral system fosters localism and pressure groups. The party system fails to develop solidarity around programs. As a consequence, ". . . those who simply lay the complications of legislative-executive relationships to the separation of powers see only part of the picture," says Lawton. "It is easy to see that the separation of powers would be something quite different . . . if it operated under the influence of a party system which developed solidarities around general programs for governmental action— equally meaningful for the members of Congress and the President . . . factors of law and usage (that) make it difficult for Congress to function as a unified and self-directed institution."[23]

CHIEF OF THE BUREAUCRACY. As administrative head of the government, the President is the chief of the bureaucracy.

To differentiate between the President as chief executive and as chief administrator is, in a sense, unreal. As chief executive, the President *is* the chief administrator, or at least the responsibility is ultimately his. On the other hand, the distinction is profitable for purposes of analysis. While the execution of the laws and the administration of the laws are practically synonymous, there is obviously a difference between the highest elective federal official whose duty it is to see that the laws are enforced and the body of appointed officials and employees who, in the aggregate, are responsible for the day-to-day enforcement and administration of the laws.

The subsystem. To differentiate between the President as chief executive and as chief administrator also makes easier the differentiation between the executive branch of the government and the bureaucracy, or the subsystem.

The bureaucracy is the body of nonelective officeholders of the executive branch of the government. The executive branch comprises the bureaucracy but includes as well the officials in the Cabinet and "little cabinet" and those of similar rank. The subsystem is different in composition. While it comprises the higher ranks of the bureaucracy, it includes also the congressional committees corresponding to the executive bureaus, as well as the private associations whose program and budgetary interests correspond in the main to those of the respective congressional committees and bureaus. A three-cornered or threefold relationship thus characterizes the subsystem—bureau, congressional committee or subcommittee, pressure group or groups.[24]

The subsystem does not operate at a lower level than that of the governmental system. The difference is to be found not so much in such terms as it is in different relationships. These are durable and are not broken ordinarily by the replacement of an old by a new administration. They are institutionalized and hold together a continuing structure composed of congressional committee (and staff), executive bureau, and special interest group personnel. But considering the executive branch as a whole, the picture is different. The subsystem is not a tightly knit set of groups but, on the contrary, is more a congeries of groups, each concerned with protecting and promoting particular values. Hence, choice of the term "subsystem" to describe these bodies of people may be misleading, since it may leave the impression that they are more highly unified than they are. It is fallacious to think of the bureaucracy as being so unified as to place in the hands of the President power to dominate Congress and get whatever legislation he wants.

The subsystem shows other characteristics of interest. It helps explain the apparent chaos which appears so often between the President and Congress in policy-making. Outweighing the political parties from the policy-making point of view, the interest groups in the subsystem represent special sets of values and constituencies, just as members of Congress do. The degree of loyalty and extent of control between the President and the bureau depend mainly on bonds of ideology and interest. They are neither uniform nor stable. Considerable autonomy exists in policy-making at the bureau level due to policy implications of program administration. This autonomy also exists in the congressional committees because of the centrifugal forces which make it impossible for Congress to control its own committees.[25]

Chairmen and members of congressional committees receive deference and respect from their bureau counterparts. There is also interdependence between party leaders and interest groups, since each can greatly benefit from the other despite the refusal of the groups to assume the label of the party and vice versa. Moreover, the relationships among committees, bureaus, and interest groups routinize the contacts and liaison among the three parties concerned, the committee staff usually being designated to deal with the groups, while bureaus, as well as departments, have informal if not formal liaison with the appropriate committees on Capitol Hill.

Tacit recognition of the effectiveness of the subsystem is to be found in criticisms made by former President Herbert Hoover. For example, in speaking before the Chamber of Commerce of the United States in May, 1955, Mr. Hoover identified the combination of bureaucratic and pressure group interests as responsible, at least in part, for the unbalanced federal budget. The implication is that resistance to the demands of these groups and cessation of the programs in which they are interested is the way to a balanced budget. The Commission which Mr. Hoover headed in 1955 recommended the termination by Congress of many of the services which were being performed by or under the supervision of numerous federal bureaus.[26]

There is no doubt that big government makes for big budgets. Back of this increase over the years are the claims made upon Congress by groups of the people organized around various interests and those required by the exigencies of our international relations. It is doubtful, however, whether the way to a balanced budget can be found in the route recommended by Mr. Hoover. These clusters of combined interests are so firmly established in the living government that to dislodge them would necessitate a virtual revolution. Such a revolution would be both economic and social, although the political changes of the New Deal, the Fair Deal, and Eisenhower's Deal may loosen and indeed dislodge a few of the clusters. But for everyone that is dislodged, two or more take its place, so generally has been accepted the philosophy of government for (groups of) the people.

Federal administration. The influence of organized groups on and in the federal government is not felt by Congress and the President alone. It is felt throughout the administrative structure as well. While further attention is devoted to this part of the subject in another chapter, three aspects may be considered here: the large number of activities performed, the great variety of these activities, and the complexity of administration.

A mere listing of the executive departments—State, Treasury, Defense, Justice, Post Office, Interior, Agriculture, Commerce, Labor, and Health, Education, and Welfare—indicates many of the main areas of administrative activity. The number of activities of the departments performing traditional functions—State, Treasury, Justice, Defense—is impressive, and in the other departments is even more so. Sample functions, selected at random, would include, for example, the Interior Department's construction and operation of irrigation projects and promotion of commerce in mineral products. The Department of Agriculture aims to enhance the farmer's economic and social conditions through many kinds of research, education, and financial subsidy. Through meat inspection and other consumer aids it benefits the public as a whole. Among the Commerce Department's functions are the developments of standards used in science, engineering, industry, and trade; investigation of foreign trade restrictions; and maintenance of navigation aids for both ocean and air commerce. Among other things, the Department of Labor mediates labor disputes and disseminates labor statistics.

The scope of federal administrative activity extends even further in the case of the independent agencies. Nine agencies regulate private enterprise in the fields of railroad transportation, electric power, interstate communications, and trading in securities, and in addition, administer the anti-monopoly laws and those governing labor-management relations. Others are active in extending credit to individuals and organizations ranging from home owners, farmers, and steamship builders and operators to cities, towns, and other public bodies. War veterans, the unemployed, bank depositors, the aged, the blind, and dependent and crippled children are other groups which come into direct or indirect contact with federal agencies. Also, the protective tariff system affects thousands of domestic producers and, indirectly, most consumers.

Numerous questions arise in connection with the independent regulatory commissions. These questions pertain to their relationships with Congress, the President, and the groups or industries purportedly regulated or marginally concerned. Most of them arise out of the nature of the job given the commission in question. The job is regulation, in one form or another, of organized economic activity.

Underlying this extension of federal authority into fields hitherto reserved to private enterprise is the assumption that the general interest will thus be furthered. Many, if not most, of the obstacles encountered develop from the varying conceptions of the public good held by Congress as a body, by the economic interests thus regulated, and by the commissioners charged with applying principles and standards fixed by Congress to a complex social situation which is constantly undergoing change.

Such commissions are composed of and staffed with commissioners and technical personnel dedicated to the public good. But the public good is conceived by them, in varying degrees, as consisting of these not altogether harmonious elements: profit, necessity, convenience, service. Regulatory commissions operate in a political atmosphere, however much the commissioners, their staffs, and defenders may protest otherwise. A defeated Senator, for example, appointed by the President to a commission regulating trade, or civil aeronautics, or communications, or common carriers does not leave behind him his convictions about economic and social policy. He brings them with him to his new post, where they influence him in his analysis and evaluation of applications for power dams, certificates for new airlines, a railroad reorganization plan, or the pleas of competing forms of transportation for equality of regulation. Other problems—organizational and administrative in nature—complicate the process by which the abstract concept of the public good is shaped in concrete terms. Should these commissions be headed by presidential appointees? Or should the chairmanship rotate among all members? Should the chairman direct the administration of the commission's work, the staffing and financing? Or should this be done by an administrator appointed by the chairman? These questions are illustrative of scores of problems arising from the situation in which these commissions operate, and about which not much is known.[27]

The above enumeration does no more than suggest the scope of federal administrative activity; yet it indicates many points where administrators and citizens come into contact. The nature of the contact varies from the mere dissemination of undisputed data to such complex functions as the development of legally enforceable administrative orders involving differing opinions of law. In between, there is a gradation running from informal personal meetings between official and citizen through semiformal conferences with few restrictions on the kinds of facts and opinions which are acceptable to highly formalized hearings suggestive of the courtroom, in which the rules of evidence govern the admissibility of material.

In general, the simpler contacts can be made by anyone, regardless of education and experience, by mail or in person. The more complex forms, on the other hand, can be exploited successfully only by those trained in the law and familiar with governmental procedure. This fact is known to every alert observer of government, and has even been recognized by the Supreme Court. In effect, the Court has said that, to be successful in dealing with the federal departments in Washington, one needs more knowledge and skill and a greater familiarity with forms and principles than the common man possesses. The conclusion is inescapable that talent of this kind will be far more readily available to those citizens and groups with resources at their disposal than to those without. If the regulation of interests growing out of the unequal distribution of property formed the principle task of legislation in Madison's day, his observation applies with even greater force today.[28]

As President, Dwight D. Eisenhower has followed a set of administrative principles which do not clash with those of the governmental subsystem previously discussed. His philosophy of administration can be summed up in this way: staff work, decentralization, responsibility of subordinates and faith in their integrity. All of these permit free range to the three components of the subsystem; the congressional committees, the bureaus in the various departments and agencies, and the clientele and associated groups of private citizens outside the government.

The Bureaucracy in the Pattern of Power

One of the most controversial subjects of politics and government is the position of the bureaucracy in the pattern of power.

Three things about bureaucracy are hardly open to dispute. In point of size, the bureaucracy is larger in contemporary times than ever before. Also bureaucracy is powerful, no matter whether in democratic, representative governments of the parliamentary or congressional types or in totalitarian government. And both the size and the power of modern bureaucracies are related in some way to the revolutions in industry, transportation, and communications which have occurred since the middle of the nineteenth century.

The nature of that relationship is vigorously debated. It has already been noted that in the United States the federal bureaucracy lacks certain characteristics popularly attributed to it. It is not subservient to the President, although he is nominally its superior and is responsible for its acts. It is neither homogeneous in composition nor unified in purpose, but is heterogeneous and divided many ways in its objectives. It is not insulated from external forces but is tied in crisscross relations to private individuals and groups and to Congress. And internally it is divided by conflicting loyalties.

However, although agreement on these points helps in a partial understanding of bureaucracy's relations with the other elements of society, it makes complete understanding more difficult. For the nature of bureaucracy and the origins and sustenance of its powers turn on different ways of reading social history. On this there is no agreement.

BUREAUCRACY AND ECONOMIC CONCENTRATION. In general, two theories are at the bottom of the controversy over bureaucracy and the problem of power. According to one, bureaucracy is regarded as the result of economic concentration; according to the other, economic concentration results from bureaucratic interference with the "normal" working of the economy.

No unanimity on theory. Neither theory of bureaucratization has escaped criticism, mainly because supporters of both are guilty of "a curious naïveté with regard to the separability of the economic and social realms, either in terms of the belief that the economic causes are basic and the political phenomena are in fact epiphenomena, or in terms of the belief that the competitive economy would work out if only it were not interfered with politically. Each view implies a theory of social change."[29] The divergence in historical interpretation is derived, in turn, from a disagreement over the nature of social facts. However, if the facts tell us anything, "they tell us both that bureaucratization is the result of economic concentration and that economic concentration is the result of governmental policies." Thus, instead of a direct cause and effect relationship, that between bureaucratization and economic concentration is due to cumulative causation, the theory of the Swedish economist Gunnar Myrdal, according to which "the ramified effects of any institutionalized social action are so far-reaching that questions of a particular historical origin frequently lose much of their significance."[30]

Light on government and interest groups. Viewed in such a light, the relation between government and interest groups is the relationship expounded throughout this work, namely, that "by *playing* the role of arbitrator (between such groups as 'business' and 'labor') government helps to consolidate these groups; and government bureaucracy, in turn, grows, inasmuch as these groups are compelled to assign new functions *to it*. This relation between government and interest groups includes an ambivalence on both sides. . . . Governmental administration can and must function, in part, independently of the 'pressures'—to the extent, at any rate, that the conflicting 'pressures' of various groups inadvertently entail the possibility of disregarding them."[31] Thus there is inertia, resistance, and pressures existing and generated by government agencies themselves. But the bureaucracy has insufficient inner resources for self-coordination and direction. Restated, the problem of bureaucracy appears as one in which ". . . the indispensability of skilled administrators makes modern bureaucracy autonomous, but professionalization makes it a subservient tool. . . . Bureaucracy is, therefore, all-powerful and, at the same time, incapable of determining how its power should be used."[32]

BUREAUCRATIC AND SUBSYSTEM ACTIONS ILLUSTRATED. Numerous examples of the operation of the bureaucracy and the subsystem can be supplied. Those which follow are not intended to be a representative sample of the actions, reactions, and interactions of and among the active groups, both official and unofficial, which characterize the day-to-day activities of the administrative bureaucracy in Washington and the country. Rather, they are offered as illustrations of such activities taken more or less at random from among a great many more which could be included. Furthermore, in later chapters on the making of public policy additional illustrations will be found.[33] And even more numerous illustrations will be found by a regular reading of the daily press and, especially, business and financial periodicals.

The government administrator is under pressure from the American people, and, especially, from the groups into which they are organized. The advice of these groups as to what administration should do is often sound, since they employ fine legal talent. Their views as to what the American people want must be taken into account, since the groups in question have ways of finding out. But these groups are not above distorting, forgetting, or even denying the existence of a general public opinion or interest when it runs contrary to their special interests.[34] "We ordinarily think," says one who has observed the administrative process from inside, "of these organizations (the National Association of Manufacturers, the American Farm Bureau Federation, the American Medical Association) as pressure groups putting heat on Congressmen; we call their spokesmen lobbyists because they do much of their work in the lobbies of legislative chambers. But they work on the administrative branch as well as the legislative. Not much goes on in the Department of Commerce that the NAM does not know about. If a regulation of the Department of Agriculture displeases a lot of farmers, the officials of the Department will hear from any of a number of organizations. The Public Health Service will think twice before it does something that the officers of the AMA might find objectionable. The Interstate Commerce Commission listens to what the Association of American Railroads has to say; members of the Federal Communications Commission sit down to dinner with officers of the National Association of Broadcasters; and high officials of the Bureau of Mines doubtless tremble at their desks when the President of the United Mine Workers bellows forth in his anger. . . ."[35]

Money and credit. Nothing illustrates the play of forces better than the constant struggle which goes on over the credit and monetary terms on which the country's economic and financial system operates. In this struggle the Treasury Department is one of the central points. The Treasury is no more immune from pressure than other government departments, bureaus, and agencies. It is in the Treasury that the ideas of individuals and interests about "hard" and "soft" money, about expansion and contraction of credit, about taxes and other imposts can be effectively presented. Tax proposals of an administration often have influence on congressional action. Hence the Treasury is subject to urging and argument by taxpayers.[36] Sometimes the Treasury will hold formal hearings at which expressions of views are invited, as in 1939 and 1944. Informal conversations are another highly valued way of bringing interested views to the attention of Treasury officials. If the key posts, in addition to that of the Secretary, were to be captured by a special interest group, the Treasury itself would become the equivalent of a pressure group rather than the representative of the general interest. Some political economists argue that this occurred in 1953 with the inauguration of the Eisenhower Administration.[37] Blough, however, maintains that the Treasury would always take a broader view than any of the major private interest groups.[38]

Pressures from Defense Department. Further indications that particular parts of the executive branch act like pressure groups is found in the way the military elements of the Department of Defense promote their vested interests. The military establishment spends more money and its impact on policy, both domestic and foreign, is greater than that of any other department or agency in the executive branch. Furthermore, it has the professional duty of maintaining and defending the territorial integrity and independence of the United States, a duty unrivaled by that of any other federal department or agency. For these reasons, for the military establishment to conduct itself like a pressure group is of unusual significance. Yet this is what happens. Like any other pressure group, military leaders intervene in the formation of policy, press both the Bureau of the Budget and the President for funds necessary to carry out and support the policies they help to make, and direct this pressure to Congress.

Moreover, military leaders seek political office and support candidacies other than their own. Also, the leaders have such tenure, status, tenacity of view, and organizational and material resources as to give them a decided advantage in their relations with civilian policy-makers, both in the State Department and in Congress. Because of their expertness and their unique status in the executive branch, they make it difficult for Congressmen to disagree. These leaders, both civilian and military, support policy through speeches and meetings and press, radio, and television interviews, in addition to testimony before congressional committees. Also, like other pressure groups, the military use civilian officials, nominally their superiors, as front men, as acceptable spokesmen for views and preferences of the professional military groups.[39]

In an era of federal budgets swollen by unprecedented military requirements, Congress may have lost control over the appropriation of funds. Two reasons have been advanced; the inadequacy of congressional organization for any broad examination of the budget, and the strength of tradition.[40] The lack of effective coordination of congressional committees over federal income and expenditure has already been pointed out. The strength of tradition here warrants an additional word. Despite the huge sums involved, in deciding what funds to recommend, congressional appropriations committees use the same method of analysis for the defense as for other parts of the budget. Subcommittees of the House and Senate Appropriations Committees "read" the parts of the federal budget dealing with defense, with justifications by witnesses from the Defense establishment, then "mark up" the bill for report to the full Committee and thence to the Congress. Under such traditional procedure, it is hard enough to get a full picture of programs when relatively small sums are involved. When a congressional subcommittee follows the same procedure for sums totaling some 60 per cent of a sixty billion dollar federal budget, as for fiscal year 1956, the tendency is to overlook the forest for the trees. "In military affairs Congress snips and Congress snipes, it drags and lags, but it follows along. This means that the executive branch, for all practical purposes, makes the decisions and bears the responsibility today."[41]

Forest Service, Fish and Wildlife. Testimony to the autonomy of the bureaus and their regional offices and to the power of interest groups over personnel, including bureau chiefs, is provided in the cases of the Forest Service and the Fish and Wildlife Service. In the former, regional offices in the West are said to have defied two Forest Service chiefs and two Presidents of the United States in resisting efforts to preserve scenic areas.[42] In the latter case, duck hunters and salmon packers are alleged to have been powerful enough to have obtained the removal of the chief of the Fish and Wildlife Service and to have caused his demotion when his administration of conservation laws was displeasing to these interests.[43]

Anti-trust enforcement, airline certificates. Administration of the anti-trust laws by the Department of Justice draws groups, legislative committees, and federal bureaus into close contact. The report of an Attorney General's committee on the anti-trust laws was attacked before a House monopoly subcommittee as the work of a group half of whose numbers were themselves involved in pending anti-trust proceedings and of a "lobby of big business and of very big business only" which was "trying to wreck the anti-trust laws" by using a "divide and conquer" technique.[44] The point is not so much the attack nor the attacker as it is the situational response and counterresponse induced by a law enforcement agency (the Department of Justice), its *ad hoc* study group (representing views about how the laws should be enforced), and the legislative committee principally concerned.

Similarly, the board regulating civil airlines, some of the airlines themselves, and members of Congress are involved in three-cornered relationships in which pressure from the latter two quarters has been felt by the former. In 1955, complaint was made by Ross Rizley, Chairman of the Civil Aeronautics Board, against the harassment of the board by "pressures." He said, . . ."and by pressures I mean extra-judicial efforts to promote or defeat a certain decision," particularly from members of Congress.[45] A former member of Congress himself, Rizley called on Congress "to cure some of these difficulties."

A further example of a governmental, legislative, and pressure group community is that of the National Rivers and Harbors Congress, the Army Engineers, and the pressure politicians of both houses of Congress, several of whom occupied key positions on committees corresponding to the public works program of the Corps of Engineers.[46]

Mention may be made of several other aspects of the three-cornered relation of pressure group, executive bureau, and legislative committee activities. Reports issued by executive agencies often provide a point around which the agency, private organizations, and members of Congress can rally in their legislative campaigns.[47] Committee reports also provide such a rallying point. There is often insincerity and deception in these reports.[48] Again, so close are relations between committee members, officials of executive bureaus, and of private organizations that as soon as congressional committees decide in executive session on their reports, committee members will meet immediately with their allies in deciding on the next step in the legislative campaign.[49] Freedom of the lobbying done by congressional staffs from any kind of regulation by law should be kept in mind.[50]

THE STAFFING OF GOVERNMENT. Recruitment, selection, and assignment of personnel are done in various ways in the federal government. Numerically, by far the largest number of jobs is filled by appointment from lists prepared by the Civil Service Commission containing names of persons who have qualified, by examination or otherwise, for the posts to be filled. As of June 30, 1955, there were slightly more than two million positions in government filled in this way. Persons in these positions are appointed by the heads of departments, agencies, and commissions. Collectively, these persons are the career civil service; they are appointed because they possess the necessary ability, training, and experience. The system is often also called the merit system. There are some exceptions to these general principles, particularly provisions for war veterans. Under legal provisions enacted by Congress, veterans are accorded certain percentage preference on the civil service lists (registers) which is added to their scores in the standard examinations. The result of such veterans' preference is shown in the large proportion of jobs in the career service which are held by veterans.

Appointment by the President. The group of positions filled by presidential appointment is much smaller numerically than that filled by appointment by the members of the President's Cabinet and others having the appointing authority. Heads of agencies, members of commissions, and Cabinet members are appointed by the President. Confirmation of such appointments by the Senate is required by the Constitution and the laws. In addition, department under-secretaries and assistant secretaries obtain their positions through presidential appointment. They, too, are appointed subject to Senate confirmation. There are also many policy-making and confidential positions below the Cabinet and sub-Cabinet level which are exempt from civil service regulations. Some of these positions, such as those among White House staff, are presidential appointments not requiring Senate confirmation. Many others, while still exempt from civil service regulations, are filled not by the President directly but by department and agency heads. In the aggregate, the number of these policy-making and confidential positions fluctuates between one thousand and eleven or twelve hundred. They are the posts which, with the Cabinet members and agency heads, are clearly outside the career government service. They exist primarily, according to the Civil Service Commission, to carry out the objectives of any national administration. As of June 30, 1955, there were 1122 such policy-making and confidential positions below the Cabinet and sub-Cabinet level.[51]

Businessmen in government. In addition to the career civil service and the policy-making body of officials just mentioned, businessmen are recruited for government service. During the two World Wars and the rearmament program caused by the hostilities in Korea, industrial mobilization necessitated bringing into the government businessmen and industrialists in large numbers. Their experience and training were of great value to the government and to the country. Without them it is doubtful whether the country's industrial system could have been mobilized for war and defense as successfully as it was.

But their contribution was not entirely altruistic. In the second World War the Senate investigating committee headed by Harry S. Truman concluded that "dollar-a-year men (as they were then called) were 'persons with axes to grind' and 'lobbyists.' " Between 1950 and 1955 such temporary government officials, now called WOC's (since they serve without compensation), were again brought into the government, and once more congressional committees found that such officials had difficulty giving undivided attention to the public business while they continued to receive salaries from their outside, private employers. In 1955 a House subcommittee investigated the standards established for the recruitment and assignment of such personnel, the sufficiency of these standards and their implementation, as they operated in the National Production Administration, the Business and Defense Services Administration (NPA's successor in the Department of Commerce), and in business advisory groups which were set up in the BDSA. Its conclusions were that employees without compensation had been misused for purposes not authorized by the Defense Production Act, although they were appointed pursuant to that law; that they were placed in positions where their governmental responsibility to serve business inherently involved conflicts with their private interests; that the "organizational arrangements of BDSA have effected a virtual abdication of administrative responsibility on the part of Government officials in charge of the Department of Commerce, in that their actions in many instances are but the automatic approval of decisions already made outside the government in business and industry"; and that in BDSA an organization was set up by the Secretary of Commerce "which in the name of the Government has been used to advance throughout the Government the cause of private interests. . . . Loose procedures concerning permissible outside activities by WOC's for their companies have resulted in abuse of Government position, conflicts of interests, and favoritism."[52] A minority dissented from these and other conclusions of the Subcommittee majority, stating that the report "belabors extensively some alleged deviations of WOC's" but "grudgingly and in passing recognizes their valuable contributions."[53] As of August 15, 1955, some 260 WOC's were employed in the Department of Commerce; of these 170 were on advising or consulting assignments.[54]

SUMMARY. The President has many roles in our constitutional and political system. Perhaps his most important role is one of guidance. He can guide the country or not, as he pleases, in his official roles—

head of state, Commander-in-Chief, party leader, legislator, Chief Executive. Operating within the bureaucracy is a semi-autonomous subsystem comprised of the officials, procedures, traditions, and mutual loyalties between executive bureau personnel, corresponding congressional committees, and outside pressure groups. In their operations many of these bureaus, and even some departments, such as the Department of Defense, frequently act like big pressure groups, that is, they have their own programs, personnel, public relations systems, propaganda, and other pressure techniques. The bureaucracy itself is a pressure group or congeries of groups. The dollar-a-year men and those employed "without compensation" are extreme examples of leaders of groups who have been absorbed into government, or who have infiltrated government, depending on the point of view adopted.

Chapter 12

THE MASS MEDIA OF COMMUNICATION

> . . . And now great pressure groups have come into be-
> ing and claim to voice the opinion of all of their members.
> These groups and interests have made a new thing of
> what we call the 'popular will' or 'public opinion.'
>
> —Lindsay Rogers
> *The Pollsters**

It is the purpose of the present chapter to consider this "new thing" to which our attention has properly been called. It is unlike anything ever before encountered by a democratic people in trying to govern themselves responsibly. Developed by pressure groups and aided by the mass communications industry and the public relations profession, propaganda has become the "new thing" for government and politics in mid-twentieth century America.

The analysis and exposition of such a subject as public opinion in all of its phases will not be undertaken here. Nor is it possible to analyze the mass communications industry or propaganda in America or public relations as a profession. To do so would take us too far afield.

Observers of government and politics must, however, be aware of the rise and emergence of these phenomena as new factors in American society. Few would deny that even in the early days of the Constitution there was something that could be called "public opinion" abroad in America. Nor would many dispute the contention that there was communication of a sort among the people. Moreover, the inspired editorial, the starter of reports and rumors, the gossip-monger, were not unknown in the early days of the Republic. Throughout our history there have always been citizens who would work to advance the interests of any individual, group, section, or

* New York: Alfred A. Knopf, Inc., 1949, p. 30.

interest that would foot the bill. "Public relations" may be a descriptive phrase of modern origin, but the idea underlying it is as old as politics.

Today, technology has revolutionized these phenomena of earlier days. Public opinion lacks the spontaneity of earlier times. Today, it is synthesized or created much, if not all, of the time. Once, the communication of ideas and opinions was restricted to word of mouth, semaphores, horseback riders, or the handbills and newspapers which could be turned out on hand presses. The communications industry today is technically capable of spanning the nation instantaneously and can convey news of events, ideas, and opinions to the great bulk of the population in a matter of minutes. Propaganda has become a device of diplomacy, domestic as well as international, consciously employed by interests, sections, regions, and groups, as well as by governmental agencies at all levels, to gain the consent or the acquiescence of the "public." Finally, public relations has emerged as a profession within the last generation, assuming a prominent position in the contemporary hierarchy of social values along with the ministry, banking, science and engineering, business, teaching, the armed services, and government service.

Nor would the astute citizen fail to recognize the effect which the revolution in the communication arts, together with the accompanying changes in public opinion, propaganda, and public relations, has had upon government and politics. When a Chief Executive can expound his philosophy of government via radio and television, when Cabinet meetings can be brought into every home by means of television, when government departments and bureaus use information officers to promote support for their policies and programs, when both the Republican and Democratic Parties hire public relations firms to advise on election campaigns, questions may well be raised as to the effects on politics in America. A somewhat closer look at these "new things" is in order.

Public Opinion

In attempting a definition of public opinion we might begin by stating what it is not. Public opinion is not the opinion of the public. Considered as a collectivity, the American people can properly be called the public. But it cannot be said that it has an opinion.

It is obvious that individuals vary greatly in their opinions. The idea of public opinion as monolithic, as a single entity, presupposes that each individual has an opinion. This, of course, is patently absurd. Not only do individual opinions vary, but many individuals have no opinions at all on many matters. In addition, even among those with opinions on any given issue or personality, there are great differences in the intensity and tenacity with which these opinions are held. At one extreme are people with opinions hardly crystallized; at the other, those whose opinions are held so intensely they become a conviction, a faith which is adhered to at all costs. But to think of all Americans as constituting a single public and attribute to it a single opinion is obviously not in accord with observable facts.

There is some question whether the current widespread use of the phrase "public opinion" contributes much to an understanding of politics; but there can be no doubt that public opinion, whatever it is, plays a part, and a large part, in politics in the United States. Elected officials at all levels of government are sensitive to it. Administrative officials are conscious of it and do not ignore it. Great government departments, such as the Agriculture Department and the State Department, go to great lengths to find out what it is. Newspapers and organs of opinion reflect it as well as help create it. Political parties try to organize it. In the struggles among business units, whether large or small, careful soundings of it are taken with a view to change or adapt it to the manipulator's advantage. Even in the field of foreign relations, public opinion is said to have a role to play, although exactly what that role is, is not easy to say. Despite all these ways in which the term is used, it is doubtful whether such usage is conducive to an understanding of public opinion.

MEANING OF PUBLIC OPINION. The doubt arises out of the varied meanings given to the phrase and out of the pretensions of those who profess the scientific study of public opinion.

No generally accepted definition. One of the more reasonable definitions is that which conceives public opinion to be simply any collection of individual opinions which are designated as such.[1] More questionable is the definition of the term as a pressure group. The publishers of the *Congressional Quarterly* expressed the hope, on the inauguration of the venture, that "by providing a link between the local newspaper and Capitol Hill . . . CQ can help make public opinion the only effective pressure group in the country. . . ."[2] For them, public opinion is editorial opinion. On the other hand, some use the term but make no attempt to describe it, perhaps assuming that everyone knows what it means. For example, in a book on the American Bar Association and its influence on public opinion and legislation, public opinion is nowhere defined. Loose usage is almost as confusing and unhelpful as using a variety of meanings.[3]

For the late Frank Buchanan, Congressman from Pennsylvania and Chairman, in 1950, of the House Select Committee on Lobbying Activities, public opinion was something which Congressmen tried to "represent." In introducing the first witness in the Committee's hearings dealing with the role of lobbying in representative self-government, Buchanan said: "On the principle that members of Congress by and large seek to represent public opinion in their districts as they interpret it, Dr. (Hadley) Cantril will discuss the factors which shape public opinion and thus, presumably, may influence the legislative process."[4]

Still another definition of public opinion connects it organically with both the rational and irrational elements of the population considered collectively: "Public opinion . . . is a deeply pervasive organic force. . . . It articulates and formulates not only the deliberative judgments of the rational elements within the collectivity but (also) the evanescent common will, which somehow integrates and momentarily crystallizes the sporadic sentiments and loyalties of the masses of the population . . ." Two main types of public opinion are identified, the static and the dynamic, the former manifesting itself in the form of traditional customs, mores, and usages, while the latter, "being predominantly rational in character, is built upon the cultivated arts of persuasion and systematic publicity, and draws upon definite historical events or contemporary happenings as the material for its propaganda and agitation. . . ."[5] It is the "product of the city."

A different conception of public opinion limits it to significant individual opinions. Seeing in the so-called "public opinion polls," and in the industry which has grown up to purvey them to the mass media, a substitute for the earlier concept of "national character," believers in this more restrictive idea deny the claims of the pollsters. They argue that public opinion is the result of significant opinions exchanged by and among individuals, each individual's opinion acting on and reacting to those of the others. Only in this way can public opinion become meaningful. Such opinion is quite different from that normally labeled "public opinion." It is difficult if not impossible to measure it. It can be located and identified only with great difficulty. Yet only thus can public opinion be regarded as a factor in the social process, only thus can the term have meaning.

Thus the term "public opinion" has different meanings for different people. Of the various definitions cited, the last seems to be the most preferable; that is, public opinion is that which results when significant opinions are exchanged among and between individuals. The term "public" is used in several different yet related senses, each of which is clear in its context. It may be used to mean the American people collectively or any part thereof, or, more particularly, a part which is alert and attentive to a given event, movement, or phenomenon and reacts to it by expressing its opinion verbally or in writing. Thus, while only an individual can have an opinion, he often expresses it as a member of a "public" group.

POLITICS AND OPINION. As a factor in politics and government, public opinion sets limits to policy and action; yet ofttimes policy and action surmount these limits. This paradox is explained by the existence, side by side, of two kinds of publics: the attentive and the inattentive. Since the public never acts as a collectivity, the inattentive parts permit the attentive parts to forge ahead with legislation which the former, if aroused, would at least question or, possibly, attempt to obstruct altogether. Thus the opinions of the inattentive public are not an effective check on those of the attentive public in the formulation of "public" opinion.

At the same time, the attentive public has its attention focused on many different objectives. A particular matter almost invariably attracts the attention of many publics, each interested for a different reason. Some want a measure advanced in Congress or the executive branch; others want it defeated or modified. The net result—rather, the proximate result—is that they usually cancel out each other's efforts, or the outcome rests on such a narrow margin as to beckon the defeated to return to the fray and the victors to defend their gains.

In this unsystematic and haphazard way a limit to policy and action is set, only to be moved forward or back at the end of the next round in the warfare of opinion. Throughout the process there is no single opinion which hovers over and penetrates the interstices of the public as a whole. On the contrary, the public opinion which is present is the opinion or opinions of various parts of the public. These parts generate the "public" opinion which makes it look as though the public as a whole were asking for something. In other words, the people as the public are misled by those who would have us believe that *the* public has *an* opinion and acts upon it. It is nearer the truth to say that most matters on which officials act and which are said to be of public concern are so labeled by one or more of the attentive, interested parts of the people. Action or inaction results not because "the people demand it" but because some part of the public has contrived to make the officials think the people demand it, when, as a matter of fact, only a small part of the people are even aware of the issue, and even fewer have an opinion on it or wish a certain action to be taken.

Opinion rarely disinterested. Much of what passes for public opinion nowadays, or is referred to as such, is merely the opinion of an individual or of a spokesman for a group which has been expressed publicly. How much of it is spontaneous and how much is synthetic or contrived is difficult to say. To trace to its source every utterance of an individual speaking for himself or for a group that appears in a daily newspaper, a periodical, a radio program, television program, or newsreel would involve a great expenditure of time, money, and effort. But it might be worth it. For we would then have some data on the significant question for politics and government: How does public opinion become what it is? Meanwhile, any curious or conscientious citizen can quickly conclude from a week's reading of a metropolitan daily newspaper that such statements are not uttered idly but are spoken with a purpose. These people have axes to grind. The corporation executive, in making his statement, wants the public to think well of his company, of its product, of its position in the community.[6] Even more generally known is the role of the advertising agency in creating good public relations for the company. In influencing collective attitudes by the manipulation of symbols, both direct means, such as sales promotion, and indirect means, such as institutional advertising, are used.

The list of possible purposes in manipulating opinion can be easily lengthened. A state wants to attract industry; a region wants to develop the tourist trade; a city wants to bring conferences and conventions to its municipal auditorium. Time and money spent in planning publicity and promotion pay off. Or a labor organization wants to promote economic security for its members. (As frequently as not, the purpose is to maintain the position of a labor leader with respect to that of his rivals or promote his economic security or increase his personal power or satisfy his ambitions.) To do so, a new concept is created: the idea or goal of a guaranteed annual wage, for example. Realization of this goal turns on acceptance of it by management, possibly by state or federal legislatures. In any event, the people as a whole, the public, must be rendered receptive to the idea, or at least not opposed. They must be acquiescent, must permit it to become part of public policy on labor-management relations generally. Acquiescence by the people is achieved by consciously conceived, deliberately planned, purposive programs of persuasion. To the extent that favorable patterns of thought along these lines exist among the people, they are taken advantage of; when they are unfavorable, they are neutralized. All media of communication are employed in the process of making the general public acquiescent while the attentive publics oppose or ally themselves with the union and its leadership in making the necessary new rules embodying the goal striven for. It is then said that the people have spoken. It has been made to appear that the public at large wanted a new idea in labor-management relations in rendering the livelihood of labor less sensitive to the hazards of the market. But the fact is quite different from the appearance. Not all of the people have spoken, by any means; only a few. These few have consciously spoken and acted for a purpose, overcoming in the even smaller group holding a different view its opposition to the formulation of a new policy. An objective of a quite small minority thus has been given the sanction of the people as a whole.

PUBLIC OPINION AND CONGRESSIONAL LOBBYING. Members of Congress investigating lobbying in 1950 were told that three aspects of opinion were significant: the direction, the intensity, and the surety with which people hold an opinion.[7] The witness, Hadley Cantril, identified two problems about lobbies for students of public opinion. First, is the question, Do lobbyists represent a public? If so, is it national, state, or local? Second, How accurately do these lobbyists reflect the views of the interest groups they claim to represent?[8] It was also said a correlation had been established between attitudes and occupation: "By and large, we find in public opinion work that the objective criteria (sic) which has most correlation with a variety of opinions is occupation. . . ."[9]

At the stage of the Committee's investigation during which these views were expressed, the Congressmen were hearing testimony on the role of lobbying in representative self-government. As so often happens in such investigations, the carefully laid plans of the Committee (majority) and staff were not allowed to materialize as planned. Lack of time, interruptions by roll calls on the floor of the House, distractions by minority committee members, differing views of what the proper role of lobbies was in representative self-government—these, among other things, prevented the ideas about public opinion expressed by witnesses from being adequately discussed and analyzed and calm conclusions reached.

The Mass Media

For Americans concerned with the state of health of their governmental and political institutions, the mass media are of central significance. By the term "mass media" is meant those means of communication which reach the masses—the newspaper and periodical press, the radio, motion pictures, and television. But the term has come to have greater meaning, and includes the use made of these means, the contents disseminated, and the way in which the content is divided.

When the First Amendment to the Constitution was adopted there were no mass media as we know them today. News and opinion were passed by word of mouth, by personal correspondence, by leaflets printed on hand presses and passed from hand to hand, by pamphlets and books, also printed and circulated by hand. These media differed greatly in degree from their present-day counterpart. By degree is meant scope, range, number of people reached, hence the impact on people. In estimating political significance, there is a great difference between a one-page handbill passed from hand to hand reaching a few dozen people (a few hundred at the most) and a daily newspaper like the *Sun,* published by Benjamin Day in New York in the 1830's with a circulation of 30,000. And the difference is magnified when comparison is made with a modern metropolitan newspaper with its circulation reaching into the hundreds of thousands or even millions. There is no need to emphasize the obvious difference in degree when we mention the up-to-date media—radio, television, motion pictures.[10]

THE NEWSPAPER PRESS. Leaving aside for the moment the relative impact of these different media on politics, the status of the newspaper press can be considered briefly. It is highly organized; there are societies of newspapers editors, publishers, and others. The publishers, for example, were organized in 1887 into the American Newspaper Publishers Association to achieve better integration in the industry and to wield direct political influence. By 1910 it had become one of the most powerful pressure groups in the country.[11]

Economically, too, the industry is highly organized, with control concentrated in fewer and fewer hands, while the number of newspapers declines. From a high point of 2600 in 1910, the number of daily newspapers had declined to 2293 in 1930, while the next twenty-five years saw 500 more disappear. Even with this decline in numbers, circulation kept increasing, until in 1956 it reached nearly 56 million. The cost of establishing a new daily has increased so as to be almost prohibitive. Financial success depends primarily on advertising, which, in turn, is a function of circulation. In the United States the press has developed a theory of press procedure, according to which a sharp division is posited between the news, the editorial, and the advertising and business departments.[12] According to this theory, the "surest way to accomplish this end (financial success) is to present the best rounded and most accurate account of the day's news and the best balanced judgments on them."[13] While the daily press does not reach as many people as a nationwide radio or television broadcast, as a purveyor of political news, it is doubtless more important. It enjoys today, as it has for over a century and a half, the constitutional guarantee of freedom from abridgment by Congress.

Most of the facts about the newspaper industry are beyond dispute; not so the interpretation of the facts. About the decline in number of newspapers there can be no dispute. But about the effect of this decline on American society there is little agreement. An unofficial Commission on Freedom of the Press reported in 1947 that the "outstanding fact about the communications industry today is that the number of its units has declined." For the Commission, this was a disturbing fact: It indicated a trend toward monopoly of opinion, an unhealthy condition and a danger to democracy. A commission free from both government and industry control was recommended to ascertain the people's aspirations for the press and determine whether they were being achieved. But the recommendation fell on deaf ears. It was opposed by the editors through their national association, which saw itself and its board of directors as "a continuing committee of the whole on self-examination and self-government."[14] Much, if not most, of the news, both national and international, is received by daily newspapers through press associations or wire services. The daily press has already established a near-monopoly on local news, and the treatment of news by these associations has tended toward uniformity.[15]

It is not difficult to refute the theory of press procedure previously mentioned, namely, that a sharp division exists between the news, the editorial, and the advertising and business departments.[16] The propaganda industry, the compulsions of headline-writing, and the practice of attempting to tell the whole story in the first sentence or paragraph are handicaps to precise reporting. Much of the news is less susceptible to objectivity than are baseball scores, stock market quotations, or election returns. Moreover, even though the press as a whole takes little direct dictation from advertising, it has a major stake in that form of salesmanship. Consequently, there is a tendency to soft-pedal any criticism of advertising or the system of economic organization out of which it grows.[17]

The press meets outside criticism by referring to its protected position under the First Amendment, a privilege which makes it the only major industry able to ignore such criticism. The normal corrective of competition fails to operate in the case of the daily press because of the financial requirements of starting new, competing units. (Ninety-four per cent of American cities and 18 states are without competing papers.) "The theory that the daily test of the market place is an expression of public criticism [as Jefferson opined in his second inaugural address] is reduced to absurdity when the public has no option, when it has to buy the newspaper that is offered or go without."[18]

RADIO, MOTION PICTURES, TELEVISION. The situation in radio, movies, and television is not too different from that of the press. Technically, the situation of the first and last media is different. Because of the limited number of wave lengths on the radio spectrum, broadcasting via radio and television is limited to those wave lengths for which licenses have been issued by the federal government (the Federal Communications Commission). But this form of governmental supervision has not been effective in keeping the channels open as wide as a full and free discussion of public issues requires. The American ideal of freedom to express diverse opinion is not attainable in a situation in which the radio and television industries are dominated by two chains, the National Broadcasting Company and Columbia Broadcasting System.[19] Moreover, for various reasons the fullest use has not been made of technical improvements. In radio, for example, the prospect of thousands of frequency modulation transmitters available in every community, small as well as large, for the expression of local and diverse opinion has not been realized.[20] In this regard, some observers have asserted that the channels of mass communication should be opened to a greater variety and quantity of opinion.[21] In press and motion pictures, as in radio and television, but for different reasons, a strong tendency toward monopoly of media, hence of opinion, exists.

For example, in the Kansas City area, the *Kansas City Star* was charged with monopolizing the dissemination of news and advertising, and was fined $5000 in August, 1955, when convicted of the charge.[22]

As to content, the outpourings of the mass media are divided unequally among news, entertainment, debate, amusement, and enlightenment. Discussion of public issues consumes but a small part of the time devoted to broadcasting and publishing.[23] Although the business community is alleged to have had difficulty in communicating its ideas to the public generally, the content of the radio is heavily weighted in favor of business.[24] The function of the mass media is not to enlighten but to entertain, not to educate but to amuse, not to encourage discussion of political and other issues but to divert attention from these issues to other and less important matters.

The Commission on Freedom of the Press summarized the factors limiting the quantity and variety of communication emanating from the mass media as follows: newspaper concentration, decreased competition in radio because of the networks, motion picture concentration, chains, local news empires, the communications empires, monopolistic practices, and the cost of new ventures.[25]

The charge that the mass media, for various reasons, are falling down on their primary job of informing and enlightening the public is not universally held. On the contrary, a widespread view holds that, on the whole, and particularly in comparison with the job done by similar media elsewhere in the world, a superb performance is being turned in. The argument runs somewhat along this line: Despite the economic and financial factors involved, the curtailing of the free dissemination of ideas, and the tendency to uniformity and conformity, the American mass media have done a fine job of informing the American people. Satisfaction with the status quo is clear in the comment by the President of the American Newspaper Publishers Association on Adlai E. Stevenson's criticism of the one-party press: "It is the responsibility of the individual editor and publisher to decide what is printed in a particular newspaper. Fortunately, there is no power in this country to standardize the editorial views of any editor or publisher."[26]

Thus, different people draw different conclusions from the facts about the communications industry. Before examining the industry in terms of propaganda and of the industry's effect on the governmental process, it is pertinent to record the warning of an eminent sociologist about monopoly in this sector of our society. After pointing out that it is power which the mass media manipulate and that the agencies of publicity take higher rank in the power structure than eminence in the creative arts, Robert M. MacIver offers this stricture against monopoly in the mass media: "Of all monopolies, the most immediately fatal to democracy is the monopoly of the media of opinion. . . . In the free conflict of opinions lies man's best antidote against the poisons of false indoctrination. . . . What, in this area, democracy has, above all, to ensure is that no opinion group lacks reasonable opportunity to find avenues through which it can, without prejudice, reach the public ear."[27]

Propaganda

In its modern form, propaganda is so different from what it used to be that we are dealing, in effect, with a new phenomenon.

In this study we mean by propaganda the attempted management of collective attitudes by the manipulation of significant symbols. This definition is adapted from one by Harold D. Lasswell, who thought of propaganda in terms of actual, rather than attempted, management of attitudes.[28] The difference is crucial. For propaganda to have some effect, it is not necessary that it succeed completely. Partial success in the management of collective attitudes satisfies most propagandists and those who employ them. If, by any chance, complete success is attained, it is regarded as exceptional. Even a modest success is sufficient justification for most managers of collective attitudes to continue their efforts. Indeed, individuals and groups, whether private, official, corporate, or philanthropic, rarely think an unsuccessful propaganda campaign a complete waste of money, effort, and talent. On the contrary, a characteristic feature of propagandists in modern times is their sanguinity. They are always hopeful of success. Both inspirers and technicians rarely give up in their attempts to impress the target publics. In the discussion which follows, therefore, the term "propaganda" will be used as referring to attempts to manage collective attitudes by the manipulation of significant symbols as well as to the management of the attitudes itself.

NOVELTY AND UBIQUITY. Were propaganda less universally used, less synthetic, less purposeful, were it regarded less as the solvent of problems, there would be less reason for insisting on the above modification in definition. As it is, propaganda may be viewed as an outstanding characteristic of the age. Its effect on the individual is unfortunate. It corrodes individual faith and conviction, we are told by Albert Schweitzer.[29] It puts the mind of man under continuous pressure from without.[30] It makes the individual doubt his own senses.[31] In the field of politics and government, propaganda is the key to an understanding of modern methods of putting American government and democracy under pressure, and gives rise to the evils of deception and coercion.[32]

THE PROFESSION OF PUBLIC RELATIONS. As used here, the term "public relations" refers to all those activities, consciously undertaken, which have for their purpose the cultivation of good will or the creation of receptive attitudes among the people as a whole, a part or class of the people, or groups of the people. When an act is spontaneous or uncontrived, it is not public relations; when an act or action is deliberate, synthetic, and is directed at an individual, a group or groups, or the public at large in order to render them sympathetic to the initiator's wishes or acquiescent to a change, then it is public relations.

To speak of public relations as a profession is, of course, technically incorrect. It is not a profession as the ministry, engineering, architecture, medicine, teaching, or the law are professions. No state authority regulates, by licensing or other means, the practice of public relations. To attempt to do so would raise questions of individual rights and the public interest, would involve freedom of speech, of the press, and of petition. In fact, such constitutional and legal questions have already been raised in connection with the public relations practices of the National Association of Manufacturers and the Committee for Constitutional Government.[33]

It may be argued that regulation of public relations as a profession does take place as a result of state and federal laws "regulating" lobbying, at least to the extent that such laws require reports of their receipts and expenditures for purposes of influencing legislation and thus bring the activities of public relations firms hired for propaganda campaigns under public scrutiny. The degree to which such requirements constitute regulation is a matter of opinion. But there can be little doubt that such public oversight, if it be conceded to be regulation at all, is not the same as the regulation exercised by state authorities over the licensed professions.

It has been unnecessary for public relations to attain the status of a profession via the route followed by other professions. Along with advertising, public relations has benefited from the protection against government regulation contained in the guarantees of a free press and freedom of speech in the federal and state constitutions. Equally important is the interdependence of advertising and publishing. Advertising revenue is the lifeblood of the mass-circulation newspapers and periodicals. Reciprocally, the advertising and the public relations professions are dependent financially on the availability of the communications channels which the newspapers and periodicals purvey at a price. Here, of course, the radio and television industry are of equal, if not greater, significance. The opening of these two channels to propaganda has been accomplished by the public relations industry, which, in turn, would never have reached its present economic or professional status without these channels.

A further factor explaining the achievement by the public relations guild of a social, if not a legal or technical, status as a profession has been the American genius for rationalizing the national interest in terms of business values. Using the term "culture" in the anthropological sense, our culture is a business culture; that is, the values associated with the production of material goods rate highest in the national scale of values. And the practitioners of public relations have been instrumental in establishing such a value hierarchy. With their talents of imagination and verbalization, they have adapted, for a fee, traditional American symbols to accommodate new products of American ingenuity and industry. A classic example is the tobacco companies' advertising campaign of the 1920's, which sanctioned cigarette smoking by women as a respectable social practice. Leaving moral and physiological considerations aside, the success of the campaign cannot be doubted. Nor can the value of its success to American agriculture and industry be gainsaid. Neither can it be denied that the success was achieved through the use of propaganda—the attempted management of collective attitudes by the manipulation of significant symbols. The rise of the advertising profession to a respectable and honored position, with the attendant emergence of public relations as a separate profession, is itself a striking example of the way a significant symbol—success in business—deliberately manipulated, can confer dignity on the very managers of these attitudes. From the days, three decades ago, when (at Ivy Lee's suggestion) John D. Rockefeller, Sr. sought to efface his public image as the personification of the oil trust and replace it with one of kindliness, courtesy, and friendly competition—by handing out dimes to urchins on railroad station platforms—the managers of collective attitudes have come far and risen high. Public relations has reached its high contemporary position because it has been able to convince the American people that they were promoting the national interest when they abandoned old ideas for new ones—whether merchandising methods, classical music, or spectator sports.

Institutional advertising. Illustrative of the resourcefulness of public relations are two ideas—institutional advertising and the engineering of consent—which are among their most successful conceptions. As the phrase suggests, institutional advertising promotes institutions through advertising.[34] The institutions may be of the widest variety: the home, the family, marriage, education, religion, public health, and business. In the latter field, the bundle of resources, techniques, skills, and values once known as capitalism has become "creative capitalism," and to it has been added the idea that advertising which promotes the private interest is also in the best public interest. Creative capitalism is the kind of economic system which we now have in the United States. Among its attributes is the recognition and acceptance of the responsibilities of business by business. By the use of advertising, the achievements of major U.S. corporations are depicted in terms of the public interest. Readers, listeners, or viewers of such advertising come to identify what is called the public interest with the activities of the corporations sponsoring it; thus "creative capitalism," a significant symbol, has been manipulated so as to obtain acceptance or lack of opposition to the desired image.[35]

Among the symbols manipulated in such "public interest" advertising are the following: good health, by the Metropolitan Life Insurance Company; the American road (to success through free enterprise), by the Ford Motor Company; highway safety (the human cost of poor roads), by the Caterpillar Tractor Company; the greatness of a good loser (Robert E. Lee), by the John Hancock Mutual Life Insurance Company; resource conservation by tree farming, by the Weyerhaeuser Timber Company. None of these corporations lose any good will by being associated in the public mind with these symbols. On the contrary, the obvious good will created for these companies by such propaganda is a tribute to their advertising agencies and to their skillful choice of symbols for manipulation.

The engineering of consent. As an advertising concept, "the engineering of consent" goes even further. Here the idea is not only that public consent can be obtained by skillful use of public relations techniques, including advertising, but also that the public can be made to feel that its consent has already been given. An illustrative example is found in the protracted struggle of the railroads with the trucking industry to achieve a more competitive position. In an article on this struggle, as it unrolled in the Commonwealth of Pennsylvania, one reporter describes "what can happen when 'opinion engineers' are given their head. It is a short step, it turns out, from wangling public consent to kidding the public into imagining its consent has already been given—a thought . . . worked up to a whole creative system for manufacturing 'situations of reality.' "[36] Judging from the recommendations of a Cabinet advisory committee in 1955 for a new transportation policy relaxing federal regulation of railroads but increasing it for other forms of transportation—highway users, waterways, airways, pipelines—and from the heightened controversy among the different forms of transport involved, the period in which they are to be engaged in efforts to "engineer consent" has not yet come to an end.[37]

As a technique or set of techniques, propaganda has been adopted extensively in America. Most major parts of our society have followed the lead of the business community in consciously attempting to manipulate significant symbols. In this way, they have tried to manage the attitudes of the American people collectively and those of its smaller, but opinion-wise more important, publics. Organized labor, agricultural producers, the wholesale and retail trade, banking and finance—are all engaged in attempts to manage collective attitudes. Similarly, inland and overseas transport (as already noted), teaching, as well as many of the other professions, newspaper and book publishing, and the other parts of the communications industry likewise do their best, with the help of public relations counsellors, to inculcate favorable attitudes in the various publics. Even some parts of organized religion have not escaped, although the affiliated

Protestant denominations have rejected propaganda as a proselytizing technique.

It would be surprising if the political parties and the federal and state bureaucracies had not adopted the new techniques of advertising and public relations, since the political interest groups, the source of pressure directed to the bureaucracies, have embraced propaganda techniques so completely. It is to the effect of the mass communications industry and, particularly, of propaganda on politics and the governmental process that we now turn.[38]

The Mass Media, Government, and Politics

What have been the effects on government and politics of the "engineering of consent," of corporate concentration in the press, radio, television, and motion picture industries, of the new tools of propaganda, and of the new professions of public relations and advertising? Has politics in America, as a consequence of the revolutions in the communications art, tended to become nothing but the manipulation of passive groups of voters by elites struggling for power?[39] Does corporate concentration in newspapers result in a narrowing of that diversity of opinion which is a necessary condition of democracy? Is another consequence of newspaper concentration the ignoring by the press of important Washington stories about what happens in terms of legislation following an election? Or do we still lack reliable information on the effect of concentration in the newspaper and other communications industries upon what people read, hear, and see?

THE TRANSFORMATION OF LOBBYING. The transformation of lobbying ranks high among the important effects of the rise of the mass communications industries on the processes of government and of politics. For many years now, the old-style buttonholing of members of Congress in the lobbies of the Capitol has taken second place to the new-style lobbying by propaganda. Congressional investigating committees, knowledgeable authors and journalists, and contemporary observers of politics all agree that the generation of propaganda is the typical modern form of lobbying. Thus, lobbying is employed to make it appear that the country wants a certain action by Congress on the pending legislation in question. "Propagandists have made the bold assertion that they represent the demands of the Great American People, and Congress has accepted the voice of Propaganda as the voice of God."[40] If this was an accurate description of the situation thirty years ago, before radio was widely used and television came on the scene, how much truer must it be today.

The creation and control of public opinion—that is, propaganda—is the long-run objective of every significant pressure group in the country. This is the conclusion of the congressional committee which investigated lobbying in 1950. "Lobbying at the grass roots" is the Committee's descriptive label for "this new emphasis in pressure tactics." "Rather than attempt to influence legislation directly, the pressure group seeks to create an appearance of broad public support for its aims. . . ." No matter whether this expression of public opinion is "genuine" or "artificial and contrived," the process is "one which has been deliberately and specifically instigated by one group or another having a particular stake in legislative issues."[41] It can be readily seen how the evils of coercion and deception may attend this process, how misrepresentation and a lack of balance are inevitable in a situation characterized by such "engineering of consent."[42]

POLITICAL REPRESENTATION MODIFIED. Still another consequence of the difference between modern means of communication and those of earlier days is the effect on political representation. It is a mixed effect not easily described, and descriptions of it lack universal corroboration. Members of the national legislature still represent their constituencies, as they have for decades. But the nature of this representation has changed. Some observers argue that, in effect, geographical representation has been replaced by functional or vocational representation, in which the manufacturing and wholesaling of opinion by voluntary groups is a main feature.[43] Others would not go quite so far. For example, the committee of the California Legislature which investigated lobby activities in 1950 argued that representation had not been changed from geographical to occupational, but that representatives elected on the basis of geography represented the balance of interests in a district; they did not reflect those interests.[44] The complex nature of modern political representation is further emphasized by recalling the way it was understood by the late Frank Buchanan, former chairman of the House Lobby Investigating Committee. The Congressman represents the public opinion in his district, he said, and his committee colleagues tacitly accepted this description of representation. But this does not advance our knowledge very much in view of the pitfalls surrounding the definition and measurement of public opinion.

Only nominally can it be said that Congressmen today represent their districts. All generalizations are hazardous and this one particularly so, for our knowledge of the nature of the relationship between members of Congress and their constituents is woefully incomplete. Much painstaking effort would be required to remedy this deficiency. Among other things, a nationwide study project would be needed, conducted periodically, identifying, analyzing, and weighing the factors—local, state, sectional, and national—which are involved in this relationship. Not the least of those factors would be the various means of mass communication, the extent to which they are effectively accessible to all members of the community, and the employment of public relations experts in election campaigns.

CHANGES IN CAMPAIGNING. Campaigning has been changed by the revolution in the communications art. For one thing, it has become much more expensive than formerly, so that now the bulk of expenditures by party committees and related groups goes for radio and television time. Also, such time must ordinarily be purchased because of the legal requirement that free time donated to one party must be donated similarly to all parties and the consequent unwillingness of network executives to extend the favor to the numerous minor parties.[45]

Another way in which campaigning has been changed is the adoption by all parties (to the extent that they have the money to do so) of all the promotional and sales techniques of public relations and advertising. Of course, not everyone agrees that sales promotion methods suitable to products are appropriate for promoting candidates for the Presidency and for Congress. Yet neither party can refrain if the other uses these techniques. A law of propaganda resembling Gresham's law of money seems to be operative here: Intrinsically inferior techniques or techniques of dubious value drive good techniques from the field. The result is that Democratic campaign managers are forced, or feel they are forced, to employ all methods, no matter how extreme or lacking in good taste, that Republican managers adopt, and vice versa. Or, like a respectable newspaper in competition with others resorting to "yellow" journalism, in order to compete for the votes of the electorate, a given party, even though striving to keep its campaign on a high level, finds itself compelled to adopt the lower level techniques of its rival.

MORE UNIFORM TREATMENT OF NEWS. The tendency toward uniformity in the treatment of news as a result of increasing concentration of control in the press and other media has already been touched on.[46] The effect on government and politics can hardly be salutary. It is not that reporters and working journalists are unable to do the job: they are too frequently not permitted to do the job they could do. Newspapermen at state capitals and at Washington know the power of the pressure groups. They know, as no other professional group in America knows, how the pressure groups manipulate the opinion of the many publics, how their lobbyists work quietly and unostentatiously among the members of the Congress and the executive departments, how the pressure groups have their vested interests in the government bureaucracy, and how the individual citizen is of very little weight in the political equation. They know the power of property, of the economic interest groups. They know the political value of activity, which pressure groups have, and the nullity of inertia and of political apathy, which reflects the attitude of most individual citizens. Reporters know the pressure groups and could tell us more about them were they permitted to do so.

There is a job to be done, according to the House Select Committee on Lobbying Activities, set up by the Eighty-first Congress, in its report filed with the House on January 1, 1951. After noting that almost half of those interviewed in a poll did not know what a lobbyist is, the Committee said: "The cherished institutions of our system of representative government can endure only if our citizens understand how our system of government works. But the filing of reports under the Lobbying Act cannot itself fulfill this need. Our two greatest educational media, the schools and the press, also have the responsibility of increasing public knowledge as to the nature and extent of pressure group operations. An informed and vigilant public is the only lasting guaranty that pressure groups will operate in an open and aboveboard manner."[47]

One Washington correspondent goes further and states that the press ignores the biggest story in the nation's capitol. Richard Strout, of the *Christian Science Monitor,* claims that the tendency toward uniform treatment of the news has resulted in the "most important story in Washington" being ignored by the press. For Strout, the story was "what intervenes between the expression of popular will at the polls and its enactment into law." He observes:

> I don't know the anatomy of the obstructive body myself, but I'd like to feel that a large force of competent journalists was digging hard to find out. How spontaneously does a 'public outcry' in defense of special privilege break out? When Senators from the South join with Republicans to vote against the nominal head of their own party, what does each southerner get and what does each Republican expect to get? The notion of Congressmen voting to 'get things for their district' is too rudimentary. I should like to know what things the obstructive Congressman wants to get (or preserve) for which people in his district.[48]

An indication of what an enterprising reporter can do when his curiosity is aroused and when he is sufficiently independent to be able to get his news printed is provided by Walter Winchell. When a congressional investigating committee in 1950 was unable to obtain from Edward A. Rumely, of the Committee for Constitutional Government, the names of purchasers of the Committee's books, Winchell obtained (or asserted he did) this information and published it.[49] The Committee and the House of Representatives never secured the information, and Rumely was upheld by the Supreme Court in his refusal to divulge it.

Corporate concentration is noticeable in the communications industry, as it is in other parts of the American economy. Nationally, television and radio broadcasting are dominated by two networks. Just what the effect is, if any, on the process of government is difficult to say. There are conflicting viewpoints on the matter. One asserts that we do not know what effect, if any, such concentration has on what people read in the press, hear over the air, and see on the screen; hence the effect on the people themselves is unknown.[50] An opposite conclusion, and one based on exhaustive testimony and studies made by the Temporary National Economic Committee in its investigation of monopoly fifteen years ago, states that "one result of the development of centralism is that individuals are no longer in contact with information which is essential to the formation of policy vital to their existence."[51] Conclusive evidence is lacking. Whether there is concentration in the communications industry and, if so, what its effect is on the content of press, radio, television, and films are questions which continue to divide Congressmen, experts, and laymen alike. Opinions there will be aplenty; facts, few.

It may be true, as the *Washington Post* claimed editorially on April 30, 1951, that a congressional inquiry makes Congress and the public increasingly aware of lobbying. There is no way of knowing whether this is the case or not. In any event, it is clear that any public awareness resulting from a congressional investigation such as that of the 1950 House Select Committee is short-lived. Rare is the editor who thinks he can afford to keep public interest alive in even an important subject when competition requires editors, generally, to find new subjects daily to feed the public.

There is additional evidence that controversy rather than enlightenment is the standard for measuring the newsworthiness of events and, consequently, that the press and the other mass media are not doing their duty of informing the people. Instead of providing a marketplace for ideas, the press is interested in a fight, according to a complaint of Senator Ralph E. Flanders (R., Vt.). He asserted that the constructive parts of his Senate speech of March 9, 1954, on Wisconsin's junior Senator, Joseph McCarthy, were slighted by the press but the polemic parts were carried around the world.[52] Similarly, in a serious study of radio, television, and society, another observer concludes that the radio and television industries have not developed a concept of public responsibility.[53]

PROPAGANDA AS NEWS. Propaganda inspired by groups, especially those of the business community, receives treatment as news in even the best newspapers, but carries no label of political advertising.

Manipulation of people by advertising, salesmanship, propaganda, and lobbying receives more emphasis now than formerly from the modern business corporation. Technological efficiency was the aim of the corporation in earlier days. Now, it aims at manipulating people, and to this end it has utilized the social and psychological sciences, as it did the physical and biological sciences earlier.[54] Groups of corporations likewise place emphasis on the manipulation of people; for example, the public relations and opinion-forming programs of the National Association of Manufacturers constituting its foremost policy function.[55]

To illustrate propaganda as news, two instances may be cited. "Socialism Seen in Hell's Canyon" was the headline of a report in *The New York Times* of May 30, 1955, attacking plans for public power development at this Snake River site. The study on which the report was based was prepared by the Council of State Chambers of Commerce, a so-called research group representing thirty-one state and regional chambers of commerce.[56] The other instance is the report of the speech of a newly elected president of the National Association of Manufacturers. This report was headlined in *The New York Times*, of December 9, 1955, "NAM Head Finds Drift to Marxism." In American politics both socialism and Marxism are symbols of things un-American, foreign, to be resisted by all who are true to the traditions of our country. Thus the public press was the means by which symbols of political significance were employed by business groups to manipulate collective attitudes. The events were worthy of being regarded as news; but the treatment they received made them propaganda as well.

Newspapers themselves are censors of news. By selecting from the mass of information which comes in over their teletypes only those parts which reflect, emphasize, and support their publishers' ideas of newsworthiness, they can present biased reports, an incomplete picture of events, distortion, and prejudice. As a consequence, the attitudes and opinions of their readers are manipulated and altered in the image of the desires of those who make newspaper publishing possible.[57]

By and large, the content disseminated by the mass media favors the existing business system. In his book *Is Anybody Listening?* William H. Whyte, Jr. reported for the editors of *Fortune* magazine on the success of American business in "selling" itself to the American people. He ridiculed the fear of business that labor and utopian theorists and collectivists were getting their incorrect theories across to the American people. He failed to understand "this preposterous claim of inferiority," and went on to say, "The most cursory check of mass media shows the hortatory content heavily weighted in favor of the business system. . . ."[58] This book reminds us, too, of the role of the public relations man, thus providing a warning to dissect carefully what the mass media disseminate. Whyte quotes one of the leaders in the field, Edward L. Bernays, as saying that the public relations man "has the responsibility of conditioning and remolding the public attitude on ideas."[59] Neither Bernays nor Whyte explains who has conferred this responsibility on the public relations man.

Access to the mass media of communication is one of the factors, according to the House Select Committee on Lobbying Activities, which has resulted in organized business gaining the greatest success in lobbying. In competition among lobbies, the Committee concluded that the advantage would always go to the group with the most money, the best organization, and the easiest access to the mass media. These were possessed by organized business in greater degree than by other groups, hence the greater success achieved by organized business.[60]

USE OF PROPAGANDA BY GOVERNMENT. The uses made of the means of mass communication by officials and agencies of the government itself have become an important factor in the governmental process. Although publicity as a tool of bureaucratic units has been treated elsewhere, it is pertinent to recall here that the same mass media through which private interests bring their message to Washington (through propaganda directed to the public at large and to the smaller publics) are employed indirectly by the coalitions of groups, bureaus, and congressional committees which work closely together for common ends. Indeed, so many of our well-organized groups are bound by ties of interest to government bureaus and congressional committees and their staffs that use of the media of communication by such coalitions may be said to be normal. Press releases issuing from the government departments ("handouts," as they are called by the working press) are frequently found to reflect attitudes and ideas promoted by groups formally external to the governmental apparatus but closely connected to it in fact. Such tactics are generally known and fail to excite concern or even interest except among a few for whom full enlightenment of the people about the operations of their government is a desirable objective.

Even more significant for the governmental-political process is the increasing employment of the means of publicity and propaganda by the Chief Executive and the failure of Congress as a body to employ these new publicity techniques. It is often forgotten that the "fireside chat" radio technique used so effectively by Franklin D. Roosevelt is little over twenty years old. The televised press conference of Dwight D. Eisenhower is another innovation in governmental publicity methods. The political impact of both techniques is great but varies with the user, the circumstances, and with other factors. The propaganda value of these new techniques is not so widely conceded. Yet it can readily be seen that anyone using the position and prestige of the office of the Chief Executive in such ways is propagandizing. Every utterance of the President, his every appearance at a press conference to make statements and answer questions, are an expression, varying from time to time as to subject, of his philosophy of government.

As yet Congress as a whole has not chosen to use the modern means of communication which the President has. However, use of these communications media by individual members of the national legislature, both members of the House and of the Senate, is common. Also, from time to time, congressional committees have consented to their hearings being broadcast and televised. Examples are the hearings conducted by Senator Estes Kefauver (D., Tenn.) into the relation between crime and politics, and by Senator Watkins (R., Utah) into charges of Senator Joseph McCarthy (R., Wis.) against the Army. But these are exceptional instances; in general, neither house nor its committees employ the radio or television. Unable to speak with a single voice, as is the Chief Executive, and preferring known and tried methods of communication to new and untried methods, Congress as a corporate body has yet to agree to being put "on the air" or televised. Any advantage to Congress in its relations to the Chief Executive and to the country as a whole would appear to Congress to be more than offset by the disadvantages which it is feared would grow out of publicizing the rivalries between the two houses, between committees of the two houses, between individuals. Congress also apparently feels it would be unwise to so publicize the lack of party unity, responsibility, and leadership, or to focus attention on its inability to discipline itself adequately for the efficient discharge of public business.

An additional factor may be the reluctance to reveal the lag between the objectives of majority opinion among the people, expressed in terms of legislation, and the action of Congress as the agency of government most fully representative of the people. According to this viewpoint, Congress lags behind majority opinion and, therefore, reflects rather than leads public opinion.[61]

RIGHT OF PETITION ALTERED. Mention should be made here of the transformation of the right of petition from a right to request from government a redress of grievances to the right to propagandize with all the means of modern communication. This is one of the major effects of propaganda on politics. (This transformation has been fully examined in Chapter 6.) Together with the other constitutional guarantees of freedom of speech, of the press, and of assembly, the right of petition in modern times has come to be considered less as a right to ask government to consider and correct injustice and grievances and more as a right "to make a case" with the public through the use of all the available means of publicity and propaganda. Amplification of the few voices usually associated with the concept of petitioning the government to either a stentorian roar or a well-modulated message expertly directed to a key public or publics is a difference of kind rather than one of degree. To gain an insight into the nature of this difference, one must keep in mind the many opportunities to manipulate symbols offered by the new means of communication. Just as every idea is an incitement, as Justice Holmes observed, so the dissemination of ideas by media which facilitate the manipulation of these ideas in symbolic form is an invitation to new thought and action by readers, auditors, and viewers.

COMMENT. The rise of the communications industries to a place of prominence in American life is a fact of major political significance. Its importance can hardly be overstated. Because of its immunity from criticism (due to the protection of the First Amendment) the communications industry is unique among industries in America. No other industry is so "affected with a public interest," yet none claims more freedom from scrutiny.

One of the anomalies of the contemporary American scene is the acceptance of so much public regulation of private activities affecting physical health, welfare, and morals, while we are reluctant in pursuing the serious and systematic analysis of private activities affecting attitudes and opinions. The dangers to representative self-government of public censorship of opinion are numerous, and there is no dearth of critics to point them out. On the other hand, those who question the effects of an essentially unregulated opinion-forming industry upon the mental health of the nation are singled out for attack as advocating censorship, if not dictatorship. A strong case can, of course, be made for free expression of opinion. Nothing said here should be understood as questioning that case. But the freedom to speak, write, and publish, which the First Amendment would protect from governmental abridgment, is freedom for full debate of public issues, not for unregulated competition to profit from purveying entertainment, with privately censored news relegated to a secondary position. If the American people are lacking in knowledge about the governmental process and are uninformed about the political nature of the world they live in, much of the blame can be laid at the door of the mass communications industry, the finest in the world, technically speaking, but one failing to measure up to its potentialities.

The availability of channels of communication through which to express a wide diversity of opinion is a prerequisite to the effective operation of political democracy in America and a safeguard against the attainment by any section, class, interest, or group of a permanent position of domination in the government.

SUMMARY. Four subjects of importance to American democracy have been discussed in this chapter: public opinion, the mass media, propaganda, and the effects of the mass media on government and politics. There is no generally accepted definition of public opinion. Whatever it is, it is agreed that it is important in the operation of government in America. Hence people and groups possessing the necessary resources, both in and out of government, put forth strenuous efforts to manipulate public opinion to their advantage. All the mass media are used in a conscious attempt to manage collective attitudes by the manipulation of significant symbols. The use of the mass media on such a scale for propaganda purposes is something new and is having an impact on the operation of governmental and political institutions. But the full effect is only beginning to be realized. Already, however, it is fairly clear that lobbying has been changed, political representation modified, and campaigning for public office transformed. In addition, it may be that treatment of the news is becoming more uniform and that much propaganda is disseminated masquerading as news. But our knowledge of the effect of concentrated control is admittedly limited. So far, Congress as a body has not yet availed itself of the mass media, as the President and the bureaucracy have done.

Chapter 13

THE MAKING OF PUBLIC POLICY —LEGISLATION

> . . . policy is present in some degree wherever there is
> activity.
>
> —Arthur W. Macmahon
> *Administration in Foreign Affairs**

Public policy in the United States is the end product of the governmental process and is made real to the average citizen in the sense of security he feels, in the public service he gets, and in the prices he pays for the things he buys.

It is difficult to say exactly how policy is made on such subjects as national defense, labor-management relations, transportation, taxation and monetary matters, immigration, or foreign relations. It is doubtful if any one person, no matter how highly placed, knows everything there is to know about any particular policy. Moreover, in the nature of things, an attempt to take apart the process of policy-making can be only partially successful. But such an attempt is made in this and the following chapters.

The Origins of Public Policy

In general public policy has its origins in either or both of two sources: the action of a foreign government, or some group within the United States. Policies result from political pressures, and much of the pressure to which American democracy is subject originates outside the United States. The response by the United States takes shape in terms of foreign policy and in some domestic policy as well. In addition, ideas generated by the American people themselves add to the pressure on American democracy. Nowadays, the line between these sources of policy is blurred. Much of what is called domestic

* University, Ala.: University of Alabama Press, 1953, p. 95.

policy is the domestic aspect of foreign policy. Most of the remainder is action by Congress in terms of legislation in response to a request by the executive branch of the government or by some domestic group which has asked Congress to redress a grievance.

POLICY AS RESPONSE TO ACTION BY FOREIGN GOVERNMENTS. American foreign relations since 1945 provide many examples of policy issues which have originated with actions of other governments, actual or feared, but which required policy decisions by the United States. The British withdrawal from Greece in 1947 necessitated decisions by the President, the State Department, and Congress. Similarly, the failure of western Europe to recover economically after the war at the expected rate, the Communist coup in Czechoslovakia in 1948, the blockade of Berlin by occupying Soviet forces, and the military attack on the UN-sponsored Republic of Korea in 1950 and the intervention of the Chinese Communists later that year—these are some of the more important acts of foreign governments which confronted the United States with the most fundamental kind of policy decisions.

POLICY AS RESPONSE TO INTERNAL STIMULI. Policy that does not result from the action of a foreign government usually originates with one of the many political pressure groups within the country. The impression in many quarters is that policy originates within Congress, with the political parties, or with public opinion. Yet this impression is hardly justified. The laws which Congress enacts originate in most cases with the informal agencies, that is, the outside pressure groups. The lawmakers rarely initiate laws.[1] Political parties remain neutral on most legislative issues.[2] Indeed, the pressure group system developed because of the default of the political parties in their task of taking a stand on issues.[3] Nor does public opinion create issues or originate legislation.[4]

Because of his messages to Congress, the President is thought to originate many ideas that ultimately are enacted into law. While this is so, it is true in a nominal way. The President speaks for himself in many instances; but more often he is the spokesman for an executive agency, a commission, or for a pressure group outside the formal structure of government. It must be remembered, too, that executive bureaus often use pressure groups to get their ideas introduced into Congress, thus bypassing the White House and the Budget Bureau, which is supposed to coordinate the President's legislative program, and increasing the proportion of policy enactments apparently originating with the groups but, in fact, having their origin in the government's executive branch.

Groups as prime originators of policy. Our numerous and varied political pressure groups are a constant factor in the shaping of issues out of which policy develops. They may raise issues which result in specific items being included in the President's legislative program. Or they may take a position on proposals set forth in the program. A summary of the items which appeared on the calendars of Congress during the second session of the Eighty-second Congress (1952) on which registered lobby groups and individuals took group positions include many of both kinds. Of particular concern were the following: the extension of the Defense Production Act, the so-called fair-trade bill, the new immigration act, universal military training, the St. Lawrence Seaway project. Spending bills also stimulated the interest of organizations, and specialized groups lobbied for or against important details of the tax and tariff programs. The American Medical Association succeeded in eliminating a section of the social security bill authorizing free examinations of disabled veterans. This section, the AMA charged, might lead to socialized medicine.

In the zeal and vision of a new-born group of citizens, the Association of the Atomic Scientists, originated the idea that the peacetime development of atomic energy, although a government monopoly, should be supervised by civilians rather than military men. One of the two fundamental questions about atomic energy development, the vesting of its control in civilian or military hands, was settled, temporarily at least, as the result of the intervention of this group of concerned citizens. Eight years later, in 1954, the other fundamental question, its development under government monopoly or private enterprise, was answered by Congress so as to permit the licensing to private industry of patents developed and owned by the government. While the Association was again active in 1954, by then other forces, largely business and financial, were more influential and were able to exploit effectively, both in Congress and through the communications media, the opposition to monopoly, particularly government monopoly, and the attachment to the myth of free competitive enterprise.[5]

Neither policy question figured in the election of the Seventy-ninth Congress in 1944, since it was not generally known at that time that atomic energy for military purposes, much less for peaceful purposes, could be successfully developed. The situation in the Eighty-third Congress was quite different. Although four congressional and two presidential elections had taken place since 1946, the proper role of private enterprise in atomic energy development was not an issue in any of them. Nor can the public information media be given a very high mark during this period for informing and explaining to the people the questions of public policy involved. Thus, when amendments were proposed in the Republican-controlled Eighty-third Congress, atomic energy control had not been the subject of public debate. Public opinion, insensitive to the consequences of the changes in the system by which vital patents were held by the government for public benefit, was largely inert and acquiescent. Only at the last minute were modifications made in the Senate, setting terms somewhat more favorable to public rather than private interest. The case is not one which shows the American system of government at its best. The two-party system failed to provide clear-cut alternatives. The electoral system failed to bring the issues into the open. The press abdicated its responsibility. The executive department, particularly the Atomic Energy Commission, did little to publicize the issues. Rather, it worked quietly with those who would benefit from the changes. Business and financial interests, in contrast with those representing a wider conception of the public interest, such as the Association of the Atomic Scientists, preferred to keep the public unalerted rather than agitated. In making policy Congress acted with no clear-cut sense of responsibility to the American people as a whole. Yet it is to be feared that the case may be typical of much policy-making.

Groups as secondary originators of policy. In creating issues and originating policy, groups are important not only as primary but also as secondary sources of policy. The relation of political, military, or strategic moves by foreign governments to American policy has already been referred to. Within the circumstances resulting from such moves, policy takes form as the government acts to meet them. Often of equal importance to the country as a whole are the actions of the groups which shape policy in specific terms within the general situation. If the Soviet Union and North Korea, for example, were the primary shapers of the American policy to rearm in 1950, with all the attendant legislation to control materials and prices, then the secondary determiners, so to speak, of specific laws governing materials allocation and price controls were the informal agencies of government, the pressure groups, which, in bloodless combat with Congress, the executive, and the courts, fixed the shape of policy which was applied to the individual citizen, the corporation, and the labor union.

The inability or failure of European countries from 1945 to 1947 to take the steps necessary to their full economic recovery was the primary reason for U.S. milling and shipping interests diluting the potential effectiveness of the Marshall Plan by obtaining amendments to the legislation as it passed in Congress. But the secondary reason was the unconcealed desire of these interests to improve or protect their economic position in the American economy.[6]

Similarly, the deteriorating security situation in Europe in 1949 caused the American recovery program to be changed into a military assistance program. Hence the ultimate reason for the favored position obtained by the American shipping interests in moving the supplies under the program can be said to have been the worsening security situation. The secondary reason, again, was the continued feeling of the organized shipowners and operators that their economic position required a favored position in the program.[7]

One reason why it is difficult to track down policy to its source is its elusiveness and subtlety. We can never be certain that our research has produced the real originator. We can never be sure that we have discovered the "real rulers" of our society.

Sometimes an idea unheralded in a presidential message to Congress turns out to have originated with an obscure or middle-echelon technician. Policy stated or proclaimed in this way is completely malleable and must be given substance in the process of legislative enactment and executive administration. Asked to contribute ideas to a presidential message to Congress, a Cabinet member turns to his private assistants and to bureau chiefs for suggestions. When the White House staff receives them, it is quick to recognize the ones with political appeal, and eagerly inserts them into a message perhaps hitherto lacking in such appeals to foreign publics. Thus, in his State of the Union Message, President Truman proposed, in 1949, that the American people share their grasp of technology with other peoples of the world, and the now-famous Point Four Program was proclaimed. But the policy was no more than a few words when proposed to Congress. The shape it took resulted from the clash of ideas among the executive branch, Congress, and the interested groups and organizations. And the spirit in which the Point Four Program was carried out overseas was not the missionary spirit of its originator but the more political spirit of skeptical, practical officials to whose hands its administration was entrusted. When we discuss the origins of policy we must be prepared to encounter subtleties of meaning and elusive origins.

If public policy may be defined as ideas embodied in legislative enactments, four definite phases emerge: origin and development of the idea; enactment by Congress; application by the executive branch; and interpretation by the courts. Only when we understand all these phases through which a policy passes can we be sure that we know something about the policy.

Legislation as Policy

Congress is the center of politics in the United States. Whether politics be thought of as partisan politics or as competition among groups to determine to their advantage the regulations by which society is governed, it is in Congress that politics has its focus.[8]

But because American politics is centered on Congress, it must not be thought that politics does not exist elsewhere. No member of Congress can afford to forget that, however much he may in fact represent interests rather than persons, he owes his position to votes in a district. The qualifications of voters and the boundaries of the districts are drawn by state legislative action. Only when a threat arises from outside the United States does the national interest override the demands of occupational, local, and sectional interests. Even then, the currents of local politics, never far below the surface, run with their usual strength.[9] However, in organizing political power, political parties fail to generate the full power of which the electorate is capable; the result is that national programs oriented nationally suffer and policy is the transitory resultant of a momentary balance of forces. It is rarely a rational choice from among rationally constructed alternatives.[10]

From the point of view of policy-making, certain facts about our governmental system need mentioning. As the law-making body, Congress is engaged in performing one of the three great traditional powers of government—the enactment of laws. Despite the separation of powers, Congress does not by itself perform the legislative function in America. Not only does it share it with the Chief Executive, but also, because of the division of powers according to the federal feature of the Constitution, the legislative power is shared with the state legislatures. Policy is "made" not only by the federal government, but also by the states through their legislatures and through their governors and state judicial systems. In this connection, the role of the states in policy-making appears to be expanding; for example, states' rights to offshore oil, right-to-work laws, and state and local regulation of power and other natural resources. In 1955, the report of the Commission on Inter-Governmental Relations sought to encourage the trend to increased policy-making by the states. While this may not be symptomatic, there can be little doubt that the return of governmental power to the states and of the federal government to a more limited role have been basic principles of the Eisenhower Administration. It is no accident that this preference for enhancing the governmental power of the states and localities at the expense of the national government coincides with the finding that the closer the points for government decision are to local communities, the better business leaders like it.

CONGRESS, AN ADJUSTER OF INTERESTS. In performing its legislative role, Congress is essentially an adjuster of interests.[11]

Congress is expected to legislate in the general interest. But it has no way of determining the general interest except in its day-to-day action on legislative and appropriation bills. Congress also expresses its understanding of the general interest by the use it makes of its investigative authority, and with respect to the Senate, of its authority to confirm presidential nominations. Consequently, it must deal either positively or by default with the proposals which are pressed upon it. At one time, it will respond to those who spend the most money in support of a bill; at another, to those who make the loudest noise; at still another, to those to whom the majority party is in political debt. Sometimes, members of Congress themselves take part in the struggle of contending groups, a role in which they depart from that of representatives of the people of their states and districts to act as representatives of occupational groups. Avocational and social, as well as occupational groups, also gain representation at times in Congress in the persons of Representatives and Senators elected on a geographical basis. Almost always, congressional politics is pressure politics, with Congress the arena of opposing interests, and policy merely the resultant of the forces of the competing groups. Always, Congress and its membership are acting in response to the dictates of the doctrine of individual rights and liberties, deciding as best they can between the demands of those emphasizing different but equally important liberties. Obviously, there is bound to be, in varying degrees, bargaining and log-rolling, or trading of votes.

More often than not, policy stems from the attempts of a group or groups constituting less than a majority of the population to write the rules by which the American people are governed. Congress rarely, if ever, acts as a collectivity. It acts through legislative majorities laboriously put together for a few moments of voting, which then dissolve, only to be brought together later, but in different proportions, for other votes.

The use of propaganda by groups should never be forgotten. Sometimes it appears that policy is what the loudest group wants it to be. Nor should the reverse be forgotten, either; namely, that propaganda by one group or groups may afford others which are operating more quietly the opportunity to get their bills validated by Congress. Diversionary tactics are of the essence of politics, and it is not an unknown practice for propaganda to be set in motion by a group for one of its objectives as a tactic to cover the pressure campaign for another.

Whatever the nature of the activity in which Congress engages, sooner or later it usually takes the form of law. Law is the statement of legislative policy in modern form, and in law is found "the most perfect expression of political power, since, by and large, it makes possible the most precise and practical guidance of political activity; or, in other words, the least fallible weighing and balancing of the behavior which constitutes political power. . . ."[12]

Congress like a diplomatic conference. Thus, as a policy-making body, Congress acts as an adjuster of interests, promoting the general interest (or the general welfare, as the Constitution terms it), not so much in each individual piece of legislation as in the aggregate of its output over the years. No longer are its members representatives of their districts and states in the classical sense. Today, they act as representatives of interests in their constituencies.[13] In a sense they are like delegates to a diplomatic conference (although the analogy breaks down in other respects), acting for the section of society delimited by districts or states composing a geographical region or section. As such, they engage in many of the usual activities of diplomatic delegations, laying and executing campaigns, seeking allies from among neutrals, cementing relations with firm allies, trying to split the opposition, employing all the stratagems and devices customarily employed by diplomats on the wider international stage, including propaganda and psychological warfare.

A modern discovery of cultural anthropology is the relativity of cultures. It is suggestive in this connection. The main contribution of the study of anthropology in the last fifty years is "the awareness of relativity among cultures," an attitude of mind which holds that "cultures—each of which contains a value system—need not be viewed as rallying points for rival emotional loyalties but can be studied as natural phenomena by methods of natural science."[14] It is not necessary to accept the latter notion in order to benefit from the insight of the former. Even though a nation, the United States can still be considered as a congeries of cultures (sections, regions) each with a more or less distinct value system, yet with certain common elements. In the Congress of the United States, the delegations representing these cultures come together periodically to parley and, from time to time, to make treaties declaring policy in the form of laws. Sir Wilmott Lewis, for many years Washington correspondent of *The Times* (London), described the conduct and output of Congress in this way to the author in a conversation in 1939.[15] It is significant that this interpretation coincides with the main contribution developed recently by students of societies as cultures and value systems.

Repeal of the federal tax on margarine. The history of federal legislation regulating manufacture and sale of margarine began between 1860 and 1870 with the discovery by Mege-Mouries that it was possible to substitute cheaper fats for butterfat in making butter. The initial legislation was based upon the general desire to prevent fraud in the sale of margarine and upon the desire of the increasingly strong dairy interests to prevent competition from this new product. The first laws were passed in the states and were either aimed at regulating or prohibiting the sale of margarine. The judiciary also took a role when the courts upheld the constitutionality of prohibitory state laws in 1888. In 1886, the first federal legislation was passed. This law aimed at regulation of the sale of margarine by imposing a tax on manufacturers, wholesalers, and retailers in the form of license fees, and a tax of two cents per pound on all margarine sold. One result of this law was the consolidation of the margarine industry; this, in turn, enabled manufacturers to spend more time and money on the improvement of their product.[16]

The dairy interests thus found that the 1886 law did not destroy the margarine industry as they had hoped it would, and various amendments to the law were soon introduced. These attempts culminated in the passage of the Grout Amendment in 1901. This new legislation introduced a new factor into anti-margarine legislation because it was based on a discriminatory tax on colored margarine. The question as to what constituted artificial coloring was debated until 1931. At first the decision rested with the Commissioner of Internal Revenue as the administrator of the tax. As a result of his decision, upheld by the Supreme Court, that margarine was artificially colored if the amount of coloring agent present was of such small quantity that it could only act as a coloring agent, the margarine manufacturers were successful in developing naturally, rather than artificially, colored margarine.

In 1930, the issue of colored margarine came to a head when the Commissioner of Internal Revenue reversed his original position against the use of palm oil as a coloring agent. The resulting sudden increase in yellow margarine on the market and the new competition to butter stirred the dairy interests to high wrath, and there was a new push to enact laws restricting all margarine sales. The issue of artificial coloring was partly resolved by the Brigham-Townsend Act, in 1931, which subjected all yellow margarine, whether artificially or naturally colored, to a ten cents per pound manufacturing tax. Federal margarine legislation remained unaltered until the final change in 1950.

In the meantime, there were several changes in the complex of interests and pressures which was concerned with margarine legislation. Both World Wars caused a shortage of real butter on the consumer market; thus the general public became better acquainted with margarine and formed definite opinions as to its acceptability and use for home consumption. In general, the public reacted favorably, and margarine was recognized as a useful and necessary substitute for butter.

Second, the margarine producers were successful in perfecting processes for utilizing domestic cottonseed oil in their production methods. This meant that the butter lobbyists could no longer use one of their most powerful arguments against the synthetic product: their demand for protection against a product using foreign imported oils.

A third development involved the interests of the various states in Congress. The nonbutter-producing states began to resent the severe regulation on margarine imposed by the powerful bloc of dairy states, and this antipathy was increased as the southern cottonseed-producing states realized their own stake in the production of margarine.

However, no further national legislation was enacted until after the second World War. By that time there had been a sufficient change in the feelings of the various pressure groups concerned with margarine, so that the stage was laid for a change in national policy.

In 1943, Representative Hampton Fulmer, of South Carolina, introduced a pro-margarine bill, which received more vocal support than most of its immediate predecessors, even though it was pigeonholed by the House Committee on Agriculture. Perhaps partly as a result of the unexpected support given to this bill, the dairy interests consolidated their strength, and the Dairy Defense Association was incorporated in the State of Illinois. Most of the major dairy organizations, including the American Butter Institute, the National Creameries Association, the National Dairy Union, the National Co-operative Milk Producers' Federation (the most conspicuously active group throughout this period), the American Dairy Association, the Dairy Industries Committee, and the United Dairy Committee, participated in the work of the Dairy Defense Association. This pressure group sponsored an educational campaign to inform the public of the merits of butter and butter substitutes by such means as surveys of the relative nutritional value of butter and other fats.

On the other side of the issue, the National Association of Margarine Manufacturers, in 1944, launched a $100,000 national advertising campaign aimed at increasing public acceptance of their product. The members of this association accounted for 85 per cent of the national margarine production. The campaign was well timed to take advantage of the wartime shortage of butter, which had forced many consumers to resort to margarine.

On the legislative front, the immediate objective of the dairy industry lobby was the defeat of a rider attached to the Senate tax bill, known as the Maybank Bill, which would have repealed certain taxes on colored margarine for the duration of the war and for six months afterward. This took on a special significance since it involved the internal pressures of the legislature itself. As a rider to a tax bill, it would go before the Senate Finance Committee, and then to the House Ways and Means Committee, both of which were more friendly to changes in margarine legislation than the two Agriculture Committees. It would also have placed the control of margarine in the Food and Drug Administration, rather than the Bureau of Internal Revenue, and would thus have restricted margarine control to products moving in interstate commerce.

The complex of pressures within the legislature was also changed when the American Soybean Association, in 1946, openly backed legislation aimed at drastic revision of the margarine law. The significance of its support lies in the fact that the soybean farmers are concentrated in the same mid-western states as the dairy farmers. Now the dairy interests were no longer able to keep the total force of the pressure on their Congressmen directed against revision of margarine legislation.

The legislative activity which directly led to the 1950 amendment to the 1886 margarine law began in 1948. In that year, Representative Mendel Rivers, of South Carolina, reintroduced his bill which had died in committee in the previous session of Congress. In spite of many maneuvers to keep the bill in committee, or to refer it to hostile committees, the over-all Senate sentiment was strong enough to invoke unusual parliamentary procedures to keep the bill alive. On June 1, 1948, the Committee on Finance reported the bill unanimously with only minor amendments. Further action was postponed until the next session because of the pressure of Senate business and the approaching presidential nominating conventions.

The 1948 congressional action was followed in 1949 by similar bitterly fought battles over the margarine tax. During the first session of Congress, forty-seven bills for the removal of the tax were introduced in the House alone. The bill which finally emerged from committee provided for removing the taxes but prohibited the manufacture and/or sale of yellow margarine. However, this bill was drastically amended on the floor of the House, so that the final law not only repealed all federal taxes on margarine but included provisions that placed colored margarine under the federal pure food and drug laws (whether produced for interstate or intrastate commerce), prohibited the serving of colored margarine in public eating places unless a prominent notice is displayed that margarine is being served or the margarine is served in triangular-shaped pats, and declared that the federal government will not "abrogate or nullify" any state law concerning margarine. This bill was passed by the House on April 1, 1949, by a vote of 287 to 89.

In the Senate the most violent opposition arose to the repeal of the margarine tax. However, a Senate bill was approved by the Finance Committee in April. But again the agenda was so full that it was shelved until the second session, in 1950. When the debate opened again, the final move by the opponents of tax repeal was to try to attach a civil rights rider to the bill, in the attempt to alienate the support of the southern states from the bill. This and other delaying amendments were all defeated, and on January 18, 1950, the Senate adopted the bill by a vote of 56 to 16. The bill successfully passed through the conference committee, and on March 7 and 8, respectively, the House and the Senate accepted the final draft. President Truman signed the bill, and the discriminatory tax that had been levied on oleomargarine and margarine for sixty-four years was repealed.

Generalizations from the federal margarine tax repeal study. The case study of the repeal of the federal tax on margarine points up numerous generalizations, which may be stated as follows:

1. Policy is expressed in law, in administrative determinations, in judicial decisions.
2. Policy is changed by changing or repealing law, altering administrative and judicial decisions.
3. Policy is rarely, if ever, fixed and unchangeable; it changes over the years, sometimes being completely reversed.
4. Invention and discovery generate new economic and political pressures which seek changes in policy.
5. In the American system of government, policy-making is an extraordinarily complicated process.
6. Congressional procedures are more easily used to maintain existing policy than to change it.

TAXES AND APPROPRIATIONS IN THE ADJUSTMENT OF INTERESTS. In supplying the government's money needs and raising revenue, Congress is handicapped by a system which lacks balance, uniformity, and equity.

Congress has not disciplined itself to the extent necessary to bring expenditure and income into balance. Although the executive budget submitted by the President estimates both income and expenditure, although he proposes congressional action necessary to raise the revenue needed to meet expenses, still, Congress has failed to display its collective willingness to bring the two sides of the federal budget into balance. Lack of legislation cannot be offered as a reason. In 1946, Congress enacted the Employment Act and the Legislative Reorganization Act. The former provides for a Council of Economic Advisers to the President, an annual economic report from the President to Congress, and a joint Senate-House committee on the economic report. Among other things, the Reorganization Act provides for the preparation by Congress of a legislative budget, appropriations in a single money bill, and a self-denying ordinance against appropriation of funds in excess of expected revenues. The experience of working under this reasonable but novel regime was more than Congress could endure. After a brief experience (1947-1949), in which appropriations procedure was greatly speeded up, and in which both Congress and the country were able to get an overview of all appropriations and all revenue, the membership of the House Appropriations Committee rebelled against its leadership, and Congress returned to the old piecemeal method of making appropriations. And it has never since attempted to live up to its self-imposed requirements.

Failure of the new system was attributed by the Chairman of the House Appropriations Committee in part to outside pressure. The importunities to which executive bureaus, the Bureau of the Budget, and the President himself are subjected have already been discussed. The alliances formed among the same bureaus, outside groups, and congressional committees have also been treated.[17] Congress is under similar pressure in making appropriations. Congressman Cannon (D., Mo.) has said: "Every predatory lobbyist, every pressure group seeking to get its hands into the United States Treasury, every bureaucrat seeking to extend his empire downtown, is opposed to the consolidated bill." He also put his finger on a basic dilemma of the American political system when he warned the House that "one weakness of our form of government is that members of Congress are political beneficiaries of federal largess distributed in their districts and their states. The more money we can vote out of the Treasury and into our respective bailiwicks, the more votes we may expect at the next election."[18]

Congress and tax pressure groups. The concentration on narrow and bureaucratic interests, which Congressman Cannon bemoaned regarding appropriations, applies also to revenue policy. Federal taxes are levied on everyone; four-fifths of the total revenue is derived from taxes on income. In the framing and administration of the revenue laws, tax pressure groups are active in all stages. Examples of such activity in administrative lobbying are offered in the next chapter. The present chapter deals with several aspects of legislative lobbying activities.

Tax pressure groups lobby incessantly. No pressure groups in the country are more adept at influencing policy-makers. Probably the most effective way by which taxpayers and taxpayers' groups press their views on Congress is through personal interviews.[19] They also present testimony at hearings of the House Ways and Means and Senate Finance Committees.

Tax pressure groups attempt to influence Congress indirectly through propaganda. Such propaganda attempts to render public opinion acquiescent, or at least, unopposed, and aims at influencing the opinion of the effective publics favorably. The targets and the techniques are not general; they are specific and selective. The targets are the members of Congress who are in a position, because of their key roles, to determine decisions and the small but powerful sections of the community who make the opinions of special interests appear to be public opinion. Like the hydraulic press, which concentrates great pressure on a small area, the representatives of tax pressure groups who contact Congressmen, testify before congressional committees, and otherwise propagandize, try to keep the attention of Congressmen concentrated on certain programs and certain proposals: "The purpose of the lobbyists is to see that the attention of the policy-maker remains focused on the 'right' facts and emotions."[20]

Tax pressure groups sometimes propose complete tax programs. Far more frequently they offer technical proposals for specific taxes or revision of specific taxes. In making tax policy, congressional decision-makers always have to decide between alternatives: Shall taxes be progressive or regressive? Shall they be uniform or selective, that is, discriminatory? Shall they be direct or indirect? In supplying policy answers, Congress is most influenced by tax proposals of a technical nature. Members appear to be less likely to think for themselves on such proposals than on rate and exemption questions. Technical proposals are not well understood even by congressional committees and command little public attention, possibly because they usually apply to only a small minority of taxpayers.

The legislative and propaganda activities of tax pressure groups are heavily weighted in favor of business and producer interests.

This emphasis is shown by an analysis of the transcripts of the 1942, 1947, and 1951 hearings before the House Ways and Means Committee. For example, in 1947, all but 12 of the 150 groups appearing represented business, labor, agricultural, or professional interests; 94 groups represented business interests, as compared with 28 for agricultural organizations, 8 for professional associations and 5 for labor.[21]

In the congressional stage of tax policy-making, it is not Congress as a whole which has the effective power of decision but a few strong members of the House Ways and Means Committee and the Senate Finance Committee. While these key members sometimes propose measures themselves, more often they consider proposals originating outside Congress, principally those of the tax pressure groups. The role of Congress is one of developing, modifying, and choosing from among proposals made by others rather than one of originating its own proposals.[22] In making decisions, the attention of key members and others on the two revenue committees are focused on the "right" things by lobbyists of the tax pressure groups. Moreover, public officials apparently make little effort to evaluate the claims of these lobbyists to group representation but, instead, simply note the arguments put forward and base decisions on their own summations, predilections, and estimates of political consequences.[23] The key members of Congress must attract voting majorities in the subcommittees, the full committees, and in the two houses themselves. In this process occur the bargaining, the compromises, the exchanges, which constitute the politics of tax policy-making.

In the complex process of tax policy-making, the executive branch, particularly the Treasury Department, plays a role which depends on the economic philosophy of the President and his Secretary of the Treasury, of other executive officials, and of the party leaders in key positions in and out of Congress. Receipts from taxes are always a preoccupation of the Treasury, particularly in an era of large federal spending for security. Officials take positions for or against proposals of tax pressure groups according to the need for revenue and the principles of taxation adhered to by the administration in power. Moreover, Treasury officials themselves make proposals to the congressional committees which, like those of tax pressure groups and individuals, are always framed in terms of the broadest interest of the nation as a whole. Administrations differ, of course, on how this interest is to be understood and promoted.

The Treasury made vigorous efforts during the Truman Administration, for example, to eliminate from the tax laws the provision, contained in every revenue act since 1926, whereby certain of the extractive industries, especially the oil industry, are permitted to deduct for tax purposes 27.5 per cent of the gross income from production as a depletion allowance. Not only was the most recent attempt, in 1951, unsuccessful, but also the provision was extended to additional extractive industries—sand and gravel, oyster shell, etc. Opposition to elimination or reduction of this provision was strong enough to prevent Congress from accepting it, and thus congressional policy on this important issue of uniformity or discrimination was made (See Table 2, p. 80).

The results of making tax policy in this way are mixed. While the tax system produces large revenue, is largely self-executing, and is based on modern principles of taxation, at the same time Congress has yielded to outside interests. By making numerous exceptions for the benefit of particular individuals, classes, or groups, especially in the income, profit, estate, and gift tax laws, Congress has departed widely from the principle of taxation according to ability to pay. Many of these exceptions can be traced to the lobbying of tax pressure groups. Not only is there the lack of coordination between tax policy and expenditure policy, noted in the preceding section, but there is also a "quality resembling schizophrenia" in the fact that very high personal and corporate income tax rates are accompanied by numerous relief measures. There is insufficient concern for the overall pattern of the tax system.[24] In addition, the laws governing imports from foreign countries contain exceptions and special provisions which have been inserted at the instance of particular producer groups. (See Table 4.) One expert described the income tax law as being "so honeycombed with the results of pressure politics that it is becoming a symbol of hypocrisy."[25] The conclusion of a former official of the research division of the Treasury Department is less critical but hardly less enlightening: ". . . Group pressures for tax proposals do have a profound influence on the development of tax policy. . . . The lobbyists for interest groups deserve the credit or the blame for many deficiencies in the tax laws."[26]

Congress and labor-management relations. In the policy field of labor-management relations, legislative policy since 1947 has reflected the proposals of the National Association of Manufacturers. The NAM may not have written the bill which became the Labor-Management Relations (Taft-Hartley) Act, as was charged by Congressmen and by the CIO and AFL, but "there is a startling similarity between the numerous NAM labor proposals since 1947 and the final version of the Taft-Hartley Act." The passage of the law "was a victory for the NAM."[27]

TABLE 4

CORRELATION OF LOBBYING, LOBBYING EXPENSES, AND LEGISLATIVE ACTION
82ND CONGRESS, 1ST SESSION

Subject	Lobbying Organizations	Reported Expenditure January–June 1951*	Legislative Action
Reciprocal Trade Agreement Act	FOR (Without "peril point")		Passed with
	U.S. Chamber of Commerce	$ 64,450.17	"Peril point"
	Congress of Industrial Organizations		restriction
	American Farm Bureau Federation	415,812.96	
		(All purposes)	
	U.S. Cuban Sugar Council		
	Cooperative League of U.S.A.		
	AGAINST (Except with "peril point"		
	retained and/or escape clause)		
	National Labor-Management Council		
	on Foreign Trade Policy		
	American Tariff League		
	National Coal Association		
	American Cotton Shippers Association		
	National Association of		
	Wool Manufacturers		
	National Renderers' Association		
	Bicycle Institute of America		
	National Milk Producers		
	Federation	91,187.93	
		(All purposes)	
	Independent Petroleum Association		
	of America		
	National Council of		
	Farmers Cooperatives	64,309.51	
	Wine Institute		
	American Knit Handwear Association		
	American National		
	Cattlemen's Association		
	National Council of American Importers		

* Expenditures are listed only for those groups which ranked among the twenty-one top-spending lobbying groups in the U.S.

Farm production policy. Federal farm policy is made in a situation no less complicated and no less political than tax and labor-management relations policy. In fact, there is more politics in farm policy. America's rural population, farm and nonfarm, is overrepresented in both houses of the Congress, particularly in the Senate. In addition, in recent years rural farm population and farm income have been decreasing relative to total national income, while farm efficiency has been increasing. Moreover, the farmer's share of the consumer's food dollar has been shrinking, while distribution costs have increased. In the congressional phase of farm production policy, the family farm is both symbol and myth; symbol of the goal to be re-captured, myth expressing the determination of economically under-represented producers and their organizational and congressional counterparts to act to redress grievances. Farm measures before Congress in 1954 attracted the attention of no less than 148 lobbyists.[28] The action and interaction of these multiple forces are the stuff from which one observer draws the conclusion that "the configuration of political power and influence which dominates agriculture (is) unhealthy from the standpoint of wise public policy and administration . . ."[29]

Commissions as a device for pre-congressional compromise. A device for working out compromises in advance of congressional policy-making is the group set up temporarily to concentrate upon a particular segment or segments of public policy. Such groups vary in size, in composition, in method of appointment, and in scope of authority. They may be described as an advisory group, a committee, a commission, or as a conference. Regardless of name, they are established to recommend new policy or suggest changes in existing policy after they have hammered out compromises both in fundamentals and in details.

A conference on primary and secondary education brought two thousand delegates to Washington in late 1955. President Eisenhower has used Cabinet committees to recommend policy on highways and transportation, and his Attorney General, Herbert Brownell, established a committee to study the enforcement of the anti-trust laws. In 1937, President Franklin D. Roosevelt's Committee on Administrative Management studied organization and procedures of the federal government with a view to increasing efficiency. Somewhat larger but still committees, not conferences, were President Harry S. Truman's Committee on Immigration and Committee on Civil Rights. Intergovernmental (federal-state) relations and economic foreign policy were the subjects for study and recommendations by other committees established by President Eisenhower. Both of the latter, as well as the education conference in 1955, were held under congressional authorization, with members appointed by the President, the Vice-President, and the Speaker of the House. The two Hoover Commissions, both headed by former President Herbert Hoover, are additional examples: the first, in 1951, to study and make recommendations to increase governmental efficiency; the second, established by the Eighty-third Congress, to scrutinize federal governmental programs as well.

The purpose of such groups involves more than ironing out differences among their members. Advisory groups, of whatever size and authority, are also responsible for educating their members about opposing attitudes. They are set up to educate the populace generally. They have propaganda value as well. Also, on occasion, they are set up to temporize, in the hope that words will dissipate pressures which otherwise would require action politically inopportune or unpalatable.

All these purposes are essentially political in nature. Hence the device of the advisory group, committee, or commission takes its place in a graduated scale of political influence in policy-making. At one extreme are the pressure groups, at the other, appointment of officials of such groups to full-time government posts. Appointment to a temporary advisory committee or to posts in government "without compensation" occupy intermediate positions in the scale. Like the Cabinet, the "little cabinet," and other policy-making posts, they are cut from the same pattern—to influence the formation of policy.

The President in legislative policy-making. Although the place of the President in policy-making has already been discussed in Chapter 11, the presidential office requires mention here as well.

As policy-maker, the President performs a dual role, sharing legislative authority with the Congress, while possessing the constitutional authority as Chief Executive to make policy in his own right. If he would really make policy by legislation, the President must be a politician. He must be able to lead or carry his own party with him and get enough support from the other to make national policy. When the President is unable to carry his own party with him, he must rely even more on the other party, if party government is to be realized. But in practice this theory breaks down as often as it works. Then another kind or theory of policy-making emerges. Policy is made from among a variety of proposals submitted not only by the President but also by outside groups, acting on their own behalf, or, frequently, at the behest of some executive bureau, or by Congressmen acting individually on their own initiative or in response to outside stimulus or pressure.

These two methods of policy-making will be recognized as but other forms of the differing ideals of government held by observers already cited: the one is party government, in the responsible sense used by Schattschneider; the other, pressure group government, in the critical yet acceptable sense understood and defended by such experts as Griffith, Galloway, Herring, and Gross. The advocates of responsible party government imply, if they do not make it explicit, that the President (as the party chief) and his administration should monopolize legislative proposals, basing them, as the British Cabinet does, on the party platform adopted in convention, and redeem the pledges made to the electorate during the last campaign. Although many, including the four just cited, would share this ideal of greater program unity accompanied by the greater party unity, cohesion, discipline, and executive leadership which it would entail, the choice for them is not seen so clearly as one between black and white. The existing situation is not so bad that procedural improvements in Congress cannot remedy it. But for Schattschneider nothing short of party reform for responsible government will do. Gross puts it in terms of legislative program when he says: "It is entirely legitimate for all contestants in the legislative process to have their own sets of legislative proposals, and there is nothing inherently desirable or at all practical in the idea that any given set of contestants be given a monopoly of the initiation of legislative proposals."[30] As this passage shows, the choice is not between responsible party and irresponsible pressure group government but between different systems of government—responsible cabinet government in the British sense, or presidential-congressional government in the American sense. The point will be further clarified in the several case studies which follow.

POLICY-MAKING BY DEFAULT. Congress makes policy in a negative sense, too. When it denies its approval to proposals for legislative action, policy is being made in a way equally significant as when it grants such approval. In this way, Congress "made" policy when congressional approval was withheld on proposals for multiple-purpose control and development of the Missouri River Basin (MVA).[31]

The proposed Missouri Valley Authority. A disastrous flood in the lower Missouri River Basin in 1951 raised anew the demand for a new approach to the problem of development of the valley and control of the river. The proposal for the creation of a Missouri Valley Authority in 1944 had provided the necessary impetus for a much-needed study of the Missouri Basin, its land, and its people. It also served to bring into focus some of the valley's major problems. The valley's history is one of alternating floods and droughts; the problem is too much water in the lower basin and too little in the upper. This water problem seems to be caused basically by the type of agricultural production pursued. The Missouri Basin has been gradually falling behind the rest of the United States in economic progress. Although considerable action has been taken by federal, state, and private agencies to solve the problems of the valley, the inadequacy of these plans is evident from the continuing waste of fertile soil, the frequent floods, and the lack of adequate development of the valley's natural resources. The Bureau of Reclamation has undertaken irrigation work, flood control has been carried out by the Army Engineers and private individuals, and some electric power has been developed. But the programs carried on by these groups have remained ineffectual because of the lack of coordination at the top levels. Until 1944, there was no concrete move toward coordination, because each agency had a special view of the river and the valley; each saw the developments for which it was responsible as all important, and hence resisted moves to coordinate and equalize the various projects.

But a different approach was presented when, in 1944, a Missouri Valley Authority bill was introduced by Senator James E. Murray, of Montana. This bill immediately received the support of President Roosevelt, but it was not backed by the governors of the states involved, or by the various government agencies already working in the valley. This latter group came forward with a plan of its own, the Pick–Sloan Compromise Plan. In order to obtain a more comprehensive view of the problems of the region and to consolidate the plans of all the interested parties, the Missouri Basin Interagency Committee was formed in 1945. But there was a strong feeling that these separate plans were still inadequate. The (First) Hoover Commission Task Force on Natural Resources published a report stating that it was quite evident that the only kind of agency that could manage the development of the Missouri Valley with the proper emphasis on all the issues involved would be an altogether new agency which would have no interests other than that of the development of the Missouri Valley.

The advocates of a Missouri Valley Authority claim that MVA is such an agency. They maintain that the essential difference between MVA and the existing Interagency Commission is one of administration or management. Under MVA there would be a single, unified management, whereas the Interagency Commission is a voluntary confederation of independent departments in the government having separate and often conflicting responsibilities. Under MVA there would be an independent administration within the valley with technical advisors on the spot. The first MVA bill, S. 555, was introduced in 1944, and a somewhat revised version has appeared each year since that date. The debates in Congress have largely centered about the forces for and against MVA.

Two powerful lobby groups developed in opposition to MVA. One, the power lobby, was represented by the National Association of Electric Companies, and was formed to oppose MVA and similar river valley proposals. The effectiveness of this group was emphasized by the fact that most of the powerful newspapers in the valley were admittedly controlled by the power companies. These companies were responsible for all the advertising against MVA. This resulted not only in a negative influence on public opinion in the very area for which MVA was proposed, but it also meant that considerable influence was exercised upon the various state legislatures, and hence upon official attitudes toward MVA.

The second powerful pressure against MVA came from the government agencies who have their own interests to protect and from those private individuals who stood to lose if a particular agency lost its control in the area. Like Senator Overton, of Louisiana, and others in the southern end of the valley, they were interested mainly in flood control and hence in protecting the program of the Army Engineers. Each of these various federal agencies also came forward to attack the MVA bill in one way or another. The Army Engineers said No in no uncertain terms. Secretary of the Interior Ickes was less direct. He stated that he favored valley authorities—many of them—but not S. 555. He proposed a bill of his own, thus helping to kill S. 555.

As it turned out, S. 555 was doomed to failure from the day it was introduced. Various moves on the floor resulted in the bill's being referred to three different committees, each of which contained factions hostile to any change in the existing system. Two committees reported unfavorably, and the third simply voted not to hold hearings. This proved to be the high point for MVA bills, for those which followed never achieved as much publicity, nor such consideration. It is significant that most of the sponsors of these various bills were Senators from states outside the Missouri Valley. The lack of popularity of the MVA in the region was notable in 1948, when, according to Governor Peterson, not a single Congressman in the basin endorsed it in his campaign.

A further factor contributing to the failure of a Missouri Valley Authority was a lack of public understanding of the issues involved. Much of the confusion, uncertainty, and contradiction of public opinion could have been dispelled by information. A poll taken in the valley itself revealed that 75 per cent of popular opinion was uninformed and disinterested in how development of the basin should be carried out. Part of this can be attributed to the strong hold which the power companies exert on the press in this region.

The pressures against MVA present a fairly close knit front which has so far successfully prevented progress in the direction of a unified approach to valley development. The interested federal agencies are each well represented on the outside by a particular lobby group. The National Reclamation Association speaks for the Reclamation Bureau, while the Army Engineers are represented by the Mississippi Valley Association, the National Rivers and Harbors Congress, and by the committees of the House and the Senate dealing with navigation and flood control. The Army's policy of not antagonizing the power companies range them on its side. Finally, hundreds of political subdivisions have interests which they believe are best advanced by the big lobbies.

The pressure group which comes closest to presenting a centralized front against MVA, while supporting the Interagency Commission, is the Missouri Valley Development Association, which is supported by contractors, farmers, ranchers, chambers of commerce, and other business, industrial, and financial interests of the region. The valley contractors have provided the largest source of funds for the Association, since they depend a great deal on Army contracts in the area. In addition to the above pressure groups there are the state administrations of most, if not all, of the basin states. Some, though they do not support Interagency, are definitely against MVA.

The common bond of all these groups, and that which is their strongest weapon, is that for one reason or another they all favor the status quo. The proponents of MVA have not as yet been able to muster enough concerted support and pressure to buck this line. Organized support for MVA was first concentrated in the Regional Committee for the Missouri Valley Authority, a once lively pressure group in the mid-1940's which has now become defunct. Its main backing came from the National Farmers' Union, the CIO, and the AFL. Support has also come from both Presidents Roosevelt and Truman. However, there seems to be a nonpartisan split over MVA, and the conservatives of both parties oppose it.

The proposal for a Missouri Valley Authority in 1944 did provide the necessary impetus for a study of the Missouri Basin, its land and its people. Though this has brought into focus some of the valley's main problems, there was, and still is, a basic disagreement over the relative importance of these problems and, above all, the way any aid should be administered. Fundamentally, there was resistance to any further over-all federal intervention in the problems of the Missouri Valley. As a result, no action has been taken. In spite of Senator Murray's repeated efforts to bring about a uniform plan for the development and control of the Missouri River Basin, until those in favor of MVA can muster effective support, public policy will continue to refute the need for a Missouri Valley Authority.

Generalizations from the case study of the MVA. From the case study of the proposed Missouri Valley Authority three generalizations may be drawn.

1. In a natural area like a river basin where vested interests are strong, traditional methods of dealing with natural catastrophes offer greater inertia and resistance to change than can be overcome by even vigorous executive leadership of the forces of change.
2. As formulators of public issues and as vehicles for program-making, political parties leave much to be desired when dealing with natural resources.
3. Mutually beneficial relations among federal bureaus, congressional committees, and outside pressure groups prove stronger in making policy by default than Congress as the law-making and policy-making body.

The sixth generalization drawn from the study of federal margarine tax repeal (see page 228) may also be drawn from the MVA study.

The issue of national health insurance.[32] The national health problem of the United States is basically one of not enough medical care because of high costs and insufficient facilities. There has been a growing awareness of the need for large-scale handling of the health problem. Some form of national health insurance is regarded as a possible solution to this problem. But with regard to national policy, the issue revolves around the question whether the United States needs major federal health legislation or whether the emphasis should be on the voluntary initiative of private groups.

The movement for national health insurance started about 1911, when the American Association for Labor Legislation began calling attention to the problem of medical care insurance. At first, emphasis was placed on the need for state legislation. The initial plans called for local administration, with funds jointly managed by employers and employees under public, not governmental, supervision. Above all, the plans were to be compulsory. The American Medical Association, later to emerge as the strongest force against national health insurance, took its initial stand at this time against any form of compulsory insurance plan administered by state or federal government.

By 1920 most of the support for compulsory health insurance legislation had died out, and during the twenty years after the first World War, the public expressed little real interest in the problem. But, beginning in the 1930's, the federal government became instrumental in initiating interest in compulsory medical insurance. The development was greatly influenced by the Depression of the 1930's and increased acceptance of the New Deal concept of federal responsibility for the general welfare. At first, there was little support for actual legislation in the field of health. In fact, the issue so endangered the Social Security Program in 1936 that it was dropped from the bill. The issue thus remained at the discussion level. It did, however, lead to a National Health Conference, held in Washington in July, 1938, to clarify the issues and stimulate constructive criticism. No specific recommendations emerged from the Conference, but it served to make compulsory medical care insurance a national issue in the sense that a large number and variety of groups became aware of the problem and took stands on the issue.

In 1939, the Wagner National Health Bill was introduced in Congress, the first bill actually to propose a comprehensive national health program. Although there was no provision for compulsory health insurance, it proposed federal grants-in-aid to states, and its coverage was much broader than all earlier proposals. It was regarded by the opposition as an extension of the authority of the federal government in the field of health and as the initial step toward compulsory health insurance. In 1943 and 1945, this and two subsequent bills died in committee. Throughout this period there was violent protest from the AMA, while the CIO and the AFL gave strong support.

In his State of the Union Message, in 1948, President Truman intensified the fight by supporting the principle of a comprehensive insurance system to protect everyone against insecurity and ill health. In his budget message a few days later, the President asked for $571 million to carry out a new welfare program, with $15 million budgeted for national health administration expenses for the next fiscal year, and for taxes amounting to $350 million for added health and social insurance. The administration subsequently gave support to the Murray–Wagner–Pepper Bill which would have established a system of insurance financed by wage and payroll deduction under an extension of the Social Security system. A substitute bill by Senator Taft would have authorized federal grants to help states provide medical services, but only for the medically indigent. This bill was supported by the AMA, thus revealing its growing awareness of the extent of the problem of medical costs and its desire to seek a solution on the basis of a prepaid system. The AMA was at this time primarily in favor of community-sponsored plans for prepaying hospital and doctor bills.

Contemporary public opinion was not behind compulsory health insurance. There was a general fear that a high degree of governmental regulation over the personnel and agencies engaged in providing medical care would discourage initiative and development. The issue was sharpened by the report issued by a National Health Assembly, composed of eight hundred representatives of public and private agencies concerned with health. Their report, *The Nation's Health—A Ten-Year Plan,* issued by Oscar Ewing, Federal Security

Administrator, strongly requested a system of national compulsory health insurance. There was considerable reaction to this report from all sides.

The Health Assembly plan was adopted by President Truman in his 1949 State of the Union Message. The administration bill proposed that a National Health Insurance Board be established within the Federal Security Administration to allocate funds to the states on the basis of estimates of their needs in order to extend complete medical, dental, hospital, and nursing care to everyone except the destitute, who would remain charity cases. The plan was to be financed by a payroll tax of 3 per cent on salaries or net income, half the tax to be contributed by employers and half by employees. Both patients and doctors would be free to join the plan as they wished.

Two other bills were introduced at the same time. One was based on the principle of state responsibility in the field of health and called for federal grants-in-aid only to relieve clear deficiencies of health care. The second emphasized the principle of voluntary prepayment, with federal aid to be granted only when it could be proved that the cost of voluntary insurance could not be met. The political battle was waged over these three bills and the divergent public philosophies behind them. The bills themselves did not emerge from committee in 1949.

Various organizations and unofficial groups vigorously supported the campaign for compulsory insurance. One was the Committee for the Nation's Health, organized by Albert D. Lasker, co-founder of the Albert and Mary Lasker Foundation to promote medical research and administration, and Michael M. Davis, Chairman of the Committee on Research in Medical Economics. This Committee lobbied in Washington directly with Congressmen. It also propagandized by issuing quantities of literature to interested groups and by answering arguments against compulsory insurance. It also worked through membership pressure groups such as those representing labor's interests, which, in turn, influenced Congress.

Another effort supporting compulsory health insurance was the Health Workshop Program. It planned conferences in several states and was influential with leaders of farm and labor organizations, women's clubs, and church groups. This program was supported by administration officials and was part of the considerable activity within government agencies to pressure Congress to pass the compulsory health insurance bill. A legislative campaign was organized within the government. Much of this activity was brought to light by the House Subcommittee on Publicity and Propaganda in the Executive Departments, which termed it a violation of the law forbidding federal employees to use federal funds to influence legislation.

Labor groups also applied pressure on Congress for the administration bill. In recent years labor has given hospital and medical care insurance a priority in collective bargaining second only to retirement income security programs. However, labor does not advocate socialized medicine with government ownership of facilities, and doctors on the government payroll. Other groups leading in support of the administration bill were the American Association of Social Workers, the ADA, the National Farmers Union, the Brotherhood of Railroad Trainmen, and the International Association of Machinists.

The opposition to the administration insurance scheme was spearheaded by the AMA. The conservative stand of the AMA toward health insurance can be attributed largely to Dr. Morris Fishbein, associated with the AMA for thirty-seven years, and for twenty-five years editor of the *Journal of the AMA*. In this position he was the virtual spokesman for the organization, in addition to being a prolific writer of books, periodical articles, columns, pamphlets, and speeches. Before 1949 the AMA could not get a reasonable hearing for its position against the government bill because of the authoritarian and rigid opinions of Dr. Fishbein. In 1949 an anti-Fishbein Committee of Physicians, under Dr. John Peters, of Yale, led a successful drive to oust Fishbein from his entrenched position. Although this eased the situation within the AMA, there were still differences of opinion which affected the internal unity and external effectiveness of its campaign.

However, there can be little doubt about the over-all impact of the AMA campaign. The organization can exercise effective control over its members, since their professional status depends on membership in it. As mouthpieces for the AMA, doctors are located in all the states and they command respect from their communities and their Congressmen. The importance of this grass-roots approach can be seen in the fact that the AMA itself had only two registered lobbyists in Washington in 1949, when it was waging its most aggressive campaign and spending a million and a half dollars to influence the outcome of the congressional elections. To organize its campaign, the AMA hired a California public relations firm, Whitaker and Baxter, specialists in political public relations, with a record of outstanding success in California.

Other organizations which participated in the campaign against national health insurance were the Committee for Constitutional Government, the Blue Cross and Blue Shield Commissions, the

Chamber of Commerce of the United States, the American Farm Bureau Federation, the National Grange, the American Legion, the Association of American Physicians and Surgeons, the American Hospital Association, the American Economic Council, and many insurance firms.

By 1951 President Truman recognized that there was no chance for early approval of the compulsory insurance scheme. In order to get public and medical support for a health program, he shifted his emphasis. He appointed the Commission on the Health Needs of the Nation to examine the status of the nation's health services and needs. In its final report the Commission recommended, first, that the principle of prepaid health services be accepted as the most feasible way of meeting the problem; second, that existing prepaid plans be expanded to include as much service as possible; and, third, that a cooperative federal-state program be established to assist in the financing of personal health services. President Truman's final position was in favor of a system of voluntary health insurance operating on the basis of more local and state initiative.

During the 1952 presidential campaign, both Stevenson and Eisenhower took strong stands against compulsory health insurance. Eisenhower had the backing of the AMA; to the AMA, the Democratic Party was associated with socialized medicine. After his election, Eisenhower came out in favor of voluntary health insurance plans. In a special message of January 29, 1954, he went further and recommended the establishment of a limited reinsurance service by the federal government to encourage private and nonprofit health insurance organizations to offer broader health protection to more families. The reinsurance idea was then the newest approach to the problem of expanding available medical services without infringing on local and private initiative and jurisdiction.

The administration bill which embodied this idea met with failure in the House in July, 1954, and it was returned to committee. It had the outspoken support of the administration, particularly the new Department of Health, Education, and Welfare. However, it was the very compromise nature of the bill which caused its failure. It was defeated by a two-pronged attack; from one side, by those who felt this effort was inadequate and, from another, by those who felt it was a step toward federal government domination in the health field. The groups which had fought each other over Truman's proposal found themselves attacking this proposal, but for exactly opposite reasons. The AMA regarded it as an entering wedge for socialism and as unnecessary, since they felt there were adequate private sums available for reinsurance. Labor groups and others called the bill inadequate. President Eisenhower did not abandon his support for the reinsurance plan, and a similar proposal was reintroduced on the opening day of the second session of the Eighty-third Congress.

As of now, however, there is no national legislative policy with regard to the health problem. The deep fissure in popular sentiment has prevented successive administrations from achieving their goal of a positive legislative answer to the demand that expanded medical facilities be made available to more people at a lower cost. However, the net result of inaction has meant that the proponents of private, voluntary systems of insurance are the winners of the battle. If only by default, the national policy becomes one of acquiescence, with the argument against federal participation as a solution to the national health problem.

Generalizations. Five generalizations may be drawn from the study of health insurance proposals:

1. Proposals for new public policy, as well as opposition, originate with private groups rather than within Congress or the executive branch of the federal government.
2. Widespread discussion of new policy proposals, stimulated by economic depression, is necessary before federal agencies assume the initiative; but such discussion and initiative do not assure congressional action.
3. Congressional enactment of new policy is hampered by the federal form of the American governmental system.
4. Combined congressional committee, pressure group, bureaucratic influence, even with strong presidential support, does not insure success for policy proposals if offset by organized professional opposition.
5. Professional public relations methods are more effective in maintaining the policy status quo than in changing it.

SUMMARY. In this chapter a realistic view has been presented of the making of public policy by Congress. Such a view requires looking more deeply into the process than the details set forth in the Constitution, which, in Article I, places the legislative power of the United States in the hands of a Congress composed of a Senate and a House of Representatives. For a comprehensive and penetrating view it is essential to look behind the formal institutions through which the legislative power is exercised to the social forces which are generated among the people and seek expression, given sufficient provocation, through the formal agencies. Moreover, even in the legislative phase of policy-making, it is rarely Congress as a whole, except in a nominal sense, that makes the laws. The key posts are occupied by committee chairmen and, to a lesser extent, by party leaders in Congress, and it is they who make the decisions upon which the making of policy is based. By the exercise of their power over legislative, taxation, and appropriations measures, over presidential nominations and treaties, the decisions are actually in the hands of a relatively few people. For the origins of legislation one must look to the interest groups in the nation, to the President, and particularly to the bureaus in the executive branch of the government.

Chapter 14

THE MAKING OF PUBLIC POLICY— ADMINISTRATION

> . . . administration is intermingled with the entire proc-
> ess of government, and with the environment in which the
> people affected by the government exist.
>
> —John M. Gaus
> *Reflections on Public Administration**

When the Secretary of the Interior directs the Commissioner of Reclamation to withdraw an application for a dam pending before the Federal Power Commission; when the Secretary of Defense lets contracts for procuring military supplies and equipment following negotiation rather than following public advertisement; when the Secretary of Health, Education, and Welfare stops the manufacture of polio vaccine pending examination and approval of methods for testing purity, strength, and viability—when such things happen, administrators are making policy.

When the Secretary of State joins with the Foreign Minister of Portugal to issue a statement regarding a Portuguese possession in the Indian subcontinent; when the President's principal foreign policy advisor delivers an address in which he declares America's intention to thwart aggression by instant and massive retaliation at places of our own choosing; when the President, at a press and radio conference, maintains that the Secretary of Agriculture and the Director of Mutual Security can reach opposite conclusions regarding the advisability of employing a land reform expert yet both be right —in these cases, too, administrators are making policy.

Administration as Policy

In a sense, policy-making begins when the legislative stage ends. There is no sharp break; there is just an extension of much the same

* University, Ala.: University of Alabama Press, 1947, p. 125.

activity. In one respect, of course, there is a difference, or, rather, different phases can be identified: the persons involved change. But even this is not entirely correct. It is not so much that the persons involved change, but that they change their positions. Legislators recede into the background. Administrators take up the responsibility for carrying out the policy declared and financed by Congress. To the old Washington saying that the President proposes but Congress disposes could be added the observation, Yes, but the bureaucracy administers, hence the bureaucracy has the last word in policy-making. But not even the bureaucracy has the last word. It is the Supreme Court under the long-hallowed custom of judicial review that commands the stage in the third of the three main phases of policy-making. It is they who "make policy," until, if the "popular" pressure is persistent enough, Congress re-emerges as the policy-maker and the cycle begins again.

But to return to consideration of administration as policy. Under the Constitution the executive branch of the federal government is separate from the legislative and judicial branches and is headed by the President, who is the Chief Executive. Moreover, it is the President's responsibility, also under the Constitution, to administer the laws enacted by Congress—whether with his approval or over his veto matters not. Thus, when the compromises have been struck, when the legislators' consciences have spoken, and when the formalities of promulgation have been met by affixing of the Great Seal and publication in the Federal Register, legislation as policy comes formally to an end and administration begins. The question now is, What can—and will—the executive branch do with the policy laid down by Congress?

TEMPORARY OR PERMANENT AGENCY? The first question facing the President, his staff, his Cabinet, and the bureaucracy is to determine how much leeway, if any, Congress has permitted them in organizing the administration of the new law. Sometimes, full discretion is allowed and in times of emergency this is common. More frequently, Congress determines the organization and the executive branch is not free to do so. In every policy formulated by Congress, it is also customary for Congress to either designate an existing administrative unit to assume the responsibility of carrying out the policy, to authorize and appropriate funds for the creation of a new unit to administer the new law, or to authorize the President to make such administrative arrangements as he sees fit. Thus, in 1948, Congress directed that a new administration be established to execute the provisions of the Economic Cooperation Act, the law underpinning the European Recovery Program. But when the Atomic Energy Act of 1946 was amended in 1954, effecting a drastic change in policy regarding private use of discoveries made by government scientists in the field of atomic energy, its administration was entrusted to the Atomic Energy Commission, an established agency. In the former instance, Congress was unwilling to allow the President to decide which agency should administer the program, especially since the prestige of the State Department in Congress was not high. In the second instance, the relations of the AEC with Congress had not suffered similarly, and therefore no change in the administration of the amended policy was deemed necessary.

In what was once called "peacetime," the normal way of providing for administration of a policy passed by Congress was for Congress itself to determine the necessary administrative framework. However, emergencies caused by economic depression, defense mobilization, and international hostilities have brought about a departure from this norm. Under such circumstances, Congress has granted much larger discretionary powers to the President. In fact, during the depression years of the 1930's, as well as before Pearl Harbor and during World War II, Congress gave complete rein to the President to determine what administrative arrangements should be made. Congress contented itself with appropriating funds to the Executive, who, in turn, decided by whom they would be spent. When Franklin D. Roosevelt, in 1933, decided to set up emergency agencies alongside the regular departments to administer the vast sums appropriated by Congress, he made a decision that was to have profound effects on the meaning of the several policies involved. For in so doing, he established a general pattern of administration not only for the depression years but for the following years in other times of emergency.

Federal assistance to the unemployed, to distressed agricultural producers, to home mortgagees, and to cities and towns unable to obtain credit from private institutions were among the emergency activities, in addition to measures for industrial recovery, that were undertaken through temporary agencies. On the other hand, administration of the new federal policy regulating the securities markets was placed in the hands of a permanent agency, as was the granting of construction and operating subsidies to the merchant marine and the guaranteeing of the rights of workers to organize and bargain collectively. While a pattern of administration was not clear in many cases, still FDR seemed to clearly prefer temporary agencies to administer activities he thought were temporary. When an emergency activity subsequently was recognized by Congress as a long-term, continuing federal job, the administrative agency was established on a permanent basis. Thus unemployment compensation was originally administered by temporary agencies. But when Congress limited federal assistance to those states which complied with certain established federal standards, the Social Security Board, a permanent agency, was set up to administer these funds.

Similarly, an Office of Defense Mobilization was established in 1952 when Congress extended economic controls originally enacted following the Korean conflict in 1950. During World War II similar controls had been administered by temporary agencies. Of the many examples of cases in which Congress has granted discretion to the President which might be cited, the development of the atomic bomb illustrates the practice most vividly. On the strength of an assurance from the President that the funds were necessary to the security of the nation, Congress appropriated two billion dollars without knowing the purpose of this expenditure. Using the unrestricted authority granted him to spend the funds, President Roosevelt authorized the immediate development of atomic weapons. For this purpose, the War Department, in 1943, established the Manhattan District project, the harmless-sounding designation behind which the stupendous efforts in atomic development were carried on. In effect, Congress abdicated its policy-making role to the President and the officials and scientists who were thus to guide the United States along a path whose end is not yet in sight.

PUBLIC ADMINISTRATION. Whether administrative agencies make policy turns on the sense in which "administration" is used. If administration is taken to mean housekeeping activities, it is largely devoid of policy. As housekeeping, administration includes planning, research, organization, staffing, budgeting, counseling, and operations. Each contributes to the efficient, economical, and nonpolitical accomplishment of a program, once it has been decided upon by the proper authority. In theory, such actions can be performed without reference to policy. Theoretically, government employees can set up programs to be administered regardless of their content. Partisan politics and patronage do not invalidate the premise on which the theory of objective administration rests. In the federal government both the General Services Administration and the Civil Service Commission have been set up on the theory that administration is housekeeping and should be nonpolitical.

But in a more significant sense administration is policy come to life. Policy is nothing unless and until it is applied. The difference is the difference between word and deed, between declaration and action, rhetoric and process. So regarded, administration acquires meaning. It ceases to be merely an organizational framework of nonpolitical individuals and becomes a stream of social activity, sanctioned by Congress and crisscrossed by currents energized by various citizen groups. Thus administration can be visualized as the product of government, the materializing of accumulated policy declarations and programs adopted by Congress.

To view administration as policy come alive is to understand its essence. Understood in this way, administration comprises the thousand-and-one protective, promotional, regulatory, managerial activities of almost unbelievable scope and variety which government at the federal level performs daily. It is the Seventh Fleet patrolling the Formosa Straits, the higher price paid for all domestic products protected by customs tariffs, the deportation of aliens illegally residing in the United States. It is also the foreign-produced dairy products not exported to the United States because of import quotas imposed by Congress. It is the Public Health Service doctor examining incoming travelers for contagious diseases, the Immigration and Naturalization Service checking passports and visas, the Coast Guard on iceberg patrol, the quarantine officials keeping out diseased plants and forest products. It is the Treasury Department's Internal Revenue Service collecting taxes on personal and corporate income, and its Bureau of Disbursement supervising the biweekly payment of the more than two million civilian employees and the three and a half million persons in the armed services. It is the Defense Department's procurement services annually spending five-sixths of the federal budget of sixty billions for military "hardware," thus directly influencing the trend of the nation's economy. Administration is the Labor Relation Board's supervision of an industry or plant election to determine a bargaining agent; the Bureau of Standards' fixing and promoting the adoption of standards for industry (not ultimate consumers); the Bureau of Labor Statistics' computing the cost-of-living index, to which industrial wages are geared; the Census Bureau's projecting the country's population growth to 1970.

It is all this and much more. A typical issue of the *U.S. Government Manual*, published by the General Services Administration, comprises five or six hundred pages of compact printed matter. Only a few pages at the beginning are needed to describe the Congress (the legislative branch) and the judiciary (the judicial branch) in the federal government. Nearly all the pages are needed to describe (in summary fashion) the workings of the executive (administrative) branch. Whether one sums it up as *Leviathan, the welfare state,* or *the service state,* or refers to it as "that gang in Washington" is not very material. Nor is it particularly relevant to refer to it as the result of the New Deal, the Fair Deal, or of President Eisenhower's "big business" Administration. These catchwords obscure thought as much as they clarify it. The point is that for one hundred sixty-six years a long and expanding succession of hopes and fears, grievances and expectations, have motivated Americans to ask their government to do things. The aggregate of these demands finds expression through the programs administered by the government. In administration, the programs of Americans are being realized every day.

ADMINISTRATORS AS POLICY-MAKERS. Administrators are important as policy-makers as well as administrators. Macmahon reminds us that ". . . policy is present in some degree wherever there is activity."[1] Since policy is action, or is dependent upon the presence or absence of action, policy is to be found throughout administration. Consequently, those who administer the laws are important to an understanding of administration considered as policy.

Administrators are important in this respect because modern legislation, in order to become policy, must be supplemented by administrative decisions. Many modern laws are complex and technical, and often embody more than one objective. It is the administrator who must work his way through the complexities to a policy. It is he who must know enough about the technical side of the legislative policy to understand it, yet not too much lest he be overwhelmed by its technology. The job of the administrator also involves making decisions from among conflicting policy objectives.

In the second place, administrators make policy because they are under a responsibility to act. Legislation is not self-executing; it must be put into effect. This calls for decisions. The public administrator, like the business executive, can be defined as one who must make many decisions, some of which may be right. To the legal obligation to act are added the compulsions of time, politics, and circumstance. No administrator has enough time; he is always forced to act under pressure. Moreover, administrators do not reach their decisions in a vacuum. The political forces and figures in Congress and out press on the administrator. He must make his decisions, too, with the possibility of court review and the certainty of congressional review in the appropriations process.

The human side of administrators also contributes to their importance as policy-makers. No administrator is a robot. Automation may threaten the livelihood of some industrial workers. But it is unlikely to cause technological unemployment among those who fashion the governmental product. Being human, the administrator has his own ideas of how the law should be carried out. Also, opportunities are present to refrain from acting, not because he wills to sabotage the law through administrative default, but simply because the law does not require him to do that which others in his place would do. Congress has never been able to draft a law so explicit that it means the same thing to all men. In these varied ways, policy takes shape under the hand of the administrator.

POLICIES MADE BY ADMINISTRATIVE DECISION. Examples were cited at the beginning of this chapter of policy being made by administrative decision in the fields of electric power development, procurement of defense supplies, polio vaccine production, foreign policy, and internal security. Additional examples will contribute to an even better understanding of the key role of the administrator in making public policy.

The supply of credit. Choices and opportunities available to administrators in the Federal Reserve System and the Treasury Department illustrate well many of the points made above. While they are not likely to be influenced in their decisions on credit policy by the possibility of challenge in the courts, pressures from political sources, both within and without the government, and along economic, sectional, and class lines as well are ever-present weights in the scales of decision. Our economy is dependent upon the availability of credit. Under authority of Congress, federal authorities create and manipulate the volume of credit and fix the terms under which it is made available to producers, distributors, and consumers of goods and services. Basically, the policy is the same today as when adopted in 1913, although additional authority in certain fields—housing, agriculture, consumer purchasing—has been added for fixed periods to meet emergencies or to meet the requirements of financing military operations. Closely related to this authority over credit is that of the Treasury in financing government operations—another authority granted by Congress. Under policies thus determined, Treasury officials are authorized to decide when, how, and under what maturity and price terms federal obligations will be sold to the investing public. Simultaneously, by raising and lowering reserve requirements of banks, by adjusting rediscount rates, and by buying and selling government bonds, Federal Reserve Board officials decide the volume and cost of credit to manufacturers, wholesalers, and retailers of the national product.

The interests represented by the Treasury and Federal Reserve Board are not always as related as the short distance separating them in Washington would suggest. The Board represents the business community in general. It is largely independent of Congress, since it pays its own bills from its profits and does not depend on appropriations from Congress. It is largely independent of the President and the executive branch as well, for, although the seven-man Board is appointed by the President and confirmed by Congress, the terms are long (fourteen years), are staggered (rarely do more than half of the Board's terms expire within a President's four-year term), and the Board's budget is established independently and is not scrutinized by the Bureau of the Budget or the Chief Executive. The Secretary of the Treasury and the department he heads tend to represent the banking community. Bankers with money to lend at interest profit more from lending at short term than at medium or long term. Thus Treasury decisions as to financing are of direct pecuniary interest to bankers, while the volume available for such investment responds to manipulation by the Reserve Board's Governors, just as the sale-ability of government obligations to the bankers depends on the yield of government bonds resulting from manipulation of the bond market by the Board.

If this necessarily summary sketch oversimplifies the situation, the point is nonetheless clear. In the decisions which must be made, many interests are involved—partisan, sectional, class, and official (not only Treasury and FRB interests but those of other departments and agencies, for example, those of the Social Security Board, since the government is trustee for Social Security account beneficiaries.) There are also economic and financial interests to be considered, as well as last and sometimes least those of the consumer. Not all of these interests are directly represented in the making of decisions; theoretically, and according to law, their voice is supposed to be heard indirectly. The interests differ and are made to harmonize only with great difficulty, if at all. The financial and social costs of making a living and of being governed turn upon the decisions made by the administrators of the nation's public debt and commercial credit policies. Policy, in these terms, results from these administrative de-cisions made within the discretionary limits necessarily permitted by Congress in fixing legislative policy.[2]

Public housing. In carrying out Congress' public housing program, administration seems to have been as important as legislation in policy-making. The Housing and Home Finance Agency is reported to have allowed cities to obtain the financial benefits of the program without meeting the legal requirements as to slum clearance, zoning, land use, and transportation.[3]

Service stations. Likewise, in anti-trust policy, administration is crucial. It was largely responsible for 65,000 failures in 1954 among the 210,000 independent automobile service stations in the United States, according to testimony given before the Senate Small Busi-ness Committee in hearings on the report of the Attonrey General's National Committee to Study the Anti-Trust Laws.[4]

Foreign oil imports. Another example of policy-making as an activity of administrators rather than as a declaration by Congress is afforded by the controversy over the amount of discretion to be permitted the President, and the limits of that discretion, in controlling foreign oil imports. In this case, lodging of such discretionary authority in the executive branch, rather than joining the issue in Congress where one or the other of the groups of domestic adversaries would have lost, was a compromise acceptable to the oil producers—both independent domestic producers and domestic companies with foreign subsidiaries, dependent on oil imports—as well as the coal producers and miners in this country.[5]

Tax exemption. The Internal Revenue Bureau makes decisions as to tax exemption. In the case of *For America,* a citizens' group founded in 1954, its application was denied.[6] Some 32,000 organizations enjoy such tax exemption. Internal Revenue officials decide whether educational activities in the field of public policy extend to attempts at influencing legislation. If it is decided that they do so, contributions to them are not granted tax exempt status.[7]

Administration of foreign policy. In foreign relations it is even truer, if possible, than in domestic matters that administration vitalizes policy. Diplomacy, the traditional tool of foreign policy, is still of great importance in the maintenance of relations with other countries despite the emergence since World War II of economic aid, propaganda, and information as supplementary tools. Resort to military power (war itself) and the threat of armed force must also be regarded as means of foreign policy. When war comes, the groups with status and strength in the making of domestic policy have a favorable opportunity to strengthen their position domestically; this is particularly true of industrial, farm, and labor groups, and, above all, of industrial producers, since success in modern war turns on success in industrial production.[8]

The imprint of private groups and especially of economic groups can be seen on foreign policy. An example is the recognition of the U.S.S.R. by the United States in 1934. American business interests exerted the chief pressure on the United States government to recognize the Soviet Union.[9] In 1955, the Committee of Endorsers of a Program to Govern Our Foreign Relations was advocating withdrawal of recognition from the U.S.S.R. and the satellites. The role played since 1949 by the so-called China Lobby in preventing the withdrawal of American recognition from the Chinese Nationalist government and its extension to the Chinese People's (Communist) government has never been thoroughly probed. But this group, comprised of importers, Nationalist Chinese leaders and American officials, pressure politicians in Congress, and private opinion leaders, aided by events, played an influential, perhaps a decisive, role.[10]

Long before the international communist conspiracy had convinced many people that the world was split between East and West, makers of American foreign policy had already felt the influence generated by activist groups among the population. On tariff and immigration policies, as well as on other so-called more political policies —recognition of new governments, intervention, protection of American rights abroad, and equality of opportunity—economic, sectional, racial, religious, and class groups had made their voices heard and their pressures felt in the halls of Congress and in administrative offices in Washington. The use of propaganda, both by government officials and by private interests seeking to influence policy, goes back to the early days of the Republic.[11] As for the weight of the impact of pressure groups on the makers of foreign policy, it is possible to interpret a large part of American foreign policy since the first World War as a succession of successful intimidations by pressure groups, with the political parties safely engaged in shadowboxing at a safe distance from the real conflicts.[12] If we sometimes forget the part played by such groups in confining administrators within strict limits in the application of the neutrality laws of the 1930's and, consequently, in the restriction of policy choices in the Spanish Civil War, the respective roles of the America First Committee and the Committee to Defend America by Aiding the Allies have perhaps not completely been lost sight of. They were influential opponents and advocates, respectively, of American policy as it developed during the twenty-seven months from the outbreak of World War II to Pearl Harbor.[13] President Franklin D. Roosevelt sought the aid of William Allen White, the Emporia (Kan.), editor and Chairman of the Defend America Committee, in explaining, promoting, and, in general, justifying the 1940 executive agreement with the British providing for the exchange of overage U.S. destroyers in return for the lease of bases in British possessions in the Western hemisphere.[14]

The two-way path of influence between administrative makers of foreign policy and political interest and pressure groups is, in fact, a characteristic and valuable feature of the modern American political system. Groups want policy shaped in their interest, while administrators and officials need the aid of such groups and broad public support for policy. Thus is democracy introduced into the conduct of foreign policy. Also, in this way, policy decisions which otherwise might not enlist widespread general support gain approval in time for it to be most valuable in America's dealings with the outside world.[15]

Sometimes domestic political pressures are so powerful that policy is remade with unseemly haste. American recognition of the new State of Israel in 1948 was such an occurrence. Within minutes of the proclamation of Israel as a state, President Truman had accorded recognition, a policy which can hardly have been unrelated to strong pressure exerted by Zionist quarters and to the approaching presidential election. The step was taken so quickly that the State Department was unable to inform the American delegation to the UN General Assembly in time to adjust to the new policy.

The military in foreign policy. It is more than a little ironic that a new structure to accommodate the War Department, deemed spacious when it was completed in the late 1930's, should now be occupied by the Department of State. There is added irony in the fact that it is farther from the White House than the old State, War, and Navy Building at 17th and Pennsylvania Avenue, and that the Department of the Army (formerly the War Department), together with that of the Navy and Air Force, under the Secretary of Defense, should command the space available in the Pentagon, the world's largest office building. In comparison with the State Department, the needs of the armed services have expanded vastly in terms of space requirements, congressional appropriations, and influence in foreign affairs.

It is not easy to exaggerate the place which strategic considerations and their advocates, the military services, have come to occupy in American foreign policy.[16]

The traditional-concept of the President making foreign policy with the advice of the Secretary of State is out of date. In the formation of present-day policy the President retains his major role but other officials have been added, making the picture not only more complex but, for this very reason, also more confusing. In 1949 there were some forty-four agencies involved in some degree in our foreign relations, hence, in foreign policy. Not all of them need be mentioned here. It is enough to describe briefly the most important.

A major force in foreign policy making is the Department of Defense. Under a Secretary who is responsible for the unified armed services, the Department of Defense operates through the component Departments of the Army, Navy, and Air Force, and the Joint Chiefs of Staff (JCS), the latter with a professional staff. The Joint Chiefs of Staff were created originally by presidential fiat in early 1942. They were given legal recognition, first, when the United Nations Charter was ratified (the JCS represents the United States in the UN Military Staff Committee), then, in 1947 and 1949, with the enactment by Congress of the National Defense Act and its amendments.

Equally important in formulating foreign policy is the National Security Council (NSC), also established by the National Defense Act of 1947. The NSC is composed of the President, under whose leadership it meets, the Vice-President, the Secretaries of Defense, State, and Treasury, the Director of the Central Intelligence Agency (CIA) and the Director of the Office of Defense Mobilization (ODM). The President may also invite others to meet with the Council. The NSC has a small staff of its own, as well as a senior staff drawn from the same agencies as the Council members themselves. The place of the NSC in the governmental structure is the Executive Office of the President.

Also in the Executive Office of the President are four special assistants to the President: for national security affairs (who also serves as executive secretary of the NSC), for foreign relations, for disarmament, and for economic foreign policy.

All federal departments headed by officials of Cabinet rank are involved in varying degrees in foreign policy formulation. Likewise, many of the independent agencies are involved; for example, the Atomic Energy Commission (AEC), the Tariff Commission, the Securities and Exchange Commission (SEC), the Federal Communications Commission (FCC), and the Civil Aeronautics Board (CAB).

Traditionally the Department of State has had the greatest responsibility for formulating policy. The other departments and agencies have made their contributions to those parts of over-all policy in which they had professional competence. Coordination was not easy and was rarely fully attained. The device for achieving it was the interdepartmental committee. A good example is the Committee for Reciprocity Information established not long after Congress (in 1934) delegated authority to the President to bargain with other countries for tariff concessions. To the interdepartmental committee as a coordinating device has been added (particularly since the end of World War II) advisory committees with a statutory base—for example, the National Advisory Committee on Financial and Monetary Policy established as part of the legislation authorizing U.S. membership in the International Bank for Reconstruction and Development and the International Monetary Fund. Before the NSC came into existence in 1947 its antecedent in the fields of defense and diplomacy was the State–War–Navy Coordinating Committee (SWNCC) and, at the Cabinet level, an *ad hoc* committee which met as occasion demanded; it had no permanent staff or secretariat. Today the NSC advises the President on grand strategy, the combination of plans, intentions, and expectations which aim at mobilizing and deploying the nation's resources so as to maximize the security of the United States, without war if possible, with the best chance of winning a war, if necessary. Policy implementation is the responsibility of the Operations Coordinating Board, an interdepartmental grouping whose members are the Under-Secretaries of State, Treasury, and Defense; the International Cooperation Administration Director; and the NSC Secretary. The State Department representative serves as chairman.

Out of this multiplicity of departments, agencies, and coordinating devices foreign policy is made, so far as the executive branch of the government is concerned, and is carried into effect. A fuller description of the policy machinery might add organizational details, but it is doubtful whether it would clarify the problem. Changes in organization, even of those features which are embedded in law, occur frequently in response to shifts in policies of other countries and as experience requires. As a major participant in international politics, America is young and immature, and is forced by the exigencies of the situation to resort to trial-and-error methods of policy-making. As a great power, the United States is little more than fifty years old; it has been a world power barely fifteen years, and the hesitant leader of that part of the world not dominated by the international communist conspiracy less than a decade. In addition, the strategic place occupied by the United States has been revolutionized with the loss of our former invulnerability, the relative weakness of our allies, and the development of new weapons. A further complicating factor is the postwar emergence of many new sovereign states, in areas that were formerly colonies or dependencies. The consequences for American diplomacy have been great; the United States has had to negotiate with these newly born, sovereign, independent states, which claim equality with older states but have little experience in statecraft and few resources, yet are jealous of their sovereignty and highly sensitive to criticism. An external situation thus unhinged from traditional factors promoting stability would tax the best organized, the most efficient and highly trained governmental system. The United States is far from having effected such an ideal deployment of its resources of materials, men, money, management, and ideals.[17]

But not even the best organization would suffice were the office of Chief Executive occupied by a man insensitive to those subtle yet significant changes in public mood which all administration of foreign policy should be attuned to detect. In our system of government no one but the President can effect changes in policy administratively to take account of changes in mood. Apparently such a change occurred between the time early in 1954 when the Secretary of State announced America's policy of "massive retaliation" and later the same year when President Dwight D. Eisenhower was reported as having abandoned this policy in favor of one of partnership with our allies and of finding a means of living with the communist world.[18] Nor is elaborate machinery for foreign policy administration any substitute for a perceptive envoy quick to seize an opportunity to promote the ideals on which the nation's foreign policy must rest. The opening afforded by the American ambassador's toast to Justice at a U.S.S.R. Foreign Ministry reception was grasped by Soviet Marshal Zhukov as the occasion to rebuke publicly a political rival, Beria, thus hastening the latter's liquidation in the intra-Kremlin struggle for power.[19] No policy paper issuing from the National Security Council's policy planning staff could predict the future so imaginatively as to provide the basis for an instruction to our ambassador in Moscow to act in this way. But by his own action the American ambassador, Charles E. Bohlen, thus made and executed policy. Such examples show clearly that administrators, too, are policy-makers.

SUMMARY. In order to become policy, congressional findings and declarations must first be applied. Much policy is made in the executive branch by administrative officials. Often policy is made administratively within wide limits permitted by Congress, as with regulatory legislation. At other times Congress prescribes rigid methods, leaving less discretion to officials in carrying out policy. The number and kinds of administrative agencies established are factors determining the ease and effectiveness with which policy is made. Foreign and defense policies, in particular, are affected by the numerous agencies concerned with political and military strategy. But a perceptive envoy abroad can also make policy on his own responsibility and without specific instructions.

Chapter 15

THE MAKING OF PUBLIC POLICY—
ADJUDICATION

> Wherever the power to govern, to make decisions on pol-
> icy, indubitably exists, it is used every bit as effectively by
> a deliberate refusal to use it as by its firm and forthright
> use.
>
> —Fred Rodell
> *Nine Men**

When public policy is made a course is set, a line of action is laid
down. Any one or all of the three branches of government can set
such a course or lay down such a line of action. In this respect the
judicial branch does not differ from the legislative and executive
branches. In the judicial branch, the Supreme Court sets the course,
it lays down the lines of action. In this way judicial interpretation
becomes policy in the large context of government as a means of adjusting varied and competing social interests.

THE JUDICIAL BRANCH IN POLICY-MAKING. When we speak of the
judicial stage of the policy-making process, we mean a course of action subject to the acquiescence, corroboration, diversion, or rejection by the federal judiciary. In point of time, the action of the federal judiciary in making policy follows that of the other main
branches of government.[1] It must be added immediately, however,
that the judicial phase is not always the last of the three stages of
policy-making. Sometimes the judicial stage precedes the others. For
policy-making is sometimes cyclical in nature, passing successively
through the legislative, administrative, and judicial stages, only to
return to the starting point and pass again through one or more of
the same three stages. To determine the sequence in a specific case
necessitates seeking the actual origin of the policy.

* New York: Random House, Inc., 1955, pp. 18-19.

Illustrations. The policy question as to where title to offshore tidelands resided—in the states, or in the federal government—ran through a complete cycle after 1937. The sequence in this case was, first, administrative, second, judicial, and, third, legislative. The legislative phase ended in 1953, when federal policy was decided by Congress in favor of the states. The policy regarding federal regulation of the sale of natural gas by producers to distributors where interstate commerce is involved is following a similar course of passing through stages. After a Supreme Court ruling in 1954 that such sales were subject to federal regulation under a law enacted by Congress in 1938, the Eighty-fourth Congress adopted legislation exempting such sales from federal regulation. The bill was vetoed by President Dwight D. Eisenhower; this, however, assures further attempts in the future to obtain favorable congressional and executive action. Federal policy regarding the compatibility of federal anti-trust laws and agreements between manufacturers and distributors fixing minimum wholesale and retail prices (resale price maintenance) is probably destined to repeat the three-phase cycle, with the agreement by the Supreme Court in 1955 to rule on the legality of these "fair-trade" agreements. In the matter of federal policy on labor-management relations, determined originally in 1935 with the enactment of the Wagner Labor Relations Act, the cycle took twelve years to run its course and start again, in 1947, with the setting of a new course by Congress in the Labor-Management Relations (Taft-Hartley) Act.

UNPREDICTABILITY OF THE JUDICIAL STAGE. The judicial stage of policy-making is erratic. In its traditional role of policy-maker by judicial review and by legal interpretation, the Supreme Court cannot itself originate policy. It must wait until some individual or corporate entity, or some group, acting through an individual, claims injury caused by the actions of others before it can enter the process.

The Court does not supply advice to the Congress when the legislative branch is making policy. Nor does the judiciary give advisory opinions to the executive branch which administrative officers might use as a gauge when making decisions as to whether their proposed actions are within the law. The result is that policy in many fields is allowed to stand as passed by Congress and administered by federal officials. But such policy lives under a constant threat, so to speak, of being challenged. In our rapidly changing society the total social situation is never constant but is always in a state of flux. Laws passed at a particular time proclaiming policy desired at the time of their enactment may appear to represent settled courses. But they can be brought under a cloud when a change of sufficient importance occurs to warrant challenging the law in the courts or seeking their amendment in the Congress. Then, as in the matter of natural gas sales, noted above, policy itself undergoes radical change without any action by the legislature; the law may be challenged or, as in the natural gas case, the legislature may be asked to return the law —that is, the policy—to the situation which existed before. A measure of stability is, however, introduced by the operation of the legal principle that the courts will not pass again on the same or similar set of facts (*stare decisis*). Also, the Supreme Court follows the practice of avoiding constitutional issues as long as possible and decides cases, to the greatest possible extent, on other grounds.

DIFFERENCE IN ACCESSIBILITY. The difference in accessibility between the judiciary and the other two branches of government is related to the erratic role of the judiciary in policy-making. Difficult though it may be for the uninitiated citizen to find his way around Congress and the great departments of government, it is even more difficult for him to engage the machinery of policy-making by the judiciary. The discretionary power of the Supreme Court to decide which of the many cases that parties are eager to have reviewed are to be granted the opportunity of review has already been mentioned. Also, the average citizen must be represented by legal counsel, and legal counsel is expensive. To say this, is not very informative when "expensive" is, indeed, a relative term. For a wealthy corporation, a $50,000 fee is not expensive, while for a poor party a fee of a fifth of this amount is exorbitant. Yet it costs, on the average, not less than $10,000 to fight a case from the court of first instance to the Supreme Court if this judicial path is necessary to determine an individual's legal rights.[2] The delay involved in the final determination of a person's rights is equally important. These two handicaps of determining policy by the judiciary are probably more characteristic of our system now than when Woodrow Wilson noted them in 1908. Even then he posed the question, Are not poor men in fact excluded from our courts by the cost and the length of their processes? He did not hesitate to answer that both simplicity and promptness were lacking in our processes of adjudication, that these processes were unnecessarily expensive, and that by leading a poor litigant through appeals and technical delays, a rich litigant could, in effect, cheat him of his rights. The constitutional principle of equal accessibility of the courts to all men had, according to Wilson, fallen into disrepair, and he called upon the country to amend and simplify the processes of justice.[3]

However, if the path of justice is no shorter now than in Wilson's time and no less expensive, it can be trod today by citizens who combine their individual strengths and resources. Thus the Supreme

Court machinery for determining policy can be put into gear more frequently and more effectively than in the past. In view of the customary right of the Court to review legislation and its veto on policy, and given the high standing of the Court among the people, rich and poor alike, it is hardly surprising that well-to-do litigants should have established at an early date the habit of resorting to the judiciary to secure their rights. Nor should it be surprising that the path thus followed should have been taken by others as soon as they were able to mobilize the necessary resources. The provocation is great. In deciding cases involving individuals, the Court is, in fact, determining policy for great social and economic groups. The records of the court rarely, if ever, disclose this fact. Yet the Court is no longer, if it ever was, only a court of law, a tribunal for the delimitation of the powers of government as against the rights of individuals, or vice versa. The Court, for better, for worse, is caught up in the power struggle. It is itself a center of power not unlike the legislative and the executive branches in its ultimate effect upon public policy, although it must, of necessity, wait upon cases involving governmental powers or individual rights before exercising its power.[4]

An Engine of Social Power. In the struggle of groups for the beneficent exercise of the power of government in their behalf, use is being made of the judicial branch of government on a widening scale. Ever since the protection of the Constitution's "due process" clause against federal and state action was extended to corporations as well as to individuals, the appearance of these creations of state law as litigants has become so common as no longer to excite interest. Yet, in thus extending to artificial persons protection intended ostensibly for former Negro slaves, the judiciary went far in verifying a major hypothesis of American society. In deciding cases involving rights of corporations, the Supreme Court is, in reality, making policy, policy regarding the rights of groups—corporations, managers, and stockholders—as well as the rights of those, considered as a group or groups, who consume the products and receive the services of corporations.

Moreover, the ramifications of this judicial legislation in connection with the powers of Congress multiply the effects on groups of the population. In particular, the power of Congress to regulate commerce between the states and the injunction against the federal and state governments' taking property without due process of law have been construed by the Supreme Court so as to alter the effective power relationship between groups. Much of its power over interstate commerce is exercised through the independent agencies established to bring under federal regulation, in varying degrees, different parts of the economic life of the country—communications, labor-management relations, surface, air, and water transportation, capital mobilization, agricultural production, terms of competition in trade. At different times, due process has been interpreted by the Supreme Court in both a procedural and a substantive sense; the former, in deciding whether agency procedure for putting rates into effect, for example, is fair and not arbitrary; the latter, in deciding whether the application of the anti-trust laws prevents "reasonable" combinations. But, whether understood in one sense or the other, due process has been given meaning by the Supreme Court so as to variously sanction, invite, or prevent existing or desired economic power relationships among groups of entrepreneurs, producers, middlemen, purveyors of services, and consumers. The individual person or corporate enterprise who is the litigant or party in action is of secondary importance; of primary importance is the group of individuals, the group of enterprises, the class or section or region whose power position, economically or politically, stands to be enhanced or weakened as a result of the appeal of the individual to the judicial power for the determination of public policy.

POLICY QUESTIONS RAISED BY SOCIAL GROUPS. In policy-making by the judiciary, even more than in policy-making by the legislative and executive branches, it is the readiness of self-conscious groups, under competent leadership and with adequate resources, to appeal to the judicial process which provides the opportunity for the courts to make policy. No matter to what part of the nation's life we turn, this fact holds true. Can fair rates be fixed and enforced and discriminatory practices prevented on the railroads? The answer turned on the readiness of aggrieved farmers to assert that they could—that public authority should regulate such actions—and upon the action of farmers as users of transportation to create an opportunity for the courts to make public policy by ruling on the issues.[5]

More recently it has been the railroads which regard themselves as aggrieved and who appeal to the public and to all agencies of government through propaganda to assist them in restoring fair, competitive conditions allegedly upset by the rise of new means of transport, particularly trucking and air transport.[6]

Can Congress, as a matter of policy, pay agricultural producers for reducing production from the proceeds of a tax levied on processors of farm commodities? The answer turned on the willingness of a processor to ask the courts. Whether he was acting solely in his own behalf or in agreement and at the behest of a processors' group is not known.[7]

Can Congress, as a matter of policy, provide for the multi-purpose development of the Tennessee River watershed, borrow and spend public funds for public enterprises that aid labor and industry, regulate utility companies which control but do not own utility operating companies? Here, too, the answers turned on the readiness of a group of utility companies to ask the courts.[8] Is a coal marketing scheme subject to federal regulation, or is it illegal under the anti-trust laws? Can manufacturers of hardwood flooring, linseed oil, maple flooring, cement, sugar, cooperate legally to fix prices, allocate sales territories, fix quality standards? If they use such practices, public policy is being determined by private authority and by default, despite provisions of federal law. But, likewise, a Federal Trade Commission inspired by concern for the public interest, or an attorney general similarly moved, investigates or prosecutes such manufacturers' groups under the anti-trust laws only after the groups themselves have moved into the field of policy-making.[9] Can the federal government grant a moratorium on farm mortgages? The answer is of prime interest to farmers whose farms are mortgaged. But it was the life insurance industry, with an obvious economic interest in the answer, which created the opportunity for the Supreme Court to make policy by answering the question in the negative.[10] In still another area, war veterans' pensions and benefits, the policy-determining function of the judiciary has operated. The spending of public funds for this purpose cannot be called into question nor impeded by an individual or group, said the trial court, avoiding a ruling on constitutionality. In refusing to hear the appeal for such a ruling, the Supreme Court said, in effect, that Congress's power in this field was unlimited.[11] In refusing to hear arguments on upsetting the decision of the lower court, the Supreme Court fixes policy as effectively, albeit negatively, as if it were to grant and hear the appeal.[12]

The National Association for the Advancement of Colored People. As a group which has used the judiciary to determine matters of public policy, the National Association for the Advancement of Colored People has been most successful. Since it was founded in 1909 the NAACP has gained no less than forty victories in the Supreme Court. Rebuffed by Congress in its efforts to secure the constitutional rights of all citizens, the Association turned to the judiciary. It is there that it has been most active in asking the questions from which the Supreme Court has been able to select those which it desired to answer.

Perhaps the question-answer which has shown the Supreme Court most clearly in its policy-making role has been that in which the

Court decided in 1954 that racial discrimination in public education is unconstitutional.[13] The impact of the Court's answers to the questions raised in the restrictive covenant cases was nationwide. Here, the Court ruled that neither federal nor state courts may issue injunctions to enforce racial restrictive covenants. The rights of Negroes to register and vote in Democratic primaries in the South, the right of Negroes to fair trial proceedings in criminal cases, their right to equal educational opportunities, the unconstitutionality of segregation of passengers in interstate transportation—these are additional areas of public policy the exact confines of which have been fixed by the Supreme Court as a result of the questions put to it in cases begun and followed through by the NAACP.[14]

The NAACP's success may be explained by the fact that the rights of individuals are a subject for suitable determination by the courts. But this is not the only explanation. The NAACP has had organization, money, respected leadership, both white and colored, and excellent legal talent. Moreover, it has pioneered in originating and developing new means of social pressure in making public policy. It has seen the value of the country's highest court for a racial minority group in its struggle for enforcement of its legal rights, an insight gained by other groups—business enterprises, labor unions, agricultural producers—in earlier times and in other connections. It has learned the tricks of the lobbying trade in a wider context than the legislative arena. By setting up a separate legal service it takes advantage, for example, of the internal revenue code, which permits deductions for income tax purposes of contributions to an organization no part of whose activities are devoted to the influencing of legislation. Thus it capitalizes on a legal fiction that amounts, in effect, to government subsidy for those who do their lobbying not in the legislature but in the judicial branch of the government.

In its resourcefulness, the NAACP went further. It did so not only by taking test cases to the Supreme Court from the trial courts but also in encouraging writings on the sociology of law, getting them printed in the law reviews of the country, and squeezing the last drop of their propaganda value by using them in briefs filed as friends of the court where judges would see and use them. In short, it has provided a superb illustration of the lobbyist's principal duty of seeing that the decision-maker's attention is kept concentrated on the "right" facts. As a friend of the court, the Department of Justice filed a brief in the restrictive covenant cases. This also illustrates another invaluable lobbying technique, namely, that of obtaining an ally in the executive branch of the government for the cause one is pleading. Thus, in a period during which the political power of Negroes was growing, particularly in northern cities where it was thought they might be sufficiently numerous to wield the balance of power in elections, the NAACP slowly, cautiously, carefully, mobilized its strength and resources to secure a series of favorable rulings. As one observer has written: "The NAACP has won more victories in the Supreme Court than any other single organization."[15] As such, its importance in shifting into gear the governmental machinery for grinding out policy has been rarely equalled and probably never surpassed.

For all the Court's protestations that it is delimiting individual rights, it is, in fact, the main actor in the adjustment of social power as generated and manipulated by and among principal groups of the nation. As one of the NAACP attorneys said recently, ". . . Supreme Court cases involving larger issues are contests between opposing forces rather than lawsuits between individuals. They are cast as individual pieces of litigation because the Constitution guarantees the rights of individuals rather than those of groups. However, as a practical matter the individual is unable to pursue his rights to the ultimate, and hence the job is done by groups of people who find themselves situated as the individual is situated and who secure their own rights by securing the rights of the similarly situated individual."[16]

The Politics of Policy-Making

In the two case studies which follow will be found additional evidence of the politics of policy-making and of the presence of those who shape policy not only in all three branches of the government but also among the populace itself and, particularly, in the political pressure groups.

THE POLICY-MAKING CYCLE. "The policy-making cycle" is a term used to describe policy-making in the United States. Less pretentious than a theory, but differing from the conventional view, the policy-making cycle expands the area within which policy is usually considered as being made. In simplified terms it has four stages: prelegislative, congressional, administrative, judicial. As contrasted with the notion of policy-making as an activity limited to Congress, the cyclical notion of policy-making would set it in a wider and deeper social context. Those holding the traditional view may deprecate this way of viewing policy, calling it sociological, or institutional, or using some other "nonpolitical" adjective. A preference for the unconventional view is admitted.

Another descriptive view of policy-making is through an application of the principle of circular response. Borrowing this term from unidentified practitioners of the biological and social sciences, the late Henry S. Dennison applied it to the field of government in his plea for "the development of political science engineering." He saw government as affected by the "continuous interaction among the factors involved. . . ." Government is more than cause and effect: "Causes do not stay causes, but are themselves altered and affected by their own effects—the principle which in the biological and social sciences has been called the principle of 'circular response.' "[17]

TIDELANDS OIL. In the tidelands oil controversy the cycle of policy-making began with the executive branch of the government. It then shifted to Congress without result, was referred to the courts on the initiative of the executive, revived in Congress, returned to the executive branch. The Courts then fixed policy until the 1952 election returned a Congress and a President who saw eye to eye. The policy of the Supreme Court was then replaced by one substituted by Congress and the Chief Executive.

For more than a hundred years prior to 1937 neither Congress nor the executive branch had considered the offshore lands below the low watermark as part of the public lands of the United States.[18] On the contrary, both had acquiesced in a situation in which the states had tacitly assumed that control, if not title, to these lands was theirs and had acted accordingly, except where federal power to control commerce and navigation was involved.

In resolutions submitted by a Senator from North Dakota and a Representative from Alabama, Congress was asked, in 1937, to assert control over the submerged lands. Prompting for these resolutions came from the Secretary of the Interior, Harold L. Ickes. They were supported by the Navy and Interior Departments, mainly on the ground that control over the exploitation of oil thought to exist under the marginal seas should, for reasons of national defense, reside in the federal government. No action was taken on the resolutions.

For reasons still not entirely clear but apparently not unrelated to politics the United States singled out the State of California in 1946 and brought suit against it in the Supreme Court. Its purpose was to obtain approval of the federal claim to title of the submerged lands. Before this suit could be tried, however, Congress, in 1945, had been asked, not by the executive departments, but by interests sympathetic to the states' claims to abandon any claim to title on the part of the federal government. The federal action against California had brought about a working political coalition of forty-six of the forty-eight states in the persons of their attorneys general to oppose federal claims to title and to support pending resolutions in Congress to quitclaim any federal right to title. In contrast to the mild opposition to quitclaim legislation, including that from the executive branch, was the strong support in both 1945 and 1946 in which the National Association of Attorneys General was prominent.[19] Congress passed the quitclaim legislation, but President Truman vetoed it.

The supporters of the quitclaim legislation saw the issue in broader terms than oil. Although the executive branch and, particularly, Secretary Ickes had attempted to narrow it to oil, a much wider and deeper issue of federal-state relations was involved, according to advocates of quitclaim legislation. Port authority officials and municipal officials, both organized nationally, contemplated with alarm the effect a successful prosecution of the federal claims would have upon control over installations below the low watermark as well as upon subsoil products other than oil. Similar concern over states' rights, rather than the hold which oil interests had over the attorneys general of the states or ignorance of the basic issue, explains the almost unanimous position of the national organization of attorneys general.[20]

Now, the judicial branch of the federal government entered actively into the policy-making picture. After much sparring between the Department of Justice and the State of California for months after October, 1945, when the suit was filed, the Supreme Court, in a divided opinion in June, 1947, decided, in effect, that the contested area (the ocean belt between low water and the three-mile limit) did not belong to California and that the rights of the United States in this area were paramount. California, supported by the National Association of Attorneys General, petitioned the Court for a rehearing, but the Court denied it. In July, the Governors' Conference petitioned Congress to pass legislation recognizing state ownership of submerged lands and resources. An order and decree implementing its decision was handed down by the Supreme Court on October 27, 1947.

Further activity of the Supreme Court in policy-making at the instance of the executive branch occurred late in 1948, when the United States instituted suits against Texas and Louisiana. Attempts of both states to differentiate their status and that of California were unavailing. Relying on its decision in the earlier California case, the Supreme Court, on June 5, 1950, decided for the United States and against Texas and Louisiana. Both states again twice requested that the Court rehear the case. All requests for a rehearing were denied, and on December 11, 1950, the Supreme Court handed down its decree: as in California, so in Texas and Louisiana, the United States had paramount rights in and full dominion and power over the lands in question. The states were enjoined from carrying on any activities for removing or taking from the submerged areas any petroleum, gas, or other valuable mineral products except under prior authorization from the United States government.

A basic question of policy remained unsettled, however. While it was clear that neither California nor Texas nor Louisiana could continue to authorize the extraction of oil, further legislation by Congress was needed before the administrative authorities of the United States could authorize such activity.[21]

Settlement of the basic question of policy, quitclaim or federal control, was continually before Congress for the next six years, from the Court's decision for the United States in the California case to the enactment of quitclaim legislation by the Eighty-third Congress and its approval by President Eisenhower in 1953. Of the scores of bills introduced beginning in January, 1948, one, S. 940 (Eighty-second Congress, first session) may be mentioned to indicate the support which it enjoyed. Behind this measure, introduced in February, 1951, to restore the situation to its pre-1947 status were ranged the following organizations: the Council of State Governments, the Governors' Conference, the National Association of Attorneys General, the American Bar Association, the National Conference of Mayors, the American Association of Port Authorities, the National Reclamation Association, the National Water Conservation Association, the National Institute of Municipal Law Officers (representing 503 cities), and the National Association of Secretaries of State. Opposing bills to vest control in the United States were also introduced in Congress, but were far fewer in number than those favoring state control. Nor did they enjoy the support of as wide a segment of the interested citizenry. Measures of this sort were introduced by Senator Alben W. Barkley, (D., Ky.), by Congressman William Lemke, (R., N.D.) and by Senator Joseph C. O'Mahoney, (D., Wyo.). These measures were introduced at the request of the Departments of Justice and of the Interior. No bill favoring federal control got out of committee during the Eightieth, Eighty-first, or Eighty-second Congress, showing conclusively the sentiment prevailing both among committee leadership and membership. In Congress itself there was a majority in both houses favoring quitclaim legislation; in fact, such a bill could have been enacted at any time. But it faced certain veto by President Truman, as in 1946, and the uncertainty of sufficient Senate votes to override a presidential veto kept its advocates from pushing the matter. President Truman's nomination of Ed Pauley, of California, as Under-Secretary of Defense sharpened the political aspect of the issue during the Eightieth Congress and gave rise to charges of lobbying by oil companies favoring quitclaim legislation.[22] Apparently, lobbying from private interests favoring federal control was not absent, either. In any event, quitclaim legislation died on the calendar of the Senate of the Eightieth Congress; nor did such legislation come to a vote in either house of the Eighty-first Congress; and while both houses of the Eighty-second Congress passed quitclaim legislation, the President once more vetoed it. By then it was clear that tidelands oil would figure as a political issue in the 1952 presidential campaign. How much it figured in the pre-nominating convention fight for delegates is not so clear. One competent observer thinks it was unimportant in the Florida and California presidential primaries; as for Texas, he attempts no estimate.[23] In the Lone Star State, Adlai E. Stevenson's position was in line with that of President Truman. But Dwight D. Eisenhower's position favoring state control over the tidelands undoubtedly did much to swing the Texas electoral vote to the Republican presidential candidate. The stand of the two parties in their platforms on this issue was also dissimilar, the Democratic platform being less than forthright, while the Republican platform made it clear that in the event of a Republican victory, rights of the states to land and resources beneath navigable inland and offshore waters within their historic boundaries would be restored. And this is what happened. Among the first enactments of the Republican-controlled Eighty-third Congress was a bill, recommended by President Eisenhower, carrying out the pledge in the Republican platform. On May 22, 1953, the President signed this bill.

Thus the cycle of policy-making had run its course. In the tidelands oil controversy it was an eccentric course, not the normal course, so to speak, of successive phases of policy-making by legislature, executive, judiciary, but an abnormal course including not only the three branches of the federal government but the entire presidential and congressional electoral process in a presidential election year as well.

RESALE PRICE MAINTENANCE. The history of resale price maintenance (RPM) as an issue of public policy extends back over a period of seventy-five years, and is still unsettled in the minds of many people. The idea first arose in the 1880's, when the introduction of specialty products, brand names, and trademarks brought about gradual change in marketing methods. As price competition became increasingly severe, retailers saw that it would be to their advantage to have a system of protected prices whereby the manufacturer would establish the price at which a particular product would be resold to the public. The retailers were able to convince the manufacturers that such a policy would be in the manufacturers' own interests, and in a few years' time the problem of price maintenance by manufacturers on their trademarked products had become an important issue in marketing and public policy.[24]

The federal government first became involved with this problem through the courts rather than through the legislature. RPM was first upheld in the courts, which found it did not involve unreasonable restraint of trade. But with the passage of the Sherman Anti-trust Act in 1890, making illegal every combination in restraint, the subject of price maintenance contracts was introduced in the courts as a violation of the Sherman Act. The first clear-cut precedent was established in 1908, in the case of *Bobbs-Merrill Co. vs. Straus,* when the Supreme Court ruled that RPM was perfectly legal for a patent-holder but not for a copyright-holder. This ruling remained in effect only a few years, however. In 1911, in *Dr. Miles Medical Co. vs. Park and Sons Co.*, the Court took the position that resale price contracts were in violation of the Sherman Act in that they substantially lessened or eliminated competition among wholesalers and retailers.

When the Courts began to respond unfavorably to RPM, the battle shifted to legislative areas. It was at this time that the proponents of "fair trade," or RPM, consolidated their efforts, and various pressure groups were formed. In 1913, the American Fair Trade League was organized to advance the cause of RPM, and on the other side, in 1915, the National Trade Association was formed. Also, in 1913, Congress established the Federal Trade Commission, which subsequently was to play an integral part in the formation of a policy of fair trade through its review of unfair competition cases and its many studies and hearings.

In 1914, the first federal legislation was introduced, and by 1932, thirty fair-trade bills had been presented to Congress. None of these was successful, partly because of disinterest and partly because of preoccupation with war problems. With economic depression, the tide began to swing; price-cutters were widely thought of as swindlers and robbers. Bills on RPM began to receive more attention, and with the passage of the National Industrial Recovery Act in 1933, RPM was established, in effect, in the retail codes of that legislation. This ended all agitation until 1935, when the NIRA was declared unconstitutional. Although Congress had not yet paid serious attention to RPM, the FTC was conducting an investigation of the price-war situation in order to gain a thorough and comprehensive understanding of the economic advantages and disadvantages of RPM legislation.

At this time manufacturers and retailers groups were the most out-spoken supporters of RPM. The National Association of Retail Druggists is generally credited with fathering the "fair-trade" move-ment. The opposition was not as clearly aligned. Some of those against "fair trade" were the Homemaker's Association of New Jer-sey, the R. H. Macy Company, the National Retail Dry Goods As-sociation, the National Grange, and Jordan Marsh and Company. The FTC study aroused other interests to agitate against RPM, among them advertising concerns, consumer organizations, and those retailers who benefited from a high degree of freedom in price policy, such as the chain store, the department store, the mail-order house, and the discount house. The FTC itself concluded that the dangers of giving the manufacturer as much power as would be con-ferred by RPM far outweighed any advantages of fair trade.

At this stage, policy formation was on the state level. Beginning in 1931, when California passed a fair-trade law, state legislation in-creasingly favored RPM. By 1936, eleven states had followed Cali-fornia's example. With this backing, the fair-trade lobbyists turned again to Washington; intense pressure was exerted on both the Presi-dent and Congress. Although the President was not pleased by the legislation before the House and managed to delay action for a time by calling the FTC to present the findings of its investigation, on June 1, 1936, S. 3822, the Tydings-Miller Bill, was reported favorably by committee and passed the Senate. However, this bill died in the House when Congress adjourned nineteen days later.

In the interim the cause of RPM was strengthened by a decision of the Supreme Court in upholding RPM laws in Illinois and Cali-fornia. In the next few years all but five of the states had passed a fair-trade law of some sort. When Congress reassembled. bills were introduced into both houses in the form of amendments to the anti-trust law. Hearings on these bills showed that the opposition was much more vocal than previously, but both bills were reported out of committee unamended.

The President, however, was not in favor of action on RPM at this time. He wanted to finish other more immediate legislation and per-haps consider RPM in conjunction with a complete revision of the anti-trust laws. Therefore the bill was continuously passed over when called up for debate. While pressure was being directed at the Presi-dent to reconsider his action in delaying the Tydings-Miller Bill an-other situation developed which laid the way for a unique form of public policy-making.

Senator Tydings, seeing that his RPM bill was making no progress, introduced it as an amendment to the pending District of Columbia appropriations bill. This bill had been passed by the House and sent to the Senate, where it was referred to the Senate Committee on the District of Columbia. There were thirty-five suggested amendments, among them Senator Tydings', entitled Amendment to the Anti-trust Laws, which stipulated that manufacturers and retailers operating under state fair-trade laws were not to be held in violation of the federal anti-monopoly laws. In effect, this would have legalized minimum resale price agreements or contracts respecting trade-marked or similarly identified goods sold in interstate commerce.

When the bill was debated in the Senate, several Senators spoke against this amendment on the grounds that it had no place in an appropriations bill and that the implications were not fully understood by Senators. A vote had to be postponed because of lack of a quorum, and when debate reopened Senator Tydings quite frankly stated that he had taken this tack because of his inability to bring his original bill to a vote. When a quorum was secured the amendment was passed, and then the bill as a whole was passed. A favorable report of the conference committee was adopted and passed again by the Senate and the House. On August 6, 1937, the bill was presented to President Roosevelt.

At this point there was much interest in the bill. It was fairly well known that the President did not greatly favor legalization of RPM and also that the Justice Department was against any fair-trade law since it would not serve the purposes intended and its effects would be the same as private price-fixing or other similar conspiracies unregulated by public authority. At the same time, it was obvious that the District of Columbia needed appropriations and that the President could not veto the RPM amendment without vetoing the whole District of Columbia Revenue Act of 1937. Therefore, on August 17, 1937, President Roosevelt signed the bill. At the same time, he severely criticized the practice of attaching unrelated riders and expressed his hesitation in approving the substance of the amendment.

Almost immediately there was agitation for repeal. Within the next few years, several federal officials and agencies had completed studies on the worth of RPM and filed statements with the Temporary National Economic Committee (TNEC) condemning the operation of the Act and urging its repeal. Generally, however, the late 1930's and early 1940's were a period of consolidation and of testing the rules of application in the courts. During the war, fair-trade issues were almost completely forgotten.

After the war, the fight was resumed, and the opposition gained momentum. The FTC conducted another study of RPM; in 1947, the desirability of RPM in the light of current conditions was studied, particularly the need for maximum economy and efficiency in the production and distribution of goods. The situation became even more unsettled when the Florida supreme court invalidated the state fair-trade act. Aside from the usual arguments, the Florida court held that conditions had changed since 1937 and that there had been no corresponding change in the act. Other state courts were examining their fair-trade laws; a bill was introduced in the federal legislature to repeal the Miller-Tydings Act; an investigation of fair-trade laws by the House Judiciary Committee was proposed to determine whether the laws were really producing the keen, healthy competition the Congress intended. During this period, the American Fair Trade Council had grown in size and, with the National Association of Retail Druggists, was hard at work protecting its gains. This can be characterized as a period of peacetime testing, re-evaluation of the conditions of the economy and of the need for RPM, and the jockeying for positions of strength on the part of pressure groups.

A shift in attitude started in 1951, when the Supreme Court again ruled on RPM laws, this time with reference to interstate commerce. On May 21, the Court handed down a decision which proved to be something of a surprise. Though the Court did not find the Miller-Tydings Act and state fair-trade laws unconstitutional, it did weaken the concept of fair trade by noting that contracts regarding price maintenance did not apply to nonsigners. While this affected many state laws which specifically expressed their application to nonsigners, no one was sure about its effect on the Miller-Tydings Act. The nub of the case became whether or not that act extended to nonsigner clauses in the state acts. The proponents of fair trade were agreed that resale price maintenance must be binding upon nonsigners, and their goal now was to make certain that a nonsigner clause was legally embodied in federal legislation. However, there was disagreement as to how this might be done. The NARD wanted to amend the Federal Trade Commission Act, while AFTC wanted to amend the Sherman Act. The AFTC feared placing too much power in the hands of the FTC, while, on the other hand, the NARD felt an amendment to the Sherman Act would be lost, since, under House rules, the bill would be referred to the Judiciary Committee whose chairman had never been sympathetic to the idea of fair trade.

The NARD planned its attack carefully by getting the McGuire Bill introduced just before the adjournment of Congress and then staging a thorough grass-roots campaign while Congressmen were in their constituencies. Their local offices were deluged with some 150,000 pieces of literature mailed out by the Bureau of Education on Fair Trade. The success of the twelve weeks' program may be summed up in the words of one Senator not so safely back in Washington in late January. Asked whether or not he would vote against fair trade his comment was, "I don't bleed good."

Hearings were opened in February, 1952. At the same time, hearings were being held on three other bills dealing with RPM, one of which was supported by governmental agencies and called for repeal of the Miller-Tydings amendment. As in the past, the proponents of fair trade were much more vocal at the hearings than were their opponents. Several of the latter were invited to appear, but most of them declined. The fight for RPM was led by the Bureau of Education on Fair Trade, with headquarters in New York, an organization backed chiefly by large drug concerns and an estimated 1300 local, regional, and national trade associations. One main argument used was that with fair-trade laws in forty-five states there should be a federal law covering the matter. Considerable stress was put on the need to protect small business. As a significant symbol, it was subject to easy manipulation. Also, the term "fair trade" had forestalled opposition on the part of consumers and the public in general.

The main opposition came from the FTC and the Department of Justice. They claimed that changed economic conditions had done away with the necessity or even the desirability of RPM legislation with respect to interstate commerce. Fair-trade restrictions would only be a hindrance in an economy geared to mass production and high turnover of commodities at reasonably low handling cost. Also, they pointed out that RPM might well be used as a cloak to hide general price-fixing activities, thereby contributing to monopoly, and was a violation of the spirit of federal anti-trust laws.

The bill was successful in the House, though there was feeling that it had been pushed through without a real quorum. When it was sent to the Senate there was some possibility of failure, partly because two-thirds of the Senators were not up for re-election, hence were less susceptible to pressure than the one-third who were, and, partly, because public feeling had been aroused by the intense lobbying activity of the fair-trade groups. The Senate hearings were more extensive and the opposition's case was argued more strongly than heretofore. Their arguments emphasized the lack of a check on RPM—the vague wording of the bill with reference to commodities in "free and open competition with commodities of the same general class." Moreover, they argued that supporters of RPM legislation had misrepresented the implications of the bill. While the bill ostensibly allowed states to follow whatever policy they wished on RPM, in reality it would have given congressional approval to RPM legislation. The CIO, the National Grange and various other farm groups, the Housewives United, and the General Federation of Women's Clubs took stands against the bill.

The bill was reported out of committee with no recommendation. On July 2, the vote was 64 in favor, 16 opposed, and 16 not voting. The vote was not divided along party lines, or even liberal or conservative lines. Having passed both houses, the bill now faced its chief opponent, President Truman. Much to everyone's surprise, he signed the McGuire Act, though the opposition had been fairly confident of his veto. The general feeling was that in an election year he had shown himself susceptible to the terrific political pressure which had been exerted through letters and telegrams to the White House. By signing he did not lose the bloc of small businessmen, while consumers did not seem to care or know enough about the bill to object.

Since the passage of this bill in 1952, activity has died down considerably. Two forces are at work, however, which indicate it may receive further consideration. One is the continual testing of the constitutionality of the McGuire Act, and the other is the growth of the discount house. Those opposed to fair trade feel that they have a good chance of getting the McGuire Act declared unconstitutional, and although the Supreme Court has refused to hear one important case, in 1952, since then various state courts have reconsidered their state fair-trade laws. Some have upheld their constitutionality, as in the cases of New York and Delaware; others have declared them unconstitutional, as in Utah, Arkansas, Florida, Michigan, and Georgia. During 1955, however, the Supreme Court refused to review fair-trade laws on constitutional grounds on no less than five occasions.

On the question of discount houses, considerable interest arose in 1955 and 1956. The Senate Small Business Committee studied the question, and there was a growing agitation to "do something" about the situation. Increasingly, retail houses have come to ignore the fair-trade prices fixed by manufacturers.

The issue of RPM is one which is closely tied to the economic structure of the country, and, as such, public policy is bound to undergo fluctuations as these economic conditions change. It is also an issue which can be easily advanced by concerted lobbying, while the opposition finds it difficult to inform the public and arouse public opinion on the potential dangers to the consumer and the economy in general. Thus national policy is rarely clearly defined; nor is the process of policy-making a clear-cut one. The considerable activity in the courts has naturally influenced legislative action. The Chief

Executive, though generally not in favor of RPM, has, in two instances, found himself forced to sign RPM legislation. At the same time, various departments of the executive branch have consistently opposed RPM. It is clear, then, that public policy on RPM is not settled and that changes will be effected as the power and influence of these various forces is consolidated.

SUMMARY. Policy is made in the nation's courts, and most particularly, in the Supreme Court, which, pursuant to the custom of judicial review, is able, in circumstances characterized by a challenge to the power of Congress or to the administrative branch, to replace the legislative and the executive by the judicial will. With population shifts, changes in technology, keener competition for greater shares of the national income, pressure groups have entered the judicial arena, where they pursue their interests with the same skill, energy, and resources they employ in the legislative and administrative fields. Also to be noted is the cyclical nature of the policy-making process, made up of four stages (pre-legislative, congressional, administrative, judicial), not all of which are encompassed by every policy, but which—since much legislation is enacted over the opposition of determined groups—must be followed before we know what policy is. Even then, with Congress ready to change policy previously made, either by repeal or amendment, a new revolution of the cycle may be started. In recent years, in the field of civil rights, when, for political reasons, Congress has not been open to groups for the redress of their grievances, the judicial process has been discovered and has been found by some of these groups to be an effective way to the making of public policy.

BIBLIOGRAPHY

Books

ADAMS, JAMES TRUSLOW. *Our Business Civilization*. New York: Charles & Albert Boni, 1929.

———. *The Living Jefferson*. New York: Charles Scribner's Sons, 1936.

ADAMS, WALTER, and GRAY, HORACE M. *Monopoly in America: The Government as Promoter*. New York: The Macmillan Co., 1955.

ALBIG, WILLIAM. *Modern Public Opinion*. New York: McGraw-Hill Book Co., Inc., 1956.

BAILEY, STEPHEN K. *Congress Makes a Law*. New York: Columbia University Press, 1950.

BARTLEY, ERNEST R. *The Tidelands Oil Controversy*. Austin: University of Texas Press, 1953.

BAUER, WILHELM. "Public Opinion," *Encyclopedia of the Social Sciences*. New York: The Macmillan Co., 1942, Vol. XII.

BENDIX, REINHARD. "Bureaucracy and the Problem of Power," MERTON, ROBERT K., *et al. Reader in Bureaucracy*. Glencoe, Ill.: The Free Press, 1952.

BENTLEY, ARTHUR F. *The Process of Government*. Bloomington, Ind.: The Principia Press of Illinois, 1949.

BERLE, ADOLF A., JR., and MEANS, GARDINER C. *The Modern Corporation and Private Property*. New York: The Macmillan Co., 1932.

BERLE, ADOLF A., JR. *The 20th Century Capitalist Revolution*. New York: Harcourt, Brace & Co., Inc., 1954.

BLOUGH, ROY. *The Federal Taxing Process*. Englewood Cliffs, N.J.: Prentice-Hall, Inc., 1952.

BOLLES, BLAIR. *How to Get Rich in Washington*. New York: Dell Publishing Co., 1953.

BRADY, ROBERT A. *Business as a System of Power*. New York: Columbia University Press, 1943.

BROGAN, DENIS W. *Politics in America*. New York: Harper & Bros., 1955.

BROWN, J. A. C. *The Social Psychology of Industry*. Baltimore: Penguin Books, Inc., 1954.

BRUCKER, HERBERT. *Freedom of Information*. New York: The Macmillan Co., 1949.

BURNS, JAMES MACGREGOR. *Congress on Trial*. New York: Harper & Bros., 1949.

BUSBEY, L. WHITE. *Uncle Joe Cannon*. New York: Henry Holt & Co., Inc., 1927.

CHAMBERLAIN, LAWRENCE H. *The President, Congress, and Legislation*. New York: Columbia University Press, 1946.

COCHRAN, THOMAS C., and MILLER, WILLIAM. *The Age of Enterprise*. New York: The Macmillan Co., 1951.

CRAWFORD, KENNETH G. *The Pressure Boys.* New York: Julian Messner, Inc., 1937.

DAHL, ROBERT A., and LINDBLOOM, CHARLES E. *Politics, Economics, and Welfare.* New York: Harper & Bros., 1953.

DAVID, PAUL A., and GOLDMAN, RALPH (eds.). *Presidential Nominating Politics in 1952,* 5 vols. Baltimore: Johns Hopkins University Press, 1954.

DEARING, MARY R. *Veterans in Politics: The Story of the GAR.* Baton Rouge: Louisiana State University Press, 1952.

DEMOCRATIC NATIONAL CONVENTION. *Official Proceedings,* 1952.

DEMOCRATIC NATIONAL CONVENTION. *Official Manual,* 1952.

DENNISON, HENRY S. "The Need for the Development of Political Science Engineering." *Papers on the Science of Administration.* eds. LUTHER GULICK and L. URWICK. 2d ed. New York: Institute of Public Administration, 1947.

DUVERGER, MAURICE. *Political Parties, Their Organization and Activities in the Modern State.* Translated by BARBARA and ROBERT NORTH, with a foreword by D. W. BROGAN. New York: John Wiley & Sons, Inc., 1955.

EBERSOLE, LUKE. *Church Lobbying in the Nation's Capital.* New York: The Macmillan Co., 1951.

EMERSON, THOMAS I., and HABER, DAVID. *Political and Civil Rights in the United States.* Buffalo: Dennis & Co., Inc., 1952.

FAINSOD, MERLE. *How Russia Is Ruled.* Cambridge: Harvard University Press, 1954.

FARLEY, JAMES A. *Behind the Ballots.* New York: Harcourt, Brace & Co., Inc., 1938.

FRIEDRICH, CARL J. "Oligarchy." *Encyclopedia of the Social Sciences.* New York: The Macmillan Co., 1942, Vol. XI.

GALBRAITH, JOHN KENNETH. *American Capitalism: The Concept of Countervailing Power.* Boston: Houghton Mifflin Co., 1952.

GALLOWAY, GEORGE B. *The Legislative Process in Congress.* New York: Thomas Y. Crowell Co., 1953.

GARCEAU, OLIVER. *The Political Life of the American Medical Association.* Cambridge: Harvard University Press, 1941.

DE GRAZIA, ALFRED. *Public and Republic.* New York: Alfred A. Knopf, Inc., 1951.

GRIFFITH, ERNEST S. *Congress: Its Contemporary Role.* New York: New York University Press, 1951.

GROSS, BERTRAM M. *The Legislative Struggle.* New York: McGraw-Hill Book Co., Inc., 1953.

HALE, ROBERT L. *Freedom Through Law: Public Control of Private Governing Power.* New York: Columbia University Press, 1952.

HARDIN, CHARLES M. *The Politics of Agriculture: Soil Conservation and the Struggle for Power in Rural America.* Glencoe, Ill.: The Free Press, 1952.

HARVEY, RAY F., et al. *The Politics of This War.* New York: Harper & Bros., 1943.

HELLER, HERMANN. "Political Power." *Encyclopedia of the Social Sciences.* New York: The Macmillan Co., 1942, Vol. XII.

HERRING, E. PENDLETON. *Presidential Leadership*. New York: Rinehart & Co., Inc., 1940.

——. *The Politics of Democracy*. New York: Rinehart & Co., Inc., 1940.

——. "Lobbying." *Encyclopedia of the Social Sciences*. New York: The Macmillan Co., 1942, Vol. IX.

HYMAN, SIDNEY. *The American President*. New York: Harper & Bros., 1954.

HYNEMAN, CHARLES. *Bureaucracy in a Democracy*. New York: Harper & Bros., 1950.

DE JOUVENEL, BERTRAND. *On Power: Its Nature and History of Its Growth*. New York: The Viking Press, Inc., 1949.

KEEZER, DEXTER M. "Press." *Encyclopedia of the Social Sciences*. New York: The Macmillan Co., 1942, Vol. XII.

KEY, V. O., JR. *Politics, Parties, and Pressure Groups*, 3d ed. New York: Thomas Y. Crowell Co., 1953.

KELLER, STANLEY, JR. *Professional Public Relations and Political Power*. Baltimore: Johns Hopkins Press, 1956.

KENT, FRANK R. *The Great Game of Politics*. New York: Doubleday & Co., Inc., 1926.

KILE, O. M. *The Farm Bureau Federation through Three Decades*. Baltimore: The Waverley Press, 1948.

KIPLINGER, W. M. *Washington Is Like That*. New York: Harper & Bros., 1942.

LASSWELL, HAROLD D. *Politics: Who Gets What, When, How*. New York: McGraw-Hill Book Co., Inc., 1936.

LAZARSFELD, PAUL, BERELSON, B., and GAUDET, H. *The People's Choice*. New York: Columbia University Press, 1948.

LEWIS, R. CRAGIN. "New Power at the Polls: The Doctors." *Politics in the United States*. ed. HENRY A. TURNER. New York: McGraw-Hill Book Co., Inc., 1955.

LUCE, ROBERT. *Congress: An Explanation*. Cambridge: Harvard University Press, 1926.

LYNCH, DAVID. *The Concentration of Economic Power*. New York: Columbia University Press, 1946.

MACIVER, ROBERT M. "Social Pressures." *Encyclopedia of the Social Sciences*. New York: The Macmillan Co., 1942, Vol. XII.

——. *The Web of Government*. New York: The Macmillan Co., 1947.

McKEAN, DAYTON D. *Party and Pressure Politics*. Boston: Houghton Mifflin Co., 1949.

MACMAHON, ARTHUR W. "Political Parties: The United States." *Encyclopedia of the Social Sciences*. New York: The Macmillan Co., 1937, Vol. XI.

——. *Administration in Foreign Affairs*. University, Ala.: University of Alabama Press, 1953.

MASON, ALPHEUS T. *The Supreme Court: Vehicle of Revealed Truth or Power Group, 1930-1937*. Boston: Boston University Press, 1953.

MERRIAM, CHARLES E. *Political Power*. New York: McGraw-Hill Book Co., Inc., 1934.

MICHELS, ROBERTO. *First Lectures in Political Sociology*. Translated by ALFRED DE GRAZIA. Minneapolis: University of Minnesota Press, 1949.

ODEGARD, PETER. *Pressure Politics, The Story of the Anti-Saloon League*. New York: Columbia University Press, 1928.

OPPENHEIMER, J. ROBERT. *The Open Mind*. New York: Simon & Schuster, Inc., 1955.

OVERSTREET, H. A. *The Mature Mind*. New York: W. W. Norton & Co., Inc., 1949.

PURDY, HARRY L., LINDAHL, MARTIN L., and CARTER, WILLIAM A. *Corporate Concentration and Public Policy*. 2d ed. Englewood Cliffs, N.J.: Prentice-Hall, Inc., 1950.

RANDALL, J. G., and CURRENT, RICHARD N. *Lincoln The President*. Vol. IV, *Last Full Measure*. New York: Dodd, Mead & Co., 1955.

RAUCH, BASIL. *The History of the New Deal, 1933-1938*. New York: Creative Age Press, Inc., 1944.

REPUBLICAN NATIONAL CONVENTION, *Official Report of the Proceedings of the Twenty-Fifth Convention*, 1952.

RIESMAN, DAVID. *The Lonely Crowd*. New Haven: Yale University Press, 1950.

RIGGS, FRED W. *Pressures on Congress: A Study of the Repeal of Chinese Exclusion*. New York: King's Crown Press, 1950.

RODELL, FRED. *Nine Men. A Political History of the Supreme Court from 1790 to 1955*. New York: Random House, Inc., 1955.

ROGERS, LINDSAY. *The Pollsters*. New York: Alfred A. Knopf, Inc., 1949.

F. D. R.: His Personal Letters. 2 vols. New York: Duell, Sloan & Pearce, Inc., 1947.

ROSEN, S. McKEE. *Political Process*. New York: Harper & Bros., 1938.

RUTHERFORD, M. LOUISE. *The Influence of the American Bar Association on Public Opinion and Legislation*. Philadelphia: University of Pennsylvania Press, 1937.

SAPIN, BURTON M., and SNYDER, RICHARD C. *The Role of the Military in American Foreign Policy*. New York: Doubleday & Co., Inc., 1954.

SCHATTSCHNEIDER, E. E. *Party Government*. New York: Rinehart & Co., Inc., 1942.

——. *The Struggle for Party Government*. College Park, Md.: University of Maryland Press, 1948.

——. *Politics, Pressures, and the Tariff*. Englewood Cliffs, N.J.: Prentice-Hall, Inc., 1935.

SCHLESINGER, ARTHUR M., JR. *The Age of Jackson*. Boston: Little, Brown & Co., 1946.

SCHRIFTGIESSER, KARL. *The Lobbyists*. Boston: Little, Brown & Co., 1951.

SCHUMPETER, J. A. *Capitalism, Socialism, and Democracy*. New York: Harper & Bros., 1942.

SCHWEITZER, ALBERT. *Out of My Life and Thought*. New York: Henry Holt & Co., Inc., 1949.

SEIPMANN, CHARLES A. *Radio, Television and Society*. New York: Oxford University Press, 1950.

SHERIF, MUZAFER, and CANTRIL, HADLEY. *The Psychology of Ego-Involvements*. New York: John Wiley & Sons, Inc., 1947.

SMELLIE, K. "Right of Petition." *Encyclopedia of the Social Sciences.* New York: The Macmillan Co., 1942, Vol. XII.

SMITH, BRADFORD. *A Dangerous Freedom.* Philadelphia: J. B. Lippincott Co., 1954.

SOREL, GEORGES. *Reflections on Violence,* Translated by T. E. HULME and J. ROTH, with an introduction by EDWARD A. SHILS. Glencoe, Ill.: The Free Press, 1950.

STAPLETON, LAURENCE. *The Design of Democracy.* New York: Oxford University Press, 1949.

STEFFENS, LINCOLN. *The Autobiography of Lincoln Steffens.* New York: Harcourt, Brace & Co., Inc., 1931.

STEINER, GEORGE A. *Government's Role in Economic Life.* New York: McGraw-Hill Book Co., Inc., 1953.

STEVENSON, ADLAI E. *Major Campaign Speeches, 1952.* New York: Random House, Inc., 1953.

STEVENSON, ELIZABETH. *Henry Adams, A Biography.* New York: The Macmillan Co., 1955.

STIMSON, HENRY L., and BUNDY, McGEORGE. *On Active Service in Peace and War.* New York: Harper & Bros., 1947.

STOCKING, GEORGE W., and WATKINS, M. W. *How Big is Big Business?* New York: Twentieth Century Fund, 1937.

SUTHERLAND, EDWIN H. *White Collar Crime.* New York: The Dryden Press, Inc., 1949.

Toward a More Responsible Two-Party System. A Report of the Committee on Political Parties of the American Political Science Association. New York: Rinehart & Co., Inc., 1950.

TRUMAN, DAVID B. *The Governmental Process.* New York: Alfred A. Knopf, Inc., 1951.

TURNER, JULIUS. *Party and Constituency: Pressures on Congress.* Baltimore: Johns Hopkins Press, 1951.

WHYTE, WILLIAM H., JR. *Is Anybody Listening?* New York: Simon & Schuster, Inc., 1952.

WILLOUGHBY, WESTEL W., and ROGERS, LINDSAY. *An Introduction to the Problem of Government.* New York: Doubleday & Co., Inc., 1927.

Periodicals and Reviews

ASCH, SOLOMON E. "Opinions and Social Pressure," *Scientific American,* 193 (November, 1955).

BARCLAY, THOMAS S. Review of DAVID D. McKEAN's *Party and Pressure Politics, American Political Science Review,* XLIII (December, 1949).

BENDINER, ROBERT. "The 'Engineering of Consent'—A Case Study," *The Reporter,* XIII (August 11, 1955).

BERDAHL, CLARENCE A. "Party Membership in the United States," *American Political Science Review,* XXXVI (April, 1942).

————. "Some Notes on Party Membership in Congress," *American Political Science Review*, XLIII (April, June, and August, 1949).

BERNSTEIN, MARVER H. "Political Ideas of Selected American Business Journals," *Public Opinion Quarterly*, Summer, 1953.

BIERSTEDT, ROBERT. "An Analysis of Social Power," *American Sociological Review*, XV (December, 1950).

CAMPBELL, ANGUS, *et al.* "The Electoral Switch of 1952," *Scientific American*, 190 (May, 1954).

CANTRIL, HADLEY. "Psychology," *Scientific American*, 183 (September, 1950).

CASSINELLI, C. W. "The Iron Law of Oligarchy," *American Political Science Review*, XLVII (September, 1953).

CHILDS, HARWOOD L. "By Public Opinion I Mean," *Public Opinion Quarterly*, III (April, 1939).

CLARK, KENNETH B. "Desegregation in the Public Schools," *Social Problems*, II (1955).

Congressional Quarterly, I, Foreword.

DREHER, CARL. "E. H. Armstrong, The Hero as Inventor," *Harper's Magazine*, 212 (April, 1956).

FRASER, HUGH RUSSELL. "Texans Don't Know Any Better," *Harper's Magazine*, 213 (June, 1956).

GABLE, RICHARD W. "NAM: Influential Lobby or Kiss of Death?" *Journal of Politics*, XV (May, 1953).

GALLOWAY, GEORGE B. "The Operation of the Legislative Reorganization Act," *American Political Science Review*, XLV (March, 1951).

"GOP Platform at Work," *Democratic Digest*, III (August, 1955).

HUITT, RALPH K. "The Congressional Committee: A Case Study," *American Political Science Review*, XLVIII (June, 1954).

KATZENBACH, EDWARD L., JR. "How Congress Strains at Gnats, then Swallows Military Budgets," *The Reporter*, XI (July 20, 1954).

KAUFMAN, HERBERT, and JONES, VICTOR. "The Mystery of Power," *Public Administration Review*, XIV (Summer, 1954).

KROEBER, A. L. "Anthropology," *Scientific American*, 183 (September, 1950).

LASSWELL, HAROLD D. "The Theory of Propaganda," *American Political Science Review*, XXI (August, 1927).

LATHAM, EARL. "The Group Basis of Politics: Notes for a Theory," *American Political Science Review*, XLVI (June, 1952).

LAWTON, FREDERICK J. "Legislative-Executive Relationships in Budgeting as Viewed by the Executive," *Public Administration Review*, XIII (Summer, 1953).

LIEBLING, A. J. "The Press," *Holiday*, VII (February, 1950).

LONG, STUART. " 'Scared Money' Wins an Election in Texas," *The Reporter*, XI (October 21, 1954).

MCKEAN, DAYTON D. "Political Machines and National Elections, 1948," *Annals of the American Academy of Political and Social Science*, No. 259 (September, 1948).

MASON, ALPHEUS T. "Business Organized as Power: the New Imperium in Imperio," *American Political Science Review*, XLIV (June, 1950).

MEANY, JOHN W. "Propaganda as Psychical Coercion," *Review of Politics*, XIII (January, 1951).

MILLER, WARREN E. "Party Preference and Attitudes on Political Issues: 1948-1951," *American Political Science Review*, XLVII (March, 1953).

MILLER, WILLIAM LEE. "Can Government Be Merchandised?" *The Reporter*, IX (October 27, 1953).

———. "Should We Fight Dirty Too? A Democrat Gives His Answer," *The Reporter*, XI (October 21, 1954).

"Our Form of Government," *Fortune*, Supplement (November, 1943).

"Political Participation in a Metropolitan District: A Study of Group Influence on Political Activity," *American Political Science Review*, XLVI (December, 1952).

PRESTHUS, R. VANCE. Review of HENRY A. WELLS's *Monopoly and Social Control*, *Journal of Politics*, XV (November, 1953).

ROBERTS, CHALMERS M. "Battle on 'the Rim of Hell': The President vs. the War Hawks," *The Reporter*, XI (December 16, 1954).

"The Roles of Congressional Leaders: National Party vs. Constituency," *American Political Science Review*, XLVI (December, 1952).

ROPER, ELMO. "Who Tells the Storytellers?" *The Saturday Review*, July 31, 1954.

ROSSITER, CLINTON L. Review of JAMES M. BURNS's *Congress on Trial*, *American Political Science Review*, XLIII (December, 1949).

SCHATTSCHNEIDER, E. E. "Party Government and Employment Policy," *American Political Science Review*, XXXIX (December, 1945).

———. "Pressure Groups versus Political Parties," *Annals of the American Academy of Political and Social Science*, No. 259 (September, 1948).

SHAYON, R. L. "Plotkin vs. the Networks," *The Saturday Review*, June 25, 1955.

SLICHTER, SUMNER H. "The Growth of Competition," *Atlantic Monthly*, 192 (November, 1953).

SMITH, CARL O., and FIELD, G. LOWELL. "The Responsibility of Parties in Congress: Myth and Reality," *Southwestern Social Science Quarterly*, XXXIV (June, 1953).

STAATS, ELMER B. "The Government Sector in the American Economy," *American Political Science Review*, XLVII (March, 1953).

STOCKING, G. W. Review of DAVID E. LILIENTHAL's *Big Business: A New Era*, *American Political Science Review*, XLVIII (March, 1954).

———. Review of T. K. QUINN's *Giant Business: A Threat to Democracy*, *American Political Science Review*, XLVIII (March, 1954).

STRONG, DONALD S. Review of FLOYD HUNTER's *Community Power Structure: A Study of Decision Makers*, *American Political Science Review*, XLVIII (March, 1954).

TURNER, JULIUS. "Primary Elections as the Alternative to Party Competition in 'Safe' Districts," *Journal of Politics*, V (May, 1953).

VOSE, CLEMENT, E. "NAACP Strategy in the Covenant Cases," *Western Reserve Law Review*, 6 (Winter, 1955).

WOODWARD, JULIAN L., and ROPER, ELMO. "Political Activity of American Citizens," *American Political Science Review*, XLIV (December, 1950).

Pamphlets

BAKER, GORDON E. *Rural versus Urban Political Power.* New York: Doubleday & Co., Inc., 1955.

BLAISDELL, DONALD C. *Government Under Pressure.* New York: Public Affairs Committee, Inc., 1942.

CHEW, ARTHUR P. *The Response of Government to Agriculture.* Washington, D.C.: Government Printing Office, 1937.

FREEMAN, J. LEIPER. *The Political Process: Executive Bureau-Legislative Committee Relations.* New York: Doubleday & Co., Inc., 1955.

KREPS, THEODORE J. *Taxes and the Human Factor.* Washington, D.C.: Public Affairs Institute, 1951.

Official Documents

BLAISDELL, DONALD C. *Economic Power and Political Pressures.* Temporary National Economic Committee, Monograph No. 26 (76th Cong., 3d. sess.) Washington, D.C.: Government Printing Office, 1941.

DEPARTMENT OF COMMERCE, *National Associations of the United States.* Washington, D.C.: Government Printing Office, 1949.

GRAVES, W. BROOKE. *Administration of the Lobby Registration Provision of the Legislative Reorganization Act of 1946.* Library of Congress, Legislative Reference Service. Washington, D.C.: Government Printing Office, 1950.

HOUSE COMMITTEE ON THE JUDICIARY, 84th Cong., 2d. sess. *Interim Report of the Anti-Trust Subcommittee,* pursuant to H. Res. 22 authorizing the Committee on the Judiciary to conduct studies and investigations relating to certain matters within its jurisdiction on WOC's and Government Advisory Groups. Washington, D.C.: Government Printing Office, 1956.

HOUSE SELECT COMMITTEE ON LOBBYING ACTIVITIES, 81st Cong., 2d sess. *Hearings.* 10 vols. Washington, D.C.: Government Printing Office, 1950.
Part 1. *The Role of Lobbying in Representative Self-Government.*
Part 2. *Housing Lobby.*
Part 3. *Contingent Fee Lobbying.*
Part 4. *National Economic Council, Inc.*
Part 5. *Committee for Constitutional Government.*
Part 6. *Americans for Democratic Action.*
Part 7. *Public Affairs Institute.*
Part 8. *Foundation for Economic Education.*
Part 9. *Civil Rights Congress.*
Part 10. *Legislative Activities of Executive Agencies.*

HOUSE SELECT COMMITTEE ON LOBBYING ACTIVITIES, 81st Cong., 2d sess. *Reports.* Washington, D.C.: Government Printing Office, 1950.
H. Rep. No. 3024. *Report citing Edward A. Rumely.*
H. Rep. No. 3025. *Report citing William L. Patterson.*
H. Rep. No. 3033. *Report citing Joseph P. Kamp.*
H. Rep. No. 3137. *Expenditures by Corporations to Influence Legislation.*
H. Rep. No. 3138. *General Interim Report.*
H. Rep. No. 3139. *United States Saving and Loan League.*
H. Rep. No. 3197. *Lobby Index, 1946-49.*
H. Rep. No. 3232. *Conference of American Small Business Organizations.*

H. Rep. No. 3233. *American Enterprise Association.*

H. Rep. No. 3234. *Lobby Index, 1950.*

H. Rep. No. 3238. *Expenditures by Farm and Labor Organizations to Influence Legislation, and Supplement to Expenditures by Corporations to Influence Legislation.*

HOUSE SELECT COMMITTEE ON LOBBYING ACTIVITIES, 81st Cong., 2d sess. *Report and Recommendations.* Washington, D.C.: Government Printing Office, 1951; Part 2, *Minority Views.* Washington, D.C.: Government Printing Office, 1951.

Organization of the Congress. Report of the Joint Committee on the Organization of Congress, pursuant to H. Con. Res. 18 (79th Cong., 2d. sess.) Washington, D.C.: Government Printing Office, 1946.

TEMPORARY NATIONAL ECONOMIC COMMITTEE. *Final Report and Recommendations* (76th Cong. 3d. sess.) Sen. Doc. 35 (77th Cong., 1st sess.) Washington, D.C.: Government Printing Office, 1941.

WILCOX, CLAIR. *Competition and Monopoly in American Industry.* Temporary National Economic Committee, Monograph No. 21. (76th Cong., 3d. sess.) Washington, D.C.: Government Printing Office, 1940.

Unpublished Dissertations

CLEVELAND, ALFRED S. "Some Political Aspects of Organized Industry." Harvard University, Department of Political Science, 1948.

GABLE, RICHARD W. "A Political Analysis of an Employers' Association, the National Association of Manufacturers." University of Chicago, Department of Political Science, 1950.

Newspapers

DESMOND, THOMAS C. "Those Dinosaurs—the State Legislatures," *The New York Times Magazine,* January 16, 1955.

DOUGLAS, PAUL H. Review of SYDNEY HYMAN's *The American President, The New York Times Book Review,* February 14, 1954.

KENNEDY, JOHN F. "To Keep the Lobbyists within Bounds," *The New York Times Magazine,* February 19, 1956.

NEVINS, ALLAN. "Our Democracy is the Hardest in the World to Spell Out in a Book," *The New York Times Book Review,* March 14, 1954.

New York *Herald Tribune,* February 11, 1955, editorial.

The New York Times, February 24, 1955, editorial.

ROCHE, JOHN P., and GORDON, MILTON M. "Can Morality Be Legislated?" *The New York Times Magazine,* May 22, 1955.

Tampa *Morning Tribune,* December 10, 1953, editorial.

Washington Post and Times Herald, March 12, 1949, editorial.

Washington Post and Times Herald, December 28, 1954, editorial.

WERNER, M. R. Review of GLYNDON G. VAN DEUSEN's *Thurlow Weed: Wizard of the Lobby, The New York Times Book Review,* February 9, 1947.

WILLIAMSON, S. T. "The Lobby on the Job," *The New York Times Magazine,* April 17, 1938.

NOTES

Chapter 1

1. John F. Kennedy, "To Keep the Lobbyists within Bounds," *The New York Times Magazine,* February 19, 1956.
2. According to a poll conducted in 1949 by the American Institute of Public Opinion. *Public Opinion Quarterly,* XIII (Fall, 1949), 552, quoted in *General Interim Report of the House Select Committee on Lobbying Activities,* H. R. Rep. No. 3138, 81st Cong., 2d sess. (Washington, D.C.: Government Printing Office, 1950), p. 2. Hereafter cited as *Interim Report.*
3. Elmer B. Staats, "The Government Sector of the American Economy," *The American Political Science Review,* XLVII (March, 1953), 182-83.
4. Elizabeth Stevenson, *Henry Adams, A Biography* (New York: The Macmillan Co., 1955), p. 173.
5. House Select Committee on Lobbying Activities, 81st Cong., 2d sess., *Hearings* (10 vols.; Washington, D.C.: Government Printing Office, 1950), Part 1, *The Role of Lobbying in Representative Self-Government,* pp. 99-100. Cited hereafter as *Lobby Hearings.*
6. *Behavior, Knowledge, Fact* (Bloomington, Ind.: The Principia Press of Illinois, 1935), p. 29.
7. E. E. Schattschneider, "Party Government and Employment Policy," *American Political Science Review,* XXXIX (December, 1945), 22.
8. David B. Truman, *The Governmental Process* (New York: Alfred A. Knopf, Inc., 1951), p. 51.
9. Charles Hyneman, *Bureaucracy in a Democracy* (New York: Harper & Bros., 1950), pp. 109-10; see also Robert M. MacIver, *The Web of Government* (New York: The Macmillan Co., 1947), pp. 298-99.
10. T. D. Weldon, *The Vocabulary of Politics* (Melbourne, London, Baltimore: Penguin Books, 1953). See also MacIver, *op. cit.,* pp. 298-99.
11. James W. Prothro, *The Dollar Decade: Business Ideas in the 1920's* (Baton Rouge: Louisiana State University Press, 1955).
12. D. W. Brogan, *Politics in America* (New York: Harper & Bros., 1955), pp. 352 ff.
13. Some students of public policy question the assumption that individuals and groups know what their interests are. For example, the stands taken by certain groups and associations on tax policy make Blough wonder whether they are well advised by the experts on taxation whom they employ. See Roy Blough, *The Federal Taxing Process* (Englewood Cliffs, N.J.: Prentice-Hall, Inc., 1952), pp. 31-32, 40-43.
14. Henry L. Stimson and McGeorge Bundy, *On Active Service in Peace and War* (New York: Harper & Bros., 1947), p. 672.
15. Fred W. Riggs, *Pressures on Congress: A Study of the Repeal of Chinese Exclusion* (New York: King's Crown Press, 1950), p. 198.
16. *Ibid.,* p. 199.
17. George A. Steiner, *Government's Role in Economic Life* (New York: McGraw-Hill Book Co., Inc., 1953), pp. 333-34.
18. Blough, *op. cit.,* p. 474.
19. *Ibid.,* pp. 40-43.
20. Ernest S. Griffith, *Congress: Its Contemporary Role* (New York: New York University Press, 1951), pp. 106, 112.
21. Tampa *Morning Tribune,* December 10, 1953.

22. *Interim Report*, p. 47. See also p. 51 and pp. 64-65.
23. Robert M. MacIver, *op. cit.*, p. 619; Karl Schriftgiesser, *The Lobbyists* (Boston: Little, Brown & Co., 1951), pp. 32-33.
24. Schriftgiesser, *op. cit.*, pp. 32-33.
25. *Interim Report*, pp. 64-65.
26. E. P. Herring, "The Lobby," *Encyclopedia of the Social Sciences* (New York: The Macmillan Co., 1942), Vol. IX, p. 567.
27. *Ibid.*
28. *Report of the Joint Interim Committee Investigating Lobbying Activities* (1950), reproduced in *Lobby Hearings*, Part 1, pp. 82-83.
29. *Ibid.*, p. 27.
30. *Ibid.*, pp. 21, 27.

Chapter 2

1. In his penetrating study of the shifts in electoral power to 1934, Arthur N. Holcombe coined the phrase "urbane politics." Urbane politics and urban politics are not synonymous, urbanity being a characteristic of much rural (rustic, for Holcombe) politics as well as of metropolitan politics. See Arthur N. Holcombe, *The New Party Politics* (New York: W. W. Norton & Co., Inc., 1933). Probably the best nontechnical story of the struggle of the Negroes for full civil rights is to be found in Walter F. White's *How Far the Promised Land* (New York: The Viking Press, Inc., 1955).
2. The United States became a member of the International Labor Organization in an unusual way. The treaty-making process was not used by President Roosevelt when the United States joined the ILO in 1934. Following Senate adoption of a resolution authorizing the President to apply for membership, the United States applied and its application was accepted by the International Labor Conference. Further congressional action was not necessary. But the President and his Secretary of Labor, Frances Perkins, had paved the way with Senate leaders for favorable Senate action on the authorizing resolution. See Frances Perkins, *The Roosevelt I Knew* (New York: The Viking Press, Inc., 1946), pp. 337-44.
3. S.J.R. 1, 83d Cong.
4. Stuart C. Dodd, "A Barometer of International Security," *Public Opinion Quarterly*, IX (1945), 196.
5. J. Robert Oppenheimer, *The Open Mind* (New York: Simon & Schuster, Inc., 1955), p. 100. Copyright 1955 by and used with permission of Simon & Schuster, Inc.
6. The entire passage is worth quoting. After noting the need for sensitivity "to all new possibilities of extending the techniques and the patterns of science into other areas of human experience," Oppenheimer says, "We become fully aware of the need for caution if we look for a moment at what are called the social problems of the day and try to think what one could mean by approaching them in the scientific spirit, of trying to give substance, for example, to the feeling that a society that could develop atomic energy could also develop the means of controlling it. Surely the establishment of a secure peace is very much in all our minds. It is right that we try to bring reason to bear on an understanding of this problem; but for that there are available to us no equivalents of the experimental techniques of science. Errors of conception can remain undetected and even undefined. No means of appropriately narrowing the focus of thinking is known to us. Nor have we found good avenues for extending or deepening our experience that bears upon this problem. In short, almost all the preconditions of scientific activity are missing, and in this case, at least, one may have a melancholy certainty that man's inventiveness will not rapidly provide them. All that we have from science in facing such great questions is a memory of our profes-

sional life, which makes us somewhat skeptical of other people's assertions, somewhat critical of enthusiasms so difficult to define and to control." *Ibid.*, pp. 100-101.

Chapter 3

1. Frank R. Kent, *The Great Game of Politics* (New York: Doubleday & Co., Inc., 1926), p. 264.
2. Arthur F. Bentley, *The Process of Government. A Study of Social Pressures* (Bloomington, Ind.: The Principia Press of Illinois, 1949). (Reissue.)
3. Now almost forgotten, except by students of the political process, the so-called "Mulhall Investigation" by a select committee of the House of Representatives uncovered the methods by which the National Association of Manufacturers (NAM) sought and achieved special rights with congressional committees and made the country believe that what was good for manufacturers was good for the country. See House Report No. 113, 63d Cong., 2d sess., Select Committee of the House on *Charges against Members of the House and Lobbying Activities of the National Association of Manufacturers of the United States and others* (Washington, D.C.: Government Printing Office, 1913).
4. Karl Schriftgiesser, *The Lobbyists* (Boston: Little, Brown & Co., 1951), p. 38.
5. Peter Odegard, *Pressure Politics. The Story of the Anti-Saloon League* (New York: Columbia University Press, 1928).
6. O. M. Kile, *The Farm Bureau Federation through Three Decades* (Baltimore: The Waverly Press, 1948).
7. See James A. Farley, *Behind the Ballots* (New York: Harcourt, Brace & Co., Inc., 1938); also Basil Rauch, *The History of the New Deal, 1933-1938* (New York: Creative Age Press, Inc., 1944).
8. *The Autobiography of Lincoln Steffens* (New York: Harcourt, Brace & Co., Inc., 1931), p. 237.
9. James Truslow Adams, *Our Business Civilization* (New York: Charles & Albert Boni, 1929).
10. Department of Commerce, *National Associations in the United States* (Washington, D.C.: Government Printing Office, 1949).
11. In his study of lobbyists, Schriftgiesser saw great value not only in Bentley's method but also in his implied conclusion of the difficulty and improbability that any one group could manage to "hold a permanent control over the government. . . ." *The Lobbyists*, p. 31. Blair Bolles, another journalist, confirms the usefulness of the method but is less sanguine than Schriftgiesser of the effects of group struggle and activity on the purpose and direction of government in Washington. "Lately," Bolles said, in concluding his study of testimony before congressional investigating committees, "the welfare state has been undergoing a subtle change into the rich man's welfare state, aiding those who don't need help or who don't deserve it, at public expense. The agencies created to end privilege have become bulwarks of privilege. The bureaus which were established originally as balance wheels for segments of the national economy—transportation, communications, land use, etc.—unbalance the economy by distributing the riches unevenly." Blair Bolles, *How To Get Rich in Washington* (New York: W. W. Norton & Co., Inc., 1953), pp. 17-18.
12. Robert M. MacIver, *The Web of Government* (New York: The Macmillan Co., 1947).
13. Stephen K. Bailey, *Congress Makes a Law* (New York: Columbia University Press, 1950); Bertram M. Gross, *The Legislative Struggle* (New York: McGraw-Hill Book Co., Inc., 1953); E. P. Herring, *Group Representation Before Congress* (Washington, D.C.: The Brookings Institution, 1928); David B. Truman, *The Governmental Process* (New York: Alfred A. Knopf, Inc., 1951).

14. E. Pendleton Herring, "Lobbying," *Encyclopedia of the Social Sciences* (New York: The Macmillan Co., 1942), Vol. IX, p. 567.
15. Schriftgiesser, *op. cit.*, p. 31.
16. Truman, *op. cit., passim*, see especially p. 535.
17. *Ibid.*, p. 535.
18. Harold Lasswell, *Politics: Who Gets What, When, How* (New York: McGraw-Hill Book Co., Inc., 1936), p. 3.
19. *Interim Report*, pp. 64 ff.
20. House Select Committee on Lobbying Activities, 81st Cong., 2d sess., *Report and Recommendations on the Federal Lobbying Act* (Washington, D.C.: Government Printing Office, 1950), Part 2, *Minority Views*, p. 2.

Chapter 4

1. New York *Herald Tribune*, February 11, 1955, p. 14.
2. *The New York Times*, February 24, 1955.
3. David Lynch, *The Concentration of Economic Power* (New York: Columbia University Press, 1946), p. 300.
4. TNEC *Final Report and Recommendations*, Sen. Doc. No. 35, 77th Cong., 1st sess. (Washington, D.C.: Government Printing Office, 1940), p. 5. Cited hereafter as TNEC *Final Report*.
5. *Ibid.*, p. 10.
6. *Ibid.*, p. 25.
7. *Ibid.*
8. *Ibid.*
9. Thomas C. Cochran and William Miller, *The Age of Enterprise, A Social History of Industrial America* (New York: The Macmillan Co., 1951), pp. 343-44. Copyright 1951 by and used with the permission of The Macmillan Co.
10. A. A. Berle, Jr., *The 20th Century Capitalist Revolution* (New York: Harcourt, Brace & Co., Inc., 1954), p. 32; Bertram M. Gross, *The Legislative Struggle* (New York: McGraw-Hill Book Co., Inc., 1953), p. 142; Harold D. Lasswell, *Politics: Who Gets What, When, How* (New York: McGraw-Hill Book Co., Inc., 1936), p. 3; Robert M. MacIver, *The Web of Government* (New York: The Macmillan Co., 1947), p. 47.
11. Hermann Heller, "Political Power," *Encyclopedia of the Social Sciences* (New York: The Macmillan Co., 1942), Vol. XI, p. 301; Charles E. Merriam, *Political Power* (New York: McGraw-Hill Book Co., Inc., 1934), p. 16.
12. Gross, *op. cit.*, p. 143. See also Robert Bierstedt, "An Analysis of Social Power," *American Sociological Review*, XV (December, 1950), where power is discussed in terms of numbers of people, social organization, and resources.
13. MacIver, *op. cit.*, p. 458. See also Bertrand de Jouvenel, *On Power: Its Nature and the History of Its Growth* (New York: The Viking Press, Inc., 1949).
14. Berle, *op. cit.*, p. 32; Laurence Stapleton, *The Design of Democracy* (New York: Oxford University Press, 1949), p. 144; *Interim Report*, p. 63.
15. On these two points see Kenneth B. Clark, "Desegregation in the Public Schools," *Social Problems*, II (1955), 197-242. On the general inadequacy of causality to explain social and political happenings, see, for example, David B. Truman, *The Governmental Process* (New York: Alfred A. Knopf, Inc., 1951), pp. 254-60; Merriam, *op. cit.*, p. 71; MacIver, *op. cit.*, pp. 91-93; and Oliver Garceau, *The Political Life of the American Medical Association* (Cambridge: Harvard University Press, 1941), introduction.
16. Berle, *op. cit.*, p. 34.
17. *Ibid.*, pp. 168-69.

18. S. K. Bailey, *Congress Makes a Law* (New York: Columbia University Press, 1950), p. 192. See also Herbert Kaufman and Victor Jones, "The Mystery of Power," *Public Administration Review*, XIV (Summer, 1954), 205 ff.

19. George W. Stocking and M. W. Watkins, *How Big is Big Business* (New York: Twentieth Century Fund, 1937); also *Monopoly and Free Enterprise* (New York: Twentieth Century Fund, 1951); Clair Wilcox, *Competition and Monopoly in American Industry*, TNEC Monograph, No. 21 (Washington, D.C.: Government Printing Office, 1940), cited in Berle, *op. cit.*, p. 27.

20. M. A. Adelman, "The Measurement of Industrial Concentration," *The Review of Economics and Statistics*, November, 1951, cited by Berle, *op. cit.*, p. 51.

21. Adelman's computation suggests that this is a static condition, varying slightly from year to year but increasing or decreasing very slowly, if at all. Berle, *op. cit.*, p. 26. Although Berle makes no direct statement, he seems to dissent.

22. R. Vance Presthus, review of Henry A. Wells's *Monopoly and Social Control* (Washington, D.C.: Public Affairs Press, 1952), in *Journal of Politics*, XV (November, 1953), 594-95; also Walter Adams and Horace M. Gray, *Monopoly in America: The Government as Promoter* (New York: The Macmillan Co., 1955).

23. Sumner H. Slichter, "The Growth of Competition," *The Atlantic Monthly*, 192 (November, 1953), 66-70.

24. David E. Lilienthal, *Big Business: A New Era* (New York: Harper & Bros., 1952).

25. George A. Steiner, *Government's Role in Economic Life* (New York: McGraw-Hill Book Co., Inc., 1953); J. Kenneth Galbraith, *American Capitalism: The Concept of Countervailing Power* (Boston: Houghton Mifflin Co., 1952).

26. Heller, *loc. cit.*, p. 303.

27. *Ibid.* See also Robert S. Lynd, foreword to Robert A. Brady's *Business as a System of Power* (New York: Columbia University Press, 1943), p. xiii.

28. TNEC *Final Report*, p. 258, footnote 75.

29. Thomas C. Desmond, "Those Dinosaurs—the State Legislatures," *The New York Times Magazine*, January 16, 1955, p. 58.

30. Floyd Hunter, *Community Power Structure: A Study of Decision Makers* (Chapel Hill: University of North Carolina Press, 1953); see also review of this book by Donald S. Strong, in *American Political Science Review*, XLVIII (March, 1954), 237.

31. Gordon E. Baker, *Rural versus Urban Political Power* (New York: Doubleday & Co., Inc., 1955), *passim*.

32. E. E. Schattschneider, "Party Government and Employment Policy," *American Political Science Review*, XXXIX (December, 1945), 1149.

33. E. E. Schattschneider, *Party Government* (New York: Rinehart & Co., Inc., 1942).

34. Paul T. David, Malcolm Moos, and Ralph Goldman (eds.), *Presidential Nominating Politics in 1952* (5 vols.; Baltimore: Johns Hopkins University Press, 1954), I, introduction.

35. Julius Turner, "Primary Elections as the Alternative to Party Competition in 'Safe' Districts," *Journal of Politics*, V (May, 1953), 197-210.

36. Karl Schriftgiesser, *The Lobbyists* (Boston: Little, Brown & Co., 1951), pp. 19-20.

37. A. A. Berle, Jr. and Gardiner C. Means, *The Modern Corporation and Private Property* (New York: The Macmillan Co., 1932).

38. Harry L. Purdy, Martin L. Lindahl, and William A. Carter, *Corporate Concentration and Public Policy* (2d ed.; Englewood Cliffs, N.J.: Prentice-Hall, Inc., 1950), pp. 681-82.

39. V. O. Key, Jr., *Politics, Parties, and Pressure Groups* (3d. ed.; New York: Thomas Y. Crowell Co., 1953), p. 180.

40. Harold D. Lasswell, *Politics: Who Gets What, When, How* (New York: McGraw-Hill Book Co., Inc., 1936), pp. 241-42.

41. "For all the vaunted power of government, it may prove to have neither the material resources nor the hard consciousness of purpose to withstand the all-out drive of well-financed, united, and determined private interests to control state power." *Interim Report*, p. 51.

Chapter 5

1. Robert M. MacIver, *The Web of Government* (New York: The Macmillan Co., 1947), pp. 410-12.
2. House Select Committee on Lobbying Activities, 81st Cong., 2d sess., *Hearings* (10 vols.; Washington, D.C.: Government Printing Office, 1950), Part 1, *The Role of Lobbying in Representative Self-Government*, p. 13. Cited hereafter as *Lobby Hearings*.
3. J. A. C. Brown, *The Social Psychology of Industry* (Baltimore, Md.: Penguin Books, Inc., 1954), pp. 48, 53.

   As Brown points out, "The new view holds that the human body is an organism which cannot be defined in terms of nonliving categories, it does not think in terms of 'mind' but of mental processes, and regards all disease as a total response to environmental threat, whether from germs, poisons, physical agents, or emotions induced by social interaction. It does not accept instinct as an adequate explanation of human behavior, and is more interested in how the biological drives are socially modified than in their mere existence; i.e., its explanations are in social rather than biological terms. Society is also regarded as an organism—as a body of organized individuals—and man as basically a social animal. All psychology is social psychology, and, without denying the existence of the superego, it is believed that the major instrument of social control is the primary group." See pp. 67-68.
4. Muzafer Sherif and Hadley Cantril, *The Psychology of Ego-Involvements* (New York: John Wiley & Sons, Inc., 1947), pp. 10-11, cited by Truman, who adds that pressure groups "develop as well as reflect uniformities in the attitudes and behavior of their members. These patterns are, or are rapidly becoming, the primary data of the social scientist. To identify and interpret these uniformities—their dynamics, their interconnections, and their relative strength—is the most effective approach to understanding a society, 'primitive' or 'complex,' or a segment of it, such as its political institutions." David B. Truman, *The Governmental Process* (New York: Alfred A. Knopf, Inc., 1951), p. 21.
5. Earl Latham, "The Group Basis of Politics: Notes for a Theory," *American Political Science Review*, XLVI (June, 1952).
6. Bradford Smith, *A Dangerous Freedom* (Philadelphia: J. B. Lippincott Co., 1954), p. 252.
7. Arthur F. Bentley, *The Process of Government. A Study of Social Pressures* (Bloomington, Ind.: The Principia Press of Illinois, 1949), p. 211. The definition continues: ". . . taken, however, not as a physical mass cut off from other masses of men, but as a mass activity, which does not preclude the men who participate in it from participating likewise in many other group activities. . . ."
8. Frank R. Kent, *The Great Game of Politics* (New York: Doubleday & Co., Inc., 1926), p. 264. Kent's estimate of sixty referred to those groups among the one hundred forty-five "special interests and groups" which maintained headquarters in Washington and which were "really effective, with sufficient financial or voting strength back of them to compel consideration."
9. Theodore J. Kreps, *Taxes and the Human Factor* (Washington, D.C.: The Public Affairs Institute, 1951), p. 18.
10. William Albig, *Modern Public Opinion* (New York: McGraw-Hill Book Co., Inc., 1956), p. 279.
11. E. E. Schattschneider, *Party Government* (New York: Rinehart & Co., Inc., 1942), p. 20.
12. U.S. Department of Commerce, *National Associations of the United States* (Washington, D.C.: Government Printing Office, 1949), p. viii.
13. Edward Conrad Smith, *A Dictionary of American Politics* (New York: A. L. Burt Co., Inc., 1924), p. 36.

14. Robert M. MacIver, "Social Pressures," *Encyclopedia of the Social Sciences* (New York: The Macmillan Co., 1942), Vol. XII, pp. 344-48.

15. Albig, *op. cit.,* p. 279.

16. The active minority is the phrase used by David B. Truman to describe the leadership situation existing as a general rule in groups. Truman, *op. cit.,* pp. 139-55.

17. See Roberto Michels, *First Lectures in Political Sociology,* trans. Alfred de Grazia (Minneapolis: University of Minnesota Press, 1949).

18. C. W. Cassinelli, "The Iron Law of Oligarchy," *American Political Science Review,* XLVII (September, 1953), 778. According to Cassinelli, any organization is an oligarchy if more than 1000 persons are involved in its activities. See p. 783.

19. Richard M. Gable, "NAM: Influential Lobby or Kiss of Death?" *Journal of Politics,* XV (May, 1953), 259; Alfred S. Cleveland, "Some Political Aspects of Organized Industry" (Ph.D. dissertation, Harvard University, Department of Political Science, 1948).

20. Donald C. Blaisdell, *Economic Power and Political Pressures,* TNEC Monograph, No. 26 (Washington, D.C.: Government Printing Office, 1941), footnote, p. 40; Oliver Garceau, *The Political Life of the American Medical Association* (Cambridge: Harvard University Press, 1941).

21. Liverpool University Survey of Conditions in the Port of Manchester (England), cited in the *Manchester Guardian Weekly* (air ed.), July 7, 1955, p. 8; Philip Taft, *The Structure and Government of Labor Unions* (Cambridge: Harvard University Press, 1954).

22. The strongest pressures on Congress are reflections primarily of minority groups of specific local, occupational, or political interests, because the majority of people do not feel strongly about such interests and do not affiliate with pressure groups. George B. Galloway, in testimony to the House Select Committee on Lobbying Activities, *Lobby Hearings,* Part 1, p. 99. The political weight, or value, of the active citizen is thus discounted twice: first, he does not take part directly in legislative affairs, but only indirectly through a representative, either territorial or functional; and second, the group to which he belongs, while "representing" him, provides effective representation for the active minority only. As for the inactive citizen who does not belong to any group, his political weight is similarly reduced by formal representation and further diminished by his Congressman's preoccupation with matters which groups importune him to dispose of to their advantage.

23. M. R. Werner, review of Clyndon G. Van Deusen's *Thurlow Weed: Wizard of the Lobby* (Boston: Little, Brown & Co., 1947), in *The New York Times Book Review,* February 9, 1947.

24. Robert M. MacIver, *The Web of Government* (New York: The Macmillan Co., 1947), pp. 292-93.

25. *Ibid.*

26. *General Interim Report of the House Select Committee on Lobbying Activities,* H. R. Rep. No. 3138, 81st Cong., 2d sess. (Washington, D.C.: Government Printing Office, 1950), p. 62. Hereafter cited as *Interim Report.*

27. Harry A. Overstreet, *The Mature Mind* (New York: W. W. Norton & Co., Inc., 1949), p. 173.

28. Hadley Cantril, in testimony to the House Select Committee on Lobbying Activities, *Lobby Hearings,* Part 1, p. 20.

29. Roy Blough, *The Federal Taxing Process* (Englewood Cliffs, N.J.: Prentice-Hall, Inc., 1952), pp. 465-66.

30. George B. Galloway, *The Legislative Process in Congress* (New York: Thomas Y. Crowell Co., 1953), p. 471.

31. Robert M. MacIver, *op. cit.,* p. 104. In MacIver's types of class structure he notes one marked similarity between the democratic pyramid and the dictatorial variety of the oligarchical pyramid: Both are determined by the discovery that organization can "counter-balance or outweigh the power attaching to property or prior

privilege of any kind." For the workers, the opportunity to organize, with technology, specialization, industry, and urbanization, meant economic power, the bargaining power of the concerted refusal to work on terms that they had rejected.
This gave them an economic role in the determination of wages, and also new
political power. "From specialized organization they moved toward more inclusive
forms of unionization, gaining thereby sufficient power to make labor an active
participant in government and even, for the first time in history, a primary determinant of government. . . ." p. 106.

32. R. Cragin Lewis, "New Power at the Polls: The Doctors," *Politics in the United
    States*, ed. Henry A. Turner (New York: McGraw-Hill Book Co., Inc., 1955), pp.
    180-85.
33. M. Louise Rutherford, *The Influence of the American Bar Association on Public
    Opinion and Legislation* (Philadelphia: University of Pennsylvania Press, 1937),
    p. 13.
34. Luke Ebersole, *Church Lobbying in the Nation's Capital* (New York: The Mac-
    millan Co., 1951).
35. Donald C. Blaisdell, *op. cit.*, pp. 125-36.
36. *Ibid.*
37. New York *Herald Tribune*, February 23, 1951.
38. *Interim Report*, p. 62.
39. See chap. vi, The Dilemma of Lobby Regulation.
40. See chap. xi, p. 182.
41. *Interim Report*, p. 2.
42. *Ibid.*, p. 23.
43. Hadley Cantril, in testimony before the House Select Committee on Lobbying Ac-
    tivities, *Lobby Hearings*, Part 1, p. 20.
44. House Select Committee on Lobbying Activities, 81st Cong. 2d sess., *Report and
    Recommendations on the Federal Lobbying Act* (Washington, D.C.: Government
    Printing Office, 1951), p. 1.
45. *Lobby Hearings*, Part 1, p. 4.
46. George B. Galloway, *op. cit.*, p. 472.
47. Alfred de Grazia, *Public and Republic* (New York: Alfred A. Knopf, Inc., 1951),
    pp. 250-51.
48. *Report of the Joint Interim Committee of the California Legislature*, printed in the
    California Legislature Assembly *Journal*, March 20, 1950, reproduced in *Lobby
    Hearings*, Part 1, p. 80.
49. *Ibid.*, pp. 82-83.
50. See chap. xii.
51. *Washington Post*, March 29, 1949. In testimony before the House Select Commit-
    tee on Lobbying Activities, authorized by a resolution of this "hag-ridden" Con-
    gress, Belle Zeller told the Committee that lobbies and pressure groups were
    legitimate and necessary in influencing legislation; were sources of information in
    making public policy; represented the public functioning in organized groups;
    played a role in forming public opinion, both through influence and education, by
    reaching out to the public through mass communication media rather than by
    direct personal appeals to legislative leaders or contributions to campaign funds.
    Lobby Hearings, Part 1, p. 59.
52. David Riesman, *The Lonely Crowd* (New Haven: Yale University Press, 1950),
    p. 243.
53. U.S. Senator Paul H. Douglas (D., Ill.), review of Sidney Hyman's *The American
    President* (New York: Harper & Bros., 1954), in *The New York Times Book Re-
    view*, February 19, 1954.
54. Bertram M. Gross, *The Legislative Struggle* (New York: McGraw-Hill Book Co.,
    Inc., 1953), p. 267.
55. Edgar Lane, cited in Galloway, *op. cit.*, p. 497, and testimony to House Select
    Committee on Lobbying Activities, *Lobby Hearings*, Part 1, p. 99.

56. Galloway, *op. cit.*, p. 472.
57. *Ibid.*, pp. 475-78.
58. "Our Form of Government," Supplement to *Fortune,* November, 1943, p. 10. By permission from *Fortune.*
59. See chap. iii, p. 39.
60. *Interim Report,* p. 4. The effectiveness of groups depends on internal factors, such as the number of members, the intensity and cohesion of this membership in group drives, the quality of leadership, geographical distribution of local branches, financing; and on external considerations, such as public opinion toward the proposals of the group, its relationship to the political parties, the alliances it can make with other groups or the opposition it meets from others, and the legislative or political situation at the time it operates. Because the American Legion meets almost perfectly each of these conditions, it obtains virtually everything it wants. "It is so generally effective that other groups may be measured against it." Dayton David McKean, *Party and Pressure Politics* (Boston: Houghton Mifflin Co., 1949), p. 623.
61. Arthur P. Chew, *The Response of Government to Agriculture* (Washington, D.C.: Government Printing Office, 1937), and Donald C. Blaisdell, *Government and Agriculture* (New York: Rinehart & Co., Inc., 1940).
62. Fred W. Riggs, *Pressures on Congress: A Study of the Repeal of Chinese Exclusion* (New York: King's Crown Press, 1950).

Chapter 6

1. Title III of the Legislative Reorganization Act of 1946 (Public Law 601, 79th Cong., 2d sess.).
2. House Select Committee on Lobbying Activities, 81st Cong., 2d sess., *Report and Recommendations on the Federal Lobbying Act* (Washington, D.C.: Government Printing Office, 1951), p. 4. Cited hereafter as *Report and Recommendations.*
3. *Congressional Quarterly,* Weekly Report, XI, No. 25 (June, 1955), p. 797.
4. See pp. 95-96.
5. *General Interim Report of the House Select Committee on Lobbying Activities,* H.R. Rep. No. 3138, 81st Cong., 2d sess. (Washington, D.C.: Government Printing Office, 1950), p. 66. Cited hereafter as *Interim Report.*
6. House Select Committee on Lobbying Activities, 81st Cong., 2d sess., *Hearings* (10 vols.; Washington, D.C.: Government Printing Office, 1950), Part 1, *The Role of Lobbying in Representative Self-Government,* p. 44. Cited hereafter as *Lobby Hearings.*
7. E. E. Schattschneider, *Party Government* (New York: Rinehart & Co., Inc., 1942), p. 198.
8. *Report and Recommendations,* p. 150.
9. *Report and Recommendations,* Part 2, *Minority Views,* p. 150.
10. *Lobby Hearings,* Part 6, *Americans for Democratic Action,* p. 104.
11. Committee counsel described the method employed as follows: "Of particular significance is the fact that Edward A. Rumely and the Committee for Constitutional Government, Inc., in recent years, have devised a scheme for raising enormous funds without filing reports pursuant to the provision of the Federal Regulation of Lobbying Act. This scheme has the color of legality, but in fact is a method of circumventing the law. It utilizes a system whereby contributions to the Committee for Constitutional Government are designated as payments for the purchase of books, which are transmitted to others at the direction of the purchaser, with both the contributor of the money and the recipients of the books totally unaware of the subterfuge." *Lobby Hearings,* Part 5, *Committee for Constitutional Government,* p. 7.

12. *Ibid.*, p. 60.
13. One witness, Belle Zeller, called the Committee's attention to the attempt in the Wisconsin statute of 1947 to establish standards in lobbying, to assure "the promotion of a high standard of ethics in the practice of lobbying, to prevent unfair and unethical practices in the practice of lobbying, to provide for the licensing of lobbyists and the suspension or revocation of such licenses." Standards were also spelled out in the 1950 report of the California State Legislature. *Lobby Hearings*, Part 1, pp. 64 and 80-96. According to Hadley Cantril, another witness, the difference between good and bad lobbying turned on whether it was open and openly acknowledged, with lobbying expenditures reported, or clandestine and secretive, with expenditures not disclosed. *Lobby Hearings*, Part 1, p. 25.
14. *Report and Recommendations*, pp. 4-5.
15. U.S. v. Rumely, 345 U.S. 41 (1953).
16. *Ibid.*
17. U.S. v. Harriss *et al.*, 347 U.S. 612 (1954).
18. *Lobby Hearings*, Part 1, p. 149.
19. *Ibid.*, p. 43.
20. *Ibid.*, p. 142.
21. *Report and Recommendations*, pp. 23-29.
22. *Ibid.*, p. 35.
23. *Lobby Hearings*, Part 1, p. 85.
24. *The New York Times*, November 10, 1954.
25. Alfred de Grazia, *Public and Republic* (New York: Alfred A. Knopf, Inc., 1951), p. 245.
26. K. Smellie, "Right of Petition," *Encyclopedia of the Social Sciences* (New York: The Macmillan Co., 1942), Vol. XII, p. 100.
27. Karl Schriftgiesser, *The Lobbyists* (Boston: Little, Brown & Co., 1951), p. xi.
28. U.S. v. Cruikshank, 92 U.S. 542 (1876).
29. U.S. v. De Jonge, 299 U.S. 353 (1937).
30. The right of petition is not dealt with as such in a volume devoted to the first freedom by Morris L. Ernst entitled *The First Freedom* (New York: The Macmillan Co., 1946). A recent collection of leading constitutional cases on civil liberties contains only two cases dealing with the right of petition. See Milton Konvitz, *Civil Rights Primer* (Ithaca: Cornell University Press, 1953). Another collection contains no cases dealing with the right of petition; see Thomas I. Emerson and David Haber, *Political and Civil Rights in the United States* (Buffalo: Dennis & Co., Inc., 1952).
31. U.S. v. Harriss *et al.*, 347 U.S. 612 (1954).
32. *Ibid.*
33. See pp. 86 ff.
34. *Lobby Hearings*, Part 1, pp. 2, 12.
35. *Ibid.*, p. 11.

Chapter 7

1. See Bibliography for titles of the ten volumes of hearings of the House Select Committee on Lobbying Activities (81st Cong., 2d sess.) and of the eleven reports, in addition to its final report, which the Committee filed with the House of Representatives.
2. Bertram M. Gross, *The Legislative Struggle* (New York: McGraw-Hill Book Co., Inc., 1953), p. 200.
3. James M. Burns, *Congress on Trial* (New York: Harper & Bros., 1949), p. 21.
4. House Select Committee on Lobbying Activities, 81st Cong., 2d sess., *Hearings* (10 vols.; Washington, D.C.: Government Printing Office, 1950), Part 1, *The Role*

of Lobbying in Representative Self-Government, p. 7. Cited hereafter as *Lobby Hearings.*

5. Donald C. Blaisdell, *Economic Power and Political Pressures,* TNEC Monograph, No. 26 (Washington, D.C.: Government Printing Office, 1941), pp. 152-56.
6. Stephen K. Bailey, in *Lobby Hearings,* Part 1, p. 36.
7. *Ibid.,* p. 39.
8. Only by searching is it possible to discover, in the lower left-hand corner, the origin of this syndicated column. The wonder was increased by reading in the transcript of the 1950 *Hearings* of the House Select Committee of Stephen K. Bailey's suggestion that the Committee study the NAM as a holding company for a variety of seemingly independent pressure groups and conditioners of rural opinion. *Lobby Hearings,* Part 1, p. 39.
9. *General Interim Report of the House Select Committee on Lobbying Activities,* H.R. Rep. No. 3138, 81st Cong., 2d sess. (Washington, D.C.: Government Printing Office, 1950), p. 11. Hereafter cited as *Interim Report.* In a study made in 1941 it was found that maintaining liaison with government offices in Washington was the most expensive activity of most trade associations. Donald C. Blaisdell, *Government under Pressure* (New York: Public Affairs Committee, Inc., 1942), p. 12.
10. Speech by Mr. Reed (R., N.Y.), 97 *Congressional Record* 2793-2801.
11. Details of advertising expenditures by thirty-one corporations of over $2 million in a three and one-half year period are to be found in Report No. 3137 of the House Select Committee on Lobbying Activities. See also chap. xii.
12. Denis W. Brogan, *Politics in America* (New York: Harper & Bros., 1955), p. 352.
13. Clarence Brown (R., Ohio), in *Lobby Hearings,* Part 1, pp. 118-19.
14. James Truslow Adams, *The Living Jefferson* (New York: Charles Scribner's Sons, 1936), pp. 220-21.
15. From "Needed now—Capacity for Leadership—Courage to Lead," Pamphlet issued by the CCG, quoted in House Select Committee on Lobbying Activities, 81st Cong., 2d sess., *Report and Recommendations on the Federal Lobbying Act* (Washington, D.C.: Government Printing Office, 1951), p. 24. Cited hereafter as *Report and Recommendations.*
16. *Interim Report,* pp. 34-40.
17. *Report and Recommendations,* p. 14.
18. W. B. Graves, *Administration of the Lobby Registration Provision of the Legislative Reorganization Act of 1946,* Library of Congress. Legislative Reference Service (Washington, D.C.: Government Printing Office, 1950), p. 37.
19. *Interim Report,* p. 63.
20. The term "pressure politician" was originated, apparently, by James M. Burns. See his *Congress on Trial.*
21. Ralph K. Huitt, "The Congressional Committee: A Case Study," *American Political Science Review,* XLVIII (June, 1954), 365.
22. W. M. Kiplinger, *Washington Is Like That* (New York: Harper & Bros., 1942), p. 288.
23. Frank R. Kent, *The Great Game of Politics* (New York: Doubleday & Co., Inc., 1926), p. 263.
24. Stephen K. Bailey, *Congress Makes a Law* (New York: Columbia University Press, 1950), appendix.
25. Burns, *op. cit.,* p. 21.
26. The literature on pressure politicians is not voluminous, the subjects themselves rarely revealing much when they write their autobiographies, their biographers usually screening out material which might reflect upon their subjects. But see Douglass Cater, "Senator Styles Bridges and his Far-Flung Constitutents," *The Reporter,* XI (July 20, 1954), 8 ff.; see also special section on McCarran's Nevada, *The Reporter,* X (June 7, 1954) 15 ff.
27. *Interim Report,* pp. 63-64.

28. *The New York Times,* November 11, 1954.

29. See pp. 71 ff.

30. Lawrence H. Chamberlain, *The President, Congress, and Legislation* (New York: Columbia University Press, 1946), p. 453.

31. George B. Galloway, *The Legislative Process in Congress* (New York: Thomas Y. Crowell Co., 1953), p. 38. Note the following from the AFL–CIO Constitution: "It shall be the duty of the Executive Council to watch legislative measures directly affecting the interests of working people and to initiate, wherever necessary, such legislative action as the convention may direct." Article VIII (Executive Council), Section 4.

32. Charles J. Zinn, *How Our Laws Are Made,* H.R. Doc. No. 210, 83rd Cong., 1st sess. (Washington, D.C.: Government Printing Office, 1953), pp. iii, 3.

33. J. G. Randall and Richard N. Current, *Lincoln the President* (New York: Dodd, Mead & Co., 1955), Vol. IV, p. 193.

34. Gross, *op. cit.,* pp. 285, 287-88, 292.

35. Roy Blough, *The Federal Taxing Process* (Englewood Cliffs, N.J.: Prentice-Hall, Inc., 1952), pp. 476-77.

36. *Lobby Hearings,* Part 1, *passim.*

37. *Report and Recommendations,* pp. 31-32.

38. "The Association's authority as industry's spokesman does not extend beyond its own membership, and that membership is at best not more than 7 per cent of the group for which representation is claimed. . . . NAM membership is predominantly concentrated among those firms having more than 100 employees, and since more than 90 per cent of all manufacturing establishments employ fewer than 100 persons, the voice of the small American manufacturer is not directly represented in NAM policies or programs." Alfred S. Cleveland, "Some Political Aspects of Organized Industry" (Ph.D. dissertation, Harvard University, Department of Political Science, 1948), pp. 128-32, 117-18.

39. *Lobby Hearings,* Part 6, *Americans for Democratic Action,* pp. 92, 97. See also page 110 for a revealing outline of ADA legislative activity given in some detail.

Chapter 8

1. From a report compiled by a member of the executive committee. See Fred W. Riggs, *Pressures on Congress: A Study of the Repeal of Chinese Exclusion* (New York: The King's Crown Press, 1950), p. 38.

2. *Ibid.,* p. 46.

3. See Lindsay Rogers' criticism of an "international political barometer" proposed by a sociologist and using opinion polling as the measuring technique. Lindsay Rogers, *The Pollsters* (New York: Alfred A. Knopf, Inc., 1949), pp. 5-6 and footnote, p. 6.

4. R. Craigin Lewis, "New Power at the Polls: The Doctors," *Politics in the United States,* ed. Henry A. Turner (New York: McGraw-Hill Book Co., Inc., 1955), pp. 180 ff.

5. See Avery Leiserson, "Organized Labor as a Pressure Group," *Annals of the American Academy of Political and Social Science,* 274 (March, 1951), 108-17; also James L. McDevitt, "The Role of the AFL in Politics," and Jack Kroll, "The CIO-PAC," in Turner, *op. cit.,* pp. 135, 138.

6. See Constitution, Article II (Objectives), Sections 5 and 12, and Article VIII (Executive Council), Section 4. Text in *The New York Times,* May 3, 1955.

7. House Select Committee on Lobbying Activities, 81st Cong., 2d sess., *Hearings* (10 vols.; Washington, D.C.: Government Printing Office, 1950), Part 2, *Housing Lobby,* p. 481. Hereafter cited as *Lobby Hearings.*

8. New York *Herald Tribune,* February 11, 1955.

9. W. M. Kiplinger, *Washington Is Like That* (New York: Harper & Bros., 1942), p. 285.

10. Frederick J. Lawton, "Legislative-Executive Relationships in Budgeting as Viewed by the Executive," *Public Administration Review*, XIII (Summer, 1953).

11. *Lobby Hearings*, Part 6, *Americans for Democratic Action*, p. 96. Besides the ADA, the other organizations were the CIO, Amvets, sleeping-car porters, New York Council for a Permanent Fair Employment Practices Committee (FEPC), AFL, machinists union, NAACP, National Community Relations Advisory Committee, and Jewish War Veterans.

12. Clement E. Vose, "NAACP Strategy in the Covenant Cases," *Western Reserve Law Review*, VI (Winter, 1955), 103-104.

13. *Ibid.*

14. Letter to Clerk of the House of Representatives, quoted in Richard W. Gable, "A Political Analysis of an Employers' Association, the National Association of Manufacturers" (Ph.D. dissertation, University of Chicago, Department of Political Science, 1950), p. 419.

15. In order to define "legislative activity," the NAM divided its activities with respect to federal legislation into five stages: (1) formulation of the NAM position or policy with respect to legislation; (2) development of an understanding of, and acceptance by, members of the Association and other business groups of the policy, viewpoint, or attitude adopted; (3) seeking to inform the public of the import and possible effect of legislation, with the definite objective of gaining public acceptance of the principles or viewpoint of the NAM; (4) acquiring and reporting information concerning the scope, effect, and prospects for legislation of particular interest to manufacturers; and (5) direct efforts to influence legislation by communication with members of Congress. It was the view of the NAM that, except for some of the activities covered by the fifth point, no other activity, treated separately, was necessarily or wholly covered by P.L. 601 (Federal Regulation of Lobbying Act). In general, the activities under point five therefore served as the basis for determining the expenditures to be reported, supplemented in some instances by expenditures under points one, two, three, or four, where such expenditures could reasonably be said to be for the purpose of directly influencing legislation. Thus calculated, a total of $85,331.52 was spent for the purpose of influencing legislation in 1947. This figure represented 3.6 per cent of total expenditures for 1947, excluding those of its public relations division; 1.9 per cent if they were included. Using the higher percentage, an additional amount of $60,954.60 was computed and included as additional administrative expense. This figure was arrived at by applying the percentage (3.6) to the total expenditures of the executive office, business management division, economic policy division, and similar divisions which made no direct legislative expenditures. Adding this additional administrative expense to the legislative expenditures gave a total of $146,186.12 for 1947. *Ibid.*, p. 411.

16. *Ibid.*, p. 419.

17. Bertram M. Gross, *The Legislative Struggle* (New York: McGraw-Hill Book Co., Inc., 1953), p. 231.

18. *Ibid.*

19. Robert Luce, *Congress: An Explanation* (Cambridge: Harvard University Press, 1926), pp. 129-30, cited in George B. Galloway, *The Legislative Process in Congress* (New York: Thomas Y. Crowell Co., 1953), p. 492.

20. George Dixon, "Washington Scene," *Washington Post and Times Herald*, August 13, 1954.

21. Oliver Garceau, *The Political Life of the American Medical Association* (Cambridge: Harvard University Press, 1941), p. 167.

22. James Loeb, Jr., Executive Secretary, before the Lobby Investigating Committee, July 12, 1950, *Lobby Hearings*, Part 6 Americans for Democratic Action, p. 106.

23. *Lobby Hearings*, Part 1, p. 85.

24. *Report and Recommendations*, p. 35.

Chapter 9

1. William Goodman, *The Two-Party System in the United States* (Princeton, N.J.: D. Van Nostrand Co., Inc., 1956), p. 129.
2. E. E. Schattschneider, *The Struggle for Party Government* (College Park: University of Maryland, 1948), pp. 13 ff.
3. Clarence A. Berdahl, "Party Membership in the United States," *American Political Science Review*, XXXVI (April, 1942), 245-59.
4. W. M. Kiplinger, *Washington Is Like That* (New York: Harper & Bros., 1942), p. 254. This estimate was made in 1943, when the country's population was 130 million people. Comparatively, this figure of a million active participants out of 130 million, or less than 1 per cent, is smaller than the corresponding figure for the Soviet Union, where it is estimated that membership in the Communist Party runs between 5 and 6 million out of a population of 220 million. Merle Fainsod, *How Russia is Ruled* (Cambridge: Harvard University Press, 1954), p. 212. Copyright 1953 by the President and Fellows of Harvard College. Reprinted by permission.
5. Berdahl, *loc. cit.*, p. 261.
6. H.R. Rep. No. 153, 74th Cong., 1st sess. pp. 21-22.
7. See pp. 61 ff.
8. Stuart Long, " 'Scared Money' Wins an Election in Texas," *The Reporter*, XI (October 21, 1954), 23.
9. Bradford Smith, *A Dangerous Freedom* (Philadelphia: J. B. Lippincott Co., 1954), p. 256.
10. Democratic National Convention, *Official Proceedings, 1952;* the *Official Manual* of the Democratic National Convention, 1952.
11. Official Report of the *Proceedings of the Twenty-Fifth Republican National Convention.*
12. See chap. x, pp. 152 ff.
13. Mitchell is said to have fixed five goals to reach before resignation: bringing the convention delegates into the making of decisions instead of hearing them from the northern city bosses; modernization of national convention proceedings, with television viewers in mind; restoration of harmony between the northern majority and the southern minority of the Party; establishment of a party journal; and elimination of the party deficit. *The New York Times*, December 5, 1954.
14. Democratic National Convention, *Official Proceedings*, 1952, pp. 5-7.
15. Paul T. David, Malcolm Moos, and Ralph Goldman (eds.), *Presidential Nominating Politics in 1952* (5 vols.; Baltimore: Johns Hopkins Press, 1954), I, preface.
16. Sidney Hyman, *The American President* (New York: Harper & Bros., 1954).
17. *The New York Times*, October 28, 1954.
18. William Lee Miller, "Should We Fight Dirty Too? A Democrat Gives His Answer," *The Reporter*, XI (October 21, 1954), 18.
19. William Lee Miller, "Can Government Be Merchandised?" *The Reporter*, IX (October 27, 1953), 16.
20. Kiplinger, *op. cit.*, p. 257.
21. *Toward a More Responsible Two-Party System.* A Report of the Committee on Political Parties of the American Political Science Association (New York: Rinehart & Co., Inc., 1950), p. 24.
22. See p. 154.
23. Tabulated by *Congressional Quarterly*, as cited in *The New York Times*, October 10, 1953.
24. *Ibid.*
25. Hadley Cantril, "Psychology," *Scientific American*, 183 (September, 1950).
26. Harry A. Overstreet, *The Mature Mind* (New York: W. W. Norton & Co., Inc., 1949), p. 185.
27. *Ibid.*, pp. 185-202.

28. Frank R. Kent, *The Great Game of Politics* (New York: Doubleday & Co., Inc., 1926), p. 269.
29. *Major Campaign Speeches of Adlai E. Stevenson* (New York: Random House, Inc., 1953), p. 19. Copyright 1953 by and used with the permission of Random House.
30. Paul Lazarsfeld, B. Berelson, and H. Gaudet, *The People's Choice* (New York: Columbia University Press, 1948), p. 27.
31. Warren E. Miller, "Party Preference and Attitudes on Political Issues: 1948-51," *American Political Science Review*, XLVII (March, 1953).
32. Angus Campbell and Others, "The Electoral Switch of 1952," *Scientific American*, 190 (May, 1954).
33. Julian L. Woodward and Elmo Roper, "Political Activity of American Citizens," *American Political Science Review*, XLIV (December, 1950), 872-75.
34. New York *Herald Tribune*, February 24, 1951.
35. E. E. Schattschneider, *Party Government* (New York: Rinehart & Co., 1942), p. 187. For differing views on the nature of parties see, for example, Robert M. MacIver, *The Web of Government* (New York: The Macmillan Co., 1947), pp. 212-13; W. W. Willoughby and Lindsay Rogers, *An Introduction to the Problem of Government* (New York: Doubleday & Co., Inc., 1927), pp. 129-30; Bradford Smith, *op. cit.*, p. 257. In James M. Burns, *Congress on Trial* (New York: Harper & Bros., 1949), pp. 33 ff. and Schattschneider, *Party Government, passim*, are to be found sharp criticisms of parties in America, both as to structure and program. Arthur W. Macmahon finds the basic issues between the two parties in their different attitudes toward wealth in land and in other means of production. "Political Parties: United States," *Encyclopedia of the Social Sciences* (New York: The Macmillan Co., 1937), Vol. XI, p. 598.
36. "Political Participation in a Metropolitan District: A Study of Group Influence on Political Activity," *American Political Science Review*, XLVI (December, 1952), 1017.
37. Dayton David McKean, "Political Machines and National Elections," *Parties and Politics: 1948, Annals of the American Academy of Political and Social Science*, 259 (September, 1948), pp. 50-51.
38. George A. Steiner, *Government's Role in Economic Life* (New York: McGraw-Hill Book Co., Inc., 1953), p. 333.
39. McKean, *loc. cit.*
40. *Ibid.*
41. Maurice Duverger, *Political Parties. Their Organization and Activity in the Modern State*, trans. by Barbara and Robert North, with a foreword by D. W. Brogan (London: Methuen & Co. Ltd., New York: John Wiley & Sons, Inc., 1955), pp. 148-50.

Chapter 10

1. Clarence A. Berdahl, "Some Notes on Party Membership in Congress," Part I, *American Political Science Review*, XLIII (April, 1949), 311.
2. Clarence A. Berdahl, "Some Notes on Party Membership in Congress," Part II, *American Political Science Review*, XLIII (June, 1949), 504, 506; Part III, XLIII (August, 1949), 721.
3. Berdahl, *loc. cit.*, Part I, p. 309.
4. George B. Galloway, "The Operation of the Legislative Reorganization Act of 1946," *American Political Science Review*, XLV (March, 1951).
5. *Organization of the Congress*. Report of the Joint Committee on the Organization of Congress, pursuant to H. Con. Res. 18, U.S. Senate, 79th Cong., 2d sess. (Washington, D.C.: Government Printing Office, 1946), p. 35. Hereafter cited as *Organization of Congress*.

6. W. W. Willoughby and Lindsay Rogers, *An Introduction to the Problem of Government* (New York: Doubleday & Co., Inc., The Odyssey Press, Inc., 1927), p. 345.
7. *Organization of Congress*, p. 26.
8. *Ibid.*
9. *Ibid.*, p. 1.
10. *Ibid.*
11. Willoughby and Rogers, *op. cit.*, p. 244 and appendix ii (pp. 493-97).
12. *Organization of Congress*, p. 1.
13. George B. Galloway, *The Legislative Process in Congress* (New York: Thomas Y. Crowell Co., 1953), p. 653.
14. Carl O. Smith and G. Lowell Field, "The Responsibility of Parties in Congress: Myth and Reality," *Southwestern Social Science Quarterly*, XXXIV (June, 1953), 35.
15. *Washington Post and Times Herald*, August 7, 1955.
16. C. O. Smith and G. L. Field, *loc. cit.*, p. 34.
17. October, 1954, p. 21.
18. *The New York Times*, February 21, 1955.
19. *The Reporter*, XI (October 7, 1954), p. 6.
20. Julius Turner, *Party and Constituency: Pressures on Congress* (Baltimore: Johns Hopkins Press, 1951), p. 23.
21. *Organization of Congress*, p. 2.
22. *Ibid.*
23. See remarks of Senator Mike Monroney (D., Okla.) in *Congressional Record*, 80th Cong., 1st sess., July 26, 1947.
24. See pp. 150 ff.
25. Former Congressman Christian Herter, of Massachusetts, as quoted in the *Washington Post and Times Herald*, December 28, 1954.
26. *Ibid.*
27. *Ibid.*
28. George B. Galloway, *op. cit.*, pp. 343-45.
29. See chap. v.
30. See chap. vi.
31. Clinton L. Rossiter, review of James M. Burns's *Congress on Trial*, in *American Political Science Review*, XLIII (December, 1949), 1280.
32. Bertram M. Gross, *The Legislative Struggle* (New York: McGraw-Hill Book Co., Inc., 1953), pp. 269-70.
33. *Ibid.*, p. 389.
34. Frank R. Kent, *The Great Game of Politics* (New York: Doubleday & Co., Inc., 1926), p. 263.
35. Dayton David McKean, *Party and Pressure Politics* (Boston: Houghton Mifflin Co., 1949), p. 623.
36. Robert Luce, *Congress: An Explanation* (Cambridge: Harvard University Press, 1926), p. 130.
37. Ralph K. Huitt, "The Congressional Committee: A Case Study," *American Political Science Review*, XLVIII (June, 1954), 365.
38. *Toward a More Responsible Two-Party System*. A Report of the Committee on Political Parties of the American Political Science Association (New York: Rinehart & Co., 1950). Measured by the criteria of (1) responsibility and accountability to the public, (2) opportunity for difference of opinion, and (3) ability to cope with the problems of modern government, the Committee decided that the two-party system as it now operates in the United States does not meet these standards. Four specific defects are noted: (1) an unwieldy, unrepresentative, and less than responsible party convention; (2) party platforms so badly defined that it is difficult to decide what elections decide, even in broadest terms; (3) absence

of a democratic relationship between the party and those called members; and
(4) the lack of research by the party organizations. The Committee wants the
United States to move "toward a more responsible two-party system." By this
phrase is meant not a party system owing responsibility to the legislature, as in
the British parliamentary system, but one "with the responsibility of both
parties to the general public, as enforced in elections," and "of party leadership
to the party membership, as enforced in primaries, caucuses, and conventions."
See pp. 20-24.

39. Notably in the written constitutions of France and Germany, while Britain operates according to an unwritten constitution.
40. Berdahl, *loc. cit.*, Part I, p. 309.
41. Julius Turner, "Primary Elections as the Alternative to Party Competition in 'Safe' Districts," *Journal of Politics*, XV (May, 1953), 210.
42. ". . . the ineffectiveness of the parties in the field of policy has shown itself both in a failure to develop institutions for the authoritative declaration of party policy and in the failure to develop an organization able to discipline or mobilize its personnel within the government. As a consequence, divisions *within* the parties are sometimes more important than the divisions between the parties." E. E. Schattschneider, "Pressure Groups versus Political Parties," *Parties and Politics: 1948, Annals of the American Academy of Political and Social Science,* 259 (September, 1948), p. 18.
43. C. O. Smith and G. L. Field, *loc. cit.,* p. 35.
44. E. E. Schattschneider, *Party Government* (New York: Rinehart & Co., Inc., 1942), p. 196.
45. C. O. Smith and G. L. Field, *loc. cit.,* p. 36.
46. *Washington Post and Times Herald,* July 28, 1955.
47. Herbert Morrison, *Government and Parliament. A Survey from the Inside* (New York: Oxford University Press, 1954).
48. Chester I. Barnard, review of Charles Hyneman's *Bureaucracy in a Democracy* (New York: Harper & Bros., 1950), in *American Political Science Review,* XLIV (December, 1950), 1004.
49. Letter to *The Reporter,* XI (November 8, 1954), 10, commenting on Martin Merson's article, "My Education in Government," *The Reporter,* XI (October 7, 1954), 27.

Chapter 11

1. U.S. Senator Paul H. Douglas (D., Ill.), review of Sydney Hyman's *The American President* (New York: Harper & Bros., 1954), in *The New York Times Book Review,* February 14, 1954.
2. James B. Reston, "Politics vs. Policy," *The New York Times,* May 5, 1955, p. 8.
3. Bertram M. Gross, *The Legislative Struggle* (New York: McGraw-Hill Book Co., Inc., 1953), p. 391.
4. Richard C. Snyder and Edgar J. Furniss, Jr., *American Foreign Policy: Formulation, Principles, and Programs* (New York: Rinehart & Co., Inc., 1954), pp. 206-7.
5. See Charles A. Beard, *President Roosevelt and the Coming of War, 1941* (New Haven: Yale University Press, 1948); Charles C. Tansill, *Back Door to War: The Roosevelt Foreign Policy, 1933-41* (Chicago: Henry Regnery Co., 1952); William L. Langer and S. Everett Gleason, *The Challenge to Isolation, 1937-40* (New York: The Council on Foreign Relations, 1952); William L. Langer and S. Everett Gleason, *The Undeclared War* (New York: The Council on Foreign Relations, 1953).
6. "A Policy in Embryo" by Franklin D. Roosevelt, in *F. D. R.: His Personal Letters* (New York: Duell, Sloan & Pearce, Inc., 1947), II, pp. 1050-1051, reproduced

in L. Larry Leonard, *Elements of American Foreign Policy* (New York: McGraw-Hill Book Co., Inc., 1953), pp. 264-65.

7. James B. Reston, review of Joseph M. Jones's *The Fifteen Weeks: February 21-June 5, 1947* (New York: The Viking Press, Inc., 1955), in *The New York Times Book Review*, October 2, 1955, p. 6.

8. But see Harry S. Truman, *Memoirs* (2 vols.; New York: Doubleday & Co., Inc., 1956), II, *Years of Trial and Hope*, pp. 325-26, 331 ff.

9. See chaps. xiii and xiv.

10. Harold Sprout, "Pressure Groups and Foreign Policy," *Annals of the American Academy of Political and Social Science*, 179 (May, 1935), pp. 114-23.

11. John W. Masland, "Pressure Groups and American Foreign Policy," *Public Opinion Quarterly*, VI (Spring, 1942), 115 ff.

12. Chaim Weizmann, *Trial and Error, the Autobiography of Chaim Weizmann* (2 vols.; Philadelphia: Jewish Publication Society, 1949).

13. Wilfred E. Binkley, *President and Congress* (New York: Alfred A. Knopf, Inc., 1947). Binkley holds the view that Congress is more responsive to conservative pressures than the President and that the Chief Executive responds to more liberal pressures.

14. Gross, *op. cit.*, p. 402.

15. James M. Burns, *Congress on Trial* (New York: Harper & Bros., 1949).

16. Frederick J. Lawton, "Legislative-Executive Relationships in Budgeting as Viewed by the Executive," *Public Administration Review*, XIII (Summer, 1953).

17. Gross, *op. cit.*, pp. 434-35.

18. Walter White, *A Man Called White, The Autobiography of Walter White* (New York: The Viking Press, Inc., 1948).

19. Matthew Josephson, *Sidney Hillman, Statesman of American Labor* (New York: Doubleday & Co., Inc., 1952); Saul D. Alinsky, *John L. Lewis, An Unauthorized Biography* (New York: G. P. Putnam's Sons, 1949); Wellington Roe, *Juggernaut; American Labor in Action* (Philadelphia: J. B. Lippincott Co., 1948).

20. Robert K. Carr, "Can the President and Congress Cooperate?" *The New York Times Magazine*, February 27, 1955, p. 9.

21. In his *Politics in America*, D. W. Brogan, Cambridge University professor of Political Science, devotes some 27 pages (out of 415) to what are called in the index "pressure 'blocs' and groups" (pp. 349-76). These pages appear in Chapter 8, entitled "President and Congress." D. W. Brogan, *Politics in America* (New York: Harper & Bros., 1955).

22. Lawton, *loc. cit.*, p. 169.

23. *Ibid.* See also Arthur F. Bentley, *The Process of Government* (Bloomington, Ind.: The Principia Press of Illinois, 1949), chap. xiv, pp. 330-59, on the pressure of interests in the executive branch.

24. J. Leiper Freeman, *The Political Process: Executive Bureau-Legislative Committee Relations* (New York: Doubleday & Co., Inc., 1955). The material on the subsystem which follows is based largely on this work.

25. These forces derive from the division of Congress into two houses; election procedures which engender responsiveness to sectional, economic, or other particularist interests, rather than a general interest; and weakness of party cohesion due to choosing committee chairmen by seniority. See chap. x.

26. The (Second Hoover) Commission on Organization of the Executive Branch was authorized and established under authority of Public Law 108 of the 83rd Congress, approved by the President July 10, 1953. Of the twelve commissioners, half official, half unofficial, four were appointed by the President, four by the President of the Senate, and four by the Speaker of the House. The Commission completed its work June 30, 1955, and submitted twenty reports to Congress, including 314 recommendations based on inquiry into seventeen functional activities of the executive branch. Among its findings were the following: federal medical services conduct 472 hospitals; the number of water developments and power projects

totals about 2000; there are probably more than 2500 government-owned commercial-type activities competitive with private enterprise in the Department of Defense alone. The Commission estimated that adoption of its recommendations in the one functional field of lending would result in ultimate annual savings of $200 million and a reduction in the national debt of $4,933,751,000. Annual savings, as estimated by the Commission's task forces, would reach $8 billion if all the Commission's recommendations were to be adopted. In the fiscal year 1955, the federal government operated at a deficit of $4,192,000,000. *Digest and Analyses of the Nineteen Hoover Commission Reports* (New York: Citizens Committee for the Hoover Report. n. d.), pp. 47, 238-39, 243.

27. Questions like those mentioned were raised by outgoing Federal Trade Commissioner James M. Mead, in 1955, before the House Small Business Subcommittee. Mead, onetime Democratic Senator from New York, was not reappointed by President Eisenhower. See also, for observations on that phase of the regulatory process which is said to have been most neglected—the political science aspects—Kenneth Culp Davis, "Reflections of a Law Professor on Instruction and Research in Public Administration," *American Political Science Review*, XLVIII (September, 1953), 728-52.

28. In *The Federalist* (No. 10), Madison said: "The regulation of these various and interfering interests (arising out of the unequal distribution of property) forms the principal task of modern legislation, and involves the spirit of party and faction in the necessary and ordinary operations of the Government."

29. Reinhard Bendix, "Bureaucracy and the Problem of Power," in Robert K. Merton and Others, *Reader in Bureaucracy* (Glencoe, Ill.: The Free Press, 1952), pp. 124-25.

30. *Ibid.*, p. 126.

31. *Ibid.*, pp. 126-27; see also Gross, *op. cit.*, p. 92.

32. *Ibid.*, p. 129.

33. See chaps. xiii and xiv.

34. Charles Hyneman, *Bureaucracy in a Democracy* (New York: Harper & Bros., 1950), pp. 163-64.

35. *Ibid.*, pp. 45-46.

36. Roy Blough, *The Federal Taxing Process* (Englewood Cliffs, N.J.: Prentice-Hall, Inc., 1952), pp. 22-24.

37. Bertram M. Gross and Wilfred Lumer, *The Hard Money Crusade* (Washington, D.C.: Public Affairs Institute, 1954).

38. Blough, *op. cit.*, pp. 40-43.

39. Burton M. Sapin and Richard C. Snyder, *The Role of the Military in American Foreign Policy* (New York: Doubleday & Co., Inc., 1954).

40. Edward L. Katzenbach, Jr., "How Congress Strains at Gnats, Then Swallows Military Budgets," *The Reporter*, XI (July 20, 1954), 2.

41. *Ibid.*, p. 35.

42. Irving Brant, "Forests and the Forest Service," letter to the editor, *Washington Post and Times Herald*, August 30, 1954, p. 12.

43. "Conservation: Growing Pressures," *The New York Times*, June 5, 1955, p. 31.

44. *The New York Times*, May 11, 1955, p. 20.

45. *The New York Times*, November 19, 1955.

46. George B. Galloway, *The Legislative Process in Congress* (New York: Thomas Y. Crowell Co., 1953), p. 515.

47. Gross, *op. cit.*, pp. 296-97.

48. *Ibid.*, p. 314.

49. *Ibid.*, p. 310.

50. In hearings before the House Select Committee on Lobbying Activities, a committee member, Joseph P. O'Hara, observed: "Over ten years a Congressman sees many forms of lobbying—many of which are exempt (from registration and reporting)—[such as that done by] our congressional legislative staffs, our own staffs. from other people's staffs." *Lobbying Hearings*, Part 1, p. 118.

51. United States Civil Service Commission, as cited in the *Washington Post and Times Herald,* August 29, 1955.
52. The House Committee on the Judiciary, 84th Cong., 2d sess., *Interim Report of the Anti-Trust Subcommittee,* pursuant to H. Res. 22, authorizing the Committee on the Judiciary to conduct studies and investigations relating to certain matters within its jurisdiction on WOC's and Government Advisory Groups (Washington, D.C.: Government Printing Office, 1956), pp. 2, 99, 101.
53. *Ibid.,* p. 108.
54. *Ibid.,* Appendix A, Table I, p. 114.

Chapter 12

1. Harwood L. Childs, "By Public Opinion I Mean," *Public Opinion Quarterly,* III (April, 1939), 327-36.
2. *Congressional Quarterly,* Vol. I (1945).
3. M. Louise Rutherford, *The Influence of the American Bar Association on Public Opinion and Legislation* (Philadelphia: University of Pennsylvania Press, 1937).
4. House Select Committee on Lobbying Activities, 81st Cong., 2d sess., *Hearings* (10 vols.; Washington, D.C.: Government Printing Office, 1950), Part 1, *The Role of Lobbying in Representative Self-Government,* p. 12. Cited hereafter as *Lobby Hearings.*
5. Wilhelm Bauer, "Public Opinion," *Encyclopedia of the Social Sciences* (New York: The Macmillan Co., 1942), Vol. XII, p. 670.
6. One of the nine powers of a corporate management mentioned by Berle (in a list admittedly not exhaustive) is "the process of forming public opinion." "Within limits, the corporate managers may enter into the process of forming public opinion, and some of them do this, though the extent of the exercise of that power is a matter of dispute." A. A. Berle, Jr., *The 20th Century Capitalist Revolution* (New York: Harcourt, Brace & Co., Inc., 1954), p. 34. One who believes that manipulation of people by appropriation of the social and psychological sciences is characteristic of the modern corporation is Edwin H. Sutherland. See his *White Collar Crime* (New York: The Dryden Press, 1949). And see below, pp. 205 ff.
7. *Lobby Hearings,* Part 1, p. 15.
8. *Ibid.,* p. 20.
9. *Ibid.,* p. 19.
10. Dexter M. Keezer, "The Press," *Encyclopedia of the Social Sciences* (New York: The Macmillan Co., 1942), Vol. XII, p. 336.
11. Thomas C. Cochran and William Miller, *The Age of Enterprise* (New York: The Macmillan Co., 1951), p. 270.
12. Keezer, *loc. cit.*
13. *Ibid.,* p. 340.
14. Quoted by Robert M. Hutchins, in an address before the American Society of Newspaper Editors, *The New York Times,* April 22, 1955.
15. Keezer, *loc. cit.,* p. 336.
16. "An imposing array of data could be mustered to indicate that the theory in its entirety bears little relation to actual press practice." *Ibid.,* p. 338.
17. *Ibid.,* p. 340. "The press is on all sides stimulated to create a setting, both material and emotional, conducive to the success of advertising effort."
18. Hutchins, *loc. cit.*
19. R. L. Shayon, "Plotkin vs. the Networks," *The Saturday Review,* June 25, 1955, pp. 33-34.
20. Carl Dreher, "E. H. Armstrong: The Hero as Inventor," *Harper's Magazine,* 212 (April, 1956), 66.

21. Thomas I. Emerson and David Haber, *Political and Civil Rights in the United States* (Buffalo: Dennis & Co., Inc., 1952), chap. vi.

22. *Washington Post and Times Herald*, August 6, 1955.

23. As to content, see "Mass Media, Content, Function, and Measurement," *Journal of Social Issues*, III (1947); on content of radio and TV programs, see "An Analysis of Radio's Programming," *Communications Research 1948-49*, eds. Paul F. Lazarsfeld and Frank N. Stanton (New York: Harper & Bros., 1949), p. 51.

24. William H. Whyte, Jr., *Is Anybody Listening? How and Why U.S. Business Fumbles when it Talks with Human Beings* (New York: Simon & Schuster, Inc., 1952), p. 15.

25. Emerson and Haber, *op. cit.*, pp. 733 ff.

26. Quoted by R. M. Hutchins, *loc. cit.*

27. Robert M. MacIver, *The Web of Government* (New York: The Macmillan Co., 1947), pp. 89-90, 219-23.

28. "The Theory of Propaganda," *American Political Science Review*, XXI (1927), 627.

29. Albert Schweitzer, *Out of My Life and Thought* (New York: Henry Holt & Co., Inc., 1949), pp. 220-22.

30. John W. Meaney, "Propaganda as Psychical Coercion," *Review of Politics*, XIII (January, 1951).

31. Solomon E. Asch, "Opinions and Social Pressure," *Scientific American*, 193 (November, 1955), 31-35.

32. E. P. Herring, "Lobbying," *Encyclopedia of the Social Sciences* (New York: The Macmillan Co., 1942), Vol. IX, p. 567.

33. See chap. vi.

34. Persuading people to accept certain ideas or abandon others by using paid space or time is another way of defining institutional advertising. See Elmo Roper, "Who Tells the Storytellers?" *The Saturday Review*, July 31, 1954, p. 25.

35. William D. Patterson (ed.), *America: Miracle at Work* (Englewood Cliffs, N.J.: Prentice-Hall, Inc., 1954). See endorsement of this work by Leo Cherne, Executive Director, the Research Institute of America.

36. Robert Bendiner, "The 'Engineering of Consent'—A Case Study," *The Reporter*, XIII (August 11, 1955), 14-23.

37. Examples of the propaganda used by these two parts of the transport industry are contained in the December, 1955 issue of *Harper's Magazine*, which carried a four-page "public interest advertisement" entitled "Competition in Transportation," by Neil J. Curry, Chairman, American Trucking Associations, Inc., followed two pages later by a one-page advertisement (not described as a public interest advertisement) entitled "How Competitive Pricing in Transportation Would Help You," by the Association of American Railroads.

38. One of the few books which recognizes the importance of the public relations profession as a new factor in the generation and use of political power is that of Stanley Kelley, Jr. See his *Professional Public Relations and Political Power* (Baltimore: Johns Hopkins Press, 1956).

39. For a development of this view, see J. A. Schumpeter, *Capitalism, Socialism, and Democracy* (New York: Harper & Bros., 1942), chaps. xxi-xxiii.

40. L. White Busbey, *Uncle Joe Cannon* (New York: Henry Holt & Co., Inc., 1927); Edgar Lane, in testimony before the House Select Committee on Lobbying Activities (1950), *Lobby Hearings*, Part 1, p. 55; George B. Galloway, *The Legislative Process in Congress* (New York: Thomas Y. Crowell Co., 1953), p. 492, quoting former Congressman Robert Luce (R., Mass.); Kenneth G. Crawford, *The Pressure Boys* (New York: Julian Messner, Inc., 1937); Karl Schriftgiesser, *The Lobbyists* (Boston: Little, Brown & Co., 1951); E. P. Herring, *loc. cit.;* Lindsay Rogers, *The Pollsters* (New York: Alfred A. Knopf, Inc., 1949).

41. *General Interim Report of the House Select Committee on Lobbying Activities,* H.R. Rep. No. 3138, 81st Cong., 2d sess. (Washington, D.C.: Government Printing Office, 1950), p. 29. Cited hereafter as *Interim Report.*

42. Herring, *loc. cit.*

43. Oliver Garceau, *The Political Life of the American Medical Association* (Cambridge: Harvard University Press, 1941), pp. 3, 5.

44. *Lobby Hearings*, Part 1, pp. 82-83.

45. Federal law (Section 315 of the Federal Communications Act) requires a radio or television network or station to grant equal time to all candidates if it offers free time to any candidate. In 1952 there were sixteen parties with candidates for the Presidency or for Congress. *The New York Times*, May 25, 1955.

46. See pp. 199-201.

47. House Select Committee on Lobbying Activities, 81st Cong., 2d sess., *Report and Recommendations on the Federal Lobbying Act* (Washington, D.C.: Government Printing Office, 1951), p. 35. Cited hereafter as *Report and Recommendations*.

48. A. J. Liebling, "The Press," *Holiday*, VII (February, 1950). Reference works also fail to cover significant stories of the political process; in F. W. Riggs, *Pressures on Congress, A Study of the Repeal of Chinese Exclusion* (New York: King's Crown Press, 1950), the failure is noted of *The American Year Book* to report the crucial part played by the Citizens' Committee for Repeal of Chinese Exclusion.

49. *Washington Post*, June 13, 1950.

50. Herbert Brucker, *Freedom of Information* (New York: The Macmillan Co., 1949).

51. TNEC, *Final Report and Recommendations*, Sen. Doc. No. 35, 79th Cong., 1st sess. (Washington, D.C.: Government Printing Office, 1940), p. 10.

52. "What Ails the Senate?" *The New York Times Magazine*, May 2, 1954.

53. Charles A. Seipmann, *Radio, Television, and Society* (New York: Oxford University Press, 1950).

54. Edwin H. Sutherland, "Crime and Corporate Organization," *White Collar Crime* (New York: The Dryden Press, 1949), reprinted in Merton and Others, *Reader in Bureaucracy* (Glencoe, Ill.: The Free Press, 1952), p. 420.

55. Alfred S. Cleveland, "Some Political Aspects of Organized Industry" (Ph.D. dissertation, Harvard University, Department of Political Science, 1948), p. 325.

56. Research institutes which emphasize one side of issues in their "fact-finding" should file under the Federal Regulation of Lobbying Act, according to a recommendation of the House Select Committee on Lobbying.

57. For example, see the article by Hugh Dressel Fraser, "Texans Don't Know Any Better," *Harper's Magazine*, 213 (June, 1956).

58. Whyte, *op. cit.*, p. 15.

59. *Ibid.*, pp. 209-10.

60. *Interim Report*, p. 63.

61. Hadley Cantril, in testimony before the House Select Committee on Lobbying Activities, *Lobby Hearings*, Part 1, pp. 19-20.

Chapter 13

1. Thomas C. Desmond, "Those Dinosaurs—the State Legislatures," *The New York Times Magazine*, January 16, 1955; George B. Galloway, *The Legislative Process in Congress* (New York: Thomas Y. Crowell Co., 1953), p. 38. Galloway states that members do not initiate much legislation but act as conduits for measures which the members' constituents, the private organizations (interest groups), and the executive departments wish introduced.

2. Bertram M. Gross, *The Legislative Struggle* (New York: McGraw-Hill Book Co., Inc., 1953), p. 235; J. Leiper Freeman, *The Political Process: Executive Bureau-Legislative Committee Relations* (New York: Doubleday & Co., Inc., 1955), *passim*.

3. E. P. Herring, "Lobbying," *Encyclopedia of the Social Sciences* (New York: The Macmillan Co., 1942), Vol. IX, p. 567.

4. Lindsay Rogers, *The Pollsters* (New York: Alfred A. Knopf, Inc., 1949), p. 27.
5. The story of neither legislative struggle has ever been told. One person in a key position in 1946, James R. Newman, was very restrained in the book he wrote on the episode. See James R. Newman and B. S. Miller, *The Control of Atomic Energy* (New York: Whittlesey House, 1948). Some of the story about the role played by the Atomic Scientists can be pieced together from material in their *Bulletin.*
6. Marshall Knappen, "Shipping Quotas and the Military Assistance Program," *American Political Science Review,* XLIV (December, 1950), 933 ff.
7. *Ibid.,* p. 933.
8. Earl Latham, "The Group Basis of Politics: Notes for a Theory," *American Political Science Review,* XLVI (June, 1952), 209.
9. Roy L. Harvey and Others, *The Politics of This War* (New York: Harper & Bros., 1943); Bruce Catton, *The War Lords of Washington* (New York: Harcourt, Brace & Co., Inc., 1948).
10. Abraham Kaplan and Harold D. Lasswell, *Power and Society. A Framework for Political Inquiry* (New Haven: Yale University Press, 1950).
11. This conclusion is drawn from a survey of the views of the following representative observers of government: Griffith, *Harper's Magazine,* Senator Paul H. Douglas (D., Ill.), Galloway, Huitt, Hale, Dahl and Lindbloom, Garceau, the House Lobby Investigating Committee (81st Cong.), Graves, Schattschneider, Bentley, David B. Truman, Gross, S. K. Bailey, and MacIver. See Bibliography.
12. Herman Heller, "Political Power," *Encyclopedia of the Social Sciences* (New York: The Macmillan Co., 1942), Vol. XII, p. 304.
13. As long ago as 1927, it was pointed out that to replace the federal feature of the Senate by an attempt to represent interests "would be little more than a legalization of the one hundred or so lobbies in Washington. . . . The issues raised by this rather fanciful suggestion . . . go to the basis of the processes of American politics." W. W. Willoughby and Lindsay Rogers, *An Introduction to the Problem of Government* (New York: Doubleday & Co., Inc., The Odyssey Press, Inc., 1927), p. 244.
14. A. L. Kroeber, "Anthropology," *Scientific American,* 183 (September, 1950), 87, 94.
15. Sir Wilmott Lewis was one of a number of distinguished Englishmen who brought rare insight into the study and exposition of American political institutions.
16. Elise Heinz, of Wellesley College, prepared, in 1955, the original paper on which this case study is based.
17. See chapter xi.
18. *Congressional Record,* January 29, 1951, pp. 796-800, quoted in Galloway, *op. cit.,* p. 659.
19. Roy Blough, *The Federal Taxing Process* (Englewood Cliffs, N.J.: Prentice-Hall, Inc., 1952), p. 24.
20. *Ibid.,* p. 476.
21. *Ibid.,* pp. 27-29.
22. *Ibid.,* pp. 22, 24.
23. According to Blough, *op. cit.,* chap. ii.
24. *Ibid.,* pp. 474-75.
25. Testimony before the Joint Committee on the Economic Report, cited in *The New York Times,* December 10, 1955.
26. Roy Blough, *op. cit.,* pp. 476-77.
27. Richard W. Gable, "NAM: Influential Lobby or Kiss of Death?" *The Journal of Politics,* XV (May, 1953), 271-73.
28. *The New York Times,* February 28, 1954, quoting lobby registration data compiled by the *Congressional Quarterly.*
29. Charles M. Hardin, *The Politics of Agriculture: Soil Conservation and the Struggle for Power in Rural America* (Glencoe, Ill.: The Free Press, 1952).
30. Bertram M. Gross, *The Legislative Struggle* (New York: McGraw-Hill Book Co., Inc., 1953), p. 428.

31. The full story has never been told. The case study given here is based on an unpublished monograph, written in 1955 by Audrey G. Corderman at Wellesley College.

32. The case study which follows is based upon a paper prepared by Lois Blatchford at Wellesley College in 1955.

Chapter 14

1. Arthur W. Macmahon, *Administration in Foreign Affairs* (University, Ala.: University of Alabama Press, 1953), p. 95.

2. G. L. Bach, *Federal Reserve Policy-Making: A Study in Government Economic Policy Formation* (New York: Alfred A. Knopf, Inc., 1950); Paul Einzig, *How Money Is Managed* (London: Penguin Books, Inc., 1954); Max Millikan, (ed.), *Income Stabilization for a Developing Democracy: A Study of the Politics and Economics of High Employment without Inflation* (New Haven: Yale University Press, 1953); Bertram Gross and Wilfred Lumer, *The Hard Money Crusade* (Washington, D.C.: The Public Affairs Institute, 1954).

3. *The New York Times,* April 1, 1955.

4. *The New York Times,* April 30, 1955.

5. *The New York Times,* May 1, 1955.

6. *The New York Times,* October 6, 1955, November 14, 1954.

7. *The New York Times,* November 25, 1955.

8. Bruce Catton, *The War Lords of Washington* (New York: Harcourt, Brace & Co., Inc., 1948). The author was information director of the War Production Board. In this book he expounds the thesis that the "lords of industry" used the war production effort to strengthen their position in the domestic economy.

9. Robert Paul Browder, *The Origins of Soviet–American Diplomacy* (Princeton: Princeton University Press, 1953).

10. "The China Lobby," *The Reporter Political Yearbook* (1952), pp. 33 ff.

11. Thomas A. Bailey, *The Man in the Street* (New York: The Macmillan Co., 1948), pp. 291-303.

12. Robert A. Dahl, *Congress and Foreign Policy* (New York: Harcourt, Brace & Co., Inc., 1950), pp. 45-57.

13. Wayne S. Cole, *America First: The Battle Against Intervention, 1940-41* (Madison: University of Wisconsin Press, 1953); Walter Johnson, *The Battle Against Isolation* (Chicago: University of Chicago Press, 1944); John W. Masland, "Pressure Groups and American Foreign Policy," *Public Opinion Quarterly,* VI (Spring, 1942), 115 ff.

14. *F.D.R., His Personal Letters* (2 vols.; New York: Duell, Sloan & Pearce, Inc., 1947), II, pp. 1050-51.

15. H. Bradford Westerfield, *Foreign Policy and Party Politics—Pearl Harbor to Korea* (New Haven: Yale University Press, 1955).

16. See Burton M. Sapin and Richard C. Snyder, *The Role of the Military in American Foreign Policy* (New York: Doubleday & Co., Inc., 1954); also, Richard C. Snyder and Edgar S. Furniss, Jr., *American Foreign Policy: Formulation, Principles, Programs* (New York: Rinehart & Co., Inc., 1954); William Y. Elliott, *United States Foreign Policy: Its Organization and Control* (New York: Columbia University Press, 1952); Bernard C. Cohen, "Foreign Policy-making: Modern Design," *World Politics,* April, 1953; Townsend Hoopes, "Civilian-Military Balance," *Yale Review,* Winter, 1954; Blair Bolles, "Who Makes U.S. Foreign Policy?" *Foreign Policy Reports,* XXXIV (November 1, 1954), 27.

17. See James L. McCamy, *The Administration of Foreign Affairs* (New York: Alfred A. Knopf, Inc., 1950). According to McCamy, the principal faults in the administration of foreign affairs are the following: diffusion of activities in the Department of State's organization; faulty organization of the executive branch of

government due to a failure to realize that U.S. foreign relations are an integral part of our domestic policy and that all agencies of government are involved; too few and inexperienced personnel; the backward state of both the practice and use of intelligence; an executive branch insufficiently checked by Congress due to lack of information and the absence of an effective opposition party; and inadequate financing of civil administration of foreign affairs. See pp. 349-53.

18. Chalmers M. Roberts, "Battle on 'the Rim of Hell,' President vs. War Hawks," *The Reporter*, XI (December 16, 1954). "The change, to be precise, has taken place in D.D.E. [Eisenhower] . . . What has happened is that the era of 'instant massive retaliation' and 'more bang for a buck' has been giving way to the 'good partners' concept with our allies and to an intensive search by the President for what he has called a *modus vivendi* with the communist world."

19. Harrison E. Salisbury, *The New York Times Magazine*, May 8, 1955, p. 33.

Chapter 15

1. On the general subject of legislation by the courts, see Fred V. Cahill, Jr., *Judicial Legislation* (New York: The Ronald Press Co., 1952).

2. Clement E. Vose, "The Impact of Pressure Groups on Constitutional Interpretation." Unpublished paper read before the American Political Science Association, Chicago, September, 1954.

3. Woodrow Wilson, *Constitutional Government in the United States* (8th ed.; New York: Columbia University Press, 1947), pp. 152-54.

4. Alpheus Thomas Mason, *The Supreme Court: Vehicle of Revealed Truth or Power Group, 1930-1937* (Boston: Boston University Press, 1953).

5. See Donald C. Blaisdell, *Economic Power and Political Pressures*, TNEC Monograph, No. 26 (Washington, D.C.: Government Printing Office, 1941), pp. 142-43 and references cited there for a discussion of the Granger cases.

6. See above, p. 206.

7. The latter supposition is suspected. See Blaisdell, *op. cit.*, p. 78.

8. *Ibid.*, pp. 77, 159-61.

9. *Ibid.*, p. 77.

10. *Ibid.*, p. 77.

11. *Ibid.*, p. 79.

12. In 1955 an author characterized this power of the Supreme Court to grant or refuse a writ of certiorari as "absolute, autocratic, and arrogant," "a free ticket to open abuse, an invitation to laziness, incompetence, even cowardice, and it has been precisely so abused in the recent past." Fred Rodell, *Nine Men. A Political History of the Supreme Court from 1790 to 1955.* (New York: Random House, Inc., 1955), pp. 14-15.

13. "While it is not perhaps customary to think of the Supreme Court as a legislative body, the cold fact is that in the desegregation cases, the nine justices have undertaken to rewrite public policy in at least seventeen states and innumerable communities. Indeed, it would be difficult to find a recent congressional enactment that equals in impact and scope these judicial holding. . . ." John P. Roche and Milton M. Gordon, "Can Morality Be Legislated?" *The New York Times Magazine*, May 22, 1955, p. 10.

14. Clement E. Vose, "NAACP Strategy in the Covenant Cases," *Western Reserve Law Review*, VI (Winter, 1955), 101-45.

15. *Ibid.*, p. 102.

16. Loren Miller, of Los Angeles, in a letter to Clement E. Vose, *ibid.*

17. Henry S. Dennison, "The Need for the Development of Political Science Engineering," *Papers on the Science of Administration*, eds. Luther Gulick and L. Urwick (2d ed.; New York: Institute of Public Administration, 1947), p. 140. Dennison admits that study of government by means of the principle of

circular response is surrounded by "peculiar difficulties (which) must be faced from the beginning and will discourage all but the strong heart. They mean, certainly, that while specialization in so complex a subject is essential, yet integration of the specialized studies must take place, as it were, simultaneously. The engineer in political science will find, as physicians have found, that the specialist is essential to progress but cannot be left to run the show alone."

18. No complete political analysis of the tidelands oil controversy has yet appeared. A full legal and historical analysis appears in Ernest R. Bartley, *The Tidelands Oil Controversy* (Austin: University of Texas Press, 1953). Except for the recitation of events following the party conventions in 1952, the sketch appearing here is based largely on Bartley's volume.

19. Bartley states: "Of 476 pages of testimony taken at the two hearings, a total of only 53 pages is devoted to the arguments and statements of the opposition; and of these 53 pages, 47 were recorded at the 1946 hearings. This is a commentary on the disorganization of those favoring federal control or ownership, as well as a demonstration of the excellently planned and executed maneuvers of those favoring the quitclaim." Bartley, *op. cit.*, p. 148.

20. *Ibid.*, p. 149.

21. "As in the case of the submerged lands off the coast of California, the question of which agency really had the authority to administer the oil operations in the marginal sea remained, like Mahomet's coffin, suspended between heaven and hell. The *Texas* and *Louisiana* cases had been decided, but the problems raised by the decisions remained." *Ibid.*, p. 212

22. Citing the tidelands oil lobby, the laundry lobby, and the China Lobby as strong contenders, a prominent reporter suggested a system of Pulitzer Prizes for lobbying. See Marquis Childs, "Washington Calling," *Washington Post*, April 9, 1948.

23. Bartley, *op. cit.*, pp. 228-30.

24. This case study of resale price maintenance is based upon a longer study made by Nancy Mueller, of Wellesley College, in 1955.

NAME INDEX

SUBJECT INDEX